AFRICANS IN EXILE

FRAMING THE GLOBAL BOOK SERIES

The Framing the Global project, an initiative of Indiana University Press and the Indiana University Center for the Study of Global Change, is funded by the Andrew W. Mellon Foundation.

AFRICANS IN EXILE

Mobility, Law, and Identity

Edited by Nathan Riley Carpenter and
Benjamin N. Lawrance

Indiana University Press

This book is a publication of

Indiana University Press
Office of Scholarly Publishing
Herman B Wells Library 350
1320 East 10th Street
Bloomington, Indiana 47405 USA

iupress.indiana.edu

The paper used in this publication meets the minimum requirements of the American National Standard for Information Sciences—Permanence of Paper for Printed Library Materials, ANSI Z39.48-1992.

Manufactured in the United States of America

Library of Congress Cataloging-in-Publication Data

Names: Carpenter, Nathan Riley, editor, author. | Lawrance, Benjamin N. (Benjamin Nicholas), editor, author.
Title: Africans in exile : mobility, law, and identity, past and present / edited by Nathan Riley Carpenter and Benjamin N. Lawrance.
Description: Bloomington : Indiana University Press, 2018. | Series: Framing the global book series | Includes bibliographical references and index. | Identifiers: LCCN 2018023836 (print) | LCCN 2018029497 (ebook) | ISBN 9780253038111 (e-book) | ISBN 9780253038074 (hardback : alk. paper) | ISBN 9780253038081 (pbk. : alk. paper)
Subjects: LCSH: Exiles—Africa—History. | Exile (Punishment)—Africa—History. | African diaspora.
Classification: LCC JV8790 (ebook) | LCC JV8790 .A668 2018 (print) | DDC 304.8096–dc23
LC record available at https://lccn.loc.gov/2018023836

1 2 3 4 5 23 22 21 20 19 18

Exile is not the end of life, but just a new beginning.

—Simon Gikandi, Washington, DC, December 2016

Contents

Part II: Geographies of Exile

Part III: Remembering and Performing Exile

Foreword

This volume is the first of its kind to introduce exile as the major theme when analyzing political developments in Africa during colonial and postcolonial times. Not only do the introduction and the sixteen chapters add new dimensions to the concept of exile and its use as a political tool, but they provide us with new interpretations and a better understanding even of well-known histories and well-researched crisis situations.

After reading this volume I was struck by how political exile has deeply affected Uganda over the centuries, even to the present day. This collection really stimulated my thinking about recasting Ugandan history in light of exile as a vehicle of power beginning with the early colonial "encounter" and continuing up into the postcolonial present. The brief survey I provide here of eight examples from Uganda where exile has been used as a political tool with dramatic and lasting effect foreshadows exile's remarkable impact as demonstrated in the various chapters in this volume, stories that span the length and breadth of African time and place.

Hardly had the British government in 1894 accepted the area west and north of Lake Victoria as a new protectorate and enrolled it in the colonial empire before it was faced with Uganda's perpetual challenge: how to turn this highly heterogeneous area with arbitrary boundaries into a functional state. Not least of the challenges was the presence of a number of kingdoms with their traditional rulers as heads of well-established hierarchies. When the colonial administration was faced with a rebellion from the Kabaka (king) of the leading kingdom Buganda they quickly turned to exile as a way of solving the crisis, and Kabaka Mwanga was deported to the Seychelles. Yet the amenities which were to be provided for him during his exile became a matter of controversy: Anglican missionaries strongly opposed the government's concession of permitting four girls as his companions. Only after a compromise allowing Mwanga to be accompanied by two girls could he be sent into exile.

The Buganda issue haunted the British administration throughout the colonial period, and it came to a head in 1953 when, during the initial negotiations for Uganda's independence, the then Kabaka Mutesa demanded secession and the full independence of Buganda. In response, the Governor returned to an old tool and deported the Kabaka to the United Kingdom. Once again a controversy regarding the "amenities" of exile unfolded as the missionaries opposed the Kabaka being accompanied by any women other than his lawful wife. Local protests enjoined the administration to allow the Kabaka to return after two years, and as independence arrived in 1962, Buganda achieved a federal status in the new constitution.

Still, Buganda's status within Uganda kept simmering, and when Kabaka Mutesa in 1966 demanded that all government institutions should vacate Buganda soil within a few weeks, the Prime Minister Milton Obote ordered the army, then under the command of the well-known General Idi Amin, to occupy Buganda and deport the Kabaka to a remote prison. He had a narrow escape and fled—this time quasi-voluntarily—into exile in London, where he later died.

It is an irony of history that the two people who forced Kabaka Mutesa into exile both suffered the same fate. In 1971 Idi Amin staged a military coup and installed himself as president forcing Milton Obote to go into temporary exile in neighboring Tanzania. Eight years later Obote retaliated and was reinstalled as president assisted by the Tanzanian army and Ugandan guerrillas—a significant deviation from the exile phenomenon as narrated in the chapters in this collection. Idi Amin was granted protection by Saudi Arabia where he was kept under house arrest for some years, dying in exile in 2003. President Yoweri Museveni refused permission for him to return, and he was buried in Jeddah in a simple grave.

For Obote his return from Tanzanian exile was but a short respite. During his second term, one of his ministers, Yoweri Museveni, shifted camps into the opposition and was forced to live in exile in Sweden. But it became a kind of migratory exile as Museveni regularly returned to Uganda to lead the ongoing guerrilla war that resulted in his rise to the presidency and in 1985 the second, and final, exile of Milton Obote, this time in Zambia.

Since then there has been no reason for Museveni to return into exile, and he is now in his fifth term as the President of Uganda. He has, however, been faced with the still very topical issue in Uganda, the status of the kingdoms. Although their functions are strictly limited by the constitution, he has restored most of them by allowing the enthronement of their kings. As a token of good will, he granted Buganda permission to repatriate the body of the late Kabaka Mutesa from London and lay it to rest in the royal tombs. Still, tensions arise now and again as Buganda continues to campaign for a proper restoration of some of its lost privileges.

In spite of all precautions these tensions have lately turned violent. In November 2016 royal guards from the relatively marginal Rwenzururu Kingdom, bordering the Democratic Republic of Congo, attacked police posts and killed several officers reflecting a tense relationship with the central government. The Ugandan army retaliated killing more than a hundred people. And before King Charles Wesley Mumbere had time to flee abroad he was arrested and removed to a distant prison, charged with treason, terrorism, and support of a secessionist movement. The government's firm and uncompromising stance shattered the peaceful accommodation of the eighteen traditional rulers. They interpreted this act as an attempt to reach a final solution of Uganda's longstanding problem of integrating the kingdoms into the modern state, and this time without extraterritorial exile as an option.

Exile in various modalities has been part and parcel of Uganda's modern history; indeed, Uganda offers almost a typology of exile. But there is also a lesson to be learned from the Ugandan experiences when we consider them together, and when viewed as part of a long and important history of exile on the African continent. The contributors to this volume describe histories where individuals and groups of people have been forced or coerced into exile. These people found themselves exiled from their homelands, like the kings exiled from Uganda, because of what they represented to the state—a threat, a glitch, an incompatible entity, something that undercut, unnerved, exposed, or otherwise destabilized reigning authority. Used as a political tool, exile tends to personalize conflict situations based on the assumption that the conflict will be solved or at least scaled down simply by deporting the ringleaders. The king himself becomes metonym. Such an approach means that the root causes of conflict are not properly addressed.

The insight and significance of this volume is in how clearly it demonstrates that the practice of exile is not about elite individuals, about kings and queens—even when those exiled are indeed nobles, royals, and rulers. This volume will certainly be of interest to those studying histories of exile in Africa and beyond. Equally important is the fact that this book offers a welcome appraisal of exile's place in the histories of colonial and postcolonial state power.

Holger Bernt Hansen
University of Copenhagen

Acknowledgments

THIS EDITED VOLUME—THE first to advance exile as a meta-theory for the study of historical and contemporary Africa—is the result of a collaborative project that began with conversations between coeditors Nate Carpenter and Benjamin N. Lawrance as Nate was finishing his PhD in 2012. As those conversations widened, and as we talked with more people, we found not only shared interests and concerns but also a vast untapped wealth of stories and experiences, and began to plan our collaboration. The first iteration of this collaborative endeavor came in 2015 as part of the fourth Conable Conference in International Studies at the Rochester Institute of Technology (RIT), in Rochester, New York. The origins of this book can be found partly in the closing session of that symposium, in which many of the contributors in this volume considered various ways of conceptualizing exile as an organizing theme.

The majority of papers in this volume were assembled from this symposium. This book, however, is certainly greater than its constituent chapters. The authors here have all read, commented on, and otherwise engaged with each other's contributions, as have numerous reviewers. The cooperation and collaboration has deepened our understanding of exile and its role in African and Global history. We have greatly benefitted from the insights, assistance, and intellectual and professional generosity of many individuals and institutions—of which we here name only a few.

The coeditors deeply appreciate the remarkable talents of the staff at Indiana University Press, particularly Stephanie Smith, Deborah Piston-Hatlen, Jennika Baines, Kate Schramm, Paige Rasmussen, Darja Malcolm-Clarke, Jamie Armstrong, Julie Marie Davis, Carl Pearson, and Dee Mortensen. We thank Phil Schwartzberg for his excellent maps, Meridith Murray for her masterful indexing, and Carl Pearson for skillful copyediting.

Beyond our marvelous contributors, the coeditors would like to thank the many individuals who were involved at various stages in the collaborative process leading to the publication of this book, including (alphabetically): Jean Allman, Abou Bamba, Gaëlle Beaujean, Gill Berchowitz, Soli Corbelle, Zéphirin Cossi Daavo, Jeremy Dell, Marcus Filippello, Jason Florio, Sean Hanretta, Stephanie Hassell, Walter Hawthorne, Catherine Higgs, Hilary Jones, Denis Lloyd, Mike McGovern, Greg Mann, Maria Marsh, Kara Moskowitz, Christine Pense, Charlie Piot, Andrew Renneisen, Richard L. Roberts, Elizabeth Schmidt, Gerhard Seibert, Lorelle Semley, Kathy Sheldon, Shobana Shankar, Keith Shear, and Corrinne Zoli.

We would like to thank our families for their patience, generosity of spirit, and limitless support. Nate would like to thank Natasha Vermaak, Kathy Matthews, and Donald Matthews. Benjamin would like to thank Cassandra Shellman, Dean James Winebrake for the generous financial support of RIT's College of Liberal Arts, Uli Linke, the Joan B. Kroc Institute for International Peace Studies and the Hesburgh Memorial Library at the University of Notre Dame, and, as always, his husband, Wilson de Lima Silva, for support and love throughout the process of bringing this to fruition.

We are very grateful for such a fruitful collaboration throughout this process.

Nate Carpenter,
Northampton Community College
Benjamin N. Lawrance,
University of Arizona

AFRICANS IN EXILE

Introduction

Reconstructing the Archive of Africans in Exile

Nathan Riley Carpenter and
Benjamin N. Lawrance

Between December 2006 and March 2007, the Musée du Quai Branly of Paris partnered with the Zinsou Foundation in Cotonou, Benin, to commemorate the centenary of the death of Béhanzin, King of Dahomey. The exhibition highlighted Béhanzin's reign (1889–94), and the history of Dahomey, with thirty royal objects loaned for the occasion by the museum to the foundation. Among the royal objects were a throne, scepters, jewelry, and two doors to the tomb of Béhanzin's father, King Glélé.[1] Notably absent from the exhibition, however, were three regal statues carved in the ateliers of the late-nineteenth-century Fon artists Sossa Dede, Bokossa Donvide, and Famille Akati, taken as the spoils of war after Dodds' campaign against Béhanzin in 1892 and then deposited in the Musée d'Éthnographie in Paris.[2] Since their transfer to the Quai Branly, the statues have been a centerpiece of the Africa exhibition gallery. The three theriomorphic sculptures of the Dahomean kings Ghezo, Glélé, and Béhanzin are undeniably among the most impressive late-nineteenth-century West African objects in the museum. Unlike some thirty or so smaller items loaned for the centenary exhibit, however, the statues remained in Paris—separated from the royal lands whence they were stolen over a century earlier. The fish-man statue of Béhanzin, left behind in Paris and standing alongside sculptures that represented Béhanzin's father and grandfather, points to an obvious, but obfuscated, fact: Béhanzin himself was not allowed to return to Dahomey. When he died in 1906, it was in exile, in Blida, Algeria.

The press release announcing the Cotonou exhibition described Béhanzin as "a king with a singular destiny."[3] Yet although Béhanzin was remarkable in many respects, not the least for his prolonged resistance to French imperial aggression, his history of exile was hardly unique. His is one of many stories of European-imposed exile during colonial rule. The list is long, and includes those who, like Béhanzin, claimed royal lineage. Ranavalona III, Queen of Madagascar, the

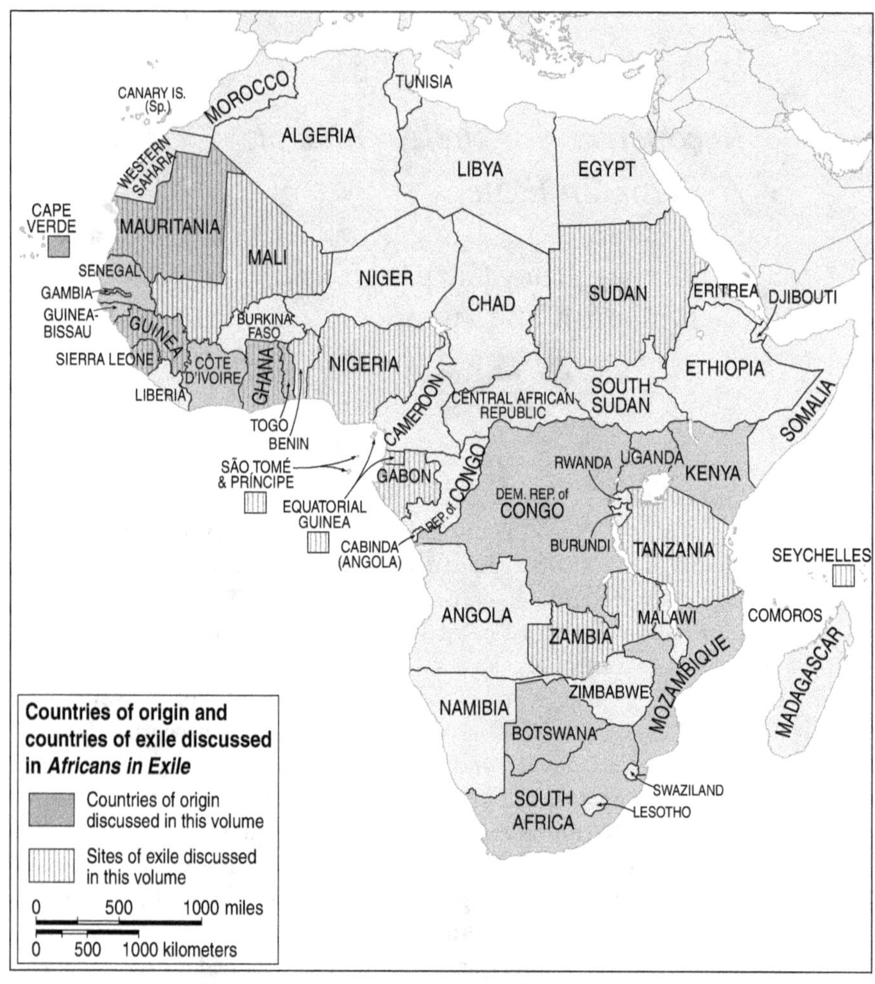

Map I.1 Africa. (Philip Schwartzberg.)

Asantehene, Prempeh I of Ashanti, Kabaka Mwanga of Buganda, and Emperor Haile Salassie of Abyssinia were but four elite Africans who found themselves forced into exile by European colonial forces, echoing displacements of European royalty by wars and revolutions. The pantheon of distinguished exiles from the African continent and its diaspora also includes many nationalist leaders and numerous political and religious dignitaries whose future return threatened to undermine the political or cultural hegemony asserted by the colonial state: Kwame Nkrumah, Oliver Tambo, Kenneth Kaunda, Aline Sitoe Diatta, Robert Resha, George Padmore, Simon Kimbangu, and countless men and women spent years in voluntary or coerced self-exile. Yet any catalogue of exiles would surely be incomplete if it omitted many lesser-known religious and political dissidents,

Fig. I.1 Sossa Dede's nineteenth-century sculpture representing Béhanzin as a fish-man. (Sossa Dede. Digital image courtesy of Myrabella. CC BY-SA 3.0 https://commons.wikimedia.org/wiki/File%3AHomme-requin_Dahomey.jpg. Currently housed at the Musée du Quai Branly, Paris.)

families of various social positions, and indeed entire communities, who chose to relocate transnationally or found themselves thrust across borders for indeterminate periods, often longing to return home.

Historians, anthropologists, and other scholars often highlight singular transformative experiences of exile.[4] But in so doing, exile itself is cast as a curious, otherwise exceptional or tangential episode in longer personal histories of political intrigue, colonial occupation, or state oppression; it is often framed as the noble choice, or alternatively as an oppositional sufferance from which a visionary ultimately recovers, or as a struggle over which a band of resisters triumphs against all odds.[5] The banishment of Bechuanaland's Kgosi Seretse Khama to London (1951–56)—ostensibly to avoid a "tribal war" among the Bangwato, but in reality to kowtow to the new apartheid regime of South Africa's Daniel Malan, a neocolonial state revolted by the image of a mixed-race monarchy on its northern border—is all too often retold ensconced within a "love conquers all" (racism, classism, elitism) trope.[6] Such routine, uncritical narration overlooks the breadth and complexity of exile and its deep and lasting impact on people across and beyond the African continent.

This volume is the first of its kind to reconsider exile in its totality and to argue for its centrality to theorizations of state power in colonial and postcolonial Africa. The contributors to this volume identify and interpret the commonalities of the experience across the continent of Africa spanning several centuries to the present day. The chapters consider specifically the question of political exile—that is, coerced or voluntary physical relocation with specified political goals in mind—and find that, rather than exceptional, exile is fundamental to any account of state power or critical rereading of colonial and postcolonial oppression. Furthermore, despite the diverse circumstances that framed individual cases, exiles often resisted displacement and suppression even when outside their homelands.

Africans in Exile offers two challenges to Africanists, with salience for historians, anthropologists, sociologists, political scientists and geographers, scholars of literature, cultural studies, and law, and indeed many others working in different locations around the globe. First, we contend that the diversity of exile experiences across the continent can be recovered and interpreted as "archive." The archive of exile is tangible, material, and rich with evidentiary insights. By uniting the diverse strands of exiled lives across time and space, we reconceptualize the instability of state authority during Africa's long engagement with European power and resituate a previously inadequately theorized predicament anew. Rather than a theory of exile, we highlight the experiences of exile as part of a continuum of African displacements beginning with the trans-Atlantic slave trade and continuing through imperialism, colonialism, independence, and up to and including contemporary events, such as the "War on Terror," an omnipresent theme in our present epoch, and one ushering in waves of new migrations.[7]

Second, this exile archive thus offers a corrective to disciplinary and interdisciplinary theories of exile that emphasize elite individuals, romantic isolation, and displacement as erasure.[8] Taken together, the essays in this book advance a counternarrative to romantic reflections on exile generally, and to the accounts of elite, royal, and singular "expatriates" preponderant in Africanist and African diaspora historiography.[9] The African experience of exile was no romance; it was torturous, arduous, debilitating, disorientating, and no less so when intentionally initiated by Africans to resist or escape authority—European, American, or African.[10] Exile was not imposed *only* on "those who count[ed]," such as kings, or "publicly important" competitors for, and critics of, state power, such as nationalists.[11]

The exile-or-conflict binary was a European conceit, a seemingly unfalsifiable fiction cementing the colonial power grab, but one continually reproduced into the postcolonial era. Exile was not confined to African elites but rather encompassed all sectors of society; exile was not a singular or individuated experience, but very frequently involved powerful group dynamics and collective contexts. And exile is not simply state oppression; not all narratives of exile are histories of erasure. As this volume demonstrates, exiles are survivors, whose stories and ordeals, when united, reshape our understanding of quotidian interactions with power by demonstrating the normative centrality of exilic displacement to political authority. The stories contained in these chapters highlight the resilience of Africans within the context of the state's capacity to "broadcast" its power and resituate exile within the *longue durée* of African mobilities.[12]

In what follows we compare prevailing treatments of exile by scholars and others with the lived experiences of African exiles broadly. We then introduce the book's contributors and their case studies in the second section and, in so doing, demonstrate the important work of recovering the archive of exile in all its complexity and diversity. And in the final section, via an exploration of the three frameworks which offer deeper understandings of how exile shaped and continues to shape the lives of Africans, we suggest ways to read and teach this volume.

Reconceiving African Exile: Beyond Nobility, Erasure, and Romantic Isolation

Broadly defined, exile is the forced removal or coerced absence from one's homeland. Over time exile in Africa has taken many forms including banishment, self-imposed expatriation, and forced resettlement, among others.[13] Exile encompasses not only political exclusion but also resettlement and migration born of environmental disaster, war, economic hardship, or fear of social persecution. Individuals are exiled, as are larger groups of people who have left their homeland for any number of reasons known and unknown.[14] They may remain permanently in exile, or return to replace, to challenge, or to overthrow existing orders; or their descendants may struggle over repatriating their remains.[15] And the productive power of the exilic experience for literary and philosophical investigations of intellectual, emotional, and spiritual disruption is profound.[16]

Exile thus defined has a long global history. It has gained particular significance over the past two centuries such that Edward Said, reflecting on the late twentieth century, suggested "our age—with its modern warfare, imperialism, and the quasi-theological ambitions of totalitarian rulers—is indeed the age of the refugee, the displaced person, mass immigration."[17] Said perhaps overstated the singularity of the late twentieth century in the history of immigration, but his recognition of the importance of displacement to recent world history is well founded.[18] While not unique to Africa, removal from one's homeland has been one of the most important historical threads in African history and a defining experience for many Africans.

But, exile has defied easy theorization. This is in part because, as Sophia McClennen argues in another context, the term is regularly employed as "a metaphor for many states of marginalization and isolation" rather than an analytically significant category.[19] Such has been the case in histories of Africa and the African diaspora where exile has often been undertheorized despite the undeniable place that removal from homeland has had for the history of the continent. Among histories of African forced displacement, the Atlantic slave trade, spanning over four hundred years, is the most significant. Even within this history however, the question of exile has largely remained unexplored. Certainly, scholars have placed exile broadly within the history of the slave trade, using it to examine the experiences of slaves in the Atlantic world as "outcasts" or as exiles of "their own nation."[20] More often, however, exile in histories of Atlantic slavery or the African diaspora has been used as suggestion, rhetorical device, and synonym for various forms of displacement or migration without sustained discussion of exile and its meanings.[21] With the important exception of pan-Africanist movements in exile, African exile is sidelined from the global encounter with colonial and imperial power.[22]

Writers from across the disciplines have employed exile in varied and sometimes conflicting ways. In discourses on exile, in Africa and beyond, three tropes are preponderant. We began this introduction with the first, namely that exiles were noble and elite. A second prevailing wisdom insists that exile erases histories, lives, and experiences, to varying degrees of completeness. And the third trope holds that the experiences of exile offer an important and uniquely romantic isolation from which *exilés* reflect profoundly on life, meaning, and existence. In various guises, and often in conversation, these tropes seek to understand human belonging and exclusion, whether physical, intellectual, emotional, or otherwise. And as tropes they contain varying degrees of truth, myth, and misrepresentation.

Historians have recognized the importance of exile in other contexts, especially in the history of earlier colonial occupations as a control strategy by European powers against indigenous political and military leaders.[23] This emphasis on royal exile is also reflected in critical engagements of displacement found in literature and film.[24] Mentions of these kings and queens, what we might call the "exiles of conquest," suggest exile as a uniquely elite sentence.[25] They also perhaps reflect the fascination of royal exile by public audiences. Béhazin's exile was widely covered by the press, as was Ranavalona's death in Algiers in 1917. Many journalists were captivated by royalty sentenced to exile on faraway tropical islands, echoing even earlier imperial exiles, such as that of Napoléon to St. Helena.[26] The emphasis on elite exiles echoes studies of early anticolonial and imperial resistance that highlighted singular, charismatic resistance leaders. But, as numerous studies have demonstrated, resistance to colonial opposition was not a uniquely, or even primarily, elite process.[27] Nor were subsequent nationalist and anticolonial movements primarily elite endeavors.[28] Exile was similarly not limited to elite figures but was a tool employed widely by and against various individuals and groups. While some exiles were elite, the majority were not; many were political agitators, local anticolonial organizers, and colonial subjects convicted of felonies or even petty crimes who were then transported across the carceral "networks of empire."[29] A focus on early military resistors, spiritual leaders, or otherwise powerful individuals who stood in the way of European aims of territorial conquest and political hegemony thus produces a very distorted view of the far-reaching experiences of exile.

By highlighting the diverse subjects of political exile, the volume also destabilizes notions of exile as a unique period of isolation and contemplation. Such representations no doubt have their origins partly in the disconnect between the imaginations of exile and the experience of forced displacement, between exile as something "strangely compelling to think about" and something "terrible to experience."[30] The robust corpus of poetry, philosophy, political theory, art, literature, mathematics, theology, music—the list goes on—points to the reflection and contemplation that has often taken place in exile. But it also belies the experience of exile. Certainly, there were cases where a person's exile allowed time for leisure, reflection, and simple living.[31] But, such cases were usually limited to elites with strong international networks and resources and did not reflect the vast majority of exile experiences. We agree, and indeed highlight below, that exile could be productive, generative, and at times catalytic. Exile could offer opportunities not available back home. And certainly there are cases where exile has allowed for introspection and inspiration. But, as Mustafah Dhada observes, "it is not easy to re-craft a life in exile" and we contend that in most cases creativity happened *in spite of* exile's dislocation, disorientation, and violence.[32]

Just as exile was not a sentence reserved for elites, and was not an experience of romantic isolation, so too not all narratives of exile are histories of erasure. It is in the experiences of those exiled and the communities left behind that we find the most forceful evidence of the tension between erasure and creation. In a 2013 interview with the French newspaper of record, *Le Monde*, the Togolese novelist and essayist Sami Tchak reflected on life in Paris. Despite having spent years in France and having been heralded for his contributions to Francophone literature, he nevertheless continued to feel out of place in his adopted home. He described his existence abroad as an exile; and that exile, he stated, was a "symbolic death."[33] Tchak's reflections signal a well-documented motif. That exile is death, like death, or worse than death itself is a common claim among those who have experienced displacement. It can be found in some of the oldest reflections on exile from the African continent.[34] The experience was almost always fraught with unease, disorientation, and suffering—both for those who found themselves in a foreign land, as well as those communities left behind. Certainly, exile was not only a figurative state. Many, such as Béhanzin, Yaa Asantewaa, and Aline Sitoe Diatta, perished while in forced or coerced exile.[35]

But, exile was also as much a state of mind as it was a physical situation. And, Tchak's own writing reveals that exile could be creative or generative. The chapters in this volume similarly demonstrate that exile was a dramatic and productive force, one wielded unevenly and unequally, and with many unintended and unanticipated consequences. As Wale Adebanwi elsewhere shows, "counter-knowledge" produced in exile challenged authority and destabilized autocracy; and oppressive states continued to feel threatened by exiles even after their departure.[36] People in exile formed or recreated national identities, they catalyzed transnational anticolonial, anti-apartheid, and anticapitalist movements, and reinforced or enhanced religious and cultural identities.[37] Certainly, exile did often mean death, an end to indigenous sovereignty, or the slow erosion of political opposition. And this is in part reflected in the claim of exile as erasure and in the trope of exile as death.[38] Such narratives are affective and address the despair and isolation that many exiles experienced. They are also problematic, however, because they substantiate the aims of states and state agents who attempted, through removal, to not only eliminate, but also excise from memory, exiles and their histories of opposition.

The Materiality of the African Exile Archive

We do not present here a theory of exile as such, so much as we posit an archive of exile. Asserting that the experiences of exiles constitute an *archive* demands a recognition of archives as something more—perhaps fundamentally different—from the archive as building or documentary repository used by states to both destroy and cleanse history, or what Achille Mbembe describes as "chronophagy."[39] African and African diaspora archival theorists have, over several decades, offered a number of important and cautionary tales about rebuilding African and African diaspora lives from problematic and dispersed sources.[40] Michel-Rolph Trouillot famously warned of a force he called "archival power," namely the power to define what is and is not a salient or worthy site of research. Trouillot also cautioned against the silences in (almost exclusively Europe-originating) historical records, silences borne by fact creation, assembly, retrieval, and significance, the very "making of history."[41] The archive of African exile, reconstructed as it may be from complex and at times confounding sources, speaks to the lived experiences of persecution in an increasingly globalized mobile migratory age. We are recreating, not creating an archive here. It already exists and is defined in the voices and experiences of exile—however diverse, fragmentary, disconnected, or scattered in space and time.[42]

Archival silences and their profound consequences—what Ann Laura Stoler has called "disabled histories"—are a reflection of the many African experiences that went unrecorded or were considered such common knowledge as to be unworthy of official notation.[43] Listening for the silences—those who forgot, those who would rather forget, and those who cannot forget—is foundational to the historiography of the archive of the African slave experience.[44] Indeed, just as the history of power is central to the history of slavery and abolition, so too, as Jacques Derrida revealed, is the history of control and political power central to the history of the archive and of archiving itself.[45] In order to reveal the reconstructed exile archive we need to become cognizant of the rewarded competency to bury the very existence of the exiled—the clerks, bureaucrats, and executives who decided "what stories could not be told"—and what lives and histories were thus buried by the punishment of exile.[46] Exiles were the recipients of punishment, and their complaints relegated to the lowest echelons of credibility by the intermediary agents of colonial power; or, as Andrew Ashforth contends in his evaluation of the colonial South African Native Affairs Commission, "the real seat of power" is "the bureau, the locus of writing" relaying orders, such as imprisonment, banishment, and deportation.[47]

But exiles are not all silenced as this collection shows; they "wrote themselves into the historical record at every opportunity" and resisted silencing with all the means they could muster.[48] Some exiles—like the trans-Atlantic Tinchant family, recovered by Rebecca J. Scott and Jean M. Hébrard, or the orphans embroiled with the infamous Amistad case—clung with "tenacious commitment" to vestiges of dignity and respect.[49] The exile archive is thus multisited and discursive. Some of the sites might be described as the "comfortable" depositories of state bureaucracies where tedious and mundane records mix with evidence of violence and dissimulation.[50] But others are located in union halls where evidence is uncovered in interviews with former liberation leaders, in repositories of memory established and maintained by those who fought against state repression, in the public sphere where song, and poetry, and rumor circulate.

In cases where information is gathered online from asynchronous conversations within communities that are at once local and global, and where information can be erased not only by state powers but also by a despotism of technological development that renders obsolete the software and hardware necessary to access that information, the "site" of research becomes even more difficult to discern and the location of the archive not singular.[51] The archive of exile is thus not primarily concerned with "archives-as-things" and does not constitute a physical space in which one breathes in documentary decay. Nor is the archive of exile primarily understood as concerning "archiving-as-process."[52] Achille Mbembe reminds us that "not all documents are destined to be in archives," and that only some meet his "criteria of archivability." Archives are routinely the "work of the state;" they are the product of judgment; they reflect the exercise of power and authority; they are coded and classified; and distributed by chronology, theme and geography; they are preidentified and preinterpreted. But for Mbembe, the archive is not data but status. We think Mbembe perhaps overreaches when he calls the archive a "sepulchre."[53] We reject the notion that death is required for institutionalization and archival status. The archive of exile is what we make of it and what we make; we need to be involved in its assemblage—*a faire parler les documents*.[54]

Part of this involvement is a mental reconfiguration of how we understand exile and its place in histories of state power. In so doing, we also consider both ruptures and continuities between colonial and postcolonial histories and the question of how to link seemingly disparate histories, across time and space, in a single discursive field. Omnia El Shakry has asked how shifting our understanding of the "moment" of decolonization might reshape how we understand the "archives of decolonization." If we see decolonization not as a clearly defined historical moment bracketed by colonialism and independence but as "an ongoing process and series of struggles" we can begin to see the diverse actors and struggles involved in decolonization, and thus also broaden our understanding of an archive of decolonization.[55] We might similarly ask what are the implications of understanding exile not as an aside or tangent in broader histories of state making, but as a critical practice that speaks to the very nature, and limits, of authority, punishment, and a state's ability to make, remake, and erase history.

The Dahomean statues remind us that the remnants of exile *and* exiles are rich and diverse. The many genres, textual forms, and media testify to the practices and experiences of displacement. The archives of exile inhabit state depositories. Administrative correspondence, frontier reports, penal codes, and legal documents provide context for understanding the use and intention of exile. These materials pinpoint some of the legal origins of exile policy. As Nathan Carpenter's discussion of exile in French West Africa in this volume suggests, there is evidence that exile was not simply another form of punishment, but a practice that had particular motives and objectives—extinction, erasure, and ultimately oblivion. These materials allow historians to trace the legal and philosophical genealogies of exile and thus challenge assumptions of the colonial state as exceptional or abnormal. Reading colonial correspondence, reports, and petitions reveals new voices from exile. Trina Hogg, in an important intervention into the history of colonial law, evaluates herein Sierra Leonean documentation to show that the processes of displacement and exile, and the experience of detention on the ground, could in fact shape European understandings of terms like "political prisoner" with implications for subsequent British colonial law.

Hidden in these administrative archives, though, is also evidence of the agency of exiles and the strategies employed to contest state power. Drawing on "random petitions," Marie Rodet's and Romain Tiquet's contribution examines letters written by those subject to French relegation, in the French Soudan and beyond, in order to show that these individuals were not only "objects of information" but also historical agents. Letters and petitions comprise a good portion of the archives of exile.[56] They give historians access to the experience of exile, however mediated.[57] Rodet and Tiquet elucidate how exiles strategically asserted citizenship rights, claiming inclusion even from spaces designed to exclude, to erase, and to silence. Exiles also contested colonial impositions and claimed local political autonomy, as Thaïs Gendry's Sanwi case study from Côte d'Ivoire demonstrates. Letter-writing campaigns were part of a political strategy that included migration from home. Thus exile was not a passive sentence. The Sanwi were "enacting exile" in order to resist French impositions and declare political sovereignty. Thus, if official state archives serve to represent the state, the archive of exile can also undercut it. It highlights the cracks and anxieties present even within official authority.

Gendry's notion of "enacting exile" signals the agency of exiles and points to the overlap between local, national, and international agendas. Personal correspondence sheds light on the various ways exiles shaped their own narratives for particular audiences. When Joanna Tague recounts how Mozambican refugees wrote to potential sponsors in the United States, for example, we see how they described themselves as legitimate liberation fighters, as incipient leaders, and as committed students and teachers. Tague's chapter, situated in the correspondence between refugees and the American Committee on Africa, finds many examples of the ways in which Mozambican exiles attempted to attain passage to an expatriate life in the United States and to create pathways for leaving and returning. In other instances, the language used to discuss communities in exile served to conceal the experience of exile. Thus Ruma Chopra, following free blacks from the Americas to Sierra Leone, brings together abolitionist notebooks, correspondence, and scientific journals to show how botany, commerce, abolition, and exile "constituted" and undergirded British empire, all the while hiding the brutality of social exclusion, displacement, and state power through language of the natural.

The archive of exile is situated internationally and transnationally. Tague's chapter, and also Kate Skinner's, note that African exiles did not qualify as refugees under the 1951 Geneva Convention on the Status of Refugees and thus had to find alternative ways to gain international support. Skinner shows how, in exile, Ewe communities engaged international aid networks, the United Nations, and the International Red Cross to address their grievances. More importantly, however, by turning to interviews and Ewe-language newspapers, she shows that refugees also tapped into longstanding regional support networks. Drawing on this less-visible archive, she highlights the ambivalence to Pan-Africanism by many Africans who did not embrace ideas of national belonging and territorial sovereignty. Many cases of exile were carried out in response to national or imperial violence. But this did not mean that such movements could be removed from local or regional contexts: exile could also be informed by local and historical struggles over economic power and political authority.

The archives of exile attest to the creative potential of exile, via poetry, prose, music, and performance. This is clearly expressed in Cape Verdean songs and poetry that, in content and creation, have served to connect exile diasporas across the globe. Marina Berthet's chapter locates in the poetry of Eugénio

Tavares a portrayal of the pain and suffering experienced by those who departed and a presentation of displacement as a "rite of passage." Exile, as Bruce Whitehouse writes, both "exposes strangers to exploitation" and offers opportunities otherwise not accessible back home.[58] It was through migration, displacement, and exile that communities were built and maintained—intellectually, spiritually, and materially. The language of exile is directed at particular audiences in distinct registers. The poetry and music created by émigré artists such as Tavares or Gabriel Mariano were created with particular audiences in mind. Songs were written in Kriol for, and about, the Cape Verdean community in exile. We see a similar process unfold in the poetry of the West African Sufi leader, and founder of the Murīd brotherhood, Cheikh Ahmadu Bamba. His poetry was similarly written to be legible to certain people, namely those who could decipher what Sana Camara describes as the "allusive and symbolic expressionism" of Bamba's "poems of the seaway." If such works were designed to be read by those "in the know," other texts have been created for the public realm, to communicate the experience of exile to broad national and international audiences. Thus, for example, while Cape Verdean exiles wrote songs in Kriol, they often wrote their poetry in Portuguese precisely because it provided an opportunity to levy a broad public critique against colonial oppression.

The archive of exile emerges in the public sphere: in newspapers, in popular song and poetry, on television and online. The arguments over belonging that Brett Shadle describes in his examination of the twentieth-century deportation of whites from colonial Kenya were played out in public, in newspaper articles and editorials. In contrast to the rhetoric employed in letter-writing campaigns, newspapers were meant for wide circulation, where questions about belonging and exclusion, of right action, exile, and deportation were to be discussed outside the bureaus of state administration. In circulated print, whites in British East Africa worked through what it meant to be a white settler in Kenya and what it meant to belong in Africa. Such public discourse could also mean that the experience of displacement, indeed one's identity, could be "announced even before it is realized."[59]

The voices of the exile archive are multivalent and often speak at cross-purposes. The experience of displacement is not uniform. It is shaped by gender, age, ethnicity, nationality, class, indeed any number of identities and factors. Aliou Ly's interviews with women involved in Guinea-Bissau's liberation war show not only how Bissau women shaped, advanced, and fundamentally altered the political strategy of the nationalists, but also how these changes were cultivated during the nationalist organization's exile in neighboring Guinea.[60] The archive of exile also resides in incomplete records of lost opportunities, failures, and disasters. Not all opportunities were constructive. Kris Inman's chapter identifies the legacy of Osama bin Laden's exile in the Islamic Republic of the Sudan throughout the archival record of subsequent terrorist activities in sub-Saharan Africa.[61] Using public statements by al-Shabaab and statements attributed to Osama bin Laden, Inman provides an alternative theory as to why al-Shabaab has focused its foreign terrorist attacks on Kenya. This is an analysis that takes seriously the public declarations of al-Shabaab and the influence of Osama bin Laden, who honed a unique political strategy and his antiwestern and anti-American rhetoric during his exile in Sudan.

The archive of exile moves and expands with exiles abroad. Exile communities were often multinational and transnational in makeup, and had shared goals to combat state oppression. Such hubs of exile—Paris, London, Accra, Conakry, Dar es Salaam—were not beyond the reach, however, of those states from which refugees had fled. States too found ways to operate beyond their territorial boundaries. Drawing on a rich trove of interviews, Susan Dabney Pennybacker's chapter demonstrates not only that hubs of exile like London offered opportunity but also that they were fraught with danger. They could be entry points for extraterritorial surveillance by oppressive regimes—South African security forces surveilled anti-apartheid activists and South African exiles in London, with the tacit consent of the British government. Meredith Terretta's reading of court petitions, memoranda, and appeals, shows the great network of transnational support for refugees such as the Zaïrian Cléophas Kamitatu, who dared push back against Congolese state oppression. Importantly, the exile archive Terretta's chapter examines emerged from an attempted deportation initiated by a transnational network that supported state oppression. Kamitatu found refuge in Paris; but Mobutu's terror extended far beyond Zaïre, and even into metropolitan Belgium and France.

The archive of exile consists of forceful challenges to received wisdom, authoritative consensus, and narratives of statecraft. Ann McDougall's study of the Mauritanian diaspora in the United States offers a nuanced intervention into studies of identity formation in exile. Identity was framed by investigative news organizations such as CNN as well as online public representations of Mauritanian groups on YouTube videos, websites, and discussion threads. Exiles in the postcolonial era have, to borrow from Dorothy Hodgson's study of Maasai identity, positioned themselves "within complex, potent, shifting fields of power, including not just the nation-state, but international NGOs, the United Nations, and transnational advocacy networks."[62] This positioning often takes place within the context of very real state oppression and violence, and thus the testimony of exiles constitutes what Benjamin N. Lawrance describes in this volume as an oral historical archive of political persecution. In the testimonies of torture from Togo presented in asylum courts, he finds documentation of the personal histories of persecution by the state. Such narratives have been informed by a host of international organizations, human rights attorneys, and country experts.

Exile is not a singular experience. Looking beyond the image created by state institutions one can find a cacophony of voices that speak to the humanity of people displaced by political forces. Thus three Dahomean statues in a Paris museum reveal not only a royal history but also a clear representation of French power. But the statues are not the only evidence of this moment in time. When Béhanzin died in exile, his wives returned to Dahomey, but his son, Ouanilo, did not. Ouanilo spent much of his life in France where he continued to advocate on behalf of his parents. To supplement this static image of statues why not consider Ouanilo's calling card? Ouanilo attached his card to a handwritten note asking for an audience with the Governor General of French West Africa. The card is noteworthy for its elegantly printed font introducing "Prince Arini Ouanilo Behanzin," its firm black border, and the handwritten address of Ouanilo's Parisian apartment. Ouanilo wrote many such letters, variously asking for the repatriation of his father's remains, advocating for his mother in Dahomey, or requesting permission to travel to Dahomey, or to his father's grave in Algeria. The exile of Béhanzin extended to his son, who remained abroad even after the death of his father, allowed only to return to Dahomey in 1921 when he was granted permission to visit his homeland for six months. Béhanzin's remains were returned seven years later, in 1928 in a tragic journey. The French government granted Ouanilo permission to repatriate his father's remains. But it was his last voyage to his homeland. Ouanilo fell sick on the return journey and died in a hospital in Dakar. He was buried in France, and his own remains were finally repatriated to Abomey eighty years later, in 2006.[63] The histories of exile extend across continents and over generations. The legacies of exile are long, and the memories of exile linger.[64]

In contrast with the static image of Dahomean statues locked away in a museum, we have here a dynamic archive comprising records scattered today across Africa, Europe, and North America, in archives housed by former colonies, hidden by erstwhile overlords, and in vibrant public debates in new metropoles. From letters and testimonies of asylum seekers, activists, and liberation fighters, the songs and poetry of émigré artists, the interviews of those who have returned home and those who remain abroad, we resuscitate individuals, families, and communities, those who have struggled and continue to struggle against attempts to erase and forget. This volume is far from a complete picture of Africans in exile.[65] The geography of Africans in exile is global. And the archive itself is much more diverse, scattered, and rich than what we can present here. We offer, though, an entry point—to see in the disconnected experiences of exile a common history, and to view in the scattered, seemingly arbitrary, and often hidden testaments of exile, a coherent archive.

How to Read and Teach this Volume

In order to make sense of the complexity and diversity of the African exile experience, we offer three analytical frameworks exploring, in turn, legality and

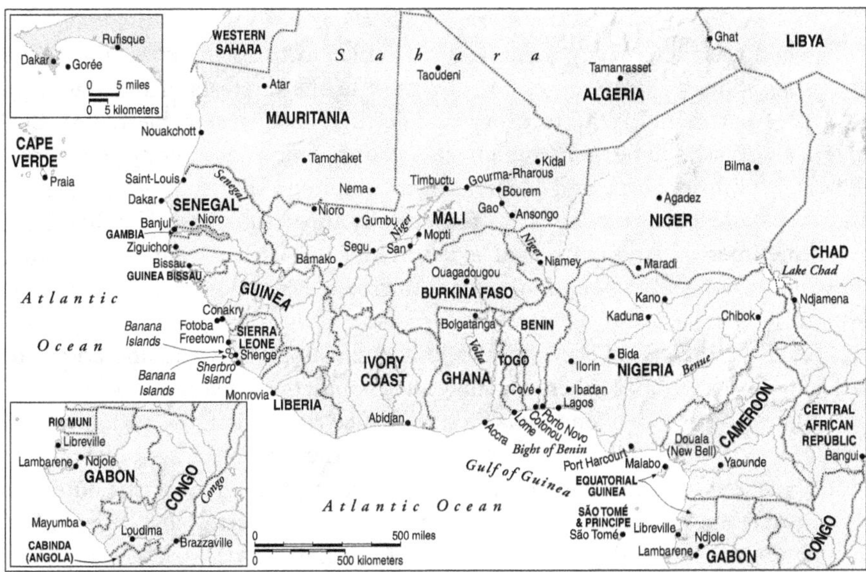

Map I.2 West Africa. (Philip Schwartzberg.)

illegality, then geography and mobility, and finally performance, identity, and memory. While there are many ways to read the archives of exile, once recovered and reconstructed, the volume is organized in three thematic sections that place narratives of exile from different time periods and political situations in conversation with one another. Though surely not the only way to think about, theorize, or categorize archives of exile, we believe they are three fundamental starting points for thinking about exile in Africa.

Part One—The Legal Worlds of Exile—brings together a series of studies that ask what were the legal genealogies of exile. Colonial spaces were "laboratories" for imperial law and often combined metropolitan codes with new and experimental legal frameworks that, while designed for specific cases, were broadly applied.[66] These chapters thus consider the ways in which exile reinforced and challenged empire through physical settlement and resettlement, as seen in Chopra's chapter, and through law, as Hogg and Carpenter describe in their chapters.[67] Because sentences of exile were rooted in law, they offered unanticipated opportunities for exiles to contest their sentences. These contestations are reveled in the archive in petitions and letters, like those uncovered by Rodet, Tiquet, and Gendry. Here, the challenge to empire came both through petition campaigns and physical demonstration. Part One concludes with Shadle's analysis of exile in colonial Kenya where the question of homeland is considered in the context of colonial white settler societies. For those settlers who claimed Africa as their homeland, was state-sanctioned displacement a sentence of deportation, or a sentence of exile?

This section questions the myriad ways states dealt with individuals who threatened their legitimacy. Exile is a particular form of coercive power. The exiled individuals were seen as so subversive to the interests of the state that their presence alone in the territory was deemed an unacceptable threat. But, they also directly challenged fundamental claims of authority; they undermined the legal, philosophical, and ideological assumptions that supported colonial and postcolonial state power.[68] This is especially apparent in cases that highlight the sometimes creative nature of exile. Where the state intent was erasure, those who were exiled often found ways to create, organize, establish, grow, or expand.

Exile was integral to the earliest colonization efforts in Africa and crucial to state attempts to control otherwise subversive populations. Every European colonial regime used exile to end dynasties, to silence rival chieftaincies, to forestall millennial religious resistance, and to facilitate the seizure of agricultural and pastoral lands for industrial enterprises or settler farmers. Historians note that European systems of exile were employed very early on during the "moment" of occupation and colonial wars of conquest.[69] These policies were part of a long history of state-sanctioned banishment by European states dating back at least as far as ostracism in ancient Greece.[70] As with these ancient policies of ostracism, exile in the colonial context served to remove those individuals or groups who threatened to undermine the very foundations upon which state power was assumed.[71] Yet, although the genealogy of colonial exile might be traced to ancient policies of banishment, the role of exile in the colonial context was worked out on the ground in an ad hoc fashion as part of a system of legal interactions that predated colonial rule.[72] Early colonial iterations of exile demonstrate that the practice was sometimes exploratory as European powers and African interlocutors began to see the capacity of removal as a mechanism of control; and sometimes, as Bala Saho has shown, Europeans disagreed as to its legality and purpose.[73] With the passage of time, however, exile developed into an explicitly political punishment, and one with distinct policy objectives.

Colonial regimes punished different people differently. The experience of exiles differed significantly from other widely employed punishments such as forced labor, confinement and incarceration, corporal punishment in the form of the notorious *chicotte* and "palm beating," or even summary execution.[74] In their examinations of the legal genealogies of exile, these essays engage a rich scholarly literature that addresses the nature of colonial law and its persistence into the postcolonial epoch. The historiography of colonial law and its application is deeply contested. On the one hand, historians have argued that law was instrumental to colonial rule. Here, law structured and limited the interactions of people on the ground. But, law could also, even if rarely, mean a sort of self-imposed limit on administrative power.[75] Because of this, historians have come

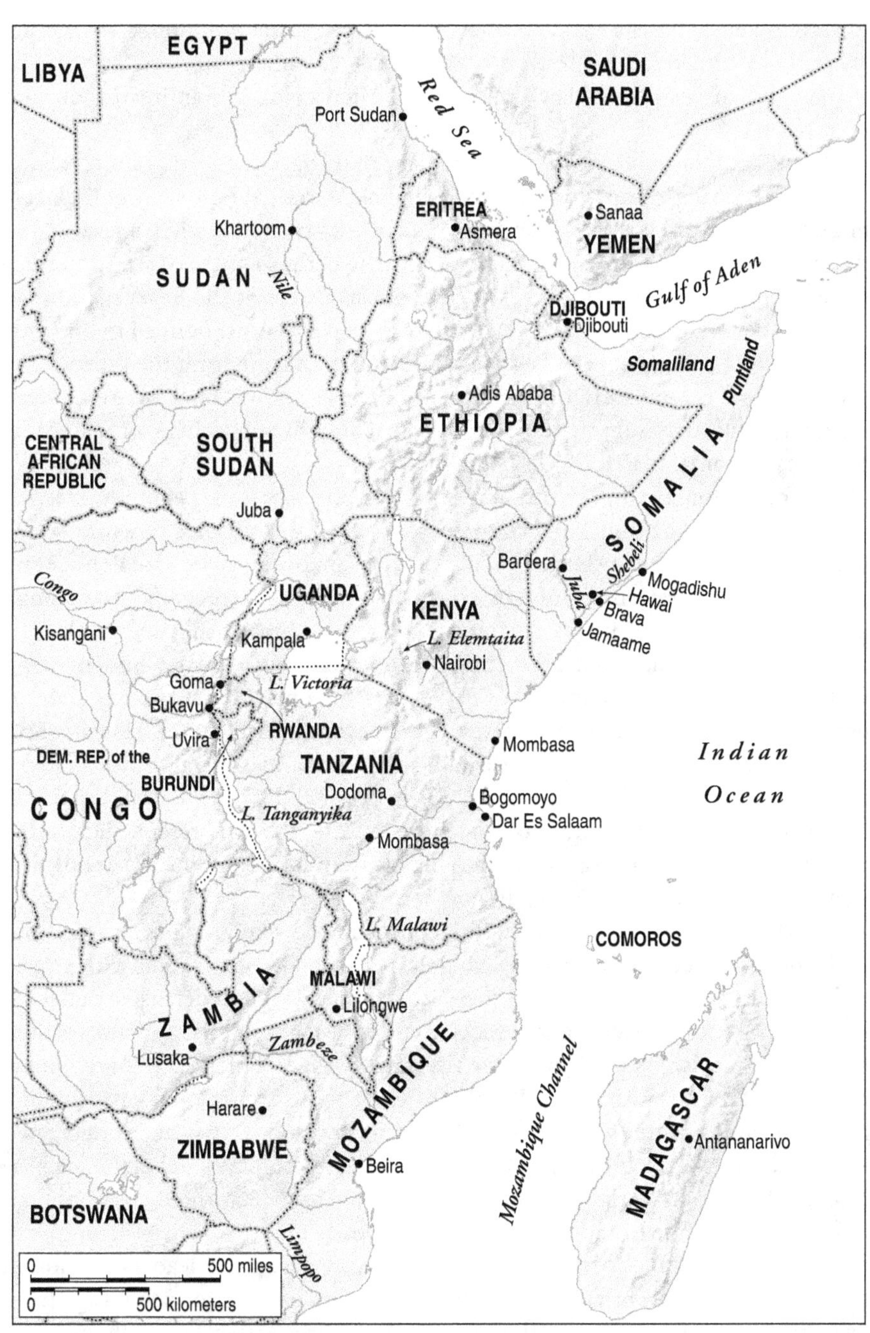

Map I.3 East Africa. (Philip Schwartzberg.)

to recognize legal claims and conflicts as markers of the limitations of colonial attempts to control people and resources.[76] The colonial realm was partly constituted by an "empire of law" that undergirded colonial administration and domination.[77]

On the other hand, however, some historians have found that an emphasis on law veils how arbitrary violence, often couched in legal terms, lay at the heart of European colonial rule.[78] Framing the debate as such, though, suggests a distinction that, in the end, likely did not exist. The perhaps unsurprising and well-documented reality is that both law and violence were at the heart of colonial rule. The colonial state in Africa, like all modern states, was founded in both law and violence; the two cannot be wholly separated, the one from the other.[79] The practice of exile demonstrates the ways in which law and violence were employed together to rule over subject populations. We highlight how policies of exile fitted into these colonial matrices of law and violence.

Under colonial administrations exile was one part of a penal regime that was meant to "tame political, economic and cultural resistance to white domination."[80] In the mid-twentieth century, and on the cusp of decolonization, colonial administrations turned to exile again as a way to preempt anticolonial political mobilization. It was during this period that many anti-imperial, anti-apartheid, nationalist, and pan-African movements moved first underground and then abroad as regimes clamped down on open dissent. Such policies extended through the colonial period and beyond. Postcolonial states subsequently employed exile as a tool of political control as struggles over government organization and constitutional power erupted during the first decades of independence, some of which continue to percolate into the present, such as the dispute over forced removals from the Chagos Islands near Mauritius or ongoing rivalries in the Emirate of Kano, in northern Nigeria.[81]

Part Two—Geographies of Exile—considers the spatial logics of exile and nodes of resistance and activism. During the period of decolonization, exile served not only as a tool of coercion and social control but also as a defensive outlet for persecuted political leaders and anticolonial parties. Nationalist and anticolonial organizations such as the Zimbabwe African National Union, the Mozambique Liberation Front, the Union of Peoples of Cameroon, and the African National Congress, among others, found voice, training, and support as they congregated at certain cities—or hubs—in Africa and across the globe.[82] Scholars, such as Michael Panzer, have rightly pointed to the ways in which these cosmopolitan hubs of resistance helped bolster nationalist politics and linked local struggles to the global political landscape.[83] But, it was not only nationalist leaders that found themselves in exile. Entire communities fled across borders to seek refuge from oppression and war. Many of the chapters here direct attention to the ways in which exile produced new affective states outside of conventional political rhetoric.

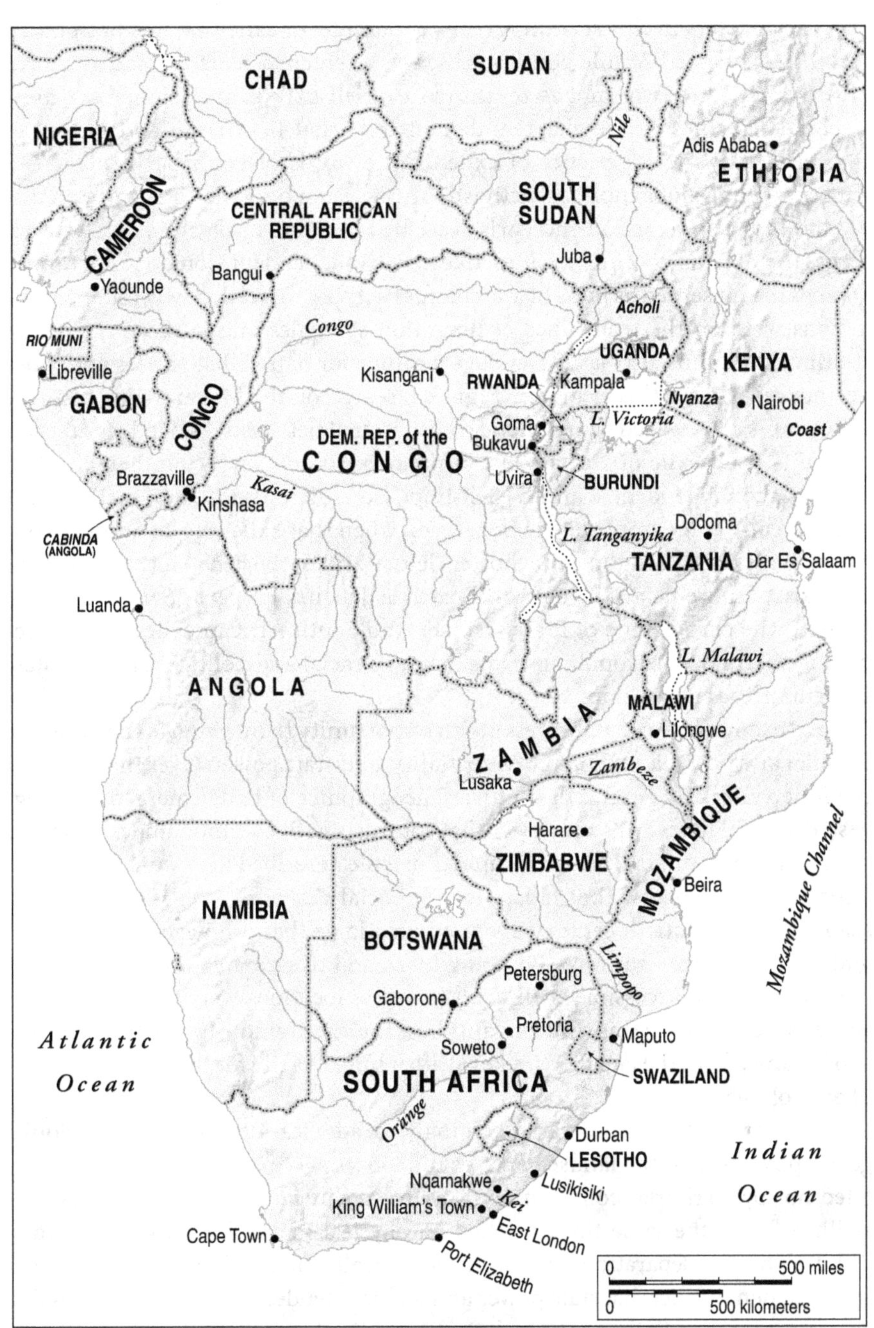

Map I.4 Southern Africa. (Philip Schwartzberg.)

The chapters in this section reveal a geography of exile that was both nodal and interconnected. While political exile was a sentence, it also served as a form of resistance. Part Two emphasizes the place of self-exile in anticolonial and anti-imperial struggles. These chapters demonstrate that in African and European sites of refuge, the experience of exile, in the words of Pennybacker, "merged with that of the global political activist." This was not only the case in the metropolitan capitals of London and Paris described by Pennybacker and Terretta, but across the African continent. Cities, like newly independent Conakry, Accra, and Dar es Salaam served as hubs of anticolonial activity. Indeed, newly independent nations were on the front lines of liberation struggles taking place across the continent and thus also served as sites of refuge for nationalist parties and those fleeing war. We see this clearly in Tague's research on the Mozambique Institute where refugees engaged sympathetic transnational networks, and in Ly's description of the self-exile of Guinea-Bissau nationalists to Conakry in neighboring, and newly independent, Guinea. Self-imposed exile did not necessarily mean, however, an escape from state terror—even when that exile was on another continent. Paris and London both hosted leftist and activist networks. But Paris also hosted more nefarious networks, such as Jacques Foccart's *Service d'Action Civique*, the cornerstone of Françafrique. And South African exiles found freedom in their new metropolitan home, but also racial and political division, state surveillance, and isolation.

An examination of exile presents an opportunity to interrogate the nature of colonial and postcolonial mobility, spatiality, and state power. Over the course of the nineteenth and twentieth centuries, geographies of exile emerged that suggested a nodal nature of state power that contrasts with common understandings of colonial territoriality. The geographies of exile described here were functional, noncontiguous spaces, "borderless foci of social activity."[84] The colonial landscapes of the twentieth century operated on a logic that privileged technologies and infrastructure—railways, shipping lines, and telegraphs for example—such that previously inaccessible or difficult to access locations were drawn into state surveillance regimes; this shift explains how the once remote Seychelles archipelago became, from the late 1800s, a key British imperial site for the exilic detention of anticolonial operatives.[85]

The geography of exile was a seemingly paradoxical extension of the colonial geography. As with the landscape of colonial occupation and control, it was dictated not by territorial continuity but rather "technical needs and physical possibilities."[86] At the same time, it relied on physical removal from state territory, linking physical separation with political neutralization. This geography of exile exposes then the fact that state power and terror extended across nation states and across continents. Exile as an analytical framework can show how postcolonial regimes exercised power that at times mapped on to prior imperial networks, such that Gregory Mann calls the post-1960 Sahelian desert "the supreme site of exile."[87] Terretta's treatment of Mobutu oppositionists in Paris and beyond demonstrates this well. The theoretical limit of modern state sovereignty—the territorial boundary beyond which the state had no legitimate jurisdiction—was never sacred.[88]

The nodal geography of exile, however, also opened up opportunities. Hubs of exile, such as Libreville, Paris, London, and Accra were cosmopolitan spaces that held out the opportunity for certain people to gain economic, political, or spiritual influence.[89] Certain cities attracted self-exiled political activists. Exiled political leaders often found greater freedom to plan, maintain, and conduct political opposition than back home. Previously isolated movements gained new support from well-connected and motivated international organizations.[90] Some nationalist movements found voice in exile.[91] The presence of these transnational groups comprised of individuals of various political persuasions could radicalize host communities in unexpected ways.[92] But it was not always the case: states may have been sympathetic to the anti-imperialist struggle, but, as Skinner points out, that did not necessarily translate into unequivocal support for political dissent, especially if that dissent threatened to undermine their own national political power.

African exilic practices are first and foremost physical movements: from home, village, "tribe," ethnic group, kingdom, state, nation, region, homeland, or continent. With this in mind our second section broadly resituates the *African* experience of exile on the continuum of distinctly African mobilities that erupt with the inception of Africa's encounter with Europe in the fifteenth century. Exile, as it is revealed in these case studies, lies between historical and contemporary bookends of the massive forced displacement of Africans characteristic of the modern epoch, between the first forced removals of African slaves up to and including the contemporary massive displacement of refugees, asylum-seekers, and victims of human trafficking networks.

Part Three—Remembering and Performing Exile—considers the characteristics and resilience of exiles in the face of adversity. This final section turns to those voices from exile and the testimonies of the displaced: testimony given in song, poetry, in international courts, on television, and online. Exile is experienced, but it is also performed. The productive forces of exile have often been unanticipated and have included trenchant critiques of state violence, arbitrary rule, and illegitimate authority.[93] These performances not only challenge state legitimacy but in so doing also, in the words of Lawrance, "instantiate" the nation. Life in exile has the ability to reify national identity as much as it erodes it. It can also serve to embolden, radicalize, and focus contemporary transnational politics and ideologies.

As the chapters in this third section demonstrate, even within this particular framework, the history of exile is diverse and multifaceted. Exile was both a political sentence meted out by state agents and apparatuses and also a deeply personal experience. It was a tool of oppression; but those who wielded it did not necessarily have control over the results. Often, sentences of exile were an attempt at erasure through removal from homeland. And, often that was the result. People lived, and died, in exile. Most will not be remembered on the centenary of their death. But in other instances, exile did not mean erasure. On the contrary, and often surprisingly, exile could be generative.

Without denying the reality of exile as death, histories of exile also point to alternative, sometimes unanticipated, outcomes. In some places, as Alysson Hobbs has shown in her history of African American racial "passing," it served as a creative force, reifying nascent identities and bolstering otherwise disparate groups.[94] In her study of Hutu nationalism in exile, Liisa Malkki depicts refugee exile as productive and reproductive of ethnic and national identities; these solidify a collective outlook even while outside of the territorial limits of the state.[95] One group of refugees can generate multiple, even fundamentally opposing, histories of their exile that include histories of death and rebirth. The space of exile then was not only one of erasure. It could also be a space in which one could create a "subversive recasting and reinterpretation" of history.[96]

The "subversive recasting" extends well beyond histories of national identity. Cheikh Ahmadu Bamba's exile is one of the best known examples of the generative potential of exile. Bamba recounted his late-nineteenth-century exile as a period of particular hardship. But, both he and his followers also later saw it as an important moment in his spiritual journey.[97] Today, the celebration of his first exile, known as the *maggal*, is marked by an annual pilgrimage to Touba, the holy city of the Murīd brotherhood, and is one of the most important celebrations of the disciples of Bamba.[98]

Just as colonial powers punished dissidents with various forms of relegation, deportation, and exile, postcolonial states wielded exile strategically, revisiting the practice to compel political dissidents into self-imposed exclusion. The decidedly unexceptional nature of exile in the African political landscape since the late twentieth century altered ways of thinking, knowing, and describing. Regional and global migration flows, camps, and ad hoc settlements meant to be temporary have in fact often become permanent in which "veritable imaginary nations henceforth live."[99] In some instances new political structures emerge out of the intersection of local, national, and global forces—both grassroots formations founded in the experience of refugee life as well as top down "decentralized despotism" driven by the responses of NGOs with humanitarian objectives.[100] The experience of exile also reminds us that it is not only the nation-state that wields political power and threatens those who might undermine control. And, it often impacts people already marginalized within their own societies. As

Aberash Bekele attests, where social relations, marriage, and kinship are closely aligned with political power and local authority, exile is both a fate and strategy for women and children faced with local oppression.[101]

This final section similarly highlights contestation over exile and memory. Life in exile has the ability to reify identities and subjectivities, national and otherwise. This occurs, as McDougall argues, through the stories that exiles tell themselves and the stories that others, especially media outlets, tell about exiled communities. How people talk about, sing about, write about, and remember exile reveals not only the great anguish that accompanied displacement but also how people operated, adapted, and lived within systems of political, economic, and spiritual oppression. Stories and memories of exile are mediated in complex ways. Informed by lawyers, activists, and engaged scholars, political exiles rehearse their narratives and instantiate themselves as national subjects. These experiences, Lawrance reminds us, challenge claims of state legitimacy today just as they have in the past.

* * *

Africans in Exile offers coherent, compelling, and original interpretations of the capacity of exile to structure political power, cultural change, and social transformation. The authors in the chapters that follow reveal, in diverse histories, a common thread of historical experience of exiles challenging fundamental assumptions of political authority and destabilizing the legal and ideological foundations of colonial and postcolonial state power. In these archives of exile we can find stories of resilience, of transformation, and of empowerment even under circumstances of oppression and hardship.

Collectively, these chapters convincingly demonstrate that far from being an exceptional experience, exile is more usefully conceived of as part of one of the defining features of the modern era: coerced displacement. While exile was experienced by elite figures, it was not uniquely, or even primarily, a sentence for kings and queens, political leaders, or individual oppositionists to authoritarian rule. The romantic notion of exile as a noble and royal sentence is a skewed vision. Nor can exile narratives be flattened into simple stories of erasure. As the Sierra Leonean poet, Syl Cheney-Coker's "Concerto for an Exile" proclaims, the experience is embodied, carried across generations:

> I have my Nova Scotian madness my tree of agony
> and let me brothers know I walk the streets of exile
> clutching their bullets in my soul![102]

For Cheney-Coker, exile is "a site for the construction of self and the interrogation of collective impulse," according to Henri Oripeloye.[103] While erasure through removal may have been the aim of states who forced or otherwise compelled individuals or groups to seek refuge outside of state boundaries, the stories here demonstrate that exiles, even though physically separated from their homeland, resourcefully resist *resection*, or being "cut out," through strategies developed to build, maintain, and recreate the social, political, and cultural bonds strained by displacement.[104]

The essays in this volume are diverse. They cover many different examples of political exile across and beyond the continent from the early colonial period and the continued ravages of the trans-Atlantic slave trade to the late postcolonial present epoch and the so-called "War on Terror." Each case is different. Even within the same empire, agents of state power treated different people differently.[105] Readers are thus encouraged to consider the particularities of each case and reflect on the various constraints and opportunities that shaped how people responded to sentences of exile. We hope readers will ponder the interconnected questions that undergird these studies: What purposes did exile serve for those in power? How did exiled subjects experience their displacement? How has exile been remembered?

At the same time, the presumption of this volume is that what has previously been viewed as disconnected instances of dislocation, these seemingly exceptional experiences scattered around through time and space, when woven together tell a compelling, coherent, and important story. We thus hope readers also see here, in the diverse experiences of individual exiles, a common thread. When Mozambican fighters set up schools in exile in neighboring Tanzania; when leftist oppositionists and anti-imperial activists converged in London and Paris; when millions of Murīds today travel annually to celebrate the exile of Bamba; when Cape Verdeans perform songs about colonial forced labor regimes in São Tomé in European music festivals; what we are witnessing is not only the brutal legacies of state-sanctioned exile, but also evidence of the limits of those states to dictate experience, history, and memory. This volume is thus a starting point to investigate a heretofore neglected tool of state power, and a common experience in African history that maintains salience in our contemporary world. Scholars and students alike will find in the following chapters stories that challenge current conceptions of exile and displacement and narratives that push us beyond the tropes of exile as life, or exile as death.

This book ends with a reflection on exile by a scholar, activist, journalist and refugee, Baba Galleh Jallow, and an Afterword by Emily Burrill. As editor of the *Daily Observer*, and then as founder and editor of *The Independent*, Jallow investigated, exposed, and wrote about state power and the abuses of the regime of Yahya Jammeh in The Gambia. He did so even after witnessing the full force of that state power—harassment, arson, imprisonment, torture, execution—levied against colleagues, friends, and family. Because of this stance, Jallow faced detention, harassment, threats to himself, his family, his fellow journalists. Following a series of attacks, including the burning of the offices and press of *The Independent*, and after Gambian security forces arrested his parents, accused him of not being a Gambian, and threatened his family, he fled the land of his birth and has lived in exile ever since. *The Independent* was eventually shut down after he left the country.[106]

As is the case with many stories of exile, Jallow's experience highlights how exile exposes fundamental state insecurities. Jammeh's dictatorship rested on the foundations of censorship, fear, and dissimulation. Journalists like Jallow and his many colleagues exposed and undercut those foundations.[107] His story is also a testimony of the ways in which communities are maintained in exile and how those communities have continued to fight back, from abroad. In early 2017, in response to a united Gambian opposition, and under the threat of a Senegal-led invasion, Jammeh himself fled The Gambia. Jammeh's hurried exile to Equatorial Guinea echoes with Burrill's rejoinder that the "exile or conflict" fiction promulgated by European colonial rulers still has salience today.

The archive of exile shows how policies and practices of exile were rooted in anxieties: concerns that certain individuals or groups threatened to undermine the fragile foundations of oppressive state control, of claimed legitimacy or right, of assumed power. Experience of exile was also fraught with personal anxiety: over unknown futures, about family or communities left behind, of the possibility of erasure, physical or otherwise. The circumstances behind individual exiles, and the experiences of exiles were diverse. But, taken collectively, these varied histories point to the Janus-faced nature of state power: at once supreme and fragile. Here, exile serves as a useful tool for examining the precariousness of power and the tensions that undergird the colonial and postcolonial state. They show too how those people, deemed so very pernicious to state power that they were forced away and abroad, continued to live, rebuild, flourish, and resist from beyond their homelands.

Notes

1. Hélène Joubert and Gaëlle Beaujean-Baltzer, *Béhanzin, Roi d'Abomey: Exposition, Cotonou (Bénin), Fondation Zinsou, 16 Décembre 2006–16 Mars 2007* (Paris: Musée du Quai Branly, 2006).

2. Gaëlle Beaujean-Baltzer, "Du trophée à l'oeuvre: Parcours de cinq artefacts du royaume d'Abomey," *Gradhiva. Revue d'anthropologie et d'histoire des arts* 6 (November 15, 2007): 70–85. For descriptions of the statues see the Quai Branly catalog, inventory numbers: 71.1893.45.1, 71.1893.45.2, 71.1893.45.3, accessed August 14, 2017, http://www.quaibranly.fr/en/explore-collections/.

3. Musée du quai Branly, "Dossier de presse: Centenaire de la mort du roi Béhanzin," Press release, accessed March 29, 2016, http://www.quaibranly.fr/uploads/tx_gayafeespacepresse/MQB-DP-centenaire-mort-du-Roi-Behanzin-Benin-FR.pdf.

4. Johnathan Bascom, *Losing Place: Refugee Populations and Rural Transformations in East Africa* (New York: Berghahn Books, 2001); André Guichaoua, ed. *Exilés, réfugiés, déplacés en Afrique centrale et orientale* (Paris: Karthala, 2004); Assefaw Bariagaber, *Conflict and the Refugee Experience: Flight, Exile, and Repatriation in the Horn of Africa* (Aldershot: Ashgate: 2006); Tricia Redeker Hepner, *Soldiers, Martyrs, and Exiles: Political Conflict in Eritrea and the Diaspora* (Philadelphia: University of Pennsylvania Press, 2009); Alice Wilson, *Sovereignty in Exile: A Saharan Liberation Movement Governs* (Philadelphia: University of Pennsylvania Press, 2016); Margaret D. Rouse-Jones and Estelle M. Appiah, *Returned Exile: A Biography of George James Christian of Dominica and the Gold Coast, 1869–1940* (St. Augustine: University of the West Indies Press, 2016).

5. For the "noble" choice, consider D. J. M. Muffett, "Legitimacy and Deference in a Tradition Oriented Society: Observations Arising from an Examination of Some Aspects of a Case Study Associated with the Abdication of the Emir of Kano in 1963," *African Studies Review* 18, no. 2 (1975): 101–115. The literature on the African National Congress is replete with the visionary triumph trope. See Paul Gready, *Writing as Resistance: Life Stories of Imprisonment, Exile, and Homecoming from Apartheid South Africa* (Lanham: Lexington Books, 2003); Tom Lodge, "State of Exile: The African National Congress of South Africa, 1976–86," *Third World Quarterly* 9, no. 1 (1987): 1–27; Raymond Suttner, "Culture(s) of the African National Congress of South Africa: Imprint of Exile Experiences," *Journal of Contemporary African Studies* 21, no. 2 (2003): 303–320; Séan Morrow, Brown Maaba, and Loyiso Pulumani, *Education in Exile: SOMAFCO, the ANC School in Tanzania, 1978 to 1992* (Cape Town: Human Sciences Research Council Press, 2004); Ngcobo Lauretta, ed., *Prodigal Daughters: Stories of South African Women in Exile* (Scottsville, S.A.: University of KwaZulu-Natal Press, 2012).

6. Ronald Hyam, "The Political Consequences of Seretse Khama: Britain, the Bangwato and South Africa, 1948–1952," *The Historical Journal* 29, no. 4 (1986): 921–947; Neil Parsons, "The Impact of Seretse Khama on British Public Opinion 1948–56 and 1978," *Immigrants & Minorities* 12 (1993): 195–219; Willie Henderson, "Seretse Khama: A Personal Appreciation," *African Affairs* 89, no. 354 (1990): 27–56.

7. Henri Oripeloye describes slavery as the "fount" of African "literature of exile" in "The Development of Exilic Poetry in Anglophone West Africa," *Tydskrif vir Letterkunde* 52, no. 1 (2015): 158. Further research—building on Liz MacGonagle's pathbreaking work—may yet push the history of exile deeper into the precolonial past, and among African communities prior to a heavy European presence, but that is beyond the scope of this present volume. See Elizabeth MacGonagle, "Living with a Tyrant: Ndau Memories and Identities in the Shadow of Ngungunyana," *The International Journal of African Historical Studies* 41, no. 1 (2008): 29–53.

8. Thomas Pavel, "Exile as Romance and as Tragedy," in *Exile and Creativity: Signposts, Travelers, Outsiders, Backward Glances*, ed. Susan R. Suleiman (Durham: Duke University Press, 1998), 25–36.

9. The romantic representation of exile is perhaps best seen in some of the most widely reproduced images of Africans in exile, including those of Béhanzin, Ranavalona, and Prempeh I. M'Baye Gueye and A. Adu Boahen, "African Initiatives and Resistance in West Africa, 1880–1914," in *UNESCO General History of Africa*, vol. 7, *Africa under Colonial Domination 1880–1935*, ed. A. Adu Boahen (London: Heinemann, 1985), 133; Schomburg Center for Research in Black Culture, Jean Blackwell Hutson Research and Reference Division, The New York Public Library, "Behanzin Captive," The New York Public Library Digital Collections, 1902, accessed February 4, 2017, http://digitalcollections.nypl.org

/items/510d47de-0ed6-a3d9-e040-e00a18064a99. For diaspora, see Elazar Barkan and Marie-Denise Shelton, eds., *Borders, Exiles, Diasporas* (Stanford: Stanford University Press, 1998); for "black expatriates," see Henry Louis Gates, Jr., "The Welcome Table: James Baldwin in Exile," in *Exile and Creativity*, ed. Suleiman, 305–321.

10. For discussion of debilitation and exhaustion, see Abena P. A. Busia, *Testimonies of Exile* (Trenton, New Jersey: Africa World Press, 1990); Manthia Diawara, *We Won't Budge: An African Exile in the World* (New York: Basic Civitas Books, 2003); Audrey Small, "Reversals of Exile: Williams Sassine's *Wirriyamu* and Tierno Monénembo's *Pelourinho*," *African Studies Review* 57, no. 3 (2014): 41–54; Andrew Hernann, "Joking Through Hardship: Humor and Truth-Telling among Displaced Timbuktians," *African Studies Review* 59, no. 1 (2016): 57–76.

11. Pavel, "Exile as Romance and as Tragedy," 27.

12. Jeffrey Herbst, *States and Power in Africa: Comparative Lessons in Authority and Control* (Princeton: Princeton University Press, 2000), 3.

13. For postcolonial political tension, see Claude E. Welch, Jr., "Ideological Foundations of Revolution in Kwilu," *African Studies Review* 18, no. 2 (1975): 116–128; for scholars in exile, see David Kerr and Jack Mapanje, "Academic Freedom and the University of Malawi," *African Studies Review* 45, no. 2 (2002): 73–91. For the most extensive survey of punishment by banishment in apartheid South Africa, see Saleem Badat, *The Forgotten People: Political Banishment under Apartheid* (Leiden: Brill, 2013), which also reprints Can Themba's essay, "Banned to the Bush!" *Drum* (August 1956): 22–24.

14. Consider the masses killed and displaced during Francisco Macias Nguema's dictatorship in Equatorial Guinea, as narrated by Ibrahim K. Sundiata, "The Roots of African Despotism: The Question of Political Culture," *African Studies Review* 31, no. 1 (1988): 9–31.

15. Godfrey Maringira, "Politics, Privileges, and Loyalty in the Zimbabwe National Army," *African Studies Review* 60, no. 2 (2017): 93–113; Bob W. White, "The Political Undead: Is It Possible to Mourn for Mobutu's Zaire?" *African Studies Review* 48, no, 2 (2005): 65–85.

16. For the disruptions spawned by the exilic movements of African colonial soldiers, see Gregory Mann, *Native Sons: West African Veterans and France in the Twentieth Century* (Durham: Duke University Presss, 2006), 79–83, 141–42, 164–65.

17. Edward Said, "Reflections on Exile," *Reflections on Exile and Other Essays* (Cambridge: Harvard University Press, 2000), 174.

18. Adam McKeown, *Melancholy Order: Asian Migration and the Globalization of Borders* (New York: Columbia University Press, 2008). And, while the displacement of tens of millions of people during the Atlantic Slave Trade may pale in comparison to the total number of people displaced across the continent in the twentieth century, its historical, cultural, and economic significance would certainly suggest its inclusion into any discussion of "an age" of mass displacement.

19. Sophia A. McClennen, *Dialectics of Exile: Nation, Time, Language, and Space in Hispanic Literatures* (West Lafayette, IN: Purdue University Press, 2004), 29.

20. Douglas B. Chambers, "'My own nation': Igbo Exiles in the Diaspora," *Slavery and Abolition* 18 (1997): 72–97; Joseph C. Miller, *Way of Death: Merchant Capitalism and the Angolan Slave Trade, 1730–1830* (Madison: University of Wisconsin Press, 1997).

21. Sylviane A. Diouf, *Slavery's Exiles: The Story of the American Maroons* (New York: New York University Press, 2014). For slave narratives, diaspora, and exile, see Pier M. Larson, "Horrid Journeying: Narratives of Enslavement and the Global African Diaspora," *Journal of World History* 19 (2008): 431–464. The dearth of critical analyses of exile in African

historical studies stands in sharp contrast to the immense literature addressing the history of European exile in the twentieth century.

22. W.E.B. Du Bois, *The Souls of Black Folk* (Oxford: Oxford University Press, 2007). For a narrative that places pan-African exile and refugee activism at the heart of transnational anticolonial, antiracist, and counterhegemonic movements in the early twentieth century, see Susan D. Pennybacker, *From Scottsboro to Munich: Race and Political Culture in 1930s Britain* (Princeton: Princeton University Press, 2009). For analyses of exile in pan-African literature, see Wendy W. Walters, ed., *At Home in Diaspora: Black International Writing* (Minneapolis: University of Minnesota Press, 2005).

23. Michael Crowder, ed., *West African Resistance: The Military Response to Colonial Occupation* (London: Hutchinson, 1978).

24. The works that have most critically engaged the question of exile among kings and queens comes not from history but from the realm of literature and film. Maryse Condé, *The Last of the African Kings*, trans. Richard Philcox (Lincoln: University of Nebraska Press, 1997); *L'exil du roi Béhanzin*, directed by Guy Deslauriers (Paris: France 2 Cinéma, 1994). Indeed, much of the literature on exile in Africa comes in the context of discussion of African literature and literary production in exile. See Roger G. Thomas, "Exile, Dictatorship and the Creative Writer in Africa: A Selective Annotated Bibliography," *Third World Quarterly* 9 (1987): 271–296.

25. Tom C. McCaskie, "The Life and Afterlife of Yaa Asantewaa," *Africa: Journal of the International African Institute* 77 (2007): 151–179.

26. See some examples of this press in Joubert and Beaujean-Baltzer, *Béhanzin*; Wendy Wilson-Fall, *Memories of Madagascar and Slavery in the Black Atlantic* (Athens, OH: Ohio University Press, 2015), 150.

27. There is a rich historiography of subaltern resistance during colonialism: A.I. Asiwaju, "Migrations as Revolt: The Example of the Ivory Coast and the Upper Volta before 1945," *Journal of African History* 17 (1976): 577–594; Leroy Vail and Landeg White, "Forms of Resistance: Songs and Perceptions of Power in Colonial Mozambique," *The American Historical Review* 88 (1983): 883–919; James F. Searing, *"God Alone Is King": Islam and Emancipation in Senegal* (Portsmouth, NH: Heinemann, 2002); Benjamin N. Lawrance, "*La révolte des femmes*: Economic Upheaval and the Gender of Political Authority in Lomé, Togo, 1931–33," *African Studies Review* 46 (2003), 43–67.

28. Susan Geiger, *TANU Women: Gender and Culture in the Making of Tanganyikan Nationalism, 1955–1965* (Portsmouth, NH: Heinemann, 1997); Elizabeth Schmidt, *Mobilizing the Masses: Gender, Ethnicity, and Class in the Nationalist Movement in Guinea, 1939–1958* (Portsmouth, NH: Heinemann, 2005); Meredith Terretta, *Nation of Outlaws, State of Violence: Nationalism, Grassfields Tradition, and State Building in Cameroon* (Athens, OH: Ohio University Press, 2014); Kate Skinner, *The Fruits of Freedom in British Togoland: Literacy, Politics and Nationalism, 1914–2014* (Cambridge: Cambridge University Press, 2015).

29. Kerry Ward, *Networks of Empire: Forced Migration in the Dutch East India Company* (Cambridge: Cambridge University Press, 2008); Uma Kothari, "Contesting Colonial Rule: Politics of Exile in the Indian Ocean," *Geoforum* 43 (2012): 697–706; Clare Anderson, "Convicts, Carcerality and Cape Colony Connections in the 19th Century," *Journal of Southern African Studies* 42, no. 3 (2016): 429–442.

30. Said, "Reflections," 137.

31. Ama Biney, "The Development of Kwame Nkrumah's Political Thought in Exile, 1966–1972," *Journal of African History* 50 (2009): 81–100.

32. Mustafah Dhada, "Frankly My Dear, We Should Give a Damn!" *Peace Review* 12, no. 3 (2000): 457.

33. Annick Cojean, "L'exil, c'est une mort symbolique," *Le Monde*, March 15, 2013.

34. R. B. Parkinson, trans., *The Tale of Sinuhe and Other Ancient Egyptian Poems, 1940–1640 BC* (Oxford: Oxford University Press, 1997).

35. Wilmetta J. Toliver-Diallo, "'The Woman Who Was More than a Man': Making Aline Sitoe Diatta into a National Heroine in Senegal," *Canadian Journal of African Studies* 39, no. 2 (2005): 338–360.

36. Wale Adebanwi, "Techno-Politics and the Production of Knowledge: Democratic Activism and the Nigerian Exile," *African Association of Political Science Occasional Paper Series* 10, no. 1. (2005): 1–35; Odhiambo Levin Opiyo, "Exiled Ngugi wa Thiong'o Was Subject of Talks," *Daily Nation*, April 23, 2017, accessed August 14, 2017, http://www.nation.co.ke /oped/Opinion/Exiled-Ngugi-wa-Thiong-o-was-subject-of-talks/440808-3900242-c3499y /index.html.

37. Sean Hanretta, "Gender and Agency in the History of a West African Sufi Community: The Followers of Yacouba Sylla," *Comparative Studies in Society and History* 50, no. 2 (2008): 478–508; Hillary Sapire and Chris Saunders, eds., *Southern African Liberation Struggles: New Local, Regional and Global Perspectives* (Cape Town: University of Cape Town Press, 2013); Stephen Ellis and Tsepo Sechaba, *Comrades against Apartheid: The ANC and the South African Communist Party in Exile* (London: James Currey, 1992); Stephen Ellis, *External Mission: The ANC in Exile, 1960–1990* (Oxford: Oxford University Press, 2013); Christian A. Williams, *National Liberation in Post-Colonial Southern Africa: A Historical Ethnography of SWAPO's Exile Camps* (Cambridge: Cambridge University Press, 2015); Louise Bethlehem, "'Miriam's Place': South African Jazz, Conviviality and Exile," *Social Dynamics* 43 no. 2 (2017): 243–258.

38. Similarly, literary examinations of exile also suggest displacement as giving life, freedom, and opportunity. Paul Tiyambe Zeleza, "The Politics and Poetics of Exile: Edward Said in Africa," *Research in African Literatures* 36 (2005): 1–22.

39. Achille Mbembe, "The Power of the Archive and its Limits," in *Refiguring the Archive*, ed. Carolyn Hamilton et al. (Dordrecht: Kluwer Academic Publishers, 2002), 19–26.

40. This includes important discussions about digitization and archives. See, for example, Keith Breckenridge, "The Politics of the Parallel Archive: Digital Imperialism and the Future of Record-Keeping in the Age of Digital Reproduction," *Journal of Southern African Studies* 40, no. 3 (2014): 499–519. See also the extended discussion of preservation of the Timbuktu libraries in Shamil Jeppie and Souleymane Bachir Diagne, eds. *The Meanings of Timbuktu* (Cape Town: Human Sciences Research Council, 2008).

41. Michel-Rolph Trouillot, *Silencing the Past: Power and the Production of History* (Boston: Beacon Press, 1995).

42. Michel Foucault, *The Archaeology of Knowledge*, trans. A. M. Sheridan Smith (New York: Pantheon, 2002), 129.

43. Ann Laura Stoler, *Along the Archival Grain: Epistemic Anxieties and Colonial Common Sense* (Princeton: Princeton University Press, 2009), 17. For a discussion of literacy and silencing see: Fallou Ngom, "Ajami Scripts in the Senegalese Speech Community," *Journal of Arabic and Islamic Studies* 10 (2010): 1–23.

44. Martin Klein "Studying the History of Those Who Would Rather Forget: Oral History and the Experience of Slavery," *History in Africa* 16 (1989): 207–219; Marie Rodet, "Listening to the History of Those Who Don't Forget," *History in Africa* 40 (2013): s27–s29; Richard L.

Roberts and Martin Klein, "The Banamba Slave Exodus and the Decline of Slavery in the Western Sudan," *Journal of African History* 21, no. 3 (1980): 375–94; Sandra E. Greene, *West African Narratives of Slavery: Texts from Late Nineteenth- and Early Twentieth-Century Ghana* (Bloomington: Indiana University Press, 2011).

45. Jacques Derrida, *Archive Fever: A Freudian Impression*, trans. Eric Penowitz (Chicago: Chicago University Press, 1996).

46. Ann Laura Stoler, "Colonial Archives and the Arts of Governance," *Archival Science* 2 (2002): 91. For colonial intermediaries, see, Benjamin N. Lawrance, Emily L. Osborn, and Richard L. Roberts, eds., *Intermediaries, Interpreters and Clerks: African Employees and the Making of Colonial Africa* (Madison: University of Wisconsin Press, 2006).

47. Andrew Ashforth, *The Politics of Official Discourse in Twentieth-Century South Africa* (Oxford: Clarendon Press, 1990), 5.

48. Randy J. Sparks, *Africans in the Old South: Mapping Exceptional Lives across the Atlantic World* (Cambridge: Harvard University Press, 2016), 163.

49. Rebecca J. Scott and Jean M. Hébrard, *Freedom Papers: An Atlantic Odyssey in the Age of Emancipation* (Cambridge: Harvard University Press, 2012), 3; Benjamin N. Lawrance, *Amistad's Orphans: An Atlantic Story of Children, Slavery, and Smuggling* (New Haven: Yale University Press, 2014).

50. Gregory Mann, "Locating Colonial Histories: Between France and West Africa," *The American Historical Review* 110 (2011): 412.

51. Jill Lepore, "The Cobweb: Can the Internet Be Archived?" *New Yorker*, January 26, 2015; Jo Guldi and David Armitage, *The History Manifesto* (Cambridge: Cambridge University Press, 2014). On inaccessible or missing archives as obstacle and "complement" see: Luise White, "Hodgepodge Historiography: Documents, Itineraries, and the Absence of Archives," *History in Africa* 42 (2015): 309–318.

52. Stoler, *Along the Archival Grain*, 20.

53. Mbembe, "The Power of the Archive," 22.

54. Catherine Coquery-Vidrovitch, *Enjeux politiques de l'histoire coloniale* (Paris: Agone, 2009). Also, Benjamin N. Lawrance, "Boko Haram, Refugee Mimesis, and the Archive of Contemporary Gender-Based Violence," *Radical History Review* 126 (2016): 159–170.

55. Omnia El Shakry, "'History without Documents': The Vexed Archives of Decolonization in the Middle East," *American Historical Review* 120, no. 3 (2015): 925.

56. Lynn Schler, "'The facts stated do not seem to be true': The Contested Process of Repatriation in British Colonial Nigeria," *The Journal of Imperial and Commonwealth History* 42, no. 1 (2014): 1–19.

57. Benjamin N. Lawrance and Charlotte Walker-Said, "Resisting Patriarchy, Contesting Homophobia: Expert Testimony and the Construction of Forced Marriage in Asylum Claims," in *Marriage by Force? Contestation over Consent and Coercion in Africa*, ed. Annie Bunting, Benjamin N. Lawrance, and Richard L. Roberts (Athens: Ohio University Press, 2016).

58. Bruce Whitehouse, *Migrants and Strangers in an African City: Exile, Dignity, Belonging* (Bloomington: Indiana University Press, 2012), 21.

59. Ann McDougall in this volume.

60. Schmidt, *Mobilizing the Masses*.

61. For a discussion of Tuareg activities in North Africa and the Arabian peninsula, see Mann, *From Empires*, 111–13; also Pierre Boilley, "Administrative Confinements and the Confinements of Exile: the Reclusion of Nomads in the Sahara," in *A History of Prison and Confinement in Africa*, ed. Florence Bernault, trans. Janet Roitman (Portsmouth, NH: Heinemann, 2003), 221–238.

62. Dorothy L. Hodgson, *Being Maasai, Becoming Indigenous: Postcolonial Politics in a Neoliberal World* (Bloomington: Indiana University Press, 2011), 5.

63. On the repatriation of Ouanilo's remains, see Didier Samson, "Ouanilo de retour à Abomey," *Radio France Internationale*, September 27, 2009, accessed February 27, 2017, http://www1.rfi.fr/actufr/articles/081/article_46428.asp.

64. Consider, for example, that while the royal statues stolen from Dahomey remain in Paris, contemporary artists in present-day Benin have recreated those statues, suggesting the continued significance of Béhanzin's exile and the place his removal has in Benin's nationalist history. For an example from the workshops of Mathieu Donvide in Abomey, see Gaëlle Beajean-Baltzer, "Du trophée à l'oeuvre," 3.

65. Indeed, this volume is informed by discussions that took place during the Conable African Studies Symposium in April 2015, at the Rochester Institute of Technology, Rochester, New York. We thank in particular the contributions from Marcus Filippello, Stephanie Hassell, Lorelle Semley, Shobana Shankar, Kara Moskowitz, and Jeremy Dell.

66. Gwendolyn Wright, "Tradition in the Service of Modernity: Architecture and Urbanism in French Colonial Policy, 1900–1930," in *Tension of Empire: Colonial Cultures in a Bourgeois World* ed. Frederick Cooper and Ann Laura Stoler (Berkeley: University of California Press, 1997), 326.

67. One infamous case was the forced deportation of two hundred sixty free people of color from Martinique in the wake of the so-called Bissette Affair, thirty five of whom were sent to Senegal. Melvin D. Kennedy, "The Bissette Affair and the French Colonial Question," *The Journal of Negro History* 45, no. 1 (January 1960): 1–10; Kelly Duke Bryant, "Black but Not African: Francophone Black Diaspora and the 'Revue des Colonies,' 1834–1842," *The International Journal of African Historical Studies* 40, no. 2 (2007): 251–282. The authors thank Lorelle Semley for highlighting the significance of this case during the fourth Conable Conference in International Studies at the Rochester Institute of Technology in 2015.

68. Or revealed colonial landscapes as "nervous places." See especially Nancy Rose Hunt's research into the practice of relegation in colonial Congo. Nancy Rose Hunt, *A Nervous State: Violence, Remedies, and Reverie in Colonial Congo* (Durham: Duke University Press, 2016).

69. Florence Bernault, "The Shadow of Rule: Colonial Power and Modern Punishment in Africa," in *Cultures of Confinement: A Global History of the Prison in Asia, Africa, the Middle-East and Latin America*, ed. Frank Dikötter (London: C. Hurst, 2007), 55.

70. Sara Forsdyke, *Exile, Ostracism, and Democracy: The Politics of Expulsion in Ancient Greece* (Princeton, NJ: Princeton University Press, 2009).

71. Sara Forsdyke, "Exile, Ostracism and the Athenian Democracy," *Classical Antiquity* 19, no. 2 (2000): 232–63; Gordon P. Kelly, *A History of Exile in the Roman Republic* (Cambridge: Cambridge University Press, 2006). Nor was exile confined to the colonial context. The French state in particular had long employed exile as a means of asserting state power even over its own subjects and linked deportation quite directly to the removal of individuals deemed dangerous to social, religious, or political stability. Paul W. Bamford, *Fighting Ships and Prisons: The Mediterranean Galleys of France in the Age of Louis XIV* (University of Minnesota Press, 1973); Almire René Jacques Le Lepelletier de la Sarthe, *Systeme penitentiare, le bagne, la prison cellulaire, la deportation* (Paris: Monnoyer, 1853); Meinrad Busslinger, *L'apport économique et culturel des Hugenots aux pays du Refuge* (Alès: Édition Ampolos, 2016); David van der Linden, *Experiencing Exile: Huguenot Refugees in the Dutch Republic, 1680–1700* (London: Routledge, 2015).

72. Richard L. Roberts and Kristin Mann, "Law in Colonial Africa," in *Law in Colonial Africa*, ed. Kristin Mann and Richard L. Roberts (Portsmouth, NH: Heinemann, 1991).

73. Bala Saho, "Banishing Colonial Agitators: The Case of Chief Mansajang Sangnia of the Gambia, 1930–1939," in *African Intellectuals and the State of the Continent: Essays in Honor of Professor Sulayman S. Nyang*, ed. Olayiwola Abegunrin and Sabelle Ogbobode Abidde (forthcoming, 2018).

74. Florence Bernault, "The Politics of Enclosure in Colonial and Post-Colonial Africa," in *A History of Prison*, 15–16; Gregory Mann, *From Empires to NGOs in the West African Sahel* (Cambridge: Cambridge University Press, 2014), 217–220.

75. John Lonsdale, "States and Social Processes in Africa: A Historiographical Survey," *African Studies Review* 24 (1981): 159.

76. Roberts and Mann, "Law in Colonial Africa," 27.

77. Emmanuelle Saada, "The Empire of Law: Dignity, Prestige, and Domination in the 'Colonial Situation,'" *French Politics, Culture and Society* 20 (2002): 98–120.

78. Isabelle Merle, "De la 'légalisation' de la violence en context coloniale : Le régime de l'indigénat en question," *Politix* 17 (2004): 137–162; Gregory Mann, "What Was the *Indigénat*? The 'Empire of Law' in French West Africa," *Journal of African History* 50 (2009): 331–353.

79. Walter Benjamin, "Critique of Violence," in *Reflections*, trans. Edmund Jephcott (New York: Schocken, 1978), 280; Thomas Blom Hansen and Finn Stepputat, introduction to *Sovereign Bodies: Citizens, Migrants, and States in the Postcolonial World*, ed. Thomas Blom Hansen and Finn Stepputat (Princeton: Princeton University Press, 2005), 20.

80. Bernault, "The Shadow of Rule," 66.

81. Owen Bowcott and Patrick Wintour, "Britain in Danger of Losing Vote of UN over Fate of Chagos Islands," *The Guardian*, June 21, 2017, accessed August 10, 2017, https://www.theguardian.com/world/2017/jun/21/britain-in-danger-of-losing-vote-in-un-chagos-islands-mauritius; Ademola Adegbamigbe, "Emir Muhammadu Sanusi may Go the Way of his Grandfather," *P.M. News* (Lagos, Nigeria), May 13, 2017, accessed August 17, 2017, https://www.pmnewsnigeria.com/2017/05/13/muhammed-sanusi-may-go-the-way-of-his-grandfather/.

82. Wazha G. Morapendi, "The Dilemmas of Liberation in Southern Africa: The Case of Zimbabwean Liberation Movements and Botswana, 1960–1979," *Journal of Southern African Studies* 38 (2012): 73–90; Ellis, *External Mission*; Terretta, *Nation of Outlaws*; Jeffrey S. Ahlman, "Road to Ghana: Nkrumah, Southern Africa and the Eclipse of a Decolonizing Africa," *Kronos* 37 (2011): 23–40; Andrew Ivaska, "Movement Youth in a Global Sixties Hub: The Everyday Lives of Transnational Activists in Postcolonial Dar es Salaam," in *Transnational Histories of Youth in the Twentieth Century*, ed. Richard Ivan Jobs and David M. Pomfret (New York: Palgrave Macmillan, 2015), 188–210.

83. Michael Panzer, "Building a Revolutionary Constituency: Mozambican Refugees and the Development of the FRELIMO Proto-State, 1964–1968," *Social Dynamics* 39, 1 (2013): 5–23. See also his doctoral dissertation, "A Nation in Name, A 'State' in Exile: The FRELIMO Proto-State, Youth, Gender, and the Liberation of Mozambique." Ph.D. dissertation, State University of New York at Albany, 2013.

84. Allen M. Howard, "Nodes, Networks, Landscapes, and Regions: Reading the Social History of Tropical Africa, 1700s–1920," in *The Spatial Factor in African History: The Relationship of the Social, Material, and Perceptual*, ed. Allen M. Howard and Richard M. Shain (Leiden: Brill, 2005), 36.

85. Kothari, "Contesting Colonial Rule," notes that over five hundred colonial subjects from Egypt, Palestine, Cyprus, the Gold Coast, and elsewhere were detained on various islands.

86. Benjamin N. Lawrance, *Locality, Mobility, and 'Nation': Periurban Colonialism in Togo's Eweland, 1900–1960* (Rochester: University of Rochester Press, 2007), 37.

87. Mann, *From Empires*, 217.

88. Janet Roitman, *Fiscal Disobedience: An Anthropology of Economic Regulation in Central Africa* (Princeton: Princeton University Press, 2005); Achille Mbembe, "At the Edge of the World: Boundaries, Territoriality, and Sovereignty in Africa," trans. Steven Rendall, *Public Culture* 12 (2000): 259–284. On sovereignty, space, and borders in the American context see Deborah A. Rosen, *Border Law: The First Seminole War and American Nationhood* (Cambridge: Harvard University Press, 2015).

89. Jeremy Rich, "Where Every Language Is Heard: Atlantic Commerce, West African and Asian Migrants, and Town Society in Libreville, ca. 1860–1914," in *African Urban Spaces in Historical Perspective*, ed. Steven Salm and Toyin Falola (Rochester: University of Rochester Press, 2005); we also appreciate Gregory Mann sharing with us a draft work entitled "Africa, France, and the Future: Exile in Ndjolé (Gabon), ca. 1900," examining how Ndjolé replaced Guyane as a site of exile in the French empire.

90. Ellis, *External Mission*.

91. Stephen R. Davis, "The African National Congress, Its Radio, Its Allies and Exile," *Journal of Southern African Studies* 35, no. 2 (2009): 349–373.

92. Ahlman, "Road to Ghana."

93. Paul Allatson and Jo McCormack, "Exile and Social Transformation," *Portal Journal of Multidisciplinary International Studies* 2, no. 1 (2005): 1–18.

94. Alysson Hobbs, *A Chosen Exile: A History of Racial Passing in American Life* (Cambridge: Harvard University Press, 2014).

95. Liisa Malkki, *Purity and Exile: Violence, Memory, and National Cosmology among Hutu Refugees in Tanzania* (Chicago: Chicago University Press, 1995).

96. Malkki, *Purity and Exile*, 56.

97. Cheikh Anta Babou, *Fighting the Greater Jihad: Amadu Bamba and the Founding of the Muridiyya of Senegal, 1853–1913* (Athens, OH: Ohio University Press, 2007), 151.

98. Christian Coulon, "The Grand Magal in Touba: A Religious Festival of the Mouride Brotherhood of Senegal," *African Affairs* 98 (1999): 195–210; Babou, *Fighting the Greater Jihad*, 167.

99. Mbembe, "At the Edge of the World," 270; also, Malkki, *Purity and Exile*, 52; Wilson, *Sovereignty in Exile*.

100. Simon Turner, "Suspended Spaces—Contesting Sovereignties in a Refugee Camp," in *Sovereign Bodies*, ed. Thomas Blom Hansen and Finn Stepputat, 332.

101. Belinda Luscombe, "11 Questions with Aberash Bekele," *Time*, September 17, 2015, accessed March 20, 2017, http://time.com/4038102/11-questions-with-aberash-bekele/.

102. Syl Cheney-Coker, *Concerto for an Exile* (Portsmouth, NH: Heinemann, 1973), 16.

103. Henri Oripeloye, "Exile and Narration of self/communal in Syl Cheney-Coker's Concerto for an Exile," *Neohelicon* 39 (2012): 423–438.

104. Oripeloye, "The Development of Exilic Poetry."

105. Jane Burbank and Frederick Cooper, *Empires in World History: Power and the Politics of Difference* (Princeton: Princeton University Press, 2010).

106. For his own account of this history see: Baba G. Jallow, *Mandela's other Children: The Diary of an African Journalist* (Louisville: Wasteland Press, 2007).

107. Niklas Hultin, Baba Jallow, Benjamin N. Lawrance, and Assan Sarr, "Autocracy, Migration, and The Gambia's 'Unprecedented' 2016 Election," *African Affairs* 116, no. 463 (2017): 321–40.

Part I

The Legal Worlds of Exile

1 "Wayward Humours" and "Perverse Disputings"

Exiled Blacks and the Foundation of Sierra Leone, 1787–1800

Ruma Chopra

Black exiles, refugees of war, became extraordinarily useful to an expanding British Empire during the late eighteenth century. An already uprooted people without means or patrons could be prepped for a second transplantation to British tropical settlements which whites found undesirable or fatal. Between 1787 and 1800, three groups of exiled blacks from England and Nova Scotia relocated to Sierra Leone to buttress British interests in the region. A geographically dispersed empire needed dependable settlers in new outposts amongst hostile African neighbors, subjects who had a stake in the British Empire. In an era of evangelical antislavery, a discourse of humanitarianism couched each subsidized migration. The strategic dispersal and concentration of exiles constituted empire.

The British government strategically promoted the settlement of black exiles in Sierra Leone. These exiles followed the trajectory established in the 1780s after the secession of the thirteen mainland American colonies. Following the War of American Independence, white and black loyalists fled to Nova Scotia to escape the enmity of the American patriots. They secured British interests by doubling Nova Scotia's population and precluding an easy conquest of the colony by the new United States to the south. British Nova Scotia was also intended to demonstrate the order of constitutional governance in contrast to the disorder of American republicanism.[1] Sierra Leone's nascent settlement spoke to another group of strategic aims: it established a British foothold in West Africa, and it showcased a formal antislavery establishment to the rest of the world. Freetown advertised the British as crusaders against the sin of slavery. Imperial and humanitarian goals went hand in hand.

Sierra Leone emerged as a solution for multiple social problems confronting metropolitan visionaries and politicians in the late eighteenth century. Men with commercial vision and philanthropic friends hoped that new colonies in

West Africa would replace the "old thirteen" lost in 1783 by exporting raw materials and becoming a new market for British manufactured items. The abolitionist Thomas Clarkson celebrated the benefits of colonizing West Africa.[2] He listed the many items that could be procured: palm oil, ivory, gold, wood including mahogany, cocoa, and tulip, spices such as nutmeg, clove, cinnamon, black pepper, and cardamom, and staples such as rice, cotton, indigo, and sugar. Clarkson imagined "black persons and others going in a body into the interior country with camels or mules . . . loaded with merchandize" and returning with exportable goods.[3]

This chapter explores the resettlement of exiled former slaves to Sierra Leone, and their role in founding a colony that the British hoped would also serve as a beacon for uncivilized and unchristian Africans. By creating an example of a flourishing settlement based on the fruits of free labor in West Africa proper, this vision for Sierra Leone followed earlier schemes, including in the former colony of Georgia in 1732. Both were based on antislavery principles and imagined industrious, sober, and moral farming families who would set a model for a new kind of British settlement. Both establishments fortified imperial presence in strategic regions and received large infusions of British public spending to sustain them.[4] Both involved the selection of immigrants who would best protect British geographical claims and promote the British antislavery vision. Protestant whites perceived as disciplined and deserving became the first settlers of Georgia while black exiles—many of whom had already shown loyalty to the empire—became selected as settlers of Sierra Leone.[5]

These blacks were both revolutionary exiles and slavery's exiles.[6] These displaced families became caught in the crosscurrents of the Atlantic world at a moment when the British were experimenting with antislavery and launching their claims to West Africa. Already uprooted blacks confronted a second migration from a perspective likely unavailable to other ex-slaves: the first exile burdened them with an awareness of imperial alternatives.

A British Vision for Sierra Leone

Zachary Macaulay, expansionist, evangelical antislavery crusader, and twenty-six-year-old governor of Sierra Leone, expressed British dreams for Africa. He idealized that the province would, with proper white supervision and an influx of black settlers, lead to new agricultural exports and, as importantly, create thousands of new consumers for British manufactured goods. Indeed, he imagined that Sierra Leone, with the most magnificent harbor in West Africa and free black workers, would soon outshine the slave colony of Jamaica. Macaulay's vision of empire is echoed in "African Prince," a moral fable about the slave trade written by abolitionist, Thomas Clarkson. Clarkson set Prince Zudor as a black

Romeo and his wife Zera as a Juliet, who, with their infant son strapped to her back, drowned in grief in the Atlantic when Zudor was betrayed and sold into slavery. Shortly after, Zudor discovered her sacrifice and threw himself into the same ocean to reunite with her.[7] Clarkson depicts the "sable and unlettered Kings of Africa" as awaiting humanitarian intervention to cease the destruction of their communities. British Sierra Leone would promise a happier ending for the prince and his bride. The mix of love, slavery, separation, and ultimately death appealed to sentimental reformers.

It was not accidental that a botanist, Henry Smeathman, suggested the peninsula of Sierra Leone for British explorations in West Africa.[8] The eighteenth-century age of botanical exploration overlapped with the era of imperial expansion; both shared in the zeal for improvement and reform. The prevalence of botanical language with its focus on the right environment (soil and climate) for transplanted seeds would become convenient shorthand for discussions of transplanted people.[9] Smeathman raved about the benefits of Sierra Leone for the average settler: "A man possessed of a change of cloathing, a wood axe, a hoe, and a pocket knife, may soon place himself in an easy and comfortable situation."[10] He imagined white settlement and minimized high white fatalities in the region. He blamed the deaths on "unwholesome" and "rancid" provisions, "intemperate lives," and "ardent spirits."[11] Despite Smeathman's assurances, it was widely known that many whites did not survive the diseases in the tropical region. The government ruled against sending white convicts to Sierra Leone even though it was sufficiently remote to preclude easy return to England. White convicts, some of whom had only committed misdemeanors or minor infractions, could not be sent wholesale to die.

Black exiles sent to Sierra Leone in 1787 set a precedent. Uprooted blacks would extend the empire's claims in regions deemed undesirable by white settlers, and settle regions where British interests exceeded British occupation. In comparison with West African communities, black settlers, many from the Americas, appeared marginally British. The blacks' complexion mattered less than their availability, their familiarity with British customs and laws, and their readiness to advance within and not outside the British Empire.

During the mid-1780s, when the evangelical lawyer Granville Sharp, who earlier became deeply invested in abolitionism through the Somerset Case, seized the opportunity to establish a free community in Sierra Leone, black emigration became irrevocably linked to British humanitarianism. It is not surprising then that the first candidates for the Sierra Leone settlement came from amongst the thousands of free black poor in London, numbered to be over fourteen thousand. In addition to domestic slaves, the influx of black refugees in England after the War of American Independence had further expanded the indigent black population. As their numbers fed class anxieties about unemployment and crime, Sharp, along with other Christian reformers, saw a chance to reduce England's burden and to launch the antislavery experiment in West Africa. Domestic order depended on expelling burdensome blacks.

Sharp's recruitment campaign invited blacks who suffered "the greatest distress" to make a home in Sierra Leone. In May 1786, widely circulated notices used Smeathman's language to emphasize the benefits of the new settlement for any hardworking emigrant: "It is found that no place is so fit and proper as the Grain Coast of Africa; where the necessaries of life may be supplied by the force of industry and moderate labour."[12] The British government would supply transportation and clothing and provisions for three months, along with tools for the cultivation of the new settlement.

The first group of migrants who left from London for Sierra Leone faced terrible difficulties and doomed Sharp's efforts in Sierra Leone. Accompanied by a captain of the Royal Navy, the group of 439 English settlers arrived in Sierra Leone in May 1787.[13] The group included the black poor and some white men, along with seventy white women. They landed in Sierra Leone during the wrong season. They faced torrential rains, inadequate housing, insufficient provisions, and the suspicion of nearby natives. Only two-thirds of those originally embarked lived beyond seven months. Some, both blacks and whites, joined the slave factories nearby; a few found employment on board slave ships.[14] In desperation, Sharp sent more settlers in April 1788 along with "live swine" to keep the colony viable.[15] But of the thirty-nine sent, only twenty-six survived. Little financial support was available for the abandoned settlers. In April 1790, when Sharp received news that the town was destroyed and the blacks had scattered, he lamented the fate of his "poor little, ill-thriven, swarthy daughter, the unfortunate colony of Sierra Leone."[16] Paternalism went hand in hand with imperialism. Fortunately for Sharp, a larger group of black exiles would become available for a second transplantation.

A Rival "New" Jamaica?

The high mortality rate in Sierra Leone could not be ignored, especially by abolitionists who had drawn sustained attention to the lack of natural increase of slaves in the West Indies. As early as 1788, Granville Sharp created a rationale for why settlers had been reduced to just 276 people within the first year. At least thirty-four people, he wrote, died in crowded ships before they reached the African coast "so the climate of Sierra Leone is not to be blamed."[17] Others died within the first four months because they "continued intemperate," lacked fresh provisions, and did not have time to build huts before the rainy season.[18] Some remained missing not due to sickness or death but to emigration; they had fled the British settlement to live in nearby African communities. By whatever means he could identify, Sharp emphasized that the deaths were due to improper precautions, and were not inevitable in a tropical climate for whites and blacks who had not acquired immunities.

After the failure of Sharp's first venture, the Sierra Leone Company, founded by merchants as much as philanthropists, attempted to revive the settlement based on a more secure foundation. Its justification was simple: "Whereas the interior kingdoms and countries of the said continent have not hitherto been explored by Europeans, nor hath any regular trade ever been carried on therewith from these kingdoms nor can such undertakings be conveniently carried on or supported unless a considerable capital joint stock is raised for that purpose."[19] The Company raised money to cultivate tropical crops and to identify useful commodities from the less-explored interior regions of West Africa. It received a monopoly to launch the settlement. In 1791, it raised £110,000 from five hundred subscribers.[20]

The potential threat represented by the Sierra Leone Company was not lost on the planters in the West Indies who confronted a sustained attack against the slave trade. The abolition of the slave trade risked shattering the edifice of their sugar economy. Tropical crops produced in West Africa, they feared would compete for metropolitan consumers. Sugar would conceivably be cheaper in Africa than that manufactured in the West Indies because it would use free labor, one-third the cost of slave labor. [21] In addition, as West Africa was only twenty days by sea from England, such produce could likely be transported more cheaply.[22]

Jamaica's hostility to the Sierra Leone Company was accompanied by a surprising enumeration of the island's advantages over West Africa. The British Empire would benefit by investing in Jamaica over West Africa. Jamaica was more easily fortified and defended because it was an island; it would be catastrophically expensive to defend a vast continent given the known volatility of the region. Sierra Leone's climate was "fatal" in comparison to Jamaica's healthier one. Jamaican slaves benefited from amelioration laws; free African laborers would receive no similar protection.[23] Reverend Cooper Willyams ended his list of enslavement's benefits by emphasizing the greater possibility of Christian conversion in the West Indies: "It is better for them to be carried to a country where they have a chance at least of better treatment, and where many of them are instructed in their duty to their God, of which before they had no idea."[24] Proslavery advocates recommended the formation of a trading company whose purpose would be restricted to commerce; a venture whose purpose was land cultivation and settlement served no commercial, military, or humanitarian purpose.[25] But the prevailing political sentiments favored Sierra Leone.

In 1791, Sierra Leone's leaders believed that the abolition of the slave trade was imminent. Their immediate object was to establish a settlement based on three categories of colonists: a small white council with regular and permanent salaries, thirty to forty skilled craftsmen or "artificers" who would receive support from the Company to build the settlement, and large numbers of settlers to whom grants of land would be made.[26] The first settlers would construct roads, cultivate crops, and build the infrastructure that would encourage a "good reputation" and invite respectable English people to seek commerce in Africa. In time, the English would cultivate connections as much as crops, build mansions, and showcase a new Jamaica in West Africa. The Company prepared to identify African commodities that would serve to replace the trade in slaves.

From Nova Scotia to West Africa

A second group of black exiles reached Sierra Leone in 1792. These individuals came from among the three thousand black loyalists who initially sought refuge in Nova Scotia after the War of American Independence. The British had promised the free blacks land in Nova Scotia in return for their loyalty; the blacks also expected to be treated as equal to whites. Instead, for eight years, between 1783 and 1791, the Nova Scotian blacks faced the hostility of white loyalists, the impossibility of sustaining themselves on barren land, and for many who never received land, a lifetime of servitude as black servants. Terrible conditions in the British colony, along with white prejudice, led over one thousand of them to seek a second relocation. They petitioned to leave the colony, for better treatment and for a better life for their families.

From the perspective of the Sierra Leone Company, the Nova Scotian blacks appeared ideal colony builders. The Company welcomed the acquisition of "free black colonists, acquainted with the English language, and accustomed to labor in hot climates."[27] In October 1791, John Clarkson, brother of the evangelical abolitionist Thomas Clarkson, and a member of the Royal Navy, arrived in Nova Scotia to recruit settlers, offering each man twenty acres for himself, ten for his wife and five for every child, along with the promise of political representation. The Company trusted the Nova Scotian black loyalists with their devout Protestant faith, their high literacy, and their clear grasp of British laws and customs. As importantly, the blacks had already proven their attachment to the empire and could serve as subordinate partners to extend British reach into Africa.

Clarkson made note of the black Nova Scotians' desperate circumstances in a tiny notebook. The blacks were forced to work as day laborers, sharecroppers, indentured servants, and, in the case of children, apprentices. They told him that "whites seldom or ever pay for work done." The blacks feared their former masters would kidnap them and return them to the United States. Others never received land and tired of living on "white men's property." Some received lower wages than promised for their work. "It is a common custom in this country," they said, "to promise a black so much per day and in evening when his work is finished" to renege on the commitment. Their children received no pay when they worked in white households because whites insisted they obliged black parents by providing children with lodging and food. None of the blacks mentioned the climate of Nova Scotia.[28]

Yet, repeatedly, the abolitionists focused on the frigid climate of the British Atlantic colony. The preoccupation with Nova Scotia's cold weather circumvented discussions of the blacks' predicament. In the abolitionists' heavy emphasis on climate, Nova Scotia appeared naturally a temporary place for blacks born in the southern colonies of Virginia, South Carolina and Georgia. No accusations were leveled at the Nova Scotia's governor, John Parr, or any white loyalists for servile treatment of free blacks. Notably, the obsession with climate appeared only when black loyalists were transported from Nova Scotia. The winters in England drew no discussion when the poor left London in 1787. If the first group of exiles were supposedly rescued from a lifetime of poverty in London, the second were rescued from endless winters in Nova Scotia.

Curiously, John Clarkson was asked to stay clear of the antislavery agenda in Nova Scotia. From London, the evangelical William Wilberforce advised Clarkson. He told him not to "tather about the abolition of the slave trade except when you are sure of your company." He recommended avoiding a conversation with the Governor on the "ill usage the blacks had received" as this would "nettle" him.[29] Also, Clarkson was to explain that the distribution of printed information promoting Sierra Leone was not intended to "spread discontent" in the colony. Avoiding sowing antislavery sentiments in Nova Scotia, Wilberforce and Clarkson sought only to remove one segment of a valuable group of free blacks for their experiment in West Africa.

White loyalists who expressed interest in Sierra Leone received no hearing. Over thirty thousand white loyalists who emigrated to Nova Scotia knew disappointment as well.[30] Although generally treated better, they also expressed dismay at the short agricultural season and the weaker economic potential of Nova Scotia. Despite early hopes, Nova Scotia failed to replace the former thirteen colonies as a supplier for the West Indian Islands. It was poorly equipped to do so; most of the produce was confined to local consumption and shipping remained scarce.[31] In addition, it produced almost nothing that Britain wanted to buy. The colony continued to depend on Britain not only for military and naval support but also to meet basic expenditures. Unlike the black loyalists who feared a return to the United States would mean re-enslavement, many of the disappointed white loyalists returned south to the new nation.

The Company categorically refused to take white loyalists from Nova Scotia to Sierra Leone. In 1791, the Director of the Sierra Leone Company, Henry Thornton, explained the restriction clearly: "In truth it is easy to perceive that none but eccentric or distressed [white] persons were very likely to go out so soon and that the peace and comfortable settlement of our colony might be much prejudiced by their party in the place."[32] Far from being grateful to the Company's founders, these men would compete with the Company's white leaders, indulge in drinking, or leave the colony.

The Company's views had not altered in 1794. A Company report emphasized that the "success of the colony depended on the exclusion of all Europeans."[33] The only white settlers permitted were those that were in the regular pay of the Company and "entirely subject" to it. The Company's directors repeated Thornton's earlier caution: "Even a few men . . . of an improper cast in the situation of independent settlers might materially prejudice or endanger the undertaking." The wrong settlers would "corrupt the morals of the colony, refuse due obedience to government, as well as excite a spirit of general discontent," and if they were excluded from the settlement, they would turn to the worst sin: they would become slave traders.[34]

In addition to describing the character flaws of potential white settlers, Thornton listed the primary reason for avoiding whites: few Englishmen would "work in the sun."[35] Thornton stressed that the Company's first object was "to procure laborers" without which the "expense of our establishment must otherwise devour us." In addition to cultivating crops, the Nova Scotian blacks would "converse with the natives and draw them to work for us." Ultimately, the Sierra Leone colony would flourish based not on whites or Nova Scotian blacks but the labor of Africans.[36] American-born loyal blacks–grateful for an alternative to Nova Scotia–would serve as middlemen and overseers to create plantations that benefitted from thousands of African "servants" whose labor cost less than slaves in the West Indies.

The founders of the Sierra Leone Company also attended to the stability that would result from "civilizing" Africans who would be socialized to British culture and values. Wilberforce noted that the colony would work best if "American settlers" would board and lodge with a few natives to teach them "language and religion, the habits of industry, the mode of cultivating lands, and the mechanical arts." As Thomas Clarkson echoed, "civilization can only take place by the natives living near a community of civilized settlers, and observing their government, customs, laws, &c."[37] The Company would also benefit from African chiefs sending their children for instruction.[38] The children would be taught the "actual practice of cultivating land, making bricks, building houses," and trades such as blacksmithing.[39]

A Second Settlement

The Nova Scotians who arrived in Sierra Leone in March 1792 confronted the same heavy casualties borne by the black poor in 1787.[40] In May 1792, the botanist Adam Afzelius reported the high mortality and sickness among them: "I found then a great confusion and want, particularly of houses and fresh provisions. . . . The evils have since that time daily increased . . . about 500 persons over the half colony is now sick and about 200 are already dead, and we have no Medical or Chirurgical assistance, but from a very young surgeon who is ill himself."[41] Within weeks, of the 1,196 who reached Sierra Leone, fewer than one thousand remained, supervised by thirty to forty white Company servants.[42]

The British surgeon's notebook from 1793 captures the imminence of death. In columns that listed the names of sick people, along with their age, complexion, and disease, the last column was labeled, "Recovered or Died."[43] Reports repeatedly revealed the vulnerability of American-born blacks to tropical diseases. Still, the reformers in the Sierra Leone Company resisted the implications of the deaths: American-born blacks, lacking childhood acquired immunities, suffered no less than whites from tropical diseases.

In light of the experience of the 1787 emigrants, the Sierra Leone Company could have anticipated the large numbers of deaths. What they had not expected, however, was the political cohesiveness of the black survivors created through their familiarity with the ideals of the American Revolution, their shared experience of servility in Nova Scotia, their removal from Nova Scotia in families and congregations, and their reconstruction of Baptist and Methodist churches in Freetown. The exiles had transformed themselves into a settler community, one that demanded the rights owed to subjects and not the benevolence extended to the saved. Starting in 1794, Nova Scotians' clamor for political representation and participation caught Sierra Leone's leaders by surprise. Some "reliable" Nova Scotians joined the British establishment and rose within its ranks as accountants and bookkeepers. But the majority opposed any actions that reduced their political or social status.[44]

Far from showing subservience to the Company, the black settlers conducted themselves like American rebels. They showed an "inadequate sense of obligation" to the Company. The Company accused them of imbibing "false and absurd notions" about their rights as freemen.[45] In 1795, the blacks submitted a petition complaining of high prices, inadequate wages, and broken promises.[46] In 1796, the settlers refused to sign their land grants suspecting foul play.[47] In frustration, Zachary Macaulay, lamented the "wayward humours, the perverse disputings, the absurd reasonings, the unaccountable prejudices, the everlasting jealousie, the presumption self-conceit [*sic*], the gross ignorance, and the insatiable demands of our settlers."[48] When they elected no European representatives in the December 1796 elections, Macaulay tellingly reported, "You see we have just the same passions in Freetown as in London and in miniature the same effects resulting from them."[49]

Black Nova Scotians' demands for equal status and participation came from their experiences in Sierra Leone as much as their American background. The Sierra Leone Company's dependence on Nova Scotians for military defense—in case of internal threat from local Africans and in case of external

French attack—provided the settlers with important leverage. The official declaration of war between France and England in February 1793 had made Sierra Leone and its one thousand settlers a low priority. British troops sailed for San Domingue to preserve the West Indies instead of protecting Sierra Leone. But in October 1794, the San Domingue rebellion spilled over to Sierra Leone. The French attacked the fragile settlement, pillaging and destroying the colony: the loss to human life was small but animals, buildings, gardens, and botanical collections were destroyed. No British troops protected the colony. The French looted and destroyed the homes and farms of the Sierra Leone Company's employees as well those of black settlers. When the French ships left after three months, the Nova Scotians regrouped systematically and rebuilt the settlement of Freetown. As the immigrants transformed into colony-builders, their tolerance of their unequal status grew yet thinner.[50]

Macaulay dignified the Nova Scotian blacks' political demands by linking them with the French Revolution. In December 1797, he reported that he had barely stopped an "insurrection" that threatened to topple the white government.[51] The settlers, he wrote, wanted to secede from the Sierra Leone Company and negotiate directly for land with African chiefs. Some Africans saw a chance to exploit the divisions between the white elites and the black settlers to advance their own claims to the region. The blacks sought an alliance that would buttress their numbers and add to their military strength. Macaulay likened the threat he faced with that of *la Guillotine* during the French Revolution: the black settlers would cut off his head "as had been done to the King of France."[52]

Macaulay did not have the legal or military power that the British state would have in Africa later in the nineteenth century—as described in Trina Hogg's chapter in this volume—and could do little about the rebels' uncompromising position. He grew impatient with the Nova Scotians' disinterest in agricultural labor. They resisted clearing rocky and forested land because the output of their cultivation "won't come to any thing in my time."[53] Instead, they established surreptitious trading relationships with natives as well as nearby slave traders.[54] Their greater interest in commerce at the expense of cultivation, mirrored that of the white settlers the Sierra Leone Company had prohibited as immigrants. Instead of comparing the black settlers to enterprising whites, Macaulay resorted to more convenient shorthand. He excoriated them for "gliding back" to the "wretched state of barbarism in which their African forefathers were sunk and from which we had fondly hoped they had now been rescued."[55]

A Third Exile Settlement

In 1800, almost six hundred Trelawney Town Maroons from northern Jamaica followed the trajectory of the black loyalists. They also emigrated as families from Nova Scotia to Sierra Leone and hoped to recreate a Jamaican-like world in another tropical environment. But the Maroons were an entirely different constituency of free blacks. They did not practice Christianity, did not read or write English, lived in polygynous households, and had more experience in the battlefield than on farmsteads or plantations. Of most relevance, the Maroons had recently proven themselves dangerous enemies of British authority in Jamaica. The Jamaican government, in fact, had deported the entire community in 1796. A people who demonstrated a "wild and lawless freedom" and would remain permanently "savage" hardly warranted imperial favor.[56]

In July 1796, Sierra Leone's leaders had opposed the Maroon settlement in the West African colony. Although they required settlers, they regarded the Maroons' military background as a threat to the fledgling colony. They worried that the Maroons and Nova Scotians would join to topple the white government in Sierra Leone. Yet in 1799, the colony negotiated a subsidy from the government to settle the Maroon families. The Company anticipated that exiled Maroons could play the same role in Sierra Leone as they had in Jamaica: they could serve as military auxiliaries to further British interests. With the help of the Maroon guerilla fighters, the small white leadership could quiet the militant Nova Scotian blacks whose military skills did not match their ideological shrillness.

By the early 1790s, the British government had officially adopted the policy of arming slave soldiers in the Caribbean. Already, by 1794, three thousand six hundred blacks and mulattoes were embodied in British infantry, cavalry, and artillery units.[57] Some in the ministry contemplated a force of nine thousand soldiers by 1795 although this did not materialize.[58] The high casualty rate of British soldiers in the Caribbean was widely known: white troops died annually at a rate of 25 percent.[59] Too many British soldiers died from sickness, not battles.[60] Some received warnings of imminent death in the ships that brought them to the West Indies. Captain Philip Thicknesse retold how, during one of his journeys towards Jamaica in the 1730s, a shipmate who had darkly warned, "God knows which of us may slip his wind first," had died within forty-eight hours of disembarkation.[61] Soldiers who survived during the first few months on the island were not necessarily safe. Some who escaped yellow fever in the first weeks of arrival contracted it with prolonged stay on the island, or died from venereal diseases, smallpox, or lung ailments. Others died of inadequate diet or toxic poisoning caused by low-quality rum.[62] Poor medical care and inadequate doctors added to the casualties. As many as two-thirds of the hospitalized soldiers did not survive and calls to station them to the healthier climate of Nova Scotia echoed during the eighteenth century.[63]

Ignoring the invitation from Nova Scotia, the government solved its problem by recruiting slave regiments and distributing them across the Caribbean. During the late 1790s, it moved from purchasing slaves from Caribbean planters to buying them directly from Africa where they were cheaper and in large supply.[64]

Between 1795 and 1808, the British bought thirteen thousand four hundred slaves, about 7 percent of the slaves imported into the British Caribbean.[65] Slave soldiers found a path to social mobility via the shortage of British troops and the growing military needs of the empire in disease-ridden contexts. The proven loyalty of these blacks to the empire ensured that the Jamaican Maroons would have an opportunity to serve in British Sierra Leone in the 1800s.

The Maroons had sustained themselves as military collaborators of the white government in Jamaica for decades before their deportation. During the 1730s, they had signed treaties with the Jamaican government, exchanging their right to autonomy and protected land in return for their service as slave catchers. The Maroons' path to security and mobility came with patronage from Jamaican whites. It is not surprising that they imagined military service as worthwhile and profitable in comparison to the servile labor they performed in Nova Scotia from 1796 to 1799.[66]

In 1791–92, unhappy black loyalists in Nova Scotia confronted a similar choice: they could serve in the British army in the West Indies as an alternative to relocating to Sierra Leone. Black men would serve under British officers and receive the same bounty, clothing, and provisions as white soldiers. Free blacks—who had already proven their allegiance in the last American war—were an ideal reserve for the war raging in San Domingue. But only sixty free blacks in Nova Scotia accepted a military assignment in the West Indies. For black refugees of the American Revolution settled in Nova Scotia, military service was a means to secure freedom and did not translate into a lifelong commitment to the empire. In contrast, the Maroons' experience led them to associate freedom with military service.

In 1800, the Maroons reached Sierra Leone in time to quell the uprising of the black Nova Scotians. They quickly restored white order and received high praise as military auxiliaries. Their refusal to identify with other blacks—Africans or Nova Scotians—made them ideal intermediaries of the empire. But like the two black groups who had arrived earlier, the Maroons suffered disastrous casualty rates. Their immunities from Jamaica were no match for the disease conditions they confronted in tropical Sierra Leone. Any British attempts to use one group of blacks as a check on another were doomed. The black loyalists who emerged during the next decade in Sierra Leone comprised a mix of poor blacks, Nova Scotian blacks, and Maroons. To distinguish them from African-born groups who resided in Sierra Leone, the exiles, along with their progeny, were called "settlers." In Sierra Leone, what mattered more than their race was their land of birth: the exiles were born inside the British Empire and—for those who survived the diseases—would find opportunity in its expansion.

Conclusion

Founded on the hopes of an imminent end to the slave trade, the Sierra Leone colony took in settlers deemed appropriate for the climate and the conditions.

The satellite settlement had not proven itself successful enough to invite desirable proprietors who would settle in the colony, build mansions, show an example of English luxury in Freetown, and eventually become absentee owners as had happened in Jamaica. Poor black families, as well as black men with military skills and guerilla experience, served the changing needs of remote zones in a dispersed empire. Their concentration facilitated British claims to the region and instantiated British antislavery sentiments.

The limits of the empire in tropical West Africa along with the rise of antislavery sentiments compelled the softening of prejudices against blacks. Free blacks, poverty-stricken and unable to return to their homes in the slave states of the United States or to the slave society of Jamaica, stood ready, in various degrees, to confront a new set of circumstances in Sierra Leone. Uprooted by war from their homes, facing isolation, and with little hope of autonomy or advancement, the exiles gambled on Sierra Leone. Their already displaced status created a deeper awareness of the plurality of British worlds. More than optimism about an idealized future, they rejected a permanent second-class status, trusted their experiences within the British Empire, and took a courageous stance towards an uncertain future. Their first exile rescued them from enslavement but not from the stigma of racism or the hardships of poverty; a second exile could save them from the wretchedness of their circumstances in London and Nova Scotia. Their supposed immunity to tropical disease and their anticipated allegiance initiated their role as British settlers in Sierra Leone.

By the early nineteenth century, black settlers in the enclave of Freetown benefited from their legal and cultural understanding of British customs and values. In 1808, global events transformed Sierra Leone's future. The end of the British slave trade brought thousands of liberated Africans into Sierra Leone. Black settlers, along with British administrators, influenced the direction of integration of these African newcomers: towards an English education, a Christian worldview, and agricultural work. Together, they invented a new model of an Atlantic African town.

Notes

1. Nova Scotia Charter, 1785, Halifax Public Archives, MG 23 C 20. The "paternal goodness" of Britain would not only encourage the zeal and ambition of true subjects but would "operate most forcibly on the revolted Americans by proving . . . what they might have enjoyed on a reunion with their careful and gracious Sovereign, and fellow-subjects."
2. Clarkson Papers, 1792, Report on Sierra Leone, Huntington Library.
3. Clarkson Papers, 1792, Report on Sierra Leone, Huntington Library.
4. Julian Gwyn, "Economic Fluctuations in Nova Scotia" in *Making Adjustments: Change and Continuity in Planter Nova Scotia, 1759–1800*, ed. Margaret Conrad (Halifax: Acadiensis

Press, 1991), 86, 73; Nova Scotia and Cape Breton, in fact, would receive £152,300 sterling in the sixty years between 1756 and 1815.

5. On the settlement of Georgia, see Christopher Brown, *Moral Capital: Foundations of British Abolitionism* (Chapel Hill: University of North Carolina Press, 2012), chap. 1; unlike the collective twentieth-century relegation process described by Marie Rodet and Romain Tiquet in this volume, these emigrants were not imagined as a form of penal forced labor.

6. Sylviane A. Diouf, *Slavery's Exiles: The Story of the American Maroons* (New York: New York University Press, 2014); Maya Jasanoff, "Revolutionary Exiles: The American Loyalist and French Émigré Diasporas," in *The Age of Revolutions in Global Context, c. 1760–1840*, ed. David Armitage and Sanjay Subrahmanyam (London: Palgrave Macmillan, 2010), 37–58.

7. Clarkson Papers, 1787–1818, "The African Prince, a Story," 1800(?), Box 2, Huntington Library.

8. In Parliamentary hearings in 1785, Smeathman had recounted the terrible climate he found in the area and the high possibility of disease and death. Still, seeing a chance to accompany the settlers and improve his own cash-strapped status, he enthusiastically supported Sierra Leone. He died on July 1, 1786. See R. Kuczynski, *Demographic Survey of the British Colonial Empire* (London: Oxford Press, 1948), 41.

9. In her visit to the island of St. Vincent, Mrs. Carmichael noted a plant she saw for the first time "growing wild by the road-side instead of being carefully cherished in a hot-house." See Mrs. A. C. Carmichael, *Domestic Manners and Social Condition of the White, Coloured and Negro Population of the West Indies*, Vol. 1 (London: Whittaker, Teacher, and Company, 1833), 8.

10. Henry Smeathman, *Plan of a Settlement to be made near Sierra Leona on the Grain Coast of Africa*, 1786, Rare Books, Huntington Library, 9.

11. Smeathman, *Plan*, 12.

12. Kuczynski, *Demographic*, 41.

13. Kuczynski, *Demographic*, 43. Importantly, in 1787, the black poor were not sent to Botany Bay. Granville Sharp to Dr. Lehsom, Clarkson Papers, October 13, 1788, Huntington Library. Initially, seven hundred people had volunteered to go to the settlement; they left on April 8, 1787 and arrived on May 9, 1787; Eveline C. Martin, *The British West African Settlements, 1750–1821* (New York: Longmans, Green, 1927), 106. Approximately seventy white women went with this first group.

14. Kuczynski, *Demographic*, 45.

15. Granville Sharp to Dr. Lehsom, Clarkson Papers, October 13, 1788, Huntington Library.

16. Martin, *The British*, 117.

17. Granville Sharp to Dr. Lehsom, Clarkson Papers, October 13, 1788, Huntington Library.

18. Ibid.

19. Martin, *The British*, 112.

20. To J. Clarkson, superintendent of Sierra Leone, from Henry Thornton, December 30, 1791, Public Archives of Canada (hereafter PAC), Ottawa.

21. Clarkson Papers, 1792, Huntington Library.

22. Reasons against a territorial grant to a Company of Merchants to Colonize and Cultivate the Peninsula of Sierra Leone on the Coast of Africa, 1791, Burns Library, Boston College; "An Essay on Colonization," Carl Wadstrom, 5 in Huntington Library, Rare Books #482157.

23. Reasons against a territorial grant to a Company of Merchants to Colonize and Cultivate the Peninsula of Sierra Leone on the Coast of Africa, 1791, Burns Library, Boston College.

24. Cooper Willyams, *Account of the Campaign in the West Indies in the Year 1794 under the Command of Their Excellencies Lieutenant General Sir Charles Grety, K. B. and Vice Admiral Sir John Jervis, K. B.* (London: Printed for T. Bensley, 1796) 114.

25. Reasons against a territorial grant to a Company of Merchants to Colonize and Cultivate the Peninsula of Sierra Leone on the Coast of Africa, 1791, Burns Library, Boston College.

26. Martin, *The British*, 114: the Company expected to make profit through land revenue from quitrents, a tax on the produce of the country, profits from land reserved to the Company, and profits on trade with the interior.

27. Martin, *The British*, 115.

28. Notebook of John Clarkson, British Library, AD MS 41262B, October 29, 1791 (other dates also possible).

29. From Wilberforce, July 8, 1791, Rothley Temple near Leicester (to Lieutenant Clarkson?), A-1981 microfilm, Ottawa, PAC.

30. Cole Harris, *Reluctant Land: Society, Space, and Environment in Canada before Confederation* (Vancouver: UBC Press, 2009).

31. Graeme Wynn, 326. Newfoundland produced more dried cod than New Brunswick and Nova Scotia combined. In Graeme Wynn, "A Region of Scattered Settlements and Bounded Possibilities: Northeastern North America, 1775–1800," *The Canadian Georgrapher* 31, no. 4 (1987).

32. To J. Clarkson, superintendent of Sierra Leone, from Henry Thornton, December 30, 1791, PAC, Ottawa.

33. Kuczynski, *Demographic*, 56; "Substance of Report;" the report from 1794 is cited in Zacahary Macaulay, *Zachary Macaulay and the Development of the Sierra Leone Company, 1793–94*, ed. Suzanne Schwarz (Leipzig: University of Leipzig Papers on Africa, 2000), vol. 1, "Journal, June-October 1793;" Indeed, when a rival group of 152 English settlers, led by William Dalrymple, tried to enter Sierra Leone colony in 1792 after having failed to establish themselves in nearby Bulama Island, the eight members of the Sierra Leone Council refused to accept them.

34. "Substance of Report," 1794.

35. To J. Clarkson, from Henry Thornton, December 30, 1791, PAC, Ottawa.

36. Ibid.

37. Thomas Clarkson to John Clarkson, July 17, 1792, ADD MS 41262A, British Library.

38. Wilberforce to John Clarkson, London, April 27, 1792, PAC, Ottawa.

39. An essay on Colonization, Wadstrom, 1794, Volume 1, Huntington Library, 94.

40. They left Halifax on January 15, 1792 and arrived March 6, 1792. See Kuczynski, *Demographic*, 66.

41. Adam Afzelius, *Sierra Leone Journal, 1795–96*, ed. and trans. Alexander Peter Kup (Studia Ethnographica Upsaliensia, 1967) printed by Almqvist and Wiksells: Uppsala, 1967, 2.

42. Kuczynski, *Demographic*, 58, 65; James W. St. G. Walker, "The Establishment of a Free Black Community in Nova Scotia, 1783–1840," in *The African Diaspora: Interpretive Essays*, ed. Martin L. Kilson and Robert I. Rotberg (Cambridge: Harvard University Press, 1976), 221.

43. Clarkson Letter Book Narrative for Dr. Charles Taylor, Surgeon of Colony, MS 41264, British Library.

44. Christopher Fyfe, ed., *Our Children Are Free and Happy: Letters from Black Settlers in Africa in the 1790s* (Edinburgh: Edinburgh University Press, 1991), 12–18.
45. "Substance of Report," 1794, 59.
46. Z. Macaulay, April 16, 1796, Huntington Library.
47. Journal of Z. Macaulay, July 26 to September 26, 1796, Huntington Library.
48. Ibid.
49. Ibid. For more on black loyalists in Sierra Leone, see Ellen Gibson Wilson, *The Loyal Blacks* (New York: Capricorn Books, 1976); and James W. St. G. Walker, *The Black Loyalists: The Search for a Promised Land in Nova Scotia and Sierra Leone, 1783–1870* (New York: Africana Publishing Company, 1976). For black loyalists in Nova Scotia, see Harvey A. Whitfield, "Black Loyalists and Black Slaves in Maritime Canada," *History Compass* 52, no. 10 (2007), 1980–1997; and especially, Whitfield, *North to Bondage: Loyalist Slavery in the Maritimes* (Vancouver: University of British Columbia Press, 2016).
50. Z. Macaulay, April 16, 1796, Box 19A, Folder 2; Z Macaulay to Selina Mills, May 20, 1796, Macaulay Papers Box 1, Huntington Library; Z Macaulay to Selina Mills, December 1, 1797, Box 2, Huntington Library; Z Macaulay, Jan 19 to May 22 1798 folder, Box 20A, Huntington Library.
51. Z. Macaulay to Selina Mills, December 1, 1797, Huntington Library.
52. Z. Macaulay to H. Thornton, December 20, 1797, Huntington Library.
53. Z. Macaulay, June 7, 1797, Huntington Library.
54. Z. Macaulay to Selina Mills, Huntington Library.
55. Ibid.
56. Answer by way of letter to Bryan Edwards, Esq., M.P., F.R.S., planter of Jamaica &c. containing a Refutation of the Historical Survey of the French Colony of St. Domingo, etc. etc. by Colonel Venault de Charmilly, 1797, 167.
57. Roger Norman Buckley, *Slaves in Red Coats: The British West India Regiments, 1795–1815* (New Haven: Yale, 1979), 15.
58. Buckley, *Slaves in Red Coats*, 24.
59. Ibid., 97.
60. Robert Sewell to Duke of Portland, November 9, 1795, Committee of Correspondence Out-Letter Book, National Archives, Spanish-Town. Of course guerilla warfare resulted in greater casualties in the Maroon War.
61. *Memoirs and Anecdotes of Philip Thicknesse, Late Lieutenant Governor of Land Guard Fort and unfortunately father to George Touchet, Baron Audley* (Graisberry and Campbell: Dublin, 1790), 46.
62. Buckley, *Slaves in Red Coats*, 102. The symptoms of toxic poisoning caused by an overconsumption of improperly distilled rum were akin to the symptoms of yellow fever, and contemporaries sometimes mistakenly confused a jaundiced complexion and dark vomit for yellow fever instead of rum intoxication.
63. Buckley, *Slaves in Red Coats*, 3, 102; Richard J. Uniacke, February 10, 1806, Halifax Public Archives, MG1 Vol. 1769, File #4; In 1808, Nova Scotian assemblyman, Richard John Uniacke, saw Nova Scotia as central to the British military effort in the Americas. The West Indies, he proposed, could have black soldiers while British soldiers in Nova Scotia would always be "ready for immediate service." The British recruits could be transferred to the West Indies in a matter of days and, after they had performed their service, could return to Nova Scotia before their health had been injured by the Southern climate.

64. Buckley, *Slaves in Red Coats*, 53.

65. Ibid., 55.

66. For more on Jamaican Maroons, see Mavis C. Campbell, *The Maroons of Jamaica, 1655–1796: A History of Resistance, Collaboration, and Betrayal* (Granby: Bergin & Garvey Publishers, 1988); and Kenneth M. Bilby, *True-Born Maroons* (Kingston: Ian Randle Publishers, 2006). For one of the foundational works, see Richard Price, *Maroon Societies: Rebel Slave Communities in the Americas* (Garden City, New York: Anchor Books, 1973).

2 From Bandits to Political Prisoners

Detention and Deportation on the Sierra Leone Frontier

Trina Leah Hogg

In 1881 five men petitioned the Colonial Office in London begging to be released from the Freetown Prison. Although the original petition has been lost, we know their time in the Freetown jail had not been easy. One prisoner suffered from smallpox; another had been diagnosed with a hernia-related disorder called hydrocele. Several men had attempted to escape and were punished by being placed in stocks, having additional bars placed on their windows, or were denied contact with the outside world.[1] The five petitioners had been delivered over by African leaders from different areas outside of the formal colony and incarcerated for a range of one to seven years. Detained as "political prisoners," these men were exiled from their homes and confined without formal charges by a government that was not their own. While some men eventually returned to their homeland, others were further exiled to other British colonies for the remainder of their lives.

Law was a key part of colonization throughout Africa. Colonizers attempted to reorder African societies through the creation of legal codes and by enforcing laws through the use of police, courts, and prisons.[2] In the formal colony of Sierra Leone, British law was implemented over its urban population who resided within the city of Freetown. Prior to 1896, the large hinterland surrounding the formal colony, which ironically produced the majority of the colony's revenue through the palm oil trade, remained sovereign African territory. As new opportunities for wealth expanded, tensions between communities living on the frontier were expressed through warfare and raiding.

This chapter explores how colonial attempts to introduce British law against banditry outside British jurisdiction produced a new type of legal category of detainee known as a "political prisoner." While at first glance this term suggests the direct importation of the same legal category in use in Europe, the classification of political prisoner in Sierra Leone emerged from negotiations between local African communities, British subject traders, and the colonial administration.[3]

The varied fates of Sierra Leone's first political prisoners reflect the dynamic legal and political landscape that existed on the frontier before the declaration of the Protectorate in 1896.

The inapplicability of formal European law beyond the borders of the formal colony compelled the colonial administration to forge diplomatic relationships with African leaders. To do so, British officials signed a series of treaties with local African headmen and chiefs. The majority of treaties signed between 1874 and 1880 had articles that stated that local leaders must turn over any person who committed crimes against British subjects living and trading in African territory.[4] Local leaders were warned not to apply their own indigenous legal codes or customary practices, particularly in cases where capital punishment was a possible outcome. Instead, local leaders were to deliver up criminals into British custody.

While these conditions suggest that imperialism reigned supreme, local factors challenged Britain's authority in the region. As Ruma Chopra's chapter in this volume demonstrates, colonial authority in Sierra Leone was thin on the ground from its inception as a British imperial outpost and resources were extremely limited. This scarcity continued well into the late nineteenth century, particularly in the southern coastal region. As Salhia Belmessous reminds us, "Europeans engaged in treaty making when the balance of power was favorable to indigenous peoples."[5] Local leaders who signed treaties were able to incorporate their own political agendas and legal ideologies into colonial law. Thus, while British officials attempted to control the frontier, the effectiveness of their power was only ever as strong as their alliances with local people. By necessity and design, the frontier was made up of "many legalities." As a result of these multiple and competing legal systems, sovereignty over the region became both shared and contested.[6]

To achieve even a moderate set of mutually intelligible laws and policies, British officials were forced to confront, and even incorporate, indigenous conceptions of justice as much as Africans were compelled to repurpose British ones. While there remained serious cultural misinterpretations, "law was a language that European and native peoples could share more easily than scholars have previously understood. . . . Cultural boundaries were porous, allowing indigenous and European peoples to translate each other's legal arguments, to draw parallels, etc."[7] Incarceration, exile, and execution were forms of punishment that the British violently imposed on Africans, but these acts did have an "approximate counterpart" in the Sierra Leone hinterland region.[8] By reconstructing the stories of Sierra Leone's earliest political prisoners, we discover that local leaders often had their own punishments in mind for bandits, but instead incorporated imperial forms of confinement and deportation into their legal repertoire. The African leaders who turned over criminals to the British in the 1870s were all attempting to assert authority in highly contentious regions. Signing treaties and delivering up "bandits" was a strategic way to eliminate those who threatened their position (in some cases only temporarily), while at the same time forging stronger diplomatic ties with the British. Although outside the confines of this chapter, it is important to note that local leaders did not adopt every British law in the same manner, and frequently defended their right to engage in their own "country customs" to punish other types of criminals within their own jurisdiction.[9]

This chapter reconstructs the stories of six of the earliest known political prisoners forcibly relocated from the Sierra Leone hinterland to Freetown between 1874 and 1882. Using archival material from Sierra Leone and London, I compare the details of the crimes, incarceration, and the outcome of each case. By uncovering previously obscured debates concerning political prisoners in Sierra Leone, this study reveals the critical role that colonial engagement with frontier communities had in constructing colonial law. In a narrative mirroring the chapter by Marie Rodet and Romain Tiquet in this volume, the legal ambiguity of Africans living outside colonial jurisdiction permitted the implementation of extralegal practices that would never have been condoned in Europe. Heightened by colonial anxiety concerning the "uncivilized" or "bloodthirsty" African, a representation that bandits most certainly embodied in the eyes of the British, colonial lawmakers fashioned a two-tier legal system with one set of laws for British subjects and another for non-British subjects.[10] British law was imposed on indigenous communities in an uneven and unilateral manner, making them particularly vulnerable to detention and deportation. Africans from outside the formal colony could be detained under British law. However, their status as foreigners effectively denied them access to the same rights and protection that subjects of the British crown would possess. While partnership with local African leaders was seen as a necessary part of early imperialism, disobedience to this "friendship" could land African leaders in the same cells as the men they had previously delivered up. This instability frequently made the operation of law both on the frontier and in the colony a volatile and violent affair.

The inherent flexibility of a category like "political prisoner" allowed colonial rulers to manipulate it for many purposes. While colonial officials often indicated that they were well aware that the detainment of African political prisoners was illegal, they continued this practice well into the twentieth century in order to further their own imperial goals and to benefit their African allies. Furthermore, the exile of two prisoners to Lagos in 1882 signals another crucial legal precedent. Following the first deportation of political prisoners from Sierra Leone, many subsequent political prisoners suffered the same fate by being exiled to Nigeria, Gold Coast, and Gambia.[11] These actions were echoed all over colonized Africa, as chapters by Sana Camara, Brett Shadle, and Nathan Carpenter in this volume underscore. Throughout various European empires, the classification of "political prisoner" allowed officials to conceal extralegal actions and legitimate the removal of any human barriers to imperialism and trade. The deportation of political prisoners established a violent geography of exile, where men were transported from protectorate to colony or from colony to colony, without the due process of law. This arbitrary, yet legally sanctioned, removal of resistors had a powerful physical and physiological impact on African colonial subjects by effectively eliminating anyone who challenged European rule.

Trading and Raiding in Sierra Leone's Sherbro Hinterland

Beginning in 1861, the southern coastal region of what is now Sierra Leone could be characterized as an imperial frontier or borderland region.[12] African and British subjects used the vast river system to navigate between two political jurisdictions commonly referred to as "Native Sherbro" and "British Sherbro." Although several maps from this period show clear lines of jurisdiction, in reality the border between colonial and indigenous territory was highly porous. At midcentury, African British subjects known as the Krio began migrating from their Freetown homes and setting up trading posts along the major rivers well outside of British territory. By the 1870s, local bandits and war captains began to target traders in increasing numbers. Krio petitions and newspaper articles made scathing attacks on British policy, arguing that these "lawless scoundrels" and "marauding savages" were destroying the fledgling colonial economy they were trying to build.[13]

As British subjects, Krio traders argued that they were entitled to the same protection from England as other European-born British travelers. These claims created a complicated legal problem for the Freetown administration. As the majority of Krio traders operated in "Native Sherbro," the majority of thefts occurred outside of British territory. However, while many Freetown Governors were keen to engage in military expeditions to reclaim Krio property, the Colonial Office in London frequently denied these requests citing the costly, ineffective, and legally questionable nature of campaigns in African territory. Policing crimes that took place outside the boundaries of the formal colony was officially discouraged and officials warned traders that if they insisted on trading in those "unsettled and turbulent districts" they did so "at their own risk."[14]

Nonintervention policies dictated by London compelled colonial officials to set up a series of diplomatic meetings with local African leaders. Although the British misunderstood significant aspects of local politics, they did perceive ongoing struggles over power and authority in the region. The new cash economy brought on by imperial trade allowed men and women outside of traditional aristocratic or elite families to gain a following and challenge old power structures.[15] Raids on Krio traders were only part of a larger series of "economic wars" happening in the region. When these conflicts reached their height in the early 1870s, many local leaders in the Sherbro region hired war captains and their soldiers to fight on their behalf. Raiding provided these hired mercenaries the opportunity to acquire wealth beyond their contracts with local leaders, and Krio warehouses were ideal targets.[16] Local leaders who protected British trade and turned over these "bandits" became identified as important friends of the colonial state, but created further tension among many of their African neighbors.

Treaty-making and other forms of diplomacy soon created a discernible set of "aligned" African leaders. Correspondence from the 1870s suggests that some aligned leaders imagined their relationship with the British much like the former war captains they had hired. They frequently solicited protection by requesting colonial police or assistance after kidnapping and raids.[17] As tensions mounted in the region, increasing numbers of leaders attended diplomatic meetings and signed treaties swearing their loyalty to the British. However, while the stipulation to turn over anyone who committed crimes against British subjects appears to have been embraced by aligned African leaders, it is clear that the British had few concrete plans about what to do with bandits once they arrived in Freetown.

Political Prisoners

Given the context of raiding and warfare on the frontier, delivering up bandits to British officials was a powerful tool for many indigenous leaders and Krio traders. However, the legal ramifications of confining non-British subjects within the formal colony was another thing altogether.[18] Policies concerning political prisoners in Freetown were improvised by legal laymen and appear to have been conceptualized through an ad hoc blend of several European criminal statuses. The legal designation of political prisoner was, of course, used in Europe throughout the nineteenth century to incarcerate men who challenged state power, most notably in Ireland.[19] Like their European counterparts, Sierra Leone's political prisoners were treated in a more lenient fashion than ordinary criminals in Freetown's prison population; they were not subject to penal labor, had a special diet, were given medical treatment, and were allowed to have visitors and engage in authorized correspondence. At the same time, political prisoners in Sierra Leone were characterized much like prisoners of war or something akin to "enemy combatants" in contemporary parlance.[20] Discussion upon their release, for example, often hinged on whether peace had been restored in the region they came from. Despite the fact that their treatment in prison appears to have been marginally better than regular prisoners, political prisoners were detained, seemingly with no legal rights, and existed in a type of legal limbo while outside of African sovereign territory.

The first reference to political prisoners in the colonial archive is in the correspondence records of the Government Interpreter George Lawson concerning the visit of two aligned leaders to Freetown in December 1877. Upon their arrival, Lawson, a Krio, wrote the Governor explaining that the two leaders were in town to see about the "*political prisoners* who were being held by the British by a general request of their own chiefs from their constantly disturbing the peace of their country and plundering territory with armed men."[21] While it is unclear if leaders from this trip were introduced to the term "political prisoner," it does appear more frequently in colonial correspondence after 1877. For example, when attempting to gain permission to mount an expedition to capture a prominent war captain in 1878, the Governor used "bandit" and "political prisoner" interchangeably, telling the Colonial Office he wanted to travel to the interior to "insist on this ruffian being given up and, in enforcing the demand, confining him as a political prisoner and a bandit, in the Freetown Gaol."[22]

Only after a substantial number of so-called "bandits" were detained in Freetown, did the colonial government attempt to define who and what political prisoners were vis-à-vis the law. One colonial official suggested that it could be "broadly stated that they are in the position of state prisoners who have been brought to and detained at S. Leone for the sake of preserving peace in their own country, and that in these circumstances a trial, in the ordinary sense of the term, would be out of place."[23] In a subsequent dispatch, the Governor wrote that the bandits who were incarcerated were regarded as "somewhat the nature of a prisoner of war" whose incarceration was "necessary for good order, but illegal."[24] These comments demonstrate how colonial law was forged from local conditions, rather than from a cohesive colonial policy or European legal principles. Despite the fact that the Colonial Office repeatedly remarked on the illegal nature of the detainment of Sierra Leone's political prisoners, they remained quite insistent that this illegality be disregarded in favor of the commercial needs and diplomatic alliances in the hinterland.

The First Political Prisoners

By 1881, at least six political prisoners were held in the Freetown prison. Leaders who handed over these men had engaged in significant diplomacy with the British and some had even provided troops for the British during several military expeditions. They had all signed the types of peace treaties outlined above that stipulated the exchange of prisoners. Each of the leaders were involved in power struggles over authority with other African leaders, either within their own family or across "ethnic" (Sherbro/Mende) lines and lived in important and contested trading regions. Delivering up bandits as political prisoners represents one significant way local leaders attempted to use diplomacy with the British to their advantage. As the stories below reveal, African leaders did not simply hand over criminals from their jurisdiction without some form of negotiation with British officials. In time, half of the early political prisoners were released back to their homes after consultation with the leaders who delivered them up initially. Mirroring many African indigenous legal systems, prisoners without the support of a powerful African patron suffered the consequences and were permanently exiled from their natal home.[25]

The first political prisoner on record was a man named Vangang who was accused of leading a raid and kidnapping two female Krio traders. In 1875, African leaders who had formed alliances with the colonial government (and received military support during the war) turned him over during the signing of a peace treaty. We know that Vangang spent at least two years in prison before two of these treaty signatories, Thomas Bongo and Gberry, traveled to Freetown to meet with the Governor to ensure that he not be freed.[26] He is not mentioned in the record again until 1880 when another aligned leader from the region petitioned that he be released into his custody.[27]

In late 1878, William Caulker, a man who could be characterized as the most prominent political prisoner, was detained in Freetown. William had become a successful trader and was well known among the Krio community. Perhaps on account of this newly acquired wealth, he was accused of trying to usurp the leadership of his cousin George's territory (the Plantain and Banana Islands) and of raiding Krio traders. Clearly understanding the power of accusations of banditry, William, in turn, accused George of "constantly violating treaties" by "the secret plunder of British subjects through the medium of several bandits."[28] William's journey from hinterland to the colonial prison was not as straightforward as a simple arrest by colonial police. Initially, his cousin George and the local American missionary, Reverend Gomer, captured and detained William for several months by keeping him bolted to a wooden cross in iron bars and chains. William's eventual incarceration as a political prisoner in Freetown occurred as the result of an extended set of negotiations between colonial officials and local African leaders, many of whom were initially reticent to release him into British custody. While George seemed initially intent on executing William himself, he appears to have changed his mind when one of his family members warned him of his "treaty obligations" to hand over William "before you shed family blood."[29] George and a council made up of local elders appear to have taken this advice to heart and so asked the Governor to "*assist* them in settling their disputes by helping to determine the 'best way of punishing him' as they wished to have William permanently removed from their country."[30]

After a series of meetings with government officials in their main town of Shenge, George and the other elders agreed to allow the British to detain William. In the letter they sent to Freetown with William, the elders wrote that while they "would have kept him for so many years in our own way . . . we have not hesitated in delivering the young man to you being well acquainted with your Excellency's justice at all times."[31] For the Caulker family, this acquiescence was critical because of their increasingly precarious hold on power in the region. Besides challenges over authority by other Caulker family members like William, ethnically Sherbro leaders were being pushed out of key leadership positions by Mende people moving southwards into traditional Sherbro territory.[32] While the Caulker family made a series of attempts to demonstrate loyalty to the British throughout the century, it became difficult to change the colonial belief that the family's infighting (highlighted no doubt by delivering up one of their own family members) had a negative and destabilizing impact on trade in the region.[33]

Like their Sherbro counterparts, important Mende leaders also attempted to strengthen their alliance with the British by delivering up prisoners. In March 1880, William Caulker and Vangang were joined by two men, Harry Mustapha and Sharkah Bollontoh, accused of raiding and stealing a canoe and its contents in Mende territory. Similar to William, Bollontoh represented the new type of African trader who had gained wealth through new forms of imperial trade.[34] In a petition that Bollontoh sent to the Colonial Office while he was in prison, he justified the theft as necessary, claiming that his sister was owed a debt from her marriage to a Krio named Mr. Mark, the owner of the canoe. Bollontoh wrote that when his sister and Mark parted, Mark had sold Bollontoh's ten-year-old niece Boih for two hundred "bushels" to purchase the canoe in question. Bollontoh explained he was merely trying to reclaim funds that he felt his sister was owed in order to retrieve his niece. Unfortunately for Bollontoh, the canoe was carrying the prominent Mende leader Gbanyah, the Government Interpreter George Lawson's daughter, and her husband John Parker who acted as an informal liaison between the colonial government and the Mende people.

When news of the raid reached the Mende capital of Sennehoo, citizens wanted revenge for the attack on their leader. Gbanyah told them they must not do this as he was "in treaty" with the British. In the meantime, Bollontoh continued to live in the region, where it appears at some point the goods in the canoe were given to Harry Mustapha.[35] According to Lawson's account of the events, as Gbanyah lay dying he instructed his son-in-law Kong to bring the matter to the Governor next time he came to Sennehoo. When this happened later in 1880, Mustapha and Bollontoh were taken back to Freetown to be detained.

In 1880, another important Mende leader, Sorie Kessebeh, delivered up a bandit named Beah Jack.[36] Like Gbanyah and Kong, Kessebeh was a Mende leader of a town within a region that was traditionally ruled by the Caulker family. In a letter to the Freetown administration, Sorie Kessebeh accused Beah Jack of being the "prime mover and perpetrator" of a recent plundering of British traders and that he continually defied the authority of those in power.[37] Like George Caulker, Kessebeh and other elders in his town pleaded with the Governor "either to cause him to be put to death or to be removed to Freetown."[38] As a consequence of this, Beah Jack was brought back to the colony and placed in the prison along with another bandit named Doombuyah, from the Port Loko area, about whom we know little.

Debates over Political Prisoners in Freetown and London

Since the late 1860s, the Freetown community had been divided on the morality of imprisoning men from outside colonial borders. Although many people argued that the detainment of political prisoners was necessary for the safety of Krio traders, others were not as sure. In one 1877 letter to a newspaper, the author wrote that he disapproved of the

> unconstitutional license the government has adopted in incarceration of certain captives brought by Governor Rowe to the Settlement May last. Whatever may be the enormity of the crimes committed by the captives, the government,

> in all justice, ought to have taken some steps to bring them to trial and award them the punishment due to their crimes.[39]

The article called for the men to be either released or put on trial, and if "no good can arise, it is useless and unjust to detain them any longer for their crimes not yet proved against them."[40]

At some point, word of the legally questionable practice of detaining political prisoners in Freetown made its way to the Colonial Office in London. In notes concerning the Bollontoh and Mustapha cases, one colonial official wrote that the detention of the political prisoners,

> was probably somewhat 'ultra vires' . . . but justified by reasons of state policy, if it is the only means of maintaining peace in the district from which they were taken. Proceedings which would be high-handed and unjustifiable in more civilized places are sometimes necessary and must be overlooked in W Africa where wars which extend over large areas are ruined to trade, and the interests of our settlements, arise from such very small matters.[41]

In the same dispatch, another official scribbled in the margin:

> Their detention is probably illegal . . . [If we are] to detain these prisoners as state prisoners should not an ordinance be passed as the other day at the Gold Coast? I have no doubt it may be sometimes advisable to detain men from such reasons but great care should be taken that the Govt has the authority for its proceedings. All such arrests should be at once reported home.[42]

Statements like these reveal the inconsistency between what was considered legal in the colony and the metropole. Officials in Freetown and London affirmed numerous times the illegality of the detention of political prisoners, yet they struggled with identifying a legal way to resolve the dilemma.[43]

While the detainees Africanness and threat to peace on the frontier was enough to justify their incarceration to Freetown officials, it was not enough to prevent somewhat of a scandal among humanitarians in London. Debates over Freetown's political prisoners moved from the desk at the Colonial Office, to the floor of the House of Commons, and finally to the pages of *The London Times*. In the summer of 1881, Charles Hopwood appears to have been informed of the men held in the Freetown prison. Taking up their cause on the floor of the House of Commons, he presented a series of questions concerning their imprisonment and its conditions, for example, "why they were not tried" and "whether [or not] they are treated like convicts."[44] Hopwood's questions were reprinted in *The London Times* on August 24, 1881, creating an embarrassing public situation for the Colonial Office. In comments attached to Hopwood's questions, one colonial official wrote, "there seems very little doubt that the Col. Govt have been acting illegally in detaining these individuals, though circumstances may have rendered the illegality justifiable."[45] The Colonial Office urged the Governor to deal with the matter at once.

This task was left to the newly appointed Governor Arthur Havelock. Being new to the cases, he relied heavily on Government Interpreter Lawson and local African leaders. While in the Colonial Office the political prisoners were characterized as a homogenous group. In Freetown each man was considered individually according to their own circumstances. Tracing this process exposes just how improvisational the construction of colonial law was. Each political prisoner's case was informed by a localized set of negotiations, not European laws or precedents. Similar to their incarceration, the fate of individual prisoners was determined through collaboration between local leaders and colonial officials. Some prisoners were returned to the custody of leaders in the hinterland, while others were exiled from the colony forever.

The first case Havelock addressed was that of Vangang, who had been in prison for seven years. After several local leaders wrote requesting his release, it was agreed that he could return home.[46] Although his departure was delayed a year because he contracted smallpox, Vangang was transferred into the custody of a local aligned leader who promised to be responsible for his future conduct.[47] Likewise, Gbanyah's successor, Kong, negotiated the release of Sharkah Bollontoh and Harry Mustapha in 1881. To solemnize the agreement, Kong and others journeyed to Freetown to "shake hands" on the agreement with the Governor personally.[48] In the end, compensation for the canoes and goods were to be paid by Bollontoh's landlord Richard Canray Bey Caulker, who was considered the "Paramount Chief" in the region. In the end, this arbitration process did much to elevate the opinion of the Mende people in the eyes of the local administration. After their meeting, Havelock remarked on the good effects that their interaction with British law had had on their "tribal nature," stating that Kong had shown a "great forbearance and a loyal desire to carry out the wishes of the Government by waiting patiently for a peaceful solution of the difficulty instead of taking the law into their own hands and making reprisals."[49]

Such law-abiding behavior on the part of Mende leaders was directly compared to the actions of Richard Canray Beh Caulker, the Paramount Chief who was ultimately accused of sanctioning Bollontoh's theft of the canoe. Richard did not attend the Freetown meeting with the Mende leaders—undoubtedly further damaging his reputation as a troublemaker. However, Richard's poor image with colonial officials appears not to have hindered his nephew William in his efforts to be released from prison. By 1882, William was removed from prison and transferred to a form of "house arrest" in Lawson's home.[50] Here, William was able to effectively use his education as a boy in the Freetown Government School to write petitions and letters proclaiming his loyalty to the Queen and her laws. Despite the fact that a variety of local leaders who had placed him in prison professed him to be "Worse than Satan in Hell" and a "demon in human shape," William returned home with only a warning.[51]

The deportation of Africans from their homelands to other British colonies prior to 1880 appears to have been a strategy of colonial rule that was reserved for elite leaders—such as the King of Elmina who was exiled from the Gold Coast to Sierra

Leone in 1873—who were perceived as a threat to the establishment of British rule. In 1881, this policy was extended in Sierra Leone to the nonelite detainees Doombuyah and Beah Jack. Lacking "responsible" custodians or mediators who would pay a penalty for their misconduct, colonial officials debated that while the men's imprisonment was necessary for "good order" it was most certainly "illegal."[52] While several colonial officials insisted that local leaders should "be made responsible for keeping in order their own ruffians," Doombuyah and Beah Jack were ultimately deported to Lagos.[53] Within the dispatch notes, permenant exile was justified as an action that benefitted the colony and favored local leaders. As one official wrote,

> We cannot detain them indefinitely in prison and I should be disposed to deport them to Lagos where after a time they could probably be let out with safety. I would say to Mr. Havelock that it is inconvenient to assume the custody of men who infest the territories of chiefs on our borders and who ought to be controlled by these chiefs themselves but . . . it would not be fair to the chiefs of the Rotifunk country after taking charge of Beah Jack to let him loose upon them, whilst there is reason to expect that he would return to his old courses.[54]

Havelock passed a special ordinance to sanction their deportation to Lagos, a legal act that would be repeated for the removal of many more political prisoners in the years that followed and indeed throughout the newly colonized continent by French, British, Belgian, German, and Portuguese regimes.[55] Although even Hopwood insisted that their deportation was tantamount to kidnapping, the plans went ahead in June 1882.[56] Both men spent the remainder of their life in detention in Lagos where they died in the early 1890s.[57]

Conclusion

As one of the oldest colonies in West Africa, events in Sierra Leone created legal precedents for the detention and deportation of African colonial subjects throughout the British Empire and provided guidance for other colonial powers. In tracing colonial legal strategies concerning banditry, this chapter challenges common assumptions about when, where, and by whom colonial law was created. The classification and treatment of "political prisoners" was not directly imported from Europe, but was forged within a complicated legal landscape that required local alliances in order to keep British trade flowing in regions outside of colonial jurisdiction. Colonial officials exploited the jurisdictional haziness of the frontier to impose unlawful measures that were clearly—and even openly—acknowledged by colonial officials as illegal. When colonial ordinances established the exile and detainment of political prisoners as lawful acts in the Colony, detainment and exile were transformed into powerful and licit tools for enforcing both British and, in some cases, indigenous authority.

In the decades following these events, Africans living on the margins of empire saw their sovereignty increasingly challenged. Soon, the status of political prisoner would no longer apply just to bandits, but to anyone who challenged imperialism in the region. Informal detention and extrajudicial transfer within colonial territories morphed into formal imprisonment and forcible removal among colonial regimes. By the late nineteenth century, the incarceration of political prisoners became an established—and frighteningly common—practice in Sierra Leone. Deportation, in particular, was a particularly violent and effective tool during the establishment of the Protectorate in 1896 and ultimately shifted the balance of power in the region to the British. Prominent leaders who had once been considered loyal to the British found themselves exiled to other British colonies. For the remainder of British colonial rule, leaders appointed to replace deportees would rule with the fear that their predessor's fate could easily become their own.

Notes

1. Lawson Report. April 10, 1880. Sierra Leone National Archives (SLNA)/ Government Interpreter Volumes (GI) 1880. Governor to CO. May 19, 1881. British National Archives (BNA)/CO 267/344/10442. Lawson report to Governor, March 4, 1881. SLNA/ GI 1881. 366. The five were William Caulker, Sharka Bollontoh, Harry Mustapha, Beah Jack and Doombuyah.

2. See Kristin Mann and Richard Roberts, *Law in Colonial Africa* (Portsmouth, N.H.: Heinemann, 1991); Richard L. Roberts, *Litigants and Households: African Disputes and Colonial Courts in the French Soudan, 1895–1912* (London: Heinemann and James Curry, *2005);* Martin Chanock, *The Making of South African Legal Culture 1902–1936* (Cambridge, UK: Cambridge University Press, 2001); Florence Bernault, "The Shadow of Rule: Colonial Power and Modern Punishment in Africa" in *Cultures of Confinement: A Global History as Prison in Asia, Africa, the Middle East and Latin America,* ed. Ian Brown and Frank Dikotter (London: Christopher Hurst 2007), 55–94; Stacey Hynd, "Killing the Condemned: The Practice and Process of Capital Punishment in British Africa, 1900s–1950s," *Journal of African History,* 49, no. 3 (2008): 403–18.

3. For more on banditry and law outside Africa but within the British Empire, see Nathan Brown, "Brigands and State Building: The Invention of Banditry in Modern Egypt," *Comparative Studies in Society and History* 32, no. 2 (1990): 258–281.

4. Edward Hertselt, *Hertslet's Commercial Treaties* (London: 1880), 30. Later treaties directly named "wanted men" that the colonial government had identified. "Treaty signed January 6, 1880 between the British Government, Boom and Jong Chiefs." BNA/CO 879/17/9. Enclosure 10. 111–112.

5. Sahlia Belmessous, *Empire by Treaty: Negotiating European Expansion, 1600–1900.* (Oxford: Oxford University Press, 2015), 9.

6. Christopher Tomlins and Bruce H Mann, *The Many Legalities of Early America* (Chapel Hill: UNC Press, 2001); Lisa Ford, *Settler Sovereignty: Jurisdiction and Indigenous People in America and Australia, 1788–1836* (Cambridge, MA: Harvard University Press, 2010); Lauren Benton, *A Search for Sovereignty: Law and Geography in European Empires, 1400–1900.* (Cambridge: Cambridge University Press, 2010).

7. Belmessous, *Native Claims*, 5.

8. Kenneth Little, *The Mende of Sierra Leone: A West African People in Transition* (London: Routledge, 1951); David Chalmers, *Chalmer's Report Part I and II*, Parliamentary Report IX, 1899.

9. Trina Leah Hogg, "'Our Country Customs': Legality, Diplomacy, and Violence on the Sierra Leone Frontier, 1861–1896," PhD dissertation, New York University, 2013.

10. For more on banditry outside Africa, but within the British Empire, see Nathan Brown, "Brigands and State Building: The Invention of Banditry in Modern Egypt," *Comparative Studies in Society and History*, 32, no. 2 (1990): 258–281; and Elizabeth Kolsky, *Colonial Justice in British India: White Violence and the Rule of Law* (New York: Cambridge University Press, 2010).

11. Chalmers Report, 1899.

12. In 1861, the British annexed a small slip of the coastal region. This became known as "British Sherbro." For more on frontiers and empire, see Jeremy Adelman and Stephen Aro, "From Borderlands to Borders: Empires, Nation-States, and the Peoples in between in North American History," *American Historical Review* 104, no. 3 (1999): 814–841; Eric Lewis Beverley, "Frontier as Resource: Law, Crime and Sovereignty on the Margins of Empire," *Comparative Studies in Society and History* 55, no. 2 (2013): 241–272.

13. "Sherbro Again," *The Independent*, June 24, 1878.

14. Colonial Office Remarks (Henning). May 18, 1878. BNA/ CO 267/334/7027.

15. Lynda Day, *Gender and Power in Sierra Leone: Women Chiefs in the Last Two Centuries* (New York: Palgrave, 2012); Allen M. Howard, "Re-making the Past: Spatial Structures and Dynamics in the Sierra Leone-Guinea Plain" in *The Spatial Factor in African History: The Relationship of the Social, Material, and Perceptual*, ed. Allan M. Howard and Richard M. Shain (Leiden: Brill, 2005). For more on this transition throughout Africa see Robin Law, ed., *From Slavery to Legitimate Commerce: The Commercial Transaction in Nineteenth-Century West Africa*. (Cambridge: Cambridge University Press, 1995).

16. Arthur Abraham, *Mende Government and Politics under Colonial Rule: A Historical Study of Political Change in Sierra Leone, 1890–1937* (Freetown: Sierra Leone University Press, 1978).

17. Some treaties demanded that aligned leaders disarm and tear down the stockades that surrounded their villages. This made them even more vulnerable to attacks and in need of colonial protection. Chiefs Bongo and Hanimo to Commandant. February 15, 1877. SLNA/ Sherbro Letterbooks (SHER) 1877.192

18. Initially, British officials appear to have been unsure as to whether bandits from the Sierra Leone frontier should even be detained in prison, as they were initially held in the private home of the Government Interpreter George Lawson. It is likely this practice drew from Lawson's housing of the King of Elmina who arrived as a prisoner in 1873 from the Gold Coast. However, it was discontinued after a notorious bandit escaped Lawson's custody and mounted a series of devastating raids on traders in the interior. George Lawson was a prominent Krio colonial administrator. See Hogg, "Our Country Customs," chapter 4.

19. Padraic Kenney, "'I felt a kind of pleasure in seeing them treat us brutally.' The Emergence of the Political Prisoner, 1865–1910," *Comparative Studies in Society and History* 54, no. 4 (2012): 863–889. For a classic article on political prisoners see Leon Radzinowicz and Roger Hood, "The Status of Political Prisoner in England: the Struggle for Recognition," *Virginia Law Review* 65, no. 8 (1979): 1421–1481.

20. Colonial officials may have been inspired by the 1874 Brussels Conference draft of the "International Declaration of the Law and Customs of War" that built on the first Geneva

Convention. For some possible historical antecedents to "enemy combatants" in British common law, see Carlton F.W. Larson, "The Forgotten Constitutional Law of Treason and the Enemy Combatant Problem," *University of Pennsylvania Law Review* 154 (2006): 863–926. The debate about whether nonstate combatants can be at war with a state, and therefore lawfully detainable is an interesting contemporary parallel to the question about whether a colonial subject can be guilty of treason.

21. George Lawson to Governor. December 31, 1877. SLNA/ GI 1877. 303. My emphasis.

22. Rowe to CO. May 18, 1878. BNA/ CO 267/334/7027.

23. Newspaper clippings re: colonial records. August 17, 1881. CO/267/346/14808.

24. Case of Doombuyah and Beah Jack. August 27, 1881. CO 267/344/16535.

25. See Bernault, "The Shadow of Rule: Colonial Power and Modern Punishment in Africa," 56–57.

26. Lawson to Rowe. April 21 1880. SLNA/ GI 1880. 503. Colonial Office to Governor. September 15, 1881. BNA/CO 267/345/17577.

27. Lawson report. April 21, 1880. SLNA/ GI 1880. 503.

28. Colonial Office to Caulker. April 22, 1881. BNA/ CO 267/347/9294.

29. William Tucker to George Caulker. October 4, 1878. Enclosure no. 5A in CO to Governor. May 12, 1881. BNA/ CO 267 344/9812. William Tucker was also an aligned leader in the 1870s.

30. Signed "With our united respects, we remain, sir, your loyal subjects Ya Coombah, Ma N'Caipor, Ba Yorgbah, Ya Bome, Ko Bess, Ko Yarma and the whole of the country." Chiefs of Shenge to Governor. October 17, 1878. Enclosure no. 5D. CO to Governor. May 12, 1881. BNA/ CO 267 344/9812.

31. Ibid.

32. Abraham, *Mende Government and Politics under Colonial Rule*, especially chapters 1–2.

33. For more on the history of the Caulker family, see Day, *Gender and Power*, and Imodale Caulker-Burnett, *The Caulkers of Sierra Leone: The Story of a Ruling Family and their Times* (Xlibris Corporation, 2012).

34. Bollontoh was a stranger to the region and had an agreement with the "Paramount Chief" Canray Beh Caulker to live and trade there. He was the brother of George Caulker mentioned above in the William Caulker case.

35. In 1880, when Bollontoh was questioned about the plundering, he said that he attacked the canoe with the consent of his landlord, Richard Canray Beh Caulker. Richard strongly denied these charges, stating that he had never received any of the stolen goods from Mustapha. In their petition to Lord Kimberly, Mustapha and Bollontoh stated that they gave Richard Caulker £12 and his "prime minister" Momodoo Carimoo (uncle to Richard Canray Beh Caulker, William and George Caulker) £10. Governor to CO. May 19, 1881. CO 267/344/10442.

36. Sorie Kessebeh assisted the British in various military expeditions in the mid-1870s.

37. Havelock to CO. August 27, 1881. BNA/ CO 267/344/16535.

38. Ibid.

39. "Sherbro," *The Independent*, January 25, 1877.

40. Ibid.

41. Colonial Office notes. May 19, 1881. BNA/ CO 267/344/10442.

42. Ibid.

43. Havelock blamed the practice of detaining political prisoners on the (very popular) former Governor Samuel Rowe. Choosing his words carefully, Havelock wrote, "The

condition of these settlements and of the native tribes in their neighbourhood is such as to render at times the detention without regular trial of persons dangerous to the peace and good order, a necessary and wholesome measure. I find my predecessor held this opinion strongly and acted upon it not infrequently." Imprisonment of Sharkah Bollontoh and Mustapha. July 29, 1881. CO/267/344/14794.

44. Transcript of House of Commons questions attached to August 17, 1881. BNA/CO/267/346/14808.

45. Ibid.

46. Lawson report. April 21, 1880. SLNA/ GI 1880. 503.

47. Lawson to CO. September 15, 1881. BNA/ CO 267/345/17577.

48. Although initially the claim they had made for the goods stolen from Mark's canoe had been £181, the party agreed on a sum of £80. Governor to CO. August 25, 1881. BNA/ CO 267/345/10534.

49. Ibid.

50. William had been educated in the Government School in Freetown and had attended school with Lawson. Throughout his detainment in Lawson's home, Hopwood demanded Caulker's "absolute freedom."

51. Chiefs of Shenge to CO. May 12, 1881. BNA/ CO 267 344/9812. Another advantage for William was the death of George Caulker. In correspondence with Havelock, the regent-chief Thomas Neale Caulker wrote that if William "stated his regret for his contumacious conduct and his willingness to submit to the head of the family, the past should be forgiven and he should be allowed to return in peace to his country and people." William stated that his cousin George has taken from him 372 slaves (described as domestic servants) and £377 pounds of merchandise and personal effects. Governor to CO. "Confiscation of Property of William Caulker by Family Members." November 25, 1881. BNA/ CO 267/346/22006. Amazingly, William joined forces with Hopwood, who continued to write letters to the colonial government on his behalf in an attempt to retrieve his personal property.

52. Colonial Notes. August 27, 1881. BNA/ CO 267/344/16535.

53. (E. Wingfield) Colonial Notes. August 27, 1881. BNA/ CO 267/344/16535.

54. Colonial Notes. August 27, 1881. BNA/ CO 267/344/16535.

55. Colonial Notes. November 28, 1881. BNA/ CO 267/347/20937. Remarks on Hopwood's remarks, various members of the Colonial Office.

56. Hopwood writes that "I forgot to point out as to these men, that they are neither of them the subjects of Her Majesty but have been kidnapped, imprisoned and ill treated, and are now to be deported, in Her Majesty's name without the semblance of a trial." Hopwood to Colonial Office. December 2, 1881. CO 267/347/21210.

57. After they landed in Lagos, the details of Doombuyah and Beah Jack's life are unclear to me. Nothing is heard of them for several years, but beginning in August 1884, Doombuyah sent a series of petitions to the Colonial Office asking for his release. There are both reported as dying in Lagos. On Beah Jack: Governor to CO. February 20, 1890. BNA/CO/267/381/5717; Parkes to Governor. February 10, 1890. SLNA/Aboriginal Letterbooks (ALB). 206. (Death) Governor to CO. June 10, 1893. BNA/CO/267/402. On Doombuyah: Governor to CO. September 6, 1887. BNA/CO/267/368/20168. Parkes to Government House. October 18, 1889. SLNA/ALB. 101. Parkes to Governor. February 10, 1890. SLNA/ALB. 206. (Death) Governor to CO. April 23, 1891. BNA/CO/267/390/10050.

3 The Path of Extinction

The Double Exile of Alfa Yaya and the Penal Regime in French Colonial Africa

Nathan Riley Carpenter

The train rolled out of Cotonou on December 7, 1905. It slowly made its way north along the freshly laid tracks through Allada, and along the fringes of the Ko forest, to its destination of Abomey—once the celebrated capital city of the kingdom of Dahomey, now but a French colonial post. At points along the route, locals came out to view the train, and to catch a glimpse of its passengers. Many came bearing gifts—sheep, chickens, fruit—hoping to be able to greet the famed group: Alfa Yaya and his entourage of exiles.[1] Though recognized by these locals, Alfa Yaya is not a well-known figure outside the history of greater Senegambia. But his story is familiar. An influential and powerful regional leader and a one-time French ally, he was arrested by the colonial administration and sentenced to exile. The government banished him along with family members and advisors to a remote location elsewhere in the empire. In the words of one French administrator, the sentence was "la voie d'extinction," the path of extinction.[2] It was a deliberate attempt to cut Alfa Yaya off from his seat of power on the northern periphery of French Guinea and thus slowly diminish his influence and extinguish his authority.

Exile was a tool that colonial agents wielded regularly during the early periods of French occupation and administration, and continued to employ well into the twentieth century. It also had specific and strategic applications. In sentencing individuals to exile, colonial administrators attempted to eliminate people who, by their very presence in the colony, threatened to undermine the foundations of colonial rule. In removing such persons, the French administration cleared obstacles to its "civilizing mission." This chapter examines some of the legal and administrative origins of exile in French colonial Africa. Many of the particularities of exile policy were worked out on the ground, in ad hoc fashion. Unlike the categories of political prisoner described by Trina Hogg in this volume, however, the legal foundations of expulsions in French colonial Africa can be found not on the colonial frontier, but in metropolitan penal codes. In this way, exile policy in Africa drew on a long history of expulsion of French citizens by the French state. An examination of the dual exiles of Alfa Yaya—his first exile to Dahomey in 1905 and a second exile to Mauritania in 1911—thus provides an opportunity to consider the ways in which the colonial state, like all modern states, was constituted in both law and arbitrary violence. The case also gives us an opportunity to consider the sometimes unexpected outcomes and consequences of exile. The excision of individuals like Alfa Yaya from society was meant as a means of erasure, of removal, of extinction. Alfa Yaya died in exile in Mauritania. But the memory of him remained and was later transformed in Guinean nationalist history. Because of his final exile, Alfa Yaya has been remembered not as an early ally of French colonial administrators, a tax collector, or brutal subregional ruler, but instead as an anticolonial resistor who continues to have relevance for contemporary national politics.

Exile, Law, and Penal Regimes

Historians of French colonial Africa have generally seen exile as one of several tools employed by advancing colonial forces during the wars of French occupation in Africa. The French particularly employed it against military resistors such as Samori Touré and African royalty such as Béhanzin. French forces arrested Touré after a long resistance and exiled him to Gabon in 1898, where he died two years later.[3] Béhanzin's presence in West Africa was deemed so threatening that his exile extended even beyond his death: French officials refused to repatriate his remains despite petitions by his son, wife, and several notables.[4] Only in 1928—two decades after his death—were his remains returned to Dahomey.[5] Exile in these cases was part of a strategy of conquest that included brutal military campaigns and punishment of various sorts levied against individuals and recalcitrant communities. Exiles included not only well-known resistors, but also many other lesser-known figures such as the Ohori leaders involved in opposing French incursions into their homeland during the early twentieth century. Mohilo, Esija, Akoagu, Eitcha, and Otutubiodjo were all sentenced to exile in 1916 to Port Etienne on the coast of Mauritania; it was for many not only a site of exile but also a death sentence.[6]

While individuals like Béhanzin and Samori Touré threatened French hegemony through military resistance, others threatened French colonialism in less direct ways. Ahmadu Bamba's rise as a spiritual leader worried the French and, because of this, the French administration arrested and exiled Bamba on spurious claims that the cleric was part of an anti-French network of radical Muslims.[7] He was sentenced to exile outside of Senegal "until the agitation caused by his teaching [was] forgotten."[8] As Sana Camara notes in this volume, however, exile brought not obsolescence, but in fact greater renown for Bamba as a spiritual resistor. The colonial state continued to employ exile even after the French military had conquered African states and leaders such as Béhanzin. It was, in the words of Florence Bernault, "a form of prolongation of the war against political opponents of colonization," and the list of those subjected to the sentence grew.[9] As Marie Rodet and Romain Tiquet describe later in this volume, the French state continued—through the penal sentence of relegation—to exile colonial subjects through the postwar period of decolonization.

The continued use of exile presents a conundrum. Why exile people at all? Carrying out sentences of exile was a time-consuming and expensive proposition. It required mobilizing sparse administrative and judicial resources to judge and then transport exiles to faraway places. Often, the colonies paid for the maintenance of elite exiles and their families for years. This included annual stipends for family members, even after terms of exile ended. Perhaps more to the point, the French colonial state had myriad other ways to deal with individuals they found difficult. Imprisonment, house arrest, forced labor, holding family members hostage, summary executions—these were all tactics that the French colonial state, not known for its leniency, regularly employed.

Sentences of exile were not uniquely colonial, and the origins of exile in the colonial context were linked to a long history of banishment as a political tool by the French state including the forced labor of the galley, the deportation of claimed enemies of the revolution, and the nineteenth-century practice of deporting French citizens to serve time in penal colonies.[10] In the case of the penal colony, condemned political prisoners, and later common-law felons and repeat offenders, were sent half way around the globe to serve out sentences dredging swamps in the jungles of New Caledonia.[11] Whether a political prisoner or a felon, it remained that the convicts were seen as potentially endangering the security of the French state at large. The one threatened to undermine the government while the other was believed to be a danger to society and future generations—a belief that reflected contemporary ideas about race, class, and social evolution. A sentence to the penal colony was not simply an act of removal, it was seen as punitive and rehabilitative. Proponents of the penal colonies believed that life and work in the tropics could rehabilitate an individual who had fallen to the degenerative effects of urban life. It would prepare individuals for reentry into society—though they were not expected to reenter metropolitan society; ex-convicts were to be reinserted into the "civil society of the colonies."[12] That rehabilitated exiled convicts were not allowed reentry into French society points to another important facet of the penal colony in the French imperial imaginary. The penal colony was also generative of empire, both through the labor of the convicts as well as the permanent settlement of colonial territory by former convicts; the 1854 law that extended deportation to petty criminals specifically referenced colonization.[13] Shortly after, imperial subjects as well as citizens were being exiled to Réunion and New Caledonia. Convicts who were sentenced to more than eight years of labor were required to remain in the colony indefinitely after having served their time. Although their punishment was temporary, their exile was permanent. Granted a plot of land, they were expected to become productive members of the colony and were seen to be serving in the interests of the state.[14]

The first attempt to create a broad-based penal code for French-claimed territories in West Africa came in March 1877.[15] The March 6 decree applied the penal code of metropolitan France to Senegal and other territories in West Africa. It was a wide-ranging ordinance that also applied the code elsewhere across the empire from Saint Pierre and Miquelon to New Caledonia.[16] The code granted judicial powers to the colonial governor and indicated that those infractions that fell within the jurisdiction of local authorities were to be punished as *contraventions*, or petty crimes, as outlined in the French penal code. Punishments were limited to fifteen days of prison and a fine of up to one hundred francs. Any extension of a punishment beyond these limits necessitated an official decree by the head of state. The law was updated ten years later by the decree of September 30, 1887. This new order gave the powers of punishment to colonial administrators as well as to the governor. Now, lower-level administrators, or *commandants*, could hand down punishments for minor infractions committed within their districts.[17]

The decree of September 30, 1887 has been cited as an example of the ways in which colonial judgment and punishment operated with very little administrative oversight. The 1887 decree was one of the foundations for the infamous *indigénat*, a regime that was employed by the French in Algeria in the late nineteenth century and was soon exported across the French empire.[18] It was born out of war and meant to be used by the French to transition from colonial occupation to colonial administration. That transition, however, never fully materialized. As A. I. Asiwaju has argued in the case of West Africa, and as Isabelle Merle has shown in her discussion of the *indigénat* in New Caledonia, this "regime" became less a state of exception than an "instrumental tool" in the everyday violence of colonial rule.[19]

The 1887 decree is an excellent example of how exile fitted into the colonial matrix of law and violence.[20] The decree served as a basis for the types of punishments usually associated with the *indigénat*. These were punishments handed down by a single colonial administrator and often for seemingly minor infractions. It should be noted, however, that the handing down of a sentence by a lower-level administrator was also not necessarily unique to the colonial setting; back in the metropole, a single magistrate had authority to determine whether a citizen would be sentenced to exile in a penal colony.[21]

In the penal colony and the *indigénat* we have examples of punitive and rehabilitative regimes—they imposed punishment on individuals or groups to effect a change in behavior. And, they were also both punishments that helped to constitute the state. They were generative in terms of the fines they imposed, in the labor they commanded and, in the case of the penal colony, the physical colonization of new territory. The sentence of exile in West Africa, in contrast, was not meant to be rehabilitative, and it might not have been primarily punitive. Nor was it seen as generative of state power. From the state's perspective, exile was a sort of excision or pruning. It was the removal of a perceived threat to state control so that the state could continue to function as intended.

Alfa Yaya, "les grands chefs," and "la voie d'extinction"

Alfa Yaya embodied the complex political environment of French colonial West Africa at the turn of the century. Born in the mid-nineteenth century, he was from the village of Foulamori, located in a rural but cosmopolitan corner of what is today northwestern Guinea, within walking distance of neighboring Guinea-Bissau. At the time, Foulamori was on the western frontier of the Futa Jallon state. He rose to power in the late nineteenth century by taking advantage of the political opening after the collapse of the neighboring kingdom of Kaabu to the west and internal divisions within Futa Jallon. After the death of his father Alfa Ibrahima in the 1880s he claimed provincial rule over Labé, the largest and most populous of the nine provinces that constituted Futa Jallon. It was by several accounts a bloody succession battle that according to Antoine Marie Jean Demougeot ended with the murder of Alfa Yaya's brother in broad daylight at a Labé mosque after Friday prayer.[22] This rise to power in Labé was accompanied by a distancing from central authority in Futa Jallon and the continuation of commercial connections with French traders on the coast, at Boké on the Rio Nuñez.

Increasing commercial interests and the perceived threat of British imperial claims prompted a French invasion of Futa Jallon in 1896 led by Robert de Beeckman, whose troops conquered the Futa resistance and killed the Futa leader, Bokar Biro.[23] France then folded Futa Jallon into Rivières du Sud, which would later become the colony of French Guinea. Labé, however, was left as an ill-defined quasi-independent entity with Alfa Yaya at its head.[24] The early alliance between Alfa Yaya and the nascent French administration was mutually beneficial. Yaya had turned away from the central Futa leadership, and France saw him as a potential bulwark against other subregional authorities in northern French Guinea and southeastern Senegal. This coupled with his substantial resources helped the French gain a foothold in the interior.

The alliance also helped Alfa Yaya secure his own authority. Having the backing of the French military was an asset. This early period of French

Fig. 3.1 Alfa Yaya. (Lucien Marie François Famechon, *Notice sur la Guinée Française* [Paris, 1900]. Digital image courtesy of the Internet Archive, University of Toronto, and University of Ottawa. http://www.archive.org/details/noticesurlaguinoofameuoft)

occupation was one characterized by selective French alliances with indigenous authorities the French saw as strategic "friends." In Alfa Yaya's case, he was supported early on by French administrators posted to Labé in the heart of the Futa Jallon highlands—most notably, as described by Emily Osborn, Ernest Noirot.[25] His most significant role in the eyes of the French was that of tax collector for Labé, an important district for tax revenue. He had a reputation for brutality; for the administration, however, this reputation was overshadowed by the fact that he was also known to be punctual, and regularly sent in his receipts to the capital in Conakry in full and on time. Yaya was also well compensated for his work. By the time of his exile he was sending more than nine hundred thousand francs a year to the treasury, taking an official cut of 10 percent for himself.[26] He very quickly amassed considerable wealth; his holdings included vast herds of cattle, large numbers of slaves, a European-style house in Kadé on the northwestern frontier, and a bank account with the Bank of West Africa in Conakry. He made requests to have a car delivered to him as soon as the roads in Futa Jallon could support it.[27]

As they did with other indigenous elites at this time, early French administrators saw Alfa Yaya as instrumental in maintaining an economic and political foothold in inland areas that were difficult to access and where European presence was always thin. But attitudes changed early in the century. Whereas previous administrators relied on indigenous intermediaries to assert authority in the colony, a new corps of colonial officials began pushing for the removal of African chiefs, clerics, and other authorities. This change in attitude is articulated by the French social historian, Jean Suret-Canale, who positions the arrest and exile of Alfa Yaya within a long history of the removal of what were referred to as "*les grands chefs*."[28] In French Guinea, the change came with the arrival of a new colonial leadership and a new lieutenant governor, Antoine Marie Frézouls.

Alfa Yaya's increasing wealth and the control he wielded in Labé worried the new lieutenant governor. Frézouls was concerned that Alfa Yaya had become too influential and had assumed a dangerous level of authority.[29] He was bolstered by the analysis of Paul Billault, who at the time was a midcareer deputy administrator posted to Labé, and who suggested several options for reducing the influence of Yaya. The lieutenant governor decided on a plan that called for the expulsion of Alfa Yaya and his son—a plan that Billault dubbed the "*voie d'extinction*," the path of extinction. The idea was that by removing Yaya and his son they would effectively cut hereditary control over Labé and the other territories claimed by Alfa Yaya. The path of extinction articulated by Billault and Frézouls was part of this broader push across the federation to root out what French administrators saw as feudal, arbitrary, and pernicious rule by indigenous elite authorities and establish a more direct control over areas that, up to that point, the French had maintained only through association with these same rulers. Frézouls invited Yaya to the colonial post at Boké with the suggestion that he would travel from Conakry and meet him there. Yaya agreed and on October 14 he left the Futa highlands accompanied by Billault and a large entourage, estimated to consist of two hundred fifty supporters. But Frézouls did not meet him. Instead, Yaya was placed aboard a boat for Conakry, leaving the majority of his partisans behind. It was a plan clearly designed to keep his supporters away from the capital city.[30] In the meantime, Frézouls deployed colonial troops in Futa Jallon to guard against uprisings once word of Yaya's arrest spread.[31] Once Yaya was in Conakry, Frézouls had him detained and then placed aboard the *Paraguay*, a boat bound for Dakar, Senegal—the capital of the Federation of French West Africa.

In Dakar, Yaya's case was brought before the Governor General and the *conseil privé*. He was accused of collaborating with others against the French, procuring arms, and fomenting discontent against French subjects in Guinea. Underlying these unfounded charges was a concern over the growing authority of Alfa Yaya both in terms of the territory he claimed and the people over whom he ruled.[32] The governor sentenced Alfa Yaya, his son Aguibou, and several advisors to five years' exile to the colony of Dahomey—at the interior post of Abomey, some several thousand kilometers from Alfa Yaya's base in the Futa Jallon highlands. After hearing of his sentence, Alfa Yaya wrote to Frézouls, pleading to be allowed to return to Futa Jallon. He reminded the lieutenant governor of his long service to France, writing that he was the "oldest of [France's] friends" in Guinea. He claimed that it was his "enemies" in Futa Jallon who were causing problems and that he only wanted to be able to return to Futa.[33] His letter seems to have gone unanswered and Yaya and his entourage of family and advisors were detained and then transported to Dahomey.

Life in Exile

State agents placed Alfa Yaya aboard the *Maranhao*, bound for the colony of Dahomey, on November 23, 1905. The ship sailed south along the coast and arrived at the port of Cotonou the following month on December 4, in the morning. Accounts from Cotonou at the time described Alfa Yaya as despondent while he and his entourage of family members and advisors stepped off the boat.[34] The group spent several days in Cotonou securing provisions and enlisting the services of a translator before being boarded on the northbound train to Abomey. If the head of Labé had been depressed by the prospect of having to spend the next five years in exile, his spirits may have been somewhat lifted by the warm greeting he received by villagers in Dahomey. As described at the beginning of this chapter, at stops along the rail line from Cotonou to Abomey, locals came out to see him and his family, to bring gifts and to greet him. In Abomey, the exiled group from Futa Jallon was quartered in a state-supplied compound adjacent to the Hausa neighborhood; it consisted of a small house, a large three-room hut, and an additional building.[35] Yaya was supported by an annual pension of twenty-five thousand francs, paid out of the annual budget of Guinea—certainly less than his previous income, but a substantial amount for an already stretched colonial treasury, and more than the annual salary of many colonial administrators.[36]

The impact of the exile on communities back in Futa Jallon was mixed. Some followers from his political base at Kadé left the colony after his deportation, moving across the border and settling in Portuguese territory. Others, however, welcomed his departure and saw his deportation as an opportunity. According to contemporary French accounts, many captives—who likely made up one-third of the population of Kadé—expressed the "greatest joy" after his departure and the subsequent suppression of his followers.[37] Twelve thousand former slaves sought out French assistance, fearing reprisals by former allies of Alfa Yaya.

The case of Alfa Yaya and others demonstrates the capricious nature of French colonial power. The official reasons for Alfa Yaya's deportation rested with claims that he had been fomenting opposition to the French and was planning an overthrow of the colonial regime. But, as was the case with Ahmadu Bamba, there was little evidence for these charges. Some within the administration recognized the seeming lack of evidence. Among them was Ernest Noirot who had served as an administrator in West Africa for many years and knew

Futa Jallon well. Writing the governor general several years into Yaya's sentence, he questioned the motives of the administration: "Invited to come to Conakry as a courtesy visit, [Alfa Yaya] was arrested. . . . [He] was immediately dragged off for Dakar where he was directed to Dahomey. What crime did he commit? Mystery."[38]

Noirot requested that the governor general commute the remainder of Alfa Yaya's sentence and let him return to his home in Futa Jallon. He reiterated that Alfa Yaya, rather than being anti-French as suggested by Frézouls, had always supported French interests. Noirot reminded the governor general that a single French official represented France in Labé from 1898 to 1903. At the time, Labé was the largest district in the colony with a population nearing two hundred thousand inhabitants. This thin administrative presence notwithstanding, taxes were always handed over in full and on time—revenues that by 1903 neared a million francs. Could a single administrator have been able to submit this sort of revenue every year had Alfa Yaya, the head of Labé, been "indifferent" to French rule?[39] The rhetorical question pointed not only to how France had depended on indigenous elites like Yaya but also to a rupture between an old guard of administrators like Noirot—who were "flexible, versatile, and able to 'make do'" and who relied upon their close relationships with indigenous elites like Yaya—and a new guard of administrators like Frézouls who saw in their predecessors an "arbitrary, and personal" approach to administration.[40] The claims of anti-French fanaticism veiled an underlying concern for Frézouls, namely the growing influence of an individual within the nascent colonial state. Yaya served his full five years.

The Second Exile

On the eve of Alfa Yaya's return, the governor general commissioned a study to determine the effects of his repatriation on the colony of French Guinea. The administration in Conakry responded with an unfavorable assessment, opposing especially his return to Labé. The lieutenant governor offered an alternative. He suggested that they place Alfa Yaya under house arrest on the Iles de Loos, a group of islands off the coast of the colonial capital, Conakry. There, he could remain with some of his entourage and tend cattle, living out his days under the watchful eye of the French administration.

The governor general rejected the idea of house arrest. His reasoning reveals in part some of the perhaps unexpected limits, or at least incongruences, of colonial rule. He may have been unwilling to commute Alfa Yaya's earlier sentence, but he also found it unreasonable to extend his sentence without cause. It would be, he argued, an unjustified prolongation and continuation of a sentence already served. Alfa Yaya may have been unwanted by the administration in Conakry, but they could not simply hold him in exile without justification. He was to return to French Guinea, with his annual stipend of twenty-five thousand francs intact.[41]

Alfa Yaya's first exile ended on November 23, 1910. He left his compound in Abomey and, two days later, boarded a boat in Cotonou bound for Conakry. Dakar had rejected Conakry's request to continue Alfa Yaya's isolation, but the lieutenant governor of French Guinea was intent on keeping the former ruler of Labé out of Futa Jallon. As soon as Alfa Yaya arrived in Conakry, the administration detained him. A month later, Lieutenant Governor Guy composed a long telegram and forwarded it to the governor general in Dakar. He claimed that Alfa Yaya had attempted to reassert his authority and had conspired with several Muslim clerics in Portuguese Guinea, Sierra Leone, and Mauritania.[42] In suggesting a region-wide conspiracy, Guy stoked an old fear of radical anti-French clerics. As Martial Merlin had done some fifteen years earlier in the case of Ahmadu Bamba, the lieutenant governor pegged Alfa Yaya as a Muslim fanatic intent on fomenting an uprising against French power. And, as was the case with Bamba, there was little evidence to support such an accusation. Nevertheless, with the accusations in place Guy arrested Alfa Yaya in February 1911 and charged him, his son Aguibou, and several others with conspiracy to "massacre Europeans" and to reinstate Futa Jallon's authority.[43]

The administration in Conakry, as well as William Ponty, then governor general in Dakar, advocated for a lifelong exile to Gabon. This was part of the continued push to suppress the authority of what he viewed as feudal indigenous elites. The case against Alfa Yaya and the recommendation of his deportation was sent up to the colonial ministry in France. But the minister balked. The laws outlining the procedures and limits for colonial exile had changed. Citing a 1904 decree addressing internment in French West Africa, he noted that exile was limited to ten years and that the place of exile must be within the federation.[44]

Following the pronouncement, Ponty sentenced Alfa Yaya, his son Aguibou, and several others to ten years' exile in Port-Étienne, Mauritania, the maximum sentence allowed under the 1904 decree. The group was to be housed in private quarters, isolated not only from outside contacts but also from other prisoners. Ponty stripped Alfa Yaya of his annual stipend and ruled that his maintenance and that of his son were to be paid through their personal resources, something allowed under article 3 of the 1904 decree.[45] Alfa Yaya's second exile was a death sentence. The following year he died in exile in Mauritania; the official reason given was scurvy. His son Aguibou served out his full sentence and ultimately returned to French Guinea in December 1921. Yaya was buried in Mauritania—his remains repatriated only in 1968, a decade after Guinea gained independence from France.[46]

Alfa Yaya's two exiles, as well as those of others in French colonial Africa, are testament to the arbitrary nature of colonial rule as well as the self-imposed limits of French authority. His first expulsion was limited to five years even though the lieutenant governor of French Guinea had argued for an indefinite extension.

Indeed, it required the fabrication of a grand conspiracy to prevent Yaya's return to Futa Jallon. That such charges could so easily be levied against a longtime ally of French colonial occupation is evidence of the power that a colonial administrator could have, even over quite influential colonial subjects. But it also demonstrates the ways in which the administration itself was limited. Once arrested, both Guy and the governor general argued for a lifetime exile outside the West African federation. But here again the will of the colonial administration ran into state decrees. In this case, the colonial ministry argued that lifetime deportation to a location outside the federation went beyond the limits laid down in law. The colonial administration then found itself constrained by forces other than ideological, personal, or economic interests.

Conclusion

The exile of Alfa Yaya is a contested history. In some places he is remembered—despite his early alliance with the French—as an anticolonial resistance figure, and part of a nationalist narrative of an independent Guinea, indeed as "the most prestigious" of early resisters to French colonialism.[47] In other arenas, his exile is remembered as an example of discord within Futa Jallon at the turn of the century. Some in the borderlands of northern Guinea believe his exile was the result of certain people "selling out" Alfa Yaya. The reconstructed narrative suggests that Alfa Yaya was duped not only by Frézouls and the French but also by those who opposed his authority in Futa Jallon—perhaps the "enemies" referenced in Alfa Yaya's 1905 letter to Frézouls. In 2010, after the second round of presidential elections in Guinea that saw Alpha Condé elected as head of state, some suggested that his victory over longtime opposition candidate Cellou Dalein Diallo, the favored candidate from Futa Jallon, was linked directly to the history of French occupation and Alfa Yaya's exile over one hundred years earlier. Tying Alfa Yaya's arrest with assertions that some within Futa Jallon had collaborated with the French government in the early 1900s to have him removed, these narratives claim that Alfa Yaya, on recognizing the deceit, asserted that no Fulbe from Futa Jallon would ever again become king of Futa Jallon. In 2010 some people from the highlands claimed that *this* was the reason why Diallo lost the election.[48] These narratives point to the long impact of exile policies and also suggest that Yaya's removal did not in the end result fully in the extinction sought by Frézouls and Billault.

The dual exile of Alfa Yaya demonstrates the arbitrary and violent nature of colonial rule operating under a thin veil of law. It could be used capriciously and without supporting evidence to remove individuals deemed too influential, too powerful, too charismatic. It also highlights changing colonial conceptions of indigenous elites in the French system. The removal of Alfa Yaya, an early ally of the French, was part of a shift in colonial policy that sought to suppress, rather than support, influential indigenous leadership. The origins of these policies of removal, of the "paths of extinction" were founded partly in French penal codes. And, as such, the case challenges the concept of the colony as an exceptional space. Rather, if the colonial state looks different it is because, as Thomas Blom Hansen and Finn Stepputat have argued, it was a "naked version of modern sovereign power."[49]

It was not, however, a direct carryover from the metropolitan case. Policy was worked out on the ground and adapted to fit administrative will. Indeed, as Trina Hogg demonstrates in her research on borderland law in Sierra Leone, the very terms and meanings of colonial law and punishment were shaped by the interactions between Africans and Europeans during these early years of colonial occupation. As always, the implications varied with the context. Take, for example, the impact on communities left behind. In some places communities certainly mourned the absence of a political or cultural leader. Thousands of people left northern Futa Jallon after Alfa Yaya's departure. But, there were also many who welcomed the deportation of an exploitative and often violent ruler. In other instances, communities back home grew stronger. As discussed by Camara in this volume, the exile of Bamba was a transformative moment in his spiritual development and a piece of colonial history reclaimed by the brotherhood. No French authority in the late nineteenth century could have foreseen Bamba's exile becoming one of the most celebrated moments in his life.[50] In the case of Yaya, his exile has helped shape the memory of a French ally and brutal authority and opposition ruler in Futa Jallon as an anticolonial resister whose betrayal by the French and some within Futa Jallon continues to resonate with contemporary national politics.

Exile served a unique purpose. It was part of the penal regime of the French colonial state and was part of a system built to suppress dissent. Unlike the notorious *indigénat* or the punishments that sent French citizens to labor in faraway penal colonies, however, exile in this instance was not primarily a punitive, rehabilitative, or generative sentence. Rather, it was a penal regime meant to rid the colony of an individual that the administration saw as someone who did, or could, undermine the very foundations of colonial authority.

Notes

1. Archives Nationales du Sénégal (hereafter ANS) 7G 96 "L'administrateur en chef, délégué du Gouverneur à Cotonou, à Monsieur le Secrétaire Général, chargé de l'expédition des affaires courantes" December 11, 1905.

2. ANS 7G 95 "L'Administrateur-Adjoint P. Billault, Commandant [de] la Région du Labé, à Monsieur le Gouverneur de la Guinée Française," May 26, 1905. An early draft of this

chapter was presented as part of an excellent panel entitled "Inclusion/Exclusion: The Politics of Belonging in French West Africa," at the 2012 French Colonial Historical Society annual meeting in New Orleans. I would like to thank Rachel Kantrowitz and Jessica Pearson for inviting me to be part of the panel and for their insightful comments. I would also like to thank Jacqueline Woodfork for comments and suggestions.

3. M'Baye Gueye and A. Adu Boahen, "African Initiatives and Resistance in West Africa, 1880–1914," in *Africa under Colonial Domination 1880–1935*, ed. A. Adu Boahen, *General History of Africa* (Berkeley: University of California Press, 1985), 7: 127.

4. ANS 8G 11 "Le Lt. Gouverneur du Dahomey et Dépendances à Monsieur le Gouverneur Général de l'Afrique Occidentale Française," March 9, 1913.

5. Mathurin C. Houngnikpo and Samuel Decalo, *Historical Dictionary of Benin* (Lanham: Rowman and Littlefield, 2013), 77.

6. Otutubiodio died in exile that same year. Marcus Filippello, *The Nature of the Path: Reading a West African Road* (Minneapolis: University of Minnesota Press, 2017), 66.

7. Cheikh Anta Babou, *Fighting the Greater Jihad: Amadu Bamba and the Founding of the Muridiyya of Senegal, 1853–1913* (Athens: Ohio University Press, 2007), 123.

8. David Robinson, "Beyond Resistance and Collaboration: Amadu Bamba and the Murids of Senegal," *Journal of Religion in Africa* 21, no. 2 (1991): 154; Babou, *Fighting the Greater Jihad*, 121–22. He was sent to Ndjolé, Gabon, a hub of political exiles at the time. Hugues Mouckaga, *Les déportés politiques au bagne de Ndjolé (Gabon): 1898–1913. L'Almamy Samory Touré, Cheikh Amadou Bamba Mbacké, Dossou Idéou, Aja Kpoyizoun, et les autres* (Paris: L'Harmattan, 2013).

9. Florence Bernault, "The Shadow of Rule: Colonial Power and Modern Punishment in Africa," in *Cultures of Confinement: A Global History of the Prison in Asia, Africa, the Middle-East and Latin America*, ed. Frank Dikötter (London: C. Hurst, 2007), 59–60.

10. Almire Rene Jacques Le Lepelletier de la Sarthe, *Systeme penitentiare, le bagne, la prison cellulaire, la deportation* (Paris: Monnoyer, 1853); Paul W. Bamford, *Fighting Ships and Prisons: The Mediterranean Galleys of France in the Age of Louis XIV* (Minneapolis: University of Minnesota Press, 1973); Miranda Frances Spieler, *Empire and Underworld: Captivity in French Guiana* (Cambridge: Harvard University Press, 2012).

11. Stephen Toth, "Colonisation or Incarceration? The Changing Role of the French Penal Colony in Fin-de-Siècle New Caledonia," *Journal of Pacific History* 34, no.1 (1999): 59; Spieler, *Empire and Underworld*.

12. Toth, "Colonisation," 61.

13. See also Ruma Chopra's discussion of exile and settlement in this volume.

14. Lorraine M. Paterson, "Prisoners from Indochina in the Nineteenth-Century French Colonial World," in *Exile in Colonial Asia: Kings, Convicts, Commemoration*, ed. Ronit Ricci (Honolulu: University of Hawai'i Press, 2016), 230–34; Toth, "Colonisation," 59–60.

15. On the development of early French colonial law in West Africa see Kristin Mann and Richard L. Roberts, eds., *Law in Colonial Africa* (Portsmouth: Heinemann, 1991); and Richard Roberts, *Litigants and Households: African Disputes and Colonial Courts in the French Soudan, 1895–1912* (Portsmouth: Heinemann, 2005), chap. 2. For the sometimes arbitrary application of Islamic law see Donal Cruise O'Brien, "Toward an 'Islamic Policy' in French West Africa, 1854–1914," *Journal of African History* 8, no.2 (1967): 305.

16. *Lois, décrets, ordonnances, règlements, et avis du Conseil D'État* (Paris: Charles Noblet, 1877), 77:65–6. Similar orders extended the penal code to French Guiana and the French outposts in India.

17. *Lois, décrets, ordonnances* (1887), 87:393–94. It was modified by the November 21, 1904 decree, limiting internment to a maximum of ten years, and it further declared, in its second article, that internment as well as sequester of belongings could be carried out only in the case of "acts of insurrection against French authority, severe political trouble, or movements susceptible to jeopardize public security" or any act that did not "fall under the application of ordinary penal laws." This portion of the law was specifically aimed at indigenous elites and gave administrators the legal cover to suppress those individuals they found the most dangerous and those whose "social influence" conflicted with the establishment of French authority. *Lois, décrets, ordonnances* (1904), 352; Ibrahima Thioub, "Sénégal: la prison à l'époque colonial. Significations, évitement et évasions," in *Enfermement, prison et châtiments en Afrique*, ed. Florence Bernault (Paris: Karthala, 1999), 287–88.

18. Olivier Le Cour Grandmaison, *De l'indigénat: Anatomie d'un "monstre" juridique: le droit colonial en Algérie et dans l'Empire français* (Paris: Zones, 2010); Jean-François Sirinelli, ed., *Dictionnaire de l'histoire de France* (Paris: Larousse, 2006), 457.

19. A. I. Asiwaju, "Control through Coercion, a Study of the Indigenat Regime in French West African Administration, 1887–1946," *Bulletin de l'I.F.A.N.* sér B, 41 (1979): 35–71. Isabelle Merle, "De la 'légalisation' de la violence en context colonial. Le régime de l'indigénat en question," *Politix* 17, no. 66 (2004): 140; see also later analyses of the indigent, which confirm these findings: Gregory Mann, "What was the Indigénat? The 'Empire of Law' in French West Africa," *Journal of African History* 50, no. 3 (2009): 331–353.

20. On the debates over the nature of the colonial state as one couched in violence or one dependent on law see: Mann and Roberts, *Law*; Walter Benjamin, "Critique of Violence," in *Reflections*, trans. Edmund Jephcott (New York: Schocken, 1978), 280; Emmanuelle Saada, "The Empire of Law: Dignity, Prestige, and Domination in the 'Colonial Situation,'" *French Politics, Culture and Society* 20, no. 2 (2002): 98–120; Thomas Blom Hansen and Finn Stepputat, eds. *Sovereign Bodies: Citizens, Migrants, and States in the Postcolonial World* (Princeton: Princeton University Press, 2005), 20.

21. Toth, "Colonisation," 60.

22. Antoine Marie Jean Demougeot, *Notes sur l'organisation politique et administrative du Labé avant et depuis l'occupation Française* (Paris: Libraire Larose, 1944), 14–15.

23. Boubacar Barry, *Senegambia and the Atlantic Slave Trade*, trans. Ayi Kwei Armah (Cambridge: Cambridge University Press, 1998), 293.

24. Jean Suret-Canale, "The Fouta-Djalon Chieftaincy," in *West African Chiefs: Their Changing Status under Colonial Rule and Independence*, eds. Michael Crowder and Obaro Ikime (Ile-Ife: University of Ife Press, 1970).

25. Emily Lynn Osborn, "Interpreting Colonial Power in French Guinea: The Boubou Penda-Ernest Noirot Affair of 1904," in *Intermediaries, Interpreters, and Clerks: African Employees in the Making of Colonial Africa*, eds. Benjamin N. Lawrance, Emily Lynn Osborn, and Richard L. Roberts (Madison: University of Wisconsin Press, 2006): 56–76; Philippe David, *Ernest Noirot (1851–1913): un administrateur colonial hors normes* (Paris: Karthala, 2012).

26. ANS 7G 96 "Lt. Gouv. de la Guinée Française à M. Le Gouv. Gén.," November 10, 1905.

27. Archives National d'Outre Mer (hereafter ANOM) FM/SG/GIN/II dossier 3a "Rapport du Capitaine Bouchez," August 25, 1902; ANS 7G 95 "Le Dir. de la Banque de l'AOF à Conakry à M. le Chef du quatrième bureau," April 14, 1905.

28. Between 1904 and WWI it became official practice to dismantle existing structures of indigenous political authority in favor of more direct control over colonial subjects.

According to Suret-Canale and others, including Martin Klein and Emily Osborn, the change can be traced to the rise of the Radical party in France in 1902. Alice Conklin emphasizes the later influence of William Ponty's *Politique des Races*. Jean Suret-Canale, "La fin de la chefferie en Guinée," *Journal of African History* 7, no. 3 (1966): 463; Martin A. Klein, *Slavery and Colonial Rule in French West Africa* (Cambridge: Cambridge University Press, 1998); Osborn, "Interpreting Colonial Power"; Alice L. Conklin, *A Mission to Civilize: The Republican Idea of Empire in France and West Africa, 1895–1930* (Stanford: Stanford University Press, 1997), 110.

29. The lieutenant governor also detested the close relationship that Yaya had developed with previous administrators. Robert Cornevin, "Alfa Yaya Diallo fut-il un heroes national de Guinée ou l'innocent victims d'un regalement de compete entire gouvernors?" *Revue Française d'histoire d'outre mer* 57, no. 208 (1970): 295; Emily Osborn, "Interpreting Colonial Power."

30. ANS 7G 96 "L'Administrateur-Adjoint P. Billault à Monsieur Le Gouverneur de la Guinée Français," October 24, 1905.

31. ANS 7G 96 "Telegrammes envoyés au Commandant de cercle de Labé par le Lieutenant Gouverneur," 23, October 30, 1905.

32. ANS 7G 96 "Le Gouverneur des Colonies, Lieutenant Gouverneur de la Guiné Française à Monsieur le Gouverneur Général," October 25, 1905.

33. ANS 7G 96 "Traduction. Alfa Yaya à Gouverneur de la Guinée Française," n.d. [1905].

34. ANS 7G 96 "Rapport sur l'arrivée et l'installation à Abomey de Yaya Alfa," December 11, 1905.

35. Ibid.

36. For comparison, the lieutenant governor's salary in Conakry in 1907 was 45,000 francs. That of the Secretary General (2nd class), 16,000 francs. Colonie de la Guinée Française, *Compte définitif des recettes et des dépenses du budget local: exercice 1907* (Conakry: Imprimerie du Gouvernement, 1909), accessed March 18, 2017, http://gallica.bnf.fr/ark:/12148/cb41270064n/date. Béhanzin had similarly received annual stipends paid by the colony of Dahomey. In his time in Martinique his annual upkeep ranged from 6000 to 10000 francs per year, a not insignificant amount. *Budget local du territoire du Dahomey* (Porto Novo: Imprimerie du Gouvernement, 1895), accessed March 18, 2017, http://gallica.bnf.fr/ark:/12148/cb412807414/date.

37. ANS 7G 96 "Rapport Politique du mois de décembre. Guinea Française, Région de Labé, cercle de Yambéring," December 1905.

38. Noirot went on to suggest that in response to Alfa Yaya's deportation, five thousand inhabitants of Labé had emigrated west into Portuguese Guinea. ANS 7G 97 "L'admin. en chef E. Noirot, à M. le Gouv. Gén.," March 1, 1909.

39. ANS 7G 97 "L'admin. en chef E. Noirot, à M. le Gouv. Gén.," March 1, 1909.

40. Osborn, "Interpreting Colonial Power," 66.

41. ANS 7G 97 "Le Gouv. Gén. de l'AOF à le Lt. Gouv. du Dahomey," October 29, 1910. See also, ANS 7G 97 "Extrait du rapport du 2ème Trimestre 1910 de la Guinée Française."

42. ANS 7G 98 "Télégramme. Guy à Gouv. Gén.," January 23, 1911.

43. ANS 7G 98 "Rapport en commission permanent du Conseil de Gouvernement," October 13, 1911.

44. ANS 7G 98 "Rapport en commission permanent du Conseil de Gouvernement," October 13, 1911. See also article 1 of the 1904 decree: *Lois, décrets, ordonnances* (1904), 104:351–352.

45. The terms of the sentence can be found in the commission report. See also: ANS 17G 47 "Ponty à M. le Commissaire du Gouv. Gén. en Territoire Civil de la Mauritanie," October 12, 1911. Ponty's order can be found in ANS 7G 98.

46. ANS 7G 98 "Télégramme. Le Gouv. Gén. à Lt. Gouv.," August 12, 1912. Alfa Yaya died on August 10, 1912. In 1968 Sekou Touré, then president of independent Guinea, sent a government delegation to Mauritania to exhume Alfa Yaya's body and repatriate his remains where they now rest in Conakry. See Robert Cornevin, "Alfa Yaya." On Aguibou's return see: ANS 2G 22/12 "Rapport politique, 1ere trimestre, Guinée," April 13, 1922.

47. Cornevin, "Alfa Yaya," 289.

48. Abdoulaye Sané, interview by the author and Marie Mané, Kankéléfa, November 2, 2010.

49. Thomas Blom Hansen and Finn Stepputat, introduction to *Sovereign Bodies*, 20.

50. Christian Coulon, "The Grand Magal in Touba: A Religious Festival of the Mouride Brotherhood of Senegal," *African Affairs* 98, no. 391 (1999): 195–210; Babou, *Fighting*, 167.

4 Reforming State Violence in French West Africa

Relegation in the Epoch of Decolonization

Marie Rodet and Romain Tiquet

Following the abolition of *indigénat* and forced labor in French West Africa in 1946, important legal reforms were undertaken for the promotion of full French citizenship in the colonies.[1] Yet sentencing to relegation—exile as punishment—continued to occur until the French West African colonies became independent in 1960. While the history of confinement in Africa has drawn increasing research interest in the past ten years, the organization and practicalities of relegation in French West Africa, and the lived experiences of those sentenced there, are still hardly known.[2] Using colonial reports and correspondence on relegation, as well as petitions addressed by exiled West African *relégués* to the colonial authorities between the 1930s and the 1950s asking for a readjustment of their sentence, this chapter aims to shed light on this specific form of exile in French West Africa. Archival files, especially those containing random petitions addressed by *relégués* to the colonial central administration, open a new window into this world. Mirroring the chapters by Trina Hogg and Marina Berthet in this volume, the narratives of exiles allow us to understand the extent to which convicts were not just objects of information (to use Foucault's terminology) but also agents attempting to challenge their status, to not be forgotten, and to make themselves visible in the face of a judicial system which aimed to "eliminate" them.

Contrary to Belgian Congo where relegation mostly targeted political prisoners, in both the French metropole and the empire relegation remained the paradoxical sentence of the "internal war" waged by the French state against its multirecidivist ex-convicts.[3] Although forcible transportation and deportation were common in the *Ancien Regime*, relegation was only systematized under the Third Republic. By then, multirecidivists were considered the worst enemies of the state, as most of them appeared to the French authorities to be incorrigible and inveterately rebellious: they had to be exiled from the body politic, hence the relegation sentence. Initially organized by the metropolitan Waldeck-Rousseau law of 1885, it was progressively extended to the colonies with two decrees in 1887 that governed both collective and individual relegations in the French empire—deportation most often to French Guiana, but also to New Caledonia and Algeria.[4] A minority of recidivists was sentenced to individual relegation, based on previously good behavior in detention and sufficient financial means to fund their own subsistence. In this case, they were allowed free movement on the relegation site and could, if they wished, enter employment or benefit from an agricultural or industrial concession. In the case of collective relegation, the French state was to provide for the *relégués*' subsistence in exchange for work (hence the use of the term "collective," since the subsistence costs had to be supported by the collectivity). Once maintenance costs had been reimbursed, the collective *relégué* could apply for a sentence to be commuted into individual relegation. Relegation normally meant "perpetual internment," but the decree of July 9, 1892 stated that after six years, individual *relégués* could apply for administrative pardon, providing that they could demonstrate good behavior, significant services rendered to colonization, and sufficient means of subsistence.[5] Yet, as the fundamental principle of the law was to "eliminate" recidivists by deportation since they were considered beyond reform, many *relégués* unaware of those provisions spent several decades in exile, making them effectively detainees of indeterminate legal status. In this chapter and in contrast with Bernault's claims, we assert that relegation in French West Africa typified the broader project of "the carceral archipelago of empire" described by Laura Ann Stoler, as it connected strategies of confinement across the empire.[6]

To date, historians of the French empire have paid considerable attention to *indigénat*, which has often been discussed as the ultimate symbol of the institutionalized ordinary violence of the colonial state, an imperial abomination in clear opposition to the republican values of the metropole. The Anglo-American "colonial turn" in French Studies in particular attempted to rethink the "French Republic" by analyzing the contradictions between progressive metropolitan policies and violence and discrimination in the colonial context. This discussion has drawn an implicit border between the metropole and its colonies, distancing arbitrary colonial violence from the metropolitan rule of law. Yet an examination of the history of relegation in French West Africa allows us to deconstruct this artificial moral barrier in terms of ordinary state violence. Relegation was a metropolitan law imposed onto the colonies and driven by the metropole, and the sentence was abolished in France only in 1970.[7] Moreover, confinement techniques and approaches to criminality were imported into Africa by European powers with colonial conquest, with the added advantage that experimentation in surveillance and punishment practices were made possible by the fallacious argument of colonizing "savage" territories and populations. The widespread metropolitan idea of the difficulty of correcting criminals was here redoubled by the racist doctrine of colonial domination, which saw Africans as a fundamentally "delinquent" race whose improvement was necessarily limited, and which thus justified perpetual subjugation under the ambiguous term of "civilizing mission." There were also sometimes necessary adaptations due to the scarcity of government in certain territories. Yet relegation within French West Africa did not lie outside the French metropolitan state of law, but was its direct prolongation. Not only did confinement—as in the metropole—become the heart of the disciplinary and surveillance system in French West Africa, but West African colonies—as we shall see—provided an environment of subjugation especially suitable for its full deployment: multirecidivists in West Africa were increasingly relegated to spaces such as Northern Mali where the state presence was scarce, except for the colonial institutions of confinement (prisons, labor camps, penal colonies etc.) which had a monopoly on legal state violence.[8]

While this chapter deals with relegation in West Africa in general, archival data indicate that most convicts sentenced to individual relegation were male citizens from the Four Communes of Senegal. In French West Africa two legal statuses coexisted: "French citizens and assimilated"—comprising French colonial settlers, Europeans, and the citizens of the Four Communes in Senegal (Saint-Louis, Gorée, Rufisque and Dakar)—and "indigènes" who were the colonial subjects. Male *relégués* from the Four Communes were the ones who left the most visible archival trace for several reasons. First, the metropolitan law of July 19, 1907 prohibited relegation for women and replaced it with a twenty-year injunction, which was made applicable in the colonies by the law of August 8, 1913.[9] Second, citizens from the Four Communes could neither be subjected to *indigénat* nor, when convicted, be employed as penal workers on public and private worksites, except when they explicitly requested such a sentence.[10] They were therefore rarely sentenced to collective relegation. The only way to leverage increased coercion against them, beyond usual imprisonment in case of conviction, was often to sentence them to individual relegation. Thus, West African relegation was not a footnote to *indigénat* targeting colonial subjects first and foremost, but was rather a direct extension of metropolitan law in the colonies. Furthermore, in the decade following World War II, the reform of the judicial system in French West Africa, made necessary by the abolition of *indigénat,* the promotion of full French citizenship, and the abolition of forced labor, did yet open up new possibilities for control and the use of ordinary state violence against local populations, using relegation in particular.[11]

Relegation always concerned a very small number of convicts, which probably also contributed to its lack of visibility in the overall penitentiary system. If the metropole had a special interest in removing French delinquents and criminals from its own territory by sending them to French Guiana or colonial Algeria, the transport of convicts from West Africa to these regions represented an enormous cost. For those colonies in great need of manpower it was especially ill-founded to deport delinquents and criminals, especially in small number. From the late 1920s, following the French Indochina model, the colonial authorities started considering organizing relegation within the French West African Federation.[12]

In this context, Northern Mali became a privileged site of relegation for convicts from other French West African colonies, reinforcing the slow transformation of this territory into a carceral archipelago. In addition to the number of already established concentration/penal camps in Bourem, Ansongo, and Gao, as well as the penal colony of Kidal, relegation to Northern Mali contributed to the extension of surveillance and control beyond the penal camps, particularly through the individual *relégués*. The individual *relégués* who formed the majority of the *relégués* deported there were not imprisoned as such, but their situation resembled the administrative confinement that Boilley described as increasingly characteristic of Northern Mali.[13] Despite Northern Mali's long tradition as a confinement site extending into the postcolonial era with the penal colony of Taoudeni, it has received insufficient scholarly attention.[14]

Relegation as Colonial Forced Labor

One of the main objectives of the colonial state was to "channel coercion" for the support of colonial economic interests in particular.[15] Under the French Third Republic, *indigénat* became a central instrument for managing and controlling the African labor force through massive imprisonment and requisition (*prestations*). Indeed, the "massification" of confinement was especially advantageous for the colonial economy since the decree of January 22, 1927 obliged convicts to work for the state.[16] As a cheap pool of workers, convicts were therefore largely used for the colonial *mise en valeur* (economic development of the colonies), not only on public but also on private worksites.[17] Thus convicts, even if limited in number, made a significant contribution to the development of French West African infrastructure.

Since collective *relégués* were forced to work in order to reimburse state maintenance, we consider collective relegation another form of penal forced labor. In 1937, a decree was even promulgated by the Colonial Ministry in order to align the earnings system of the collective *relégués* with that of those sentenced to hard labor.[18] As analyzed by most scholars of colonial justice in the French empire, the system of relegation potentially helped to provide the colonial state with manpower, especially in desolated and isolated places that did not appeal to colonial settlers.[19] In French Guiana, both individual and collective *relégués* were used with the clear objective of developing the colony.[20] Yet in French West Africa, despite the centrality of *mise en valeur* in the colonial rhetoric of the 1920s, sentences to relegation always remained quite marginal and therefore could not be used to expand forced labor. In Senegal between 1889 and 1930, a total of forty-seven recidivists (thirty-five of whom had been previously convicted of theft) were sentenced to relegation to French Guiana.[21] From 1921 to 1929, in the region of

Dakar, sixteen persons were sentenced to relegation.[22] The number of sentences averaged between four and five a year for French West Africa in the 1920s.[23] From the late 1920s, following the pattern in Indochina, the colonial authorities decided to stop sending individual *relégués* to Guyane. At this time, only convicts sentenced to collective relegation were still being sent to Guyane.[24] However, due to transportation costs, it was finally decided to keep most of them in West Africa.[25] While collective *relégués* were sent to penal camps and prisons in other colonies of French West Africa where they had to work alongside ordinary convicts, individual *relégués* could move freely within the site of relegation and had only to report regularly to authorities.[26] The majority of West African recidivists seem to have been sentenced to individual relegations. Indeed, in 1929, the Minister of the Colonies warned the Governor General of French West Africa that individual relegation was too easily granted and should instead, as in the metropole, be granted exceptionally and only under strict conditions.[27] By the time this comment was made, convicts sentenced to individual relegation appear to have been mainly citizens from the Four Communes. More generally, sentencing to relegation in French West Africa, even when it involved Guyane, seems to have occurred primarily in Senegal, where the justice of the peace as well as the courts of first instance could sentence citizens to relegation.[28] In the case of citizens of the Four Communes, sentences of relegation were used to apply increased coercion while remaining within the metropolitan state of law. Relegation here is an extension of the metropolitan carceral archipelago to the rest of the empire, in which state violence was used to "eliminate" populations who were not considered amenable to correction.

Even when convicts were considered amenable to reform, the path from relegation to freedom was long and cumbersome. First, a convict needed to apply for individual relegation following sentencing. Then, it fell on the convict to apply for administrative pardon after six years of individual relegation, by proving good behavior during incarceration. Furthermore, until 1948, freed *relégués* were normally banned for twenty years.[29] Thus, the main goal of relegation in West Africa remained the elimination of recidivists and the sanctioning of disruptive behaviors. West Africans were usually sentenced to relegation because of repeated petty crimes such as theft or vagrancy. Those sentenced to individual relegation were convicts judged at odds with authority; isolated, they had to dedicate themselves to work to demonstrate their reformation. Thus, while colonial justice often proved to be crucial for "leveraging" a workforce in West African colonies, relegation does not appear to correlate. The small numbers suggest forced labor was not the main objective. And the fact that relegation continued in the postwar era, despite the abolition of forced labor in 1946, tends to reinforce this hypothesis. The abolition of *indigénat* in 1946 and the subsequent introduction of the French metropolitan penal code in French West Africa prompted the colonial authorities to launch a series of internal consultations regarding relegation.[30] However, they remained primarily concerned with the technicalities of reorganizing the judicial and administrative hierarchy. The consultations did not foster humanitarian questioning of the relegation system per se. In practice, the abolition of *indigénat* gave new powers to local jurisdictions, as they automatically became justices of peace. Until then, local courts were not able to pronounce relegation sentences. But with the 1946 reform of the justice system in French West Africa, every local jurisdiction could potentially propose convicts for relegation. Thus, at a time when important legal reforms were undertaken for the promotion of full French citizenship in the colonies, the same reforms also opened up new possibilities for control and the use of ordinary state violence against local populations, using deportation in particular. Indeed, in 1951 the Governor of French West Africa (hereafter FWA) had already noticed an increase since 1946 of the number of recidivists sentenced to relegation by the penal courts of FWA.[31] To some extent, this move also reinforced what was denounced by Ya Doumbia, Soudan's representative at the Assembly of the Union in July 1950, as the creation of a second-class citizenship for former imperial subjects. Doumbia argued that these new citizens had clear obligations and rights in criminal courts and to some extent in politics, but factual inequality in other matters continued in practice, due to systematic racial discrimination and the lack of a clear legal protection of their personal status.[32] In 1955 the central authorities in Dakar found that "relégués individuels" in FWA had until then enjoyed too much freedom of movement, especially in urban centers.[33] It led to the promulgation of a decree of October 14, 1955 which reorganized individual relegation and further constrained individual *relégués* in their movement.[34]

Furthermore, now that no difference existed between citizens from the Four Communes and the rest of the population of FWA, the metropolitan law could be widely used—particularly to impose collective relegation—despite the official abolition of forced labor. In the same vein, the judicial reform of 1946 made the application of the metropolitan law of 1941, regarding compulsory penal work outside penal institutions, easier to implement directly in French West Africa. However, in this case African political representatives attempted to oppose the decree as they feared "that this provision would provide a convoluted way of reintroducing forced labor."[35] Yet this opposition, despite the partial rewriting of the text in 1947 and 1948, did not prevent its final promulgation. Its main objective was to fight against recidivism by promoting the reeducational virtues of penal work. Relegation as well as penal work formed a central part of the metropolitan culture of state coercion, and could therefore not be conceived as subjects of reform. Thus, the colonial penal system was so closely linked to the French culture of punishment that it could not be in practice "decolonized."

The location of the execution of the relegation sentence was always strategic and contributed to the construction of specific colonial territories, such as Guyane for metropolitan France. In French West Africa, the precise relegation location was never determined by decree, but was decided by the Governor General based on the profile of the *relégué*. As we shall see, French Soudan, and especially the North, were to be increasingly designated as particularly appropriate locations for the execution of such sentences. Relegation to Northern Mali contributed to the establishment of a specific region as the ultimate carceral archipelago, where the scarce state presence was mainly represented by institutions whose leading mission was clearly linked to the exercise of legal state violence, such as military garrisons, prisons, penal colonies, and forced labor camps.[36]

The Invisible Construction of the Carceral Archipelago in French Soudan

From the 1930s onwards, French Soudan was often proposed as an appropriate relegation site for colonial subjects from other colonies and especially from Senegal. Yet the authorities in French Soudan regularly expressed reservations, especially where individual *relégués* were concerned, as the possibility for them to work and maintain themselves in the colony were limited and ultimately represented a burden on the local budget. Indeed, the authorities of the *cercle* where *relégués* had been sent were often left with no choice but to employ them in miscellaneous odd jobs. In 1937, two *relégués* from Senegal were sentenced to relegation in French Soudan, but the authorities tried to oppose the decision by explaining that they had few skills enabling them to find work.[37] The previous *relégué* sent to the colony from Senegal in 1935, who was first sent to Mopti, was arrested for theft soon afterwards and sentenced to one year's imprisonment in Bamako. He was then sent to Gourma-Rharous in Northern Mali, where he requested a relocation because he could not find any work. His request was denied.

The hosting of collective *relégués* also represented a burden for the local administration, even if they were to be used on colonial building sites. In 1942, the Governor of Senegal notified the Governor of French Soudan of his intention to send a total of twenty-four collective *relégués*.[38] The authorities in French Soudan decided to relocate them to Ansongo, so that they could work on the *Mer-Niger* building sites, the Trans-Saharan Railway project which was reactivated under Vichy.[39] Yet no host facility was available and extra credit had to be allocated to build provisional accommodation. The Trans-Saharan Railway project was abandoned soon after, leaving the *relégués* of Ansongo without work; they then had to be supported by the local administration, with insufficient personnel to supervise them.

In short, the small numbers of collective and individual *relégués* and the kind of work they undertook made them not terribly productive in economic terms and largely useless for *mise en valeur*. Yet for the central colonial authorities, the difficult economic situation in which individual and collective *relégués* sometimes found themselves was unimportant, as it was part of the process both of redemption and of social (if not physical) elimination. In practice, the central colonial authorities tended to ignore the economic difficulties of *relégués* and complaints about costs borne by local authorities. They demonstrated the clear goal of continuing to promote the success of the relegation system in Northern Mali, even using the argument that the *relégués* in this region had fully adapted in order to propose further relegation there. The economic imperative here was not about how to use these convicts to the benefit of the *mise en valeur*, but how to make sure that their deportation would remain as low cost as possible. It is this priority which led to their administrative "disappearance" in the carceral landscape of Northern Mali or other isolated places.[40]

The choice to relegate convicts to French Soudan was primarily motivated by strategic issues. Indeed, *relégués* were increasingly sent north beyond Mopti and Segu, which had been usual places of deportation in the previous decades with deportees such as Sheikh Anta Mbakke, as highlighted by Jeremy Dell.[41] The development of the road network in the colony, and the expansion of these cities as important economic hubs, meant that these regions were no longer appropriate sites for relegation. The colonial authorities were especially concerned with keeping troublesome subjects away from urban centers. Indeed, they were increasingly anxious about an idle and "detribalized" African proletariat on the margins of big colonial centers.[42]

As already mentioned, one consequence was that most individual *relégués* encountered difficulties in finding work. Not surprisingly, these convicts regularly asked to be relocated to less isolated and economically deprived areas of the colony.[43] In Bourem or Ansongo, the only remunerative possibilities were work on construction projects in the region, such as road building or the Trans-Saharan Railway project. This work was therefore undertaken alongside penal workers and other forced laborers including *prestataires*: for example, Amadou, an individual *relégué* from Dakar, chose to work as a builder on the road repair sites of the district of Bourem.[44] They could also be recruited as foremen on the same building sites. Abdoulaye, an individual *relégué* from Senegal, was sent to Bourem in 1936 and took up a post as a supervisor at the STAPS (*Service des Travaux d'Aménagement des Pistes Sahariennes*).[45] The carceral archipelago was thus constructed with overseers and convicts living and working alongside one another.

The main objective of deportation to Northern Mali was to "eliminate" recidivists, by rendering them to some extent invisible in the main public space. Yet, although they were deported to isolated and deprived places, they were nonetheless not exiled into a void. They had social lives in those places, even family lives in some cases.[46] Unfortunately we do not have sources testifying to the ways local populations from Northern Mali perceived these *relégués*. But one can suspect that the deportation of these foreigners in these places may have reinforced the experience of those territories and their inhabitants as places of relegation, desolation and deprivation. Although their numbers were small, the *relégués'* foreignness and their penal status could not go unnoticed in these underpopulated places. It reinforced a process of marginalization and territorial exceptionalism which had already begun in the early years of colonization as Northern Mali—in the same way as Niger which would also be used as relegation destination—was instituted as a military territory.[47] Only in 1911 had Gao and Kidal been detached from the military territory of Niger to officially become civil territories, even though they would not be administered by a civilian until 1948. In 1938, the *relégués* camp in Ansongo was extended. In 1940 it hosted the deported Hamallist leaders from Nioro, following the Nioro-Assaba upheavals. In 1955, three collective *relégués* who had served their imprisonment sentence in Fatoba (Guinea), were sent to Northern Mali.[48] Collectively over time former military territories were reconstructed as places of physical and symbolic relegation. Similarly to penal colony imprisonment, *relégués* had normally to serve their sentence in a colony other than their colony of origin, and certainly not in the territory where the crime was committed.[49] An individual from Dakar could, for example, be sent to Fatoba.[50] But there were a few instances when *relégués* who had committed crimes in French Soudan were nonetheless sent to Northern Mali, notably Kidal.[51] Relegation within the same colony also contributed to the establishment of this region as a territorial exception, building on its initial institution as a military territory. In the postwar era, as colonial authorities grew more confident in their ability to control Northern Mali, the region became the ultimate site of exile, a role cemented in the postcolonial era.[52] Thus, while relegation was banished from other colonies (the penal colony of Guyane was closed in 1953), French West African colonial authorities were paving the way for the further establishment of Northern Mali as a carceral archipelago. However, archival files containing isolated petitions addressed to the central administration by individual *relégués* attest to the diverse strategies employed by those convicts to make themselves visible and remembered in the face of a judicial system which aimed to "eliminate" them.

Against Invisibility: Relégué Petitions

In 1934, Teuw, a citizen of Saint-Louis, was sentenced to twenty months' imprisonment for theft and, as a recidivist, to supplementary relegation. Following his release, he was sent to Nema (French Soudan) as individual *relégué* in 1936. However, one year later in Bamako he was sentenced to ten years' imprisonment for theft and fraud.[53] It was during this second conviction that he wrote several times to the Governor of the Colony and to the Governor General of FWA to complain about the conditions of his Bamako imprisonment. In his first petition of 1937, he insisted heavily on his citizen status and the rights to which he was entitled in prison, compared to colonial subjects.[54] Following this petition, an inquiry was launched and the Bamako authorities systematically rejected Mansour's allegations of mistreatment. They highlighted the fact that he never complained during the prison's inspection by the commandant and the general prosecutor, despite the fact that "[he] is literate, he can decently write and express himself in French and that he knows the rights and duties of a French citizen."[55] Teuw wrote five further petitions from 1938 to 1940, the last of which was a four-page petition to the Governor of French Soudan. In this last petition he complained, as in the previous ones, about the fact that he was not allowed to work.[56] A colonial report stated that Teuw had initially been recruited as a prison nurse at his own request, but that he had to be removed from this position because of various thefts he committed at the expense of inmates. The Bamako administrator suggested he be transferred to Northern Mali to work on the Trans-Saharan railway. This assignment often represented a capital sentence, due to the high mortality rate.[57] Yet as a French citizen, Teuw could not be subjected to penal work except at his own request, as stated by article 3 of the general decree of January 22, 1927. He was ultimately sent to Gao prison, a move orchestrated by the authorities to rid themselves of a vociferous objector.

Niang and Baka, both citizens from the Four Communes, were sentenced to *relégation* in March 1942 and June 1944 respectively, both for multiple thefts.[58] They were initially incarcerated in Saint-Louis to serve their sentences. Subsequently, they wrote to the Governor of Senegal to request their relegation sentence be changed to individual relegation.[59] Both requests were written in a very rhetorical, almost florid style, following the traditional French codes of formal hand-written letters. Baka's petition started as follows: "I have the honor to request your kind indulgence for an individual relegation."[60] Niang ended his missive in similar terms: "Hence, I dare to hope that you will deign to have pity of my soul, which since so many years rues its misdeeds by suffering in jail."[61]

These discursive practices (marks of deference, rhetoric of repentance) were in a way mandatory in order for the prisoners' petition to be read and considered by the colonial authorities. Those petitions must be understood here as "public transcripts."[62] The letters produced by the "dominated" had to reproduce everyday colonial subordination, in order to be allowed into the space/landscape of the "dominant." Upon their receipt, the colonial machinery systematically launched a commission to adjudicate requests. The prison director and physician were asked their views on a prisoner's morality and behavior. In both Niang's and Baka's files, one can read that each of them "has shown good will and good spirit" during their incarceration, and that this "good behavior" demonstrates that it is likely that the prisoner can "amend himself."[63] These kinds of appraisals were central to decision-making which could lead the relegation sentence to qualify as individual relegation.

Interestingly, Niang and Baka both complained that they had been kept in prison in Saint-Louis for an additional year, despite the fact that their sentence of imprisonment had officially come to an end. It looks as if, without their efforts to petition for the transformation of their relegation sentence into individual relegation, they risked being further forgotten in the Saint-Louis prison until the official release of the administrative decision allowing their deportation to another territory. Ultimately, they were both granted the sentences of individual relegation.

Abdoulaye was an individual *relégué* assigned to Bourem from 1935 to 1954. He was almost "forgotten" there, despite his repeated petitions to the colonial authorities complaining about his economic situation and the impossibility of finding any work and requesting relocation to a more viable part of the colony, in order to be able to support not only himself but also his family. His letters give a unique insight into the life of individual *relégués*, demonstrating that, despite a clear administrative attempt to isolate them, they were nonetheless able to adapt and rebuild a family and social life. Abdoulaye complained about his financial situation in the very first months of his assignment to Bourem, sending two petitions to the Governor of French Soudan in 1936.[64] He repeatedly asked for a readjustment of his sentence in 1941, 1945 and 1946, each time requesting a better salary, or some credit, or a relocation to a less expensive area.[65]

The colonial authorities systemically refused relocation, with the view that *relégués* should not be allowed to live in larger urban centers nor to return to their country of origin. In their refusal letters, they claimed that Abdoulaye was qualified enough to find work by himself, showing little concern about his fate. When confronted with such issues, the central administration often insisted on the fact that the *relégués* had to experience an "evolution towards a new life of hard work," as though they were explicitly considering that the difficulties they had to go through were actually part of a necessary redemption process, even if the local authorities were also requested to assist the *relégué* in settling in and finding work.[66] In 1953, Abdoulaye's wife petitioned for his release. Indeed, according to the decree of July 9, 1892, he could be granted administrative pardon. He was ultimately granted administrative pardon in 1954, and probably left Bourem immediately after to return to Senegal.

As Trina Hogg's chapter shows, the colonial machinery made exiled prisoners disappear in an anonymous collective, and often reduced them to bureaucratic statistics in prison records. However, petitions from prisoners made a claim for their own identity and individuality, breaking away from the colonial power's attempts to make them invisible. Just as Thaïs Gendry's chapter in this volume demonstrates the capacity of a community to navigate their own destiny in the face of colonial violence, the very existence of petitions shows us that the colonized were not just objects of control, but also individuals who attempted to be active subjects of their own history.

Conclusion

The exportation of metropolitan state violence through relegation in French West Africa had dramatic consequences, as it slowly drowned convicts into administrative lapses in the carceral archipelago of northern Mali in particular. Petitions automatically entailed the launch of official inquiries, which could lead us to believe that the colonial authorities had a certain degree of interest in *relégués'* fates and in respecting the state of law. In practice, however, official responses instead testify to how much annoyed they were by those petitions.

The response to such petitions only reinforces a picture of the colonial obsession and obstinacy with clearly eliminating too vociferous and incorrigible convicts, by making sure that they would get lost in the maze of the penal administration. Furthermore, the institution was so closely linked to metropolitan penitentiary violence that petitions could not have any impact on possible reform, even at a time when the French authorities were entering the decolonization process. On the contrary, the decolonization process facilitated the full use of metropolitan relegation as an efficient punitive lever, to increase coercion beyond usual imprisonment sentences and to "eliminate" undesirable new citizens.

Notes

1. The code of *indigénat* was implemented in all French West Africa on November 21, 1904. It proved to be an extremely "efficient" means of asserting administrative power, and so it soon became an important mode of government. See Gregory Mann, "What was the Indigénat? The 'Empire of Law' in French West Africa," *The Journal of African History* 50, no. 3 (2009): 331–353; Bénédicte Brunet-Laruche and Laurent Manière, "De 'l'exception' et du 'droit commun' en situation coloniale: l'impossible transition du code de l'indigénat vers la justice indigène en AOF," in *Droit et justice en Afrique coloniale : traditions, productions et réformes*, ed. Bérengère Piret, Charlotte Braillon, Laurence Montel, and Pierre-Luc Plasman (Brussels: Publications de l'Université Saint-Louis, 2013), 117–141.

2. See Florence Bernault, ed., *Enfermement, prison et châtiments en Afrique du 19e siècle à nos jours* (Paris: Karthala, 1999); Ibra Sène, "Colonisation française et main-d'oeuvre carcérale au Sénégal: de l'emploi des détenus des camps pénaux sur les chantiers des travaux routiers (1927–1940)," *French Colonial History* 5 (2004): 153–171; Daniel Branch, "Imprisonment and Colonialism in Kenya, c. 1930–1952: Escaping the Carceral Archipelago," *International Journal of African Historical Studies* 38, no. 2 (2005): 239–265; Dior Konaté, "On Colonial Laws and the Treatment of Young Female Delinquents in Senegal: The Case of Léonie Guèye," *Stichproben. Wiener Zeitschrift für kritische Afrikastudien* 7 (2007): 35–60; Mamadou Dian Cherif Diallo, *Répression et enfermement en Guinée. Le pénitencier de Fotoba et la prison centrale de Conakry de 1900 à 1958* (Paris: L'Harmattan, 2005); Hugues Mouckaga, *Les déportés politiques au bagne de Ndjolé (Gabon): 1898–1913. L'Almamy Samory Touré, Cheikh Amadou Bamba Mbacké, Dossou Idéou, Aja Kpoyizoun, et les autres* (Paris: L'Harmattan, 2013); Emmanuel Blanchard and Joël Glasman, "Introduction générale: Le maintien de l'ordre dans l'Empire français: une historiographie émergente," in *Maintenir l'ordre colonial. Afrique, Madagascar, XIXe-XXe siècles*, ed. Jean-Pierre Bat and Nicolas Courtin (Rennes: Presses Universitaires de Rennes, 2012). On the renewal of the studies of confinement and deportation in imperial context and beyond, see Frank Dikötter and Ian Brown, ed., *Cultures of Confinement: A History of the Prison in Africa, Asia and Latin America* (Ithaca: Cornell University Press, 2007); Sherman Taylor, "Tensions of Colonial Punishment: Perspectives on Recent Developments in the Study of Coercive Networks in

Asia, Africa and the Caribbean," *History Compass* 7, no. 3 (2009): 659–677; Marie Morelle and Frederic Le Marcis, "Pour use pensée pluridisciplinaire de la prison en Afrique," *Afrique Contemporaine* 253 (2015): 117–129.

3. Nancy Rose Hunt, *A Nervous State: Violence, Remedies, and Reverie in Colonial Congo* (Durham, NC: Duke University Press, 2016); Miranda Frances Spieler, *Empire and Underworld: Captivity in French Guiana* (Cambridge: Harvard University Press, 2012).

4. On the chronology of the history of transportation, deportation, and relegation in France, see Louis-José Barbançon, "Chronologie relative à la déportation, transportation et relégation française," *Criminocorpus* [Online], Les bagnes coloniaux, instruments de recherche, January 1, 2006, accessed November 18, 2014, http://criminocorpus.revues.org/142.

5. Archives du Ministère des affaires territoriales et des collectivités locales (hereafter MATCL) Bamako, box 6: Relégation individuelle des prisonniers. Letter #832 INT/AP. November 3, 1953. Haut Commissaire de la République Gouverneur général de l'AOF à Gouverneur du Soudan.

6. Florence Bernault, "The Shadow of Rule: Colonial Power and Modern Punishment in Africa," in Dikötter and Brown, *Cultures of Confinement*, 55. Ann Laura Stoler, *Along the Archival Grain. Epistemic Anxieties and Colonial Common Sense* (Princeton: Princeton University Press, 2010), 130–139. On the development of the carceral archipelago in France from the nineteenth century onward, see Michel Foucault, *Discipline and Punish: The Birth of the Prison* (London: Penguin Books, 1977).

7. The Bagne of Cayenne in Guyane was closed in 1953 but sentences to relegation continued to be pronounced and executed in the metropole until 1970. See Jean-Lucien Sanchez, "The Relegation of Recidivists in French Guiana in the 19th and 20th Centuries," in *Global Convict Labour*, ed. Christian G. de Vito and Alex Lichtenstein (Leiden: Brill, Studies in Global Social History, 2015), 222–248.

8. Ibrahima Thioub, "Sénégal: la prison à l'époque colonial. Significations, évitement et evasions," in Bernault, *Enfermement*, 205–226.

9. See the law of July 19, 1907, accessed October 13, 2015, https://criminocorpus.org/en/legislation/textes-juridiques-lois-decre/textes-relatifs-a-la-deportati/acces-aux-textes/loi-du-19-juillet-1907/.

10. Article 3 of the decree on work in the prisons of French West Africa, *Journal Officiel de l'AOF*, January 22, 1927.

11. Forced labor was abolished in French West Africa with the promulgation of the Houphouët Boigny law of 1946. However, it did not abolish penal forced labor nor penitentiary work in the colonies. Forced labor sentences are still regularly pronounced in contemporary Mali, Senegal, Niger, and Mauritania.

12. Service régional des archives de Dakar, Senegal (hereafter SRAD) 1D5/1. On the relegation system in French Indochina, see Martine Fabre, "La condamnation des indigènes aux travaux forcés ou à la relégation," *Histoire du Droit des Colonies* [online] 2008, accessed November 28, 2017, https://www.histoiredroitcolonies.fr/IMG/pdf/MF2008TravauxForces.pdf. See also Peter Zinoman, *The Colonial Bastille: a History of Imprisonment in Vietnam, 1862–1940* (Berkeley: University of California Press, 2001), 33, 58–59, 66.

13. Pierre Boilley has analyzed Northern Mali as a major place of social and administrative confinement. See Pierre Boilley, "Enfermements administratifs, enfermements d'exil: la chaîne des réclusions sahariennes," in Bernault, *Enfermements*, 366–385.

14. Boilley only deals with the issue of social and administrative confinement, not imprisonment. Mann has a chapter on Malian Saharan prisons, but it is mostly centered on the

postcolonial period. Gregory Mann, *From Empires to NGOs in the West African Sahel: The Road to Nongovernmentality* (Cambridge: Cambridge University Press, 2014), chap. 6. Sy has related in his realistic novel *Toiles d'araignées* the horrific carceral conditions in northern Mali based on his own experience there in the 1970s: Ibrahima Sy, *Toiles d'araignées* (Paris: Actes Sud, 1997).

15. Blanchard and Glasman, "Introduction générale," 13.

16. Thioub, "Senegal," 288. Archives nationales du Sénégal (hereafter ANS), 3F86: Arrêté du 14 mars 1892 réglementant le travail pénal. Arrêté relatif au travail dans les prisons de l'Aof, *Journal Officiel de l'Aof*, 22 janvier 1927. A similar decree had already been promulgated in 1892, but only for the colony of Senegal.

17. Under *mise en valeur* the Ministry of the Colonies began a series of major construction projects in French West Africa with the primary aim of providing raw materials to France. Penitentiary work on colonial roads was common colonial practice. See Romain Tiquet, "Challenging Colonial Forced Labor: Resistance, Resilience and Power in Senegal," *International Labor and Working-Class History*, 43 (2018): 135–150; Babacar Fall, *Le travail forcé en Afrique occidentale française (1900–1946)* (Paris: Karthala, 1993); Sène, "Colonisation française." For convict labor on private worksites, see Babacar Fall, "Manifestations of Forced Labor in Senegal: as Exemplified by the Société des Salins du Sine-Saloum Kaolack 1943–1956," in *Forced Labour and Migration: Patterns of Movement within Africa*, ed. Abebe Zegeye and Shubi Ishemo Shubi (London, 1989), 269–288.

18. MATCL 6: Réglementation du pécule des relégués collectifs. Rapport au Président de la République française. October 16, 1937.

19. For the role of the French penal colony, see Stephen Toth, "Colonisation or Incarceration? The Changing Role of the French Penal Colony in Fin-de-Siècle New Caledonia," *Journal of Pacific History* 34, no. 1 (1999): 59–74.

20. Martine Fabre, "La condamnation des indigènes," 17.

21. "Les relégués internés au pénitencier de Saint-Jean-du-Maroni," *Criminocorpus* [online], September 24, 2013, accessed March 5, 2015, https://criminocorpus.org/en/ref/25/16947/.

22. SRAD 1D5/1: Letter of December 30, 1929. Administrateur en chef p.i Dakar à Gouverneur général AOF.

23. SRAD 1D5/1: Letter #824 A.P/3 of April 24, 1930. Gouverneur général AOF à Ministre des colonies.

24. SRAD 1D5/1: Letter #158 of November 6, 1929. Ministre des colonies à Gouverneur général AOF.

25. SRAD 1D5/1: Letter #824 A.P/3 of April 24, 1930. Gouverneur général AOF à Ministre des colonies.

26. MATCL 6: Telegram #2309 A.G. of April 23, 1936. Gouverneur général AOF à Chef subdivision Bourem.

27. SRAD 1D5/1: Letter #158 of November 6, 1929. Ministre des colonies à Gouverneur général AOF.

28. The justice of the peace was a tribunal equivalent to that of the metropole. On the justice of the peace, see Maïté Lesné-Ferret, "Une juridiction spécifique: le juge de paix à compétence étendue," in *Le Juge et l'Outre-mer, Tome 5. Justicia illitterata: aequitate uti? Les dents du dragon*, ed. Bernard Durand, Martine Fabre, and Mamadou Badji (Lille: Centre d'histoire judiciaire éditeur, 2010).

29. Archives nationales d'Outre mer, France (hereafter ANOM), Fonds ministériel (hereafter FM), Affaires politiques (hereafter affpol) 1192: Circulaire Dispense de l'interdiction de séjour en faveur des relégués relevés de la relégation, undated but probably 1948.

30. MATCL 6: Letter #92/INT/AP2 of February 12, 1951. Haut Commissaire de la République Gouverneur général de l'AOF à Gouverneurs des Territoires de Groupe.

31. Centre des archives diplomatiques de Nantes, France (thereafter CADN) box 183PO/1/353 Fond Dakar AOF Dossier relégation application du décret de 1885: Letter #184 of June 29, 1951. Gouverneur général AOF à Haut Commissaire en commission du Conseil de gouvernement.

32. Frederick Cooper, *Français et Africains? Être citoyen au temps de la décolonisation* (Paris: Payot, 2014), 205–206.

33. CADN 183PO/1/353: Letter #3289 of August 31, 1955. Procureur général à Directeur général des affaires politiques.

34. CADN 183PO/1/353: Letter #1123 of March 3, 1956. Direction services sécurité AOF à Chefs de service police.

35. ANOM, Inspection générale du travail (hereafter IGT) 103-D1.

36. Mann, *From Empires*, 217–218.

37. MATCL 6: Letter of June 16, 1937. Gouvernement Soudan français à Secrétaire général gouvernement AOF.

38. MATCL 6: Situation juridique des relégués collectifs, APAS/4. Undated but probably 1942.

39. See Monique Lakroum, "Les projets français de transsaharien (XIXe–XXe siècles) un challenge pour l'industrie," accessed August 15, 2015, http://documents.irevues.inist.fr/bitstream/handle/2042/31932/C&T_1989_19_295.pdf?sequence=1.

40. SRAD 1D5/1: Letter #824 AP/3 of April 24, 1930. Relégation des indigènes en Afrique occidentale française. Gouverneur général AOF à Ministre des colonies.

41. Jeremy Dell, "'The Eternal Agitator': Sheikh Anta Mbakke's Exile to Segu and the Early Years of the Post-Bamba Muridiyya" (paper presented at the Conable African Studies Symposium "Exile, Deportation, and Forced Labor in Colonial Africa," April 2–4, 2015). See also MATCL 6: Letter of June 16, 1937. Gouvernement Soudan français à Secrétaire général gouvernement AOF.

42. ANOM, FM, Commission Guernut 59 B 32: Rapport annuel sur le fonctionnement de la justice indigène, 1931.

43. See individual *relégués*' petitions in MATCL 6.

44. *Indigénat* involved taxes paid in the form of forced labor mostly performed on road repair sites (*prestation*). MATCL 6: Telegram-letter #2023 of July 1940. Cercle Gao à Gouverneur; Telegram-letter #306 of May 5, 1941. Subdivision Bourem à cercle Gao. Due to privacy concerns raised by the regulation issued by the Republic of Mali in 2002 restricting the use of any records held by the National Archives of Mali that might "implicate the private lives of citizens," we use only the first name to identify *relégués* in correspondence. For more information on court cases and privacy, see Richard Roberts, *Litigants and Households: Colonial Courts and African Disputes in the French Soudan, 1895–1912* (Portsmouth, N.H.: Heinemann, 2005), xi–xii.

45. MATCL 6: Telegram-letter confidential #70/c of September 17, 1953. Chef subdivision à Administrateur commandant cercle Gao.

46. On the importance of family life in forced labor camps, see Marie Rodet, "Forced Labor, Resistance, and Masculinities in Kayes, French Sudan (1919–1946)," *International Labor and Working-Class History* 86 (2014): 1–17; Marie Rodet and Romain Tiquet, "Genre, travail et migrations forcées sur les plantations de sisal du Sénégal et du Soudan français (1919–1946)," in *Le travail colonial. Engagés et autres mains-d'oeuvre migrantes dans les empires 1850–1950*, ed. Issiaka Mandé and Eric Guerassimoff (Paris: Riveneuve, 2016), 353–381.

47. MATCL 6: Telegram-letter #1906/AD of March 19, 1937. Commandant cercle Bamako à Gouverneur Soudan.

48. See Diallo, *Répression.*

49. Mouckaga, *Déportés.*

50. In 1948, Sékou Coulibaly from Dakar was sentenced to relegation by the justice of peace of Sikasso in French Soudan. He was then sent to Fatoba. A few Mauritanians were also sentenced to relegation in Fatoba according to Diallo, *Répression.*

51. MATCL 6: Relégation individuelle des prisonniers. 1942.

52. Mann, *From Empires*, 217.

53. MATCL 6: Telegram-letter #940 APA/3 of February 13, 1940. Gouverneur p.i. Soudan à Cercle Bamako.

54. MATCL 6: Letter of June 26, 1937.

55. MATCL 6: Rapport d'enquête plainte détenu. July 13, 1937. Administrateur des Colonies P. Jouret à Administrateur Commandant Cercle Bamako.

56. See in MATCL 6: five hand-written letters of June 16, 1938, August 3, 1938, July 3, 1930, February 5, 1940, and February 17, 1940.

57. Mann, *From Empires*, 218.

58. ANOM, FM Affpol 1192.

59. It is likely that the few petitions found in the archives are only the tip of the iceberg. Written by individuals or professional letter writers (*agents d'affaires*), petitions were common in the colonial period. See, for instance, Benjamin N. Lawrance, "Petitioners, 'Bush Lawyers', and Letter Writers: Court access in British-Occupied Lomé, 1914–1920," in *Intermediaries, Interpreters, and Clerks: African Employees in the Making of Colonial Africa*, ed. Benjamin N. Lawrance, Emily Lynn Osborn, and Richard L. Roberts (Madison: University of Wisconsin Press, 2006), 94–114.

60. ANOM, FM Affpol 1192: Hand written letter of June 10, 1946.

61. ANOM, FM Affpol 1192: Hand written letter of May 9, 1946.

62. For "public transcripts" see James C. Scott, *Domination and the Arts of Resistance: Hidden Transcripts* (New Haven: Yale University Press, 1990), 2.

63. ANOM, FM Affpol 1192.

64. MATCL 6: Letters of June 6, 1936 and September 5, 1936.

65. MATCL 6: Letters of May 5, 1941, October 2, 1945, and February 26, 1946.

66. The phrase "*une évolution vers une nouvelle vie de labeur*" is used twice in two different instances of official correspondence dealing with the assignment of two *relégués* in June and July 1936. MATCL 6: Telegram-letter #3631 A.G. of June 30, 1936. Governor French Sudan to Administrator Cercle Tombouctou; Telegram-letter #3928 A.G. of July 16, 1936. Governor French Sudan to Administrator Cercle Nema.

5 A Kingdom in Check

Exile as a Strategy in the Sanwi Kingdom, Côte d'Ivoire, 1915–1920

Thaïs Gendry

In the final weeks of 1916, nearly twenty thousand inhabitants of the French colony of Côte d'Ivoire crossed eastward into the neighboring British colony of the Gold Coast, abandoning their homes, and leaving their crops and land behind. This mass movement was the explosive result of an ongoing confrontation between a colonial state and an African kingdom. The specific ground was southeast colonial Côte d'Ivoire in the middle of World War I, where the Sannvin, inhabitants of the Sanwi Kingdom openly challenged colonial authorities over living conditions and colonial impositions. This confrontation evolved through different stages over a four-year period, developing into a complex strategy of resistance with exile at its core.

In the first month of 1914, the kingdom's chieftaincy started a petition campaign, trying to negotiate the terms of colonial rule in their region through official and administrative channels. When it proved ineffective, their next move was to threaten French authority with the self-exile of the entire population of the region. They waited until the end of 1916 when, in light of the failure of this first stage of the movement, they asserted their determination and enacted the exile.

The exile lasted about two years and served a dual purpose. First, by leaving, the Sannvin removed themselves from the daily violent retaliations of French agents against their people and political movement. Second, because their exodus testified to the political unrest of the region and drew wide attention to the confrontation, the Sannvin hoped to trigger negotiations towards a new regional order. As the chieftaincy explained in a petition exposing their struggle to the British Governor of the Gold Coast: "We set out to enlighten French public opinion, Parliament and Central Government as to the violence and troubles we are subjected to, until France grants us the liberal treatment we deserve."[1] In asking for liberal treatment they undoubtedly were demanding some degree of territorial and political sovereignty. But, the second stage of the movement did not yield any result in that direction either and, upon the population's return in 1918, colonial repression was swift. Not only were the Sannvin not granted political autonomy, their chiefs were sentenced by the colonial administration to decade-long deportations across French West Africa.

The goal of this chapter is to understand the stakes and objectives of the Sanwi movement and the means mobilized by the population to reach them. How did the Sannvin use petitioning? What situation were they trying to render visible? What demands were they putting forth? How did they respond and adapt to colonial violence? What were they trying to achieve in creating this sequence of political movements? And, what were these networks of migration, which enabled the exile of twenty thousand people, on foot and by boat, in just over a week? In this chapter, we will explore how imperial policies, writing practices, regional African networks, colonial borders, and exile were invested with an innovative political praxis. This movement of resistance to an array of colonial impositions, first among them the loss of power and autonomy of the elites, the violent behavior of on-the-ground administrators, and the overwhelming demands for forced labor, offers fertile insights into tensions shaping the incipient colonial order of the early twentieth century.

Formal Colonialism and the Rise of Political Discontent

The Sannvin, or Anyi-Sannvin, were the inhabitants of an Akan kingdom located on the eastern border of the French Côte d'Ivoire. This border had been designed over a decade of negotiations between French and British administrators and officially implemented on May 11, 1905. It was drawn without much consultation of the villagers in the area, but the treaty specified that "any natives who may not be satisfied with the assignment of their village to one of the two Powers shall have, for the period of one year, the right to emigrate to the other side of the frontier."[2] The inhabitants of the borderland lived in between French and British imperial spaces and more importantly within a complex, long-standing and still operational inter-African network throughout which Sannvin claimed multiple affiliations.[3] What this meant was that well after the deadline Akans, among them the Sannvin, kept travelling and settling quietly on both sides; going to the territories across the border was a routine trip. Fishermen would daily navigate the waters belonging to each colonial power, trading on both shores.[4] Archival documents testify to the vibrancy of these movements. While colonial borders were envisioned and drafted on paper, they lived on the ground.[5] In the southern region of the Ivory Coast-Gold Coast border, Akan families and businesses were spread across French and British domains and mostly ignored this "paper border."

The Anyi-Sannvin were historically a large community when they settled in the Aowin region located on the western frontier of today's Ghana. At the

Map 5.1 Akan Speaking Peoples in Côte d'Ivoire and Gold Coast. (Philip Schwartzberg.)

beginning of the eighteenth century, they were driven away from eastern territories by a series of wars led by another Akan power, the Asante Confederation.[6] Ongoing pressure led to their spread westward and with the authorization of the main Aowin lineage (*afilie*), the Sannvin created a new *afilie*, which gave rise to the Sanwi kingdom. According to European testimonies in the eighteenth and nineteenth century, "everything suggests a persisting link between the new master of the [Sanwi] region and their original chief called the King of Aowin."[7] Yet, the relations of domination and subordination varied over time. The unprecedented development of Sanwi political and commercial power under the rule of Amon N'Duffu (1845–1888) led to its differentiation from the Aowin in the middle of the nineteenth century.

The consolidation of Sanwi power did not lead to its isolation. On the contrary, Krinjabo, its capital, became an important regional hub of connection with other Akan states as French and British colonial powers were reshuffling the political game. An interesting example is the impact of the successive wars between the Asante Confederation and the British. In the neighboring regions of the Asante, the British established protectorates and colonial domination, under which they forbade the sale of arms and gunpowder. The Asante Confederation needed to find alternative routes so that its firearms and ammunition could reach its soldiers and they turned to the Sanwi. By the end of the nineteenth century, most major commercial regional roads passed through Krinjabo and the population of the kingdom was increasing with emigration from different parts of the Akan regions. This partnership with the Asante benefited the Sanwi economically and politically, as they were gaining independence from the Aowin and other powerful Akan states. The wealth of the kingdom also sprang from participation in the colonial trade of rubber and mahogany, which were abundant in the forest belt, ensuring sustained revenue and important trade with both the French and the British. Until a decade into the twentieth century, the Sanwi Kingdom was an independent and wealthy African kingdom, a commercial crossroads, and a respected kingdom within the Akan's constellation of regional powers.

For sixty years, the sovereignty of the Sanwi Kingdom had effectively been underwritten by an advantageous treaty concluded with French envoys in 1843: the Traité de protectorat d'Assinie. This *traité de protectorat* (protectorate treaty) postulated two distinct sovereignties: an interior one, through which the king kept authority over his subjects, and an exterior one, which disempowered royal authority to engage in international matters and open its territory to non-French citizens, i.e. other Europeans. But as Isabelle Surun observes, such treaties were written in an ink which became invisible over time. Consequently, the layers of sovereignty they established soon blurred and faded into one: the colonial authority.[8] Until 1904, the internal sovereignty of the Sanwi was respected, embodied for instance in the customary tax the French State paid to the King of Sanwi for French merchants to trade and travel across his territory. In 1895, the unification of West African French colonies—Afrique Occidentale Française (AOF)—started the deconstruction of the balance reached by treaties. In October 1904, the "pays de protectorat" were dismantled which meant that "all great native commands and all great chiefs . . . were stripped of real authority" and "became mere instruments of the colonial administration's policies."[9] Consequently, the Sanwi Kingdom was fully integrated into "Greater France" as a *domaine public*, official French territory, and underwent an administrative and political overhaul. Over a period of ten years, Sannvin experienced the full force of new rules and obligations, such as forced labor, cultivation, taxation, and war recruitment. Political interference, along with the partial collapse of their economy following a fall in the price of rubber, the opening of a new commercial road supplanting their own, and the consequent destruction by French administrators of their main commercial city, Aboisso, all contributed to the impact.[10] Yet, as Danielle Domergue points out, "the Sanwi Kingdom was a small regional power which intended to keep its traditions along with a number of prerogatives inherited from early and fruitful contacts with France."[11] The Sannvin, and first among them, the King and nobility, refused to recognize an annexation to the French empire as they quite simply refused the status of a subordinated, colonized region and people.

Therefore, Sanwi nobility negotiated in the capacity of political leaders of an independent kingdom. They believed it was their right to negotiate as a sovereign entity and launch into official talks with the colony and with France. It is doubtful whether French administrators ever thought the Sanwi kingdom could make a legitimate case for regional autonomy, especially given how the colonial order was framed by the 1910s and 1920s. Regardless of how they were viewed by different parties, my point is neither to determine whether their demands were realistic, nor if they could all have been met with success. Rather, it is to understand the political stakes from the side of the Sannvin chieftaincy: what they saw as their main objectives as representatives of an independent community and hence to better understand the strategy developed to attain their goal. If we understand their goal to be sovereign, the different strategic phases we will analyze in the rest of the chapter fall into place. First, the Sanwi chieftaincy questioned colonial practices on their territory, thus asserting that they sought to regain control of the land and resources. Second, in choosing self-imposed exile for the entire society, the Sanwi chieftaincy demonstrated that another kind of sovereignty, sovereignty over the people, if not over the land, remained.

The first step towards official negotiations took the form of a letter campaign addressed to the French metropolitan authorities. For two years, the Sanwi chieftaincy petitioned the French government, thoroughly listing their complaints and demands, creating a public testimony of colonial practices as they were carried out on the ground. They, in other words, were making their situation known outside of the colony. As Marie Rodet and Romain Tiquet argue in this volume, petitions were commonly used as strategic means to fight the "invisibilization" process to which African populations were subjected by the colonial machinery. More generally, there is a growing body of research that uses public writing—understood as writing addressed to public figures or public institutions, anonymously or not—as historical sources.[12] As Sheila Fitzpatrick notes, "in periods and places when information flow was sharply restricted, citizens' letters constitute one of the few nodes of transmission of public opinion."[13] Whether personal testimonies as analyzed by Trina Hogg in early colonial Freetown, or prisoners' requests as examined by Marie Rodet and Romain Tiquet, such public writings always shed new light on the contentious construction of colonial orders across Africa.

In our case, criticism and demands as formulated in the petitions pertained to two specific domains. First, the petitions criticized the daily treatment by the

French administration, especially the use of the *Indigénat* regime, which enabled fining and imprisoning in order to coerce people into providing head taxes, forced labor, and soldiers for the war. *Prestations* (days of forced labor) were at the center of most of Sanwi's complaints. The Sannvin chieftaincy argued against the extravagance of the *prestations*, which were imposed to such a degree that there were no men or women left to work during the fishing season or to harvest the crops. The stated opposition to the *prestations* is but one example of how, throughout their letters, the Sanwi chieftaincy protested the material and social hardship endured by their community because of daily colonial obligations.

A second set of demands focused on sovereignty. As the "Sannvin [had] no reasons to believe that they [were] no longer the masters of their lands," they demanded the restoration of autonomy in local politics such as the right to freely choose their king.[14] Serious interference had started as early as 1908, when Borobah, King of the Sanwi, was arrested and condemned for refusing to recognize the authority of colonial courts. Indeed, he kept administering justice as before, refused to pay taxes or to send men for labor on the roads—one of the most common and resented kinds of forced labor in French colonies.[15] After his arrest, an even more rebellious king, Amon Assemyin, was enthroned. He too was arrested and found dead in his cell a few weeks later. This suspicious death nearly triggered an open rebellion. This led in 1912 to the installation of Kodia Kassi, a new king chosen by the French administration. Suffering from a lack of legitimacy, he was never considered fit to rule by the population who resisted his attempts at collaboration with colonial administrators.[16] This interventionist policy in local affairs was made worse by other losses of power which the Sannvin chieftaincy regarded as diminishing their status, namely denying the Sannvin their right to administer justice outside of colonial courts and to collect anew the yearly customary tax formerly paid by the French State, both of which the Sannvin sought to restore.

As early as 1914, the Sanwi chieftaincy acquired the services of a former French administrator who had worked as a Customs Police Officer for several years between Côte d'Ivoire and the Gold Coast before being dismissed for alleged fraud. After his demise, Frédéric Lambert Sainte Croix Martinin stayed in Grand-Bassam, a town near the Sanwi Kingdom, and established himself as an "homme d'affaires," i.e. a businessman and consultant for the colony's subjects, on matters administrative and legal. He was, in other words, a public writer with valuable inside knowledge about the colonial system, who was willing to put that knowledge at the disposal of whomsoever would pay a good price.[17] Very quickly, Lambert came to be considered an adversary by the colonial administration. In a report, Governor Gabriel Angoulvant accused him of purposefully upsetting the colonial balance by advocating in favor of rebellious populations, requesting that he be returned to France, by force if necessary.[18]

Indeed, Lambert proved to be as much of a thorn in the side of the colonial administration as he was useful to the Sannvin. He provided the Sannvin with the language and codes necessary to address administrative, judicial and parliamentary metropolitan authorities. Thus, rather than the Sannvin openly calling for the end of colonialism or the departure of French agents from their lands, they instead worked with Lambert to draft petitions subtly dealing with local issues by framing them in the larger colonial ideology of the French civilizing mission. Sannvin were portrayed as legal actors and faithful subjects asking for the application of a just colonial rule. They invoked their faith in French justice and enlightenment as well as their desire for freedom of worship and freedom of labor for the constructive exploitation of the land.[19]

Even with a careful internal analysis of the letter campaign, it is impossible to determine to what degree the different actors shared the values expressed in the documents: did Lambert really think African people should regain some autonomy? Was the hardship of forced labor, experienced by common people, properly conveyed through the preoccupations of the chieftaincy and the language of Lambert? Did the Sanwi chieftaincy really want to adopt some French institutions? Regardless, the argumentative strategies were meant to be operational within the framework of colonialism. To some degree they were successful, as petitions did get to the desk of the *Ministre des Colonies* and were addressed by deputies of the French Parliament.[20]

Despite those efforts, Inspector Ernest Bourgine, the agent dispatched by the metropolitan government to investigate the situation, affirmed that the Sannvin had mostly been spared the increased hardships of the war in terms of taxes and recruitment, because the administration was well aware they held the possibility of cross-border migration to avoid conscription and war efforts. The whole political campaign was dismissed as a caprice on behalf of a population accustomed to being pampered by colonial officials and who still obstinately refused to recognize France's authority over their land and people. When the Sannvin realized the French would not yield to their political letter campaign, they developed a new strategy and spectacularly defied France. After two years of lobbying and a very unpromising administrative response, the Sannvin simply left.

The Political Stakes of Exile

Migration as revolt has long been a template for studies of resistance in colonial Africa, starting with the scholarship of A. I. Asiwaju, who defined migrations in the region as highly political.[21] Migrations have been interpreted as embodying political responses to colonial violence and impositions such as heavy taxation, forced labor, and conscription, which populations refused by absconding from the territory where such measures were enforced.[22] In colonial West Africa, there are numerous examples of such forms of resistance driving people away from French ruled colonies towards British ones, testifying to an awareness of African peoples that regional colonial rules differed.[23]

But migrating should not necessarily be analyzed as either the beginning or the end of a protest, nor seen simply as the essence of a political movement. Rather, the Sanwi protest migration is best viewed as part of a wider strategy. It was not intended to be a permanent migration, but rather a display of power, will, and autonomy in order gain greater leverage in negotiations with the colonial power. We see echoes of this in the strategies described by Aliou Ly's and Kate Skinner's chapters in this volume. Migration and exile can be tools used to revitalize the political game. In Ly's example, exile provided a second wind yielding unexpected results in the case of the Guinea-Bissau struggle for independence. The exile of the PAIGC into neighboring Guinea enabled the organization to redevelop their strategy, notably by including women and forming new alliances, which Ly convincingly argues was determinant in the successful subsequent struggle for independence. And although the Ewe exiles in Togo were unsuccessful, Skinner's analysis shows how exile operated as a powerful vehicle of collective resistance to state authority. Similarly, the Governor of Côte d'Ivoire did not mistake it for something else, writing, "It is the very principle of our domination that is at stake. I consider this mass departure as a rebellion, a very serious manifestation of insubordination, a muffled act of war more dangerous in consequence than an armed rebellion."[24]

Tellingly, 1917 was not the first occurrence of a collective movement away from the French colonial Côte d'Ivoire by the Sanwi population. French administrators had noted three previous exoduses of a few hundred people between 1908 and 1912.[25] Yet, before the middle of World War I, it seems little political defiance was attached to these migrations towards Akan territories in the Gold Coast and these mostly took place under the radar of the authorities. It was a circumscribed refusal by some families to live under French rule but without an open challenge, or demands addressed to French authorities. The actions undertaken were infrapolitical in the sense given by James C. Scott—hidden forms of insubordination, which did not appear in French documents outside of dull descriptive footnotes.[26] In comparison, the exile that took place in the last weeks of 1916 was an open act of defiance, a political challenge organized by the chieftaincy, and followed by the population who had suffered under violent colonial rule and practices. The Sannvin chieftaincy used it as a lever to force French colonial administrators into negotiating for their return, for unlike previous small and discreet exoduses, it created a difficult situation for colonial Côte d'Ivoire on at least three intertwined levels.

First, inside the colony of Côte d'Ivoire, French administrators feared the exile would trigger political unrest and help spread a rebellious mood already surging in response to the hardship of war conditions, especially the massive recruitment of soldiers for the battlefields of Europe.[27] It became vital to stifle the movement as the numbers of administrative punishments linked to the *indigénat*—fines, forced labor, and imprisonment—skyrocketed after each levy of taxes and round of conscription in the colony, testifying to increasing resistance from the populations. Administrators felt these expeditious punishments soon would not be enough of a deterrent to stop an outbreak of violent discontent.[28]

The second level was regional. In seeking refuge in the Gold Coast colony, the Sannvin involved British authorities. In their letter to the Governor of the Cold Coast, they officially asked for asylum and protection, from "brutal and authoritarian" representatives of French colonial power.[29] The British Government of the Gold Coast seized on this opportunity to present itself as a land of "liberation" and fair rule in West Africa and, in his correspondence with the British mainland, Governor Clifford Hughes entertained the idea of granting the Sannvin refugee status. Eventually, their position as war allies with France weighed more heavily in the balance but they steadfastly refused to hand Sannvin chiefs over to French envoys or to force the Sannvin off British land.

During World War I, there were numerous occurrences of French subjects crossing into British colonies to avoid conscription.[30] The French Governor even asked the British counterpart to perform a simultaneous draft of soldiers to defuse the idea that by crossing the border French subjects could avoid military conscription. Not only did Governor Clifford refuse, he also argued that French conscription methods resembled the slave trade, which the British had banned decades earlier, and that they would have no part in it. Governor Clifford wanted the border between the two colonies to embody a clear demarcation between French and British "native policies" in the minds of the regional African populations. He pointed out in a report that he wanted to assert that difference to avoid suspicion and tension in his own colony.[31] Actually, the Sannvin protest movement created an interesting political opportunity to rehabilitate colonial practices in the Gold Coast since—as scholars of the Gold Coast, Kwabena O. Akurang-Parry and David Killingray in particular, have made abundantly clear—conditions of recruitment and forced labor were extremely hard on the population there as well.[32]

While the French and the British saw the exile as a matter of avoiding conscription, hence a problem specifically arising from the war situation, this was only one of several grievances made by the Sannvin, who consistently tried to shake off the idea that their movement was against recruitment. Because they did not want to be depicted as deserters, they even persuaded Blaise Diagne, the first African deputy to the French Parliament, who, during World War I was in charge of organizing military recruitments in West Arica, to support their cause.[33]

Finally, for the French, this massive exile was a blow in the long-standing interimperial fight over human resources. Indeed labor was scarce in West Africa, especially in the coastal region where farm laborers and construction workers were in high demand.[34] British and French administrations were competing to attract seasonal workers and long-term migrants from northern territories and the Upper Volta and in this fight over labor supply, the British repeatedly had the upper hand.[35] For the French administration, having thousands of workers and peasants walk out of the colony put a serious strain on labor and the economy. Moreover, it exposed them to political embarrassment insofar as the exile was portrayed both by the British Government and Sanwi chieftaincy as a critique of French rule in a highly competitive region.

While many actors seized on the Sanwi protest movement to promote and justify their agenda, focusing mainly on the war, this fact should not obscure the complex protest against numerous aspects of French colonial rule and indigenous policies. As we have pointed out, the battle over sovereignty was embodied in the different ways in which the Sanwi chieftaincy fought colonial impositions. While they initially chose petitioning to reassert their right to rule and work the land in the way they saw fit, it was only when they had reached the conclusion that their territorial sovereignty would not be upheld within the French empire that the nobility along with most subjects exiled themselves.

Enacting Exile

It is possible to reconstruct the migration routes used by the Sannvin thanks to the numerous telegrams British officers sent to Accra as they saw thousands pouring into their districts. More than fifteen thousand Sannvins were reported to have crossed simultaneously over the length of the border in just a few days, from a total population in the Sanwi Kingdom estimated to be twenty-two thousand by the French administration.

Sannvins crossed the border in multiple locations thus finding themselves exiled in different administrative provinces of the British colony. Yet, only in the Sefwi Province, reached by the northernmost migration pass, did the District Commissioner consider this massive crossing as an illegal action that required "active measures." In response to the migration "all chiefs and headman of villages were informed through the *Omanhin* [Paramount Chief of the Sefwi region] that the offering of facilities to these people evading their military obligations was tantamount to aiding the enemy. Patrols of civil and preventive police have been moving all along the frontier villages distributing instructions and prevailing upon natives to return."[36] But in every other district, officers were more circumspect. One argued that: "In some districts indeed, where local feeling is opposed to the immigration the District Commissioner has been able to assume the responsibility of taking forcible measures to deport the immigrants but I must emphasize the fact that such action has been outside the law and could not prudently be taken in any other districts."[37] From Boinso to Newtown, District Officers awaited orders from Accra and let Sannvin protest migrants settle.

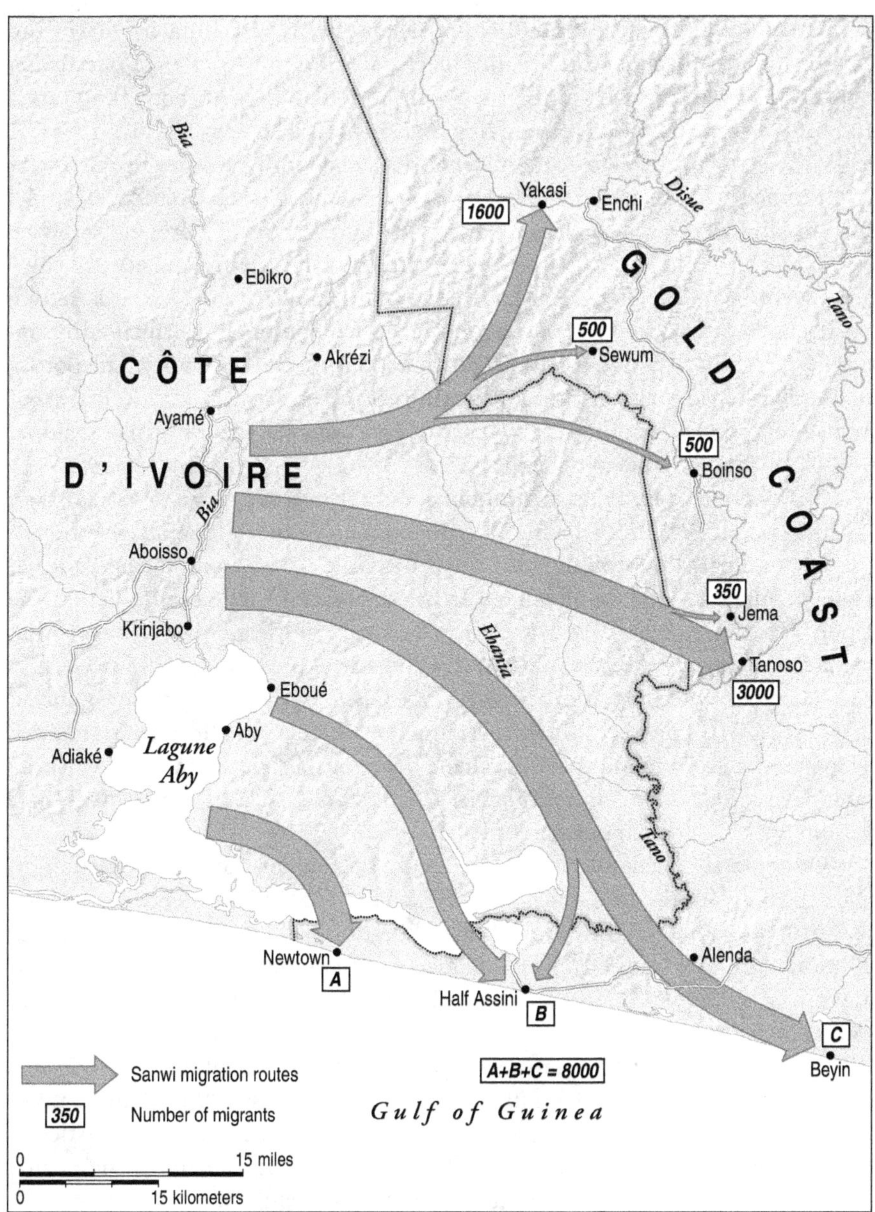

Map 5.2 Sanwi Migration from Côte d'Ivoire to Gold Coast. (Philip Schwartzberg.)

From the inception, they understood the political situation was delicate—surely about more than escaping military recruitment—and that since powerful paramount chiefs had agreed on sheltering these political refugees, deporting them across the border would be tantamount to mirroring French policies.

In fact, regarding the Côte d'Ivoire-Ghana frontier, the materiality of the border strengthened once the Sannvin crossed it. Prior to the protest exile, little control was enforced along the Akan borderlands, with both the French and British administrators recognizing that this was a zone over which spread a regional network central to economic, political, and family life they had no interest in impeding.[38] In 1916, by investing the border with their political struggle, the Sannvin turned the colonial paper border into an effective protective device from French colonial rule. The Sannvin entrenched the separation between colonial spaces. Whereas they had been free to move about, French administrators, agents, and troops were not allowed to breach the border; and British administrators steadfastly refused to allow French actions on their territory. The border also strengthened politically since asserting the difference between treatments of indigenous populations on each side became an inherent part of British regional policies during the time of the exile.

It is difficult to find documentation about the everyday lives of the Sannvin in the Western Provinces during this period. On an official level, several ordinances were passed, forbidding chiefs of the Gold Coast from letting Sannvin build permanent habitations. They further demanded that Sannvin actions be reported to authorities.[39] From what can be found in the archives, it seems that the chiefs disregarded these orders and that many of the migrants did settle, and had started to work the mines and the fields. One British administrator reported that "the Aowin chiefs are all for sheltering the refugees, and little assistance can be looked for from them, the Omanhene here voiced the general view when he said that all these were originally subject to his stool, and look upon him as their paramount chief; this appears to be so."[40]

Quite possibly this situation was uncomfortable for the Sanwi chieftaincy. Over the previous decades, they had acquired regional independence from older, powerful Akan centers of power. Was asking for shelter a setback in regional politics? Exiling themselves was intended to regain autonomy from the colonial power, not lose it on another front. It is hard to know what the relationship was between Sannvin chiefs and Gold Coast chiefs, but British archives reveal the time in exile did not necessarily come with regained authority. For example, common rights cases were judged by the Gold Coast rather than Sannvin chiefs after a few months there, and we know that the right to render justice to their people was a central demand by the Sanwi chieftaincy made to the French colonial administration, a power they did not regain while in exile.[41]

The Sanwi chieftaincy probably had not planned for the exile to last as long as it did. And after two years in the Gold Coast they had already suffered greatly—materially and symbolically. *Afilie* of the Western Regions had reinforced their authority in the Akan networks spreading between French and British colonies. The exiles held a neutral position towards the British and had not made any progress with the French administration. The long wait in the Gold Coast proved to be a slow but fatal blow to the movement. By the end of 1918, the Sanwi chieftaincy had to recognize the strategy of the exile had yet to bear fruits; they began to negotiate a return onto Côte d'Ivoire. The stalling of negotiations was to add to the dire economic and political situation in the Gold Coast, especially in the Western Regions where they had migrated. The cocoa economy was collapsing due to the fall in price, famines were starting in different parts of the colony, and the British authorities had to implement a series of economic measures to regulate the price of everyday foodstuffs.[42] Understandably, the influx of the Sannvin population did not ease the strain put on local economics and supplies. It was time for a new move.

Returning from Exile

The Sannvin return at the end of 1918 coincided with a noticeable personnel reshuffle in Côte d'Ivoire and the AOF. The end of the First World War was reviving an appetite for change and promotion within the empire. Retirements, promotions, and newcomers in the colonial administration were upsetting the old organization. In just a few months Governor of Côte d'Ivoire Lapalud was replaced by Raphaël Antonetti, as were the Governor of the AOF and the *Commandant de Cercle*. From their exile, it is likely Sannvin chiefs entertained the hope it would bring about a change in rule, more favorable to their cause, or at least renewed political opportunities. They chose this strategic moment to come back.[43]

The return was also linked to an indigenous political struggle over Sanwi power itself. King Kodia Kassi, chosen and imposed by the administration in 1912, died on January 21, 1918.[44] His death predates the return of the exiles by only a few months and marked the beginning of one of the most important political events in the kingdom: the selection and enthronement of a new king. While new kings were traditionally chosen by an assembly of chiefs, most of them had gone into exile in 1916.[45] Probably, this conjuncture of events was seen as a new political opportunity, which could enable the exiles to restart negotiations after the stalemate in the Gold Coast.

In the middle of 1918, an assembly of chiefs and notables elected Borobah King of Sanwi. As seen above, Borobah had already been King of Sanwi until his arrest by the French administration who had nominated Kodia Kassi a few years later. Borobah was legitimated by his lineage and by his having previously stood up to the French authorities as king. The colonial administration could not but resent and refuse this choice, especially after years of open conflict. The new Governor of Côte d'Ivoire, Antonetti, branding this election a coup d'état, officially deposed Borobah, stating that "since the population cannot find anyone suitable,

I would rather not name anyone. It is with regret that I suppress an indigenous command but given the general entourage of the king, I think it preferable."[46] The entourage of the king was no other than the chieftaincy that had returned from exile.

Though French authorities had guaranteed there would be no charges or reprisal for the exile, by framing this election as a coup they were effectively able to punish the leaders of the exile and the political campaign in general.[47] Thirteen chiefs, all of whom had gone into exile, were arrested and deported to other colonies of the A.O.F. for periods ranging from three to ten years: Joseph Anoma and Ala Amarama were sentenced to five years in prison and ten more years of *interdiction de séjour* from Côte d'Ivoire (banishment from the territory but without forced residence), while N'gata Kan, Se Kakou, Eoue Koffi, Soumien Anvo, and Jean Amon were sentenced to three years of prison in Haut-Sénégal-Niger and five years of banishment; Amon Koutoua, Nianvo Bleoue, Eba Kadio, Aswa Kouame, Akoua Bkin Bile, and Alye Elike served two years in Côte d'Ivoire. Unexpectedly, they were not convicted for anti-French actions or disturbing the colonial public order. Rather, they were opportunistically condemned under charges of misusing the political customs of their land to elect a tyrant unwanted by the population.[48] In establishing this line of argument, the administration was framing the Sanwi movement as an issue of "tyrannical indigenous rule." In their words, thanks to the administrative deportation of these "abusive chiefs," they were able to restore peace in the region and protect the Sannvin population from further hardship. By this condemnation, the administration established the official discourse on the Sanwi case and discredited the political struggle of the past three years. It would have been the only available record, had not Sanwi chieftaincy so adamantly petitioned metropolitan authorities.

Despite the political and judicial backlash, Borobah never acknowledged the administration's decision. In his subsequent interactions with the colonial power in the years 1919 and 1920, he systematically presented himself as "King of the Sannvin" or "King of Sanwi" and dealt with the envoys and administrators as a King. He relentlessly demanded the liberation of the chiefs who had elected him, and asked for the 1843 Treaty to be honored until his death in 1922. In a 1924 political report on Côte d'Ivoire, an administrator wrote "in the Assinie cercle, the Krinjabo stool [of the Sanwi kingdom] has been without a tenure holder since the death of Borobah.[49] Nevertheless, most of the notability is favorable to the named Koadio Adou, who will be officially enthroned at the beginning of 1925."[50] Though Borobah was never officially endorsed, the colonial administration did not manage to put another king in his place and over time started dealing with him as their rightful intermediary for all matters concerning taxation, labor, and the ruling of the region.

A Conclusive Sequence of Resistance?

Maintaining their chosen King on the ground was no small victory for the Sannvins, and the administration continued to feel threatened years after the movement had ceased. Well into the 1920s, judiciary archives show they were strongly opposed to granting sentence remissions to the chiefs they had sentenced and exiled in distant colonies.[51] Local administrators argued before the Governor General of the AOF that the political situation on the ground was as volatile as ever and sending back the praised and rebellious chiefs would be a most unwelcome political signal. Perhaps one of the achievements of the Sanwi movement was to have maintained an atmosphere of engagement in the region, forcing successive administrations to rule them with tact along with being granted a number of taxation and labor privileges.

The Sannvin never lost their sense of being a coherent community that ought to be embodied in a sovereign state. After asserting their independence from other Akan kingdoms in the nineteenth century and resisting integration into the colony of Côte d'Ivoire in the first half of the twentieth century, once again, the Kingdom of Sanwi asked for sovereignty when Côte d'Ivoire achieved independence in 1960. Faced with the refusal of President Félix Houphouët-Boigny, the king and chiefs once again migrated to the newly independent Ghana. With the permission of Prime Minister Kwame Nkrumah, they stayed there for a year before accepting recognition of the Ivorian national state and returning to their land.

In the 1910s and 20s, the movement failed to obtain a specific administrative status, and how could it have been otherwise? France was in the process of strengthening the grip on its empire and defining its assimilationist indigenous policies.[52] This political campaign is striking for the innovative political forms it contained. The Sannvin forged weapons out of material initially designed to rule over them: indigenous policies, treaties, and borders. They tried for a time to express their discontent and demands in the colonial framework, hoping to gain recognition as a political and social entity. The subsequent exile showed their demands for what they really were: dissident and uncompromising.

Carving their way through the colonial political spheres enabled the Sannvin to mobilize the potential of a regional Akan network for the purpose of a confrontation with the colonial system. They developed this possibility into a complex political scenario, where they would be the leaders and French authorities would have to comply with their demands. It should be noted here that the administrative battle, later enacted in a defiant exile, was a complementary part of what we can call a sequence of political endeavors, a strategy of resistance shaped by both colonial and regional African tools.

That the immediate results were small should not keep the historian from appreciating the potential of such a "case" for learning about the tensions that shape colonial worlds on a daily basis. This moment was neither one of armed and heroic resistance, nor a low intensity confrontation led with the everyday weapons of the weak. It was its own daring, evolving, innovative attempt to tackle the issues arising from the development of colonialism in the Sanwi region.

Notes

1. The National Archive (TNA), CO 96/580, Registry of In-letters, June 1917.
2. TNA, CO 96/569, August 11–September 17, 1916.
3. Pierluigui Valsecchi, "Formation des États et alliances intercommunautaires dans la Côte d'Or (17ème-18ème siècles)," *Journal des Africanistes*, 75, no. 1 (2005): 77–100.
4. TNA, CO 96/582/61918.
5. Paul Nugent, *Smugglers, Secessionists and Loyal Citizens on the Ghana-Togo Frontier* (Athens: Ohio University Press, 2002), 5.
6. Traditionally described as the most powerful center of the Akan world from the seventeenth century until the war with the British in the early twentieth century. See for example: Gérard Chouin, Claude-Hélène Perrot, and Gérard Pescheux, eds., "Approches croisées des mondes akan: Archéologie, Histoire, Anthropologie, Partie I: Anthropologie et Histoire," *Journal des Africanistes* 75, no. 1 (2005): 12.
7. Henriette Diabate, "Le Sannvin: un royaume Akan de la Côte d'Ivoire, 1701–1901, Sources orales et histoire," (PhD diss., Université Panthéon-Sorbonne, 1984), 172.
8. Isabelle Surun, "Une souveraineté à l'encre sympathique, Souveraineté autochtone et appropriation territoriale dans les traités franco-africain au XIXe siècle," *Annales. Histoire et Sciences Sociales*, 69, no. 2 (2014): 313–348.
9. Alice L. Conklin, *A Mission to Civilize: The Republican Idea of Empire in France and West Africa, 1895–1930* (Stanford: Stanford University Press, 1995), 113; Babacar Fall, *Le travail forcé en Afrique Occidentale Française 1900–1946* (Paris: Karthala, 1993), 45.
10. Archives Nationales d'Outre-Mer (ANOM), FM/1AFFPOL/566, May 20, 1917, Rapport des chefs d'Assouba, d'Aébo, d'Adaou et d'Ahegnabo relatifs aux évènements qui ont eu lieu dans le Sanwi.
11. Danielle Domergue, "La Côte d'Ivoire de 1912 à 1920, Influence de la première guerre mondiale sur l'évolution politique, économique et sociale," *Annales Universitaires d'Abidjan* 1, no. 4 (1976): 41.
12. Agnès Benoît, "Le 'pétitionnaire universel': Les normes de la pétition en France et au Royaume-Uni pendant la première moitié du XIXe siècle." *Revue d'histoire moderne et contemporaine* 58, no. 4 (2011): 45–70; Yves-Marie Bercé, *La dernière chance: histoire des suppliques du Moyen Âge à nos jours* (Paris: Perrin, 2014); Lianjiang Li, "Political Trust and Petitioning in the Chinese Countryside," *Comparative Politics* 40, no. 2 (2008): 209–26.
13. Sheila Fitzpatrick, "Supplicants and Citizens: Public Letter-Writing in Soviet Russia in the 1930s," *Slavic Review* 55, no. 1 (1996): 80.
14. ANOM, FM/1AFFPOL/566, May 20, 1917, Rapport des chefs d'Assouba, d'Aébo, d'Adaou et d'Ahegnabo relatifs aux évènements qui ont eu lieu dans le Sanwi.
15. Henriette Diabaté, *Le Sannvin*, 715–718.
16. Henry Mouezy, *Assinie et le royaume de Krinjabo: Histoire et coutumes* (Paris: Larose, 1942).

17. ANOM, FM/1AFFPOL/566/659, May 16, 1917, Lettre du Gouverneur Général de l'AOF (Clozel) au M. le Ministre des Colonies (Maginot).

18. ANOM, FM/1AFFPOL/566, note de Gabriel Angoulvant, annexée à la lettre 222.

19. For a description of the French *Mission Civilisatrice*, see Conklin, *Mission*, 38–71.

20. ANOM, FM/1AFFPOL/566/68, January 30, 1918, Rapport administrative pour Monsieur le Gouverneur de la Côte d'Ivoire.

21. A. I. Asiwaju, "Migration as Revolt, the Example of the Ivory Coast and the Upper Volta before 1945," *Journal of African History* 17, no. 4 (1976): 577–594.

22. Jon Abbink, Mirjam de Bruijn, and Klaas van Malraven, eds., *Rethinking Resistance, Revolt and Violence in African History* (Boston: Brill, 2003).

23. Benjamin Lawrance, *Locality, Mobility and "Nation": Periurban Colonialism in Togo's Eweland, 1900–1960* (Rochester: University of Rochester Press, 2007), 47; Jean Rouch, "Migrations au Ghana (Gold Coast), Enquête 1953–1955," *Journal de la Société des Africanistes* 26, no. 1 (1956): 33–196.

24. ANOM, FM/1AFFPOL/566, note de Gabriel Angoulvant, annexée à la lettre n°222.

25. TNA, CO 96/579/23855, February 27, 1917, The Commissioner of the Western Province Atterbury to the Governor of the Gold Coast.

26. James C. Scott, *Domination and the Arts of Resistance: Hidden Transcripts* (New Haven: Yale University Press, 1990), 16.

27. There were five recruitments between January 1915 and July 1918, which amounted to 23,000 men for Ivory Coast, 211,000 for the A.O.F and A.E.F., and 590,000 for the whole of the French Empire. René Pierre Anouma, *Aux origines de la nation ivoirienne, 1893–1960* (Paris: L'Harmattan, 2005).

28. Simon Pierre Ekanza, "L'oppression administrative en Côte d'Ivoire (1908–1920)," *Bulletin de l'Ifan* B 37, no. 3 (1976): 667–684.

29. TNA, CO 96/580/35943, June 10, 1917, Lettre des chefs à son Excellence le Gouverneur de la Gold Coast.

30. TNA, CO 96/565/4592, Despaches, January-February 1916.

31. TNA, CO 96/579/31547, June 22, 1917, Report of Govenor Clifford Hugh.

32. Kwabena O. Akurang-Parry, "Colonial Forced Labour Policies for Road Building in Southern Ghana and International Anti-Forced Labour Pressures, 1900–1940," *African Economic History* 28 (2000): 1–25; Kwabena O. Akurang-Parry, "African Agency and Cultural Initiatives in British Imperial Military and Labor Recruitment Drives in the Gold Coast (Colonial Ghana) during the First World War," *African Identities* 4, no. 2 (2006): 214–219; David Killingray, "Repercussions of World War I in the Gold Coast," *Journal of African History* 19, no. 1 (1978): 39–59.

33. ANOM FM/1AFFPOL/520/13, Extrait de rapports politiques, 3ème et 4ème semestre 1918; Chantal Antier, "Le recrutement dans l'Empire colonial français, 1914–1918," *Guerres Mondiales et Conflits Contemporains*, 230 (2008): 27.

34. Fall, *Le travail forcé*, 44–45.

35. Asiwaju, "Migration as revolt," 582–584; Rouch, "Migrations au Ghana," 25.

36. TNA, CO 96/578, February 30, 1917, Report from Chief Commissioner Howard Ross.

37. TNA, CO 96/579/31547, Introduction of a report by Gold Coast Governor Hugh Clifford to the Secretary of State for Colonies Walter Long.

38. TNA, CO 96/578/23855, February 24, 1917, The Governor of Côte d'Ivoire to the Governor of the Gold Coast

39. TNA, CO 96/579/23855, "To all chiefs in the Districts."

40. TNA, CO 96/578/12640, Confidential Report, Immigration of French subjects to avoid military service.

41. TNA, CO 96/688, Reports for 1918.

42. Kwabena O. Akurang-Parry, "'Untold Difficulties:' The Indigenous Press and the Economic Effects of the First World War on Africans in the Gold Coast, 1914–1918," *African Economic History* 34 (2006): 58–61.

43. TNA, CO 96/592/46751, Enclosure 2, À son Excellence, Monsieur le Gouveneur de la Gold Coast, Afforenou, 4 juillet 1918, "Lettre des chefs exilés."

44. ANOM, FM/1AFFPOL/520/13, Rapport politique du 3ème et 4ème semestre 1918

45. TNA, CO 96/579/31547, "Liste des chefs à arrêter en priorité."

46. ANOM, FM/1AFFPOL/520/13/349B.M., September 8, 1918, Rapport Antonetti au Gouverneur Général à Dakar, fait à Bingerville.

47. TNA, CO 96/584/42121, August 22, 1917, Foreign Office à l'Ambassadeur de France à Londres.

48. ANOM, FM/1AFFPOL/520/13, August 26, 1919, Rapport de la Commission sur l'Internement d'indigènes du cercle d'Assinie.

49. Cercles were small administrative units of the French Empire.

50. ANOM, FM/1AFFPOL/527, Rapport politique sur la Côte d'Ivoire, 1924.

51. ANOM, FM/1AFFPOL/145.

52. Conklin, *A Mission to Civilize*, 198–199.

6 "As If I Were in Prison"

White Deportation and Exile from Early Colonial Kenya

Brett L. Shadle

"Exile" implies that one has been removed (or, under duress, has removed oneself) from one's home. Exile may be temporary, as was that of Ahmadu Bamba as narrated by Sana Camara in his chapter in this volume, or permanent as Ruma Chopra's chapter demonstrates. In either case, the implication is that one is *out of place*—that one's real home is somewhere else, somewhere one is prevented from living. Exile ends only when one returns to one's home. In contrast, "deportation" removes a person from where (according to the state) he does not belong, where he has no claim as native or citizen. A state deports a person "back" to where he came from, to his *real* home.

The distinction between exile and deportation is more complicated when considering settler colonialism. A settler, especially in the earliest years of a colony, is not "native." The land of his birth is somewhere else, over the ocean. Yet the central conceit of settlers is that they are creating a new home. They are not wayfarers, they are not transients, but they have come to *settle*, to sink roots in a new land. Nonetheless, there are occasions when a government sees fit to remove—deport—a settler from that new land in order to preserve the peace or excuse itself of a financial burden. In early colonial Kenya, relatively well-off, well-established, politically vocal settlers alternately embraced some removals as the necessary *deportation* of undesirable whites, and hotly protested others as the illegitimate *exile* of settlers who were refashioning east Africa into a home.

Elite settlers and government officials concurred that some whites had no business in Kenya and (enthusiastically or reluctantly) agreed that deportation must be their fate. According to virtually all whites, their safety relied on "prestige," a kind of aura emanating from white skin that prevented Africans from even imagining violence, disobedience, or "insolence." Yet some whites acted in ways that damaged prestige. Vagrants, criminals, the insane, the flagrantly immoral: such folks led Africans to wonder if Europeans really were superior.

Thus the bulk of settlers believed that if poor whites and ruffians could not be uplifted, they must be deported.

When the government ordered the removal of the Honorable Galbraith Cole, settlers could hardly contain themselves. Cole had murdered an African but had been found not guilty by a white jury; his continued presence in the colony could only, London and Nairobi decided, inflame racial discord. He must be deported. Cole's fellow settlers understood this not as a deportation, but as exile. Cole, it was argued, had committed himself to developing Kenya, he had invested his time and money, his heart and soul, in the colony. "Ne'er do wells" could be sent *back* whence they had come, for they had contributed nothing, and could make no claim to Kenya. Cole, however, was being sent *away* from what was, after eight productive years in the colony, his *home*. Such stories of white deportations from Kenya offer an opportunity to reconsider forced removal in Africa, and provide useful counternarratives to the petitions and letter-writing campaigns explored in chapters by Trina Hogg, Meredith Terretta, and Marie Rodet and Romain Tiquet in this volume.

The colonial government in Kenya only rarely exiled its African challengers, and most likely never across the ocean. In the early decades of the colony, jails and the lash sufficed to deal with those who did not welcome their new overlords. Officials were also blessed to rule a colony of which large portions were closed to travel, sparsely inhabited, and generally disconnected from events in Nairobi and the more populous agricultural lands. Rather than send Africans to a deserted isle, officials could dispatch them to the margins of the colony. Thus were the prophets of Mumbo, a millennial movement based in the southwest, exiled to backwaters in the east of the colony, as were several Mazrui during World War One "owing to suspicions of their loyalty."[1] So too Harry Thuku, leader of the pan-ethnic (and hence dangerous) East African Association. His 1922 arrest attracted several thousand protesters outside the jail; their presence in turn attracted the bullets of police as well as of tea-sipping white settlers on a hotel verandah. Thuku was bundled up and sent to Kismayu on the coast, and later to Marsabit in the arid Northern Frontier District.[2] Thuku managed to stay in contact with people downcountry, but in his isolation he quickly diverted his energies to education, trade, farming, and raising ponies.[3] Upon his release in 1930, the district commissioner noted that Thuku's "interests [were] those of the country gentlemen."[4]

As much as Thuku or millenarian preachers gave officials pause, much more troublesome were their fellow whites. White settlers never constituted a very large percentage of the East African population. There were but a few dozen in 1901. The next year, the Commissioner of the Protectorate, Sir Charles Eliot, surveyed his domain and concluded that his African subjects stood too far down the social evolutionary ladder to be able to serve as a productive peasantry, the economic foundation of a colony. He required white men. Eliot sought Britons and (white) South Africans to come and bring forth riches from the land—provided that these men already had enough riches to invest in proper agricultural methods, not merely survive through hardscrabble prospecting or subsistence farming. Whites responded to his call and though small in number—in 1911 the total white population, including missionaries and government officials, totaled 3175—they quickly made themselves central to politics. Over the decades, officials in Kenya usually supported settler interests, though never to the extent settlers wished; officials in London sometimes dreamt of ending the settler experiment altogether, what with the constant scandals and inquiries and missives over land, labor, political control, and violence. But settlers would not so easily be made to leave their new homes.

Prestige and Deportable Whites

Virtually all whites in Kenya—officials, missionaries, and settlers, wealthy and poor—placed enormous faith in "prestige."[5] Prestige came from a mixture of fear, awe, respect, and trust. Africans, so the theory went, feared the violence of rifles and Maxim guns, they stood in awe of trains and phonographs, they respected whites' character and honor, they trusted white leadership and paternalism. Prestige was what allowed the solitary district official in an isolated corner of the colony to rule tens of thousands of Africans. Prestige protected the lone white man traipsing through the bush, and the lone white woman on a farm "back of beyond." Prestige was, as settler author Elspeth Huxley described it, a kind of "invisible coat of mail, or a form of magic" that permitted whites to walk about unarmed.[6] Of course, the daily reproduction of white rule was somewhat more complicated than this. But chalking up their supposed inviolability to prestige flattered colonial whites, some of the least immune to the sins of pridefulness: it made sense to settlers that their character, their individual and racial accomplishments, would induce Africans to submit.

The seeming omnipotence that prestige granted whites was counterbalanced by its apparent fragility. Any real or imagined act of resistance by an African—from a smirk or snide remark up to murder or rape—could be construed as a dangerous, perhaps fatal, strike against prestige. Whites religiously studied Africans for such bits of "insolence," devilish incantations that could render the magic worthless. Yet whites also surveilled one another. For Africans must be given no reason to doubt that whites were superior beings. They must not be faced with examples of whites behaving in ways that did not inspire awe and respect.

Thus did virtually all whites in Kenya engage in spirited critiques of each others' failings. Many were the cardinal sins against the god of prestige. Vagrancy and extreme poverty clearly would set Africans pondering the nature of the white man. How could white men be superior, how could they have prestige, if some lived in degrading conditions, ate little, and wore rags? Criminals and the mentally ill too could undermine prestige. Alcoholics, drug addicts, wife-swappers, check bouncers, the violently ill-tempered, the slothful, those who took African lovers: all these were, by many fellow whites, condemned as dangerous. Their actions, their very existence, might reveal to Africans that white prestige was not a god but a hallucination. Individual whites, and white rule itself, could not long survive the loss of prestige.

All European settler colonial states despised and feared and pitied the poor white, the oxymoron, the thing that logically should not exist. And yet across the colonized world, they existed.[7] As a member of the South African parliament explained in 1924, "in this country, there is a small number of whites against the natives, a few civilised people against uncivilised hordes, and for that reason it is so important that not a single white person be allowed to go under . . . There is no greater problem than this, because the existence of the European civilisation in this country hinges on it."[8] Doris Lessing articulated the "first law" of white southern Africa: "Thou shalt not let your fellow whites sink lower than a certain point; because if you do, the nigger will see he is as good as you are."[9] Plans, often shared internationally, for dealing with this dangerous category included education, wage protection, uplift, and scientific-medical programs to counter the pathologies of poor whites.[10]

Uplift and charity had their places, but the preservation of white rule in Kenya could best be accomplished through the physical removal of bedraggled and criminal whites. Vagrants would be rounded up and jailed. Under the 1900 Vagrancy Regulations, they would be put to work and earn the cost of their passage back from whence they had come, or at least someplace else.[11] Thus in August 1903, a "poor European with no means of livelihood" stood before the Mombasa town magistrate, who ordered him into hospital where he could regain his health and earn his passage to either Suez or India. A month later, two whites arrived, penniless, in Mombasa, having come from South Africa via Somaliland. They would call the jail home for three months as they earned their return passage.[12] Criminals sentenced to imprisonment could be sent to "a place in some part of His Majesty's dominions out of the United Kingdom" where their presence behind bars would not draw Africans' attention.[13]

Mentally ill whites would be very briefly confined to a prison or, after 1910, the Mathare mental hospital, before being sent on to Britain or South Africa.[14] Whites of exceptionally poor personal morality too might be sent away. Authorities discovered a Swedish woman in Mombasa reputed to sleep with nonwhites; she was at risk of deportation before she disappeared. In 1928, elite settler women (and, crucially, the governor's wife) lobbied successfully to deny reentry to two members of the "Happy Valley" set for fear of the damage their bed-hopping, pill-popping escapades might have on white prestige.[15]

Most settlers (excluding, presumably, those deported) fully supported the deportation of vagrants and various ruffians. In November 1903, the editors of the *East Africa and Uganda Mail* condemned the jailing of vagrants whose only crime was unemployment, for both vagrancy and imprisonment lowered prestige.[16] When two weeks later "half a dozen or so of working men" in Mombasa Prison were put aboard ships for South Africa, the *Mail* "hoped sincerely that they will secure honest, if not lucrative employment and never again be subjected to the humiliation of earning their living in prisons or work houses."[17] If the honest poor white working man could not be found employment, better that he become the problem of some other land. Preventing the immigration of "the undesirable" was also applauded. The *Times of East Africa* congratulated the government for passing legislation to regulate immigration by mandating a surety. "It is a timely enactment," the paper editorialized, "and will be welcomed by every true colonist, desirous as he must be of keeping the country as free as possible from the presence of the individual known as the undesirable." Such people included those "who toil not neither do they spin" and "South African 'characters.'"[18]

Kenya as Home

The removal of undesirable whites (undesirable from the perspectives of officials and the more successful settlers) was made easier due to the fact that they were not native to Kenya. Francis George Kikuyu Wallace was probably the first settler child born, in 1896, in what would become the White Highlands.[19] Few followed him. It would be some years before more than a handful of whites could stake a claim to Kenya as the land of their birth. Thuku and the Mumboites, in contrast, were sons of East African soil. Once they had proved themselves more amenable to colonial rule they could return to the hills and plains where, by birth, ancestry, race, they *belonged*. White settlers, however, could not point to the corner of the farm where their ancestors lay, their blood had not dampened the earth at initiation. Their childhood memories were of schoolbooks, not of watering cattle at the stream. Kenya could never be *home* to settlers in the same way it could be to Thuku.

Yet very many settlers did claim Kenya as their home, albeit in different ways than did Africans. Some whites were, of course, simply passing through, the residuum of empire. Uninvested in the country, they might seek a fortune hunting ivory or in trade, and move along. An Englishman and a "Scotchman" had come up from South Africa, which was "boomed out," and were prepared to seek their fortunes elsewhere if Kenya did not provide for them.[20] Colonial officials and missionaries might spend decades in East Africa, but their dedication was to God or King, and to their African charges. But settlers, whether on their farms or in the towns, conceived of Kenya as their permanent home. They built stone houses as soon as their finances permitted. They planted gardens with flowers imported from England. Settlement in Kenya was more than an economic venture. Indeed, most settlers survived on overdrafts from local banks, and many failed in their financial struggles. Yet their purses sagged with the coin of rootedness, their wallets were thick with the notes of belonging.

For those whites who avoided penury, Kenya promised a wonderful life. Settlers gloried in the vistas, the hunting, their outsized voice in government, and the army of African servants who attended to their needs. Alyse Simpson once asked her husband John "if he thought that we would one day be able to make money here, but his reply had been slightly off-hand. To make money did not seem to be his ultimate concern. It was as though he were a pioneer for the joy of it, for its own blessed sake."[21] Karen Blixen, famed author of *Out of Africa*, found emotional comfort in her retinue of servants, whom she treated and referred to as her children—the only children she would ever have. Indeed, *Out of Africa* itself could be read as a novel of exile from her Kenyan home, though written in the country of her birth. There was an incipient sense also of being *Kenyan*.[22] Although individuals might refer to Britain as "back home," Kenya had become, simply, home.[23] John Simpson, Karen Blixen, and hundreds of others created deep bonds with Kenya and Kenyans. Bonds twisted by racism, violence, and land appropriation, to be sure, but no less real for that.

Simply wishing to makes one's home in a particular place does not necessarily imply any *right* to do so. Settlers had several arguments to bolster their claim to Kenya. The first, and the one most often used when chastising the government, was that Sir Charles Eliot had invited the settlers to Kenya to forge a white man's country. Settlers had patriotically answered his plea. It was only fair, settlers reasoned, that government continue to support their efforts to remake Kenya in the way they saw fit.

More important to settlers' conception of Kenya as home were the discourses of civilization and development. Settlers understood themselves to be part of a great historical moment. White civilization had been spreading across the globe for decades, through trade, imperialism, and settler colonialism. This was all now, finally, coming to equatorial Africa. Settlers subject to the Crown saw themselves as pioneers bringing all the benefits of British civilization to the wilds of East Africa. Settlers from the US and other European countries brought their own racial genius to the project. An important part of this was development of the land, especially through "modern" agricultural production and cattle raising. Russell Bowker, an early and outspoken immigrant from South Africa, advised Eliot against inviting in capitalists and speculators. They would only extract their profits and leave the country impoverished. "I want to see the land go direct to the men who will cultivate it," Bowker stated, "the men who will help to lift and develop the country."[24]

Assured that they alone could civilize and make prosperous British East Africa, settlers understood themselves to have a right, perhaps a destiny, to make it their home. The *Leader* condemned those who would promote African rights at the expense of settlers. Such thinking ignored that "the few thousand white settlers who are planted here—and thriving—are the 'Pilgrim Fathers' or forerunners of an established superior caste who are going to rule the destinies of this portion of the African continent." Only the "Pilgrim Fathers" could make the colony flower, ensure its contribution to the global expansion of civilization and wealth: "while the endeavor of the European is to create permanent sources of fruitfulness and value the only endeavor of the Kavirondo [Luo] or Masai is to perpetuate his old savage life of idleness and periodic starvation. If he has any money he buries it."[25] Such an argument also served to counter African claims to the land. Certainly Africans had arrived first in eastern Africa, but they had not improved the land, and they had left vast swathes empty. The land was thus, settlers imagined, free for the taking.[26]

If the civilizing mission justified, necessitated, white settlement, all the more reason to send penurious and criminal whites on their way. Although settlers were always anxious to increase their numbers, an unemployed man did nothing to improve the country. Even setting aside the damage a vagrant did to white prestige, his value to the white man's country was precisely zero. "W. S." of Nairobi explained that whites—certain whites—had a right and duty to live in Kenya: "the inter-penetration of black and white . . . (subject always to such a degree of exclusion of the baser elements of white civilization as is effectively practised in Kenya) is desirable in the general interests of the African and the economic interests of humanity."[27] Human progress required white settlers in Kenya, but only those who could make a positive contribution.

In their ongoing political battles with Indians, settlers pointed to their own permanence to assert their superior claim over the colony. Indian immigrants had preceded whites (there had long been a south Asian presence along the coast) and they significantly outnumbered the latecomers.[28] Through their connections with the Indian National Congress and with the paternalistic interest of the India Office, Indians had the skill to make uncomfortable political demands. White settlers rightly understood that any advancement by Indians must come at some cost to whites. They thus turned to questions of developing and creating a home. Settlers insisted that, unlike themselves, Indians had no attachment to Kenya. Whether born in India or east Africa, the argument went, their fellow non-Africans viewed the colony as a business venture, nothing more. Indians sent their profits to India, rather than using it to build up Kenya. As traders, they exploited their African customers, those whom whites strove to civilize. The image of the Indian was the counterpoint to the settlers' image of themselves: Indians were in Kenya to make a quick rupee, whites were in Kenya to make a home.[29] As the *Mail* complained, substantial sums paid to Indian railway workers had gone directly to India. Would not it have been wiser to use Britons, who "with the money so earned could have made permanent homes for themselves" in Kenya?[30]

This was the home settlers had created for themselves. From deep within welled a love for the land, the flora and fauna, the lifestyle that Kenya offered them. This emotional attachment to their new homes complemented the great burden they had undertaken, that of developing and civilizing Africa. Through this painstaking work, settlers explained, they had secured the right to claim Kenya as their home. Poor, immoral whites could make no such claim, and in fact their very presence made Kenya an unsuitable home for all white people. Deportation would be their fate. In this context, settlers could not but be outraged when the state concluded that a leading settler, one in the vanguard of developing the country, one who no longer had any other home, was a menace.

Galbraith Cole: Deported, Exiled

In another era, in another part of the world, Galbraith Cole might have seemed an unlikely colonist. Born in 1881, he was the son of the Earl of Enniskillen, and married Eleanor Balfour, the British prime minister's niece. Yet Kenya offered something to men like Cole, something they could find nowhere else. In 1903, after having served in the South African War, he visited his sister who had recently moved to British East Africa with her new husband, Hugh Cholmondeley (Lord Delamere). There, Eleanor would later write, Cole quickly became "fascinated with all the problems of developing a new country."[31] He claimed a vast fifty thousand acres, later moving to a slightly less-vast thrity thousand acre farm. Here Cole, like his brother Berkeley, Delamere, and other honorables, could create a world of safaris and servants on a regal estate, free from the modern world and the crumbling of their feudal pretensions in Britain.

Cole, in common with other elite settlers, invested in herding, in his case sheep. In common with many herders, Cole suffered from stock theft. Also in common with many herders, he took the law into his own hands. Around two in the afternoon on April 10, 1911, he, with several African servants and his farm manager Alexander Wright, came upon three Africans. They were, Cole said, caught in the act of skinning several of Cole's sheep. (Later, Wahatha wa Chichia testified that they had spent the morning collecting honey, and were simply cooking maize when Cole arrived.)[32] Sionga wa Mithura and Wangi wa Kabrie ran. Cole fired two shots. One bullet entered Sionga's back and exited through his stomach. Wright and Cole then went over to (as Wright put it) "examine" Sionga. Sionga was alive, lying facedown. The white men either did not notice or disregarded his spilled intestines, the evidence of which, even a dozen days later, could still be found on the spot.[33] Sionga would not live to see the sunset.

Word eventually reached the authorities by way of Wahatha. A European constable and medical officer examined the site and collected evidence, and at a preliminary hearing in early May Cole was committed to trial for murder or culpable homicide.[34] On May 31, after testimony by Wahatha, Wangi, Wright, the constable, and the doctor, Cole was sworn in.[35] He began by telling the judge and jury facts that they surely already knew: he had served in the military, he had come to east Africa in 1903, and the theft of his sheep was "a common occurrence." On April 9 he had lost yet another animal, and had "given up the attempt to catch the thieves as hopeless." On April 10 his luck changed. Cole freely admitted to having discharged two bullets, the first striking a tree, the second cutting down Sionga. He "saw the boy [*sic*] and the wound as stated [by Wahatha and Wright], he was alive when I left." Cole testified that he "left [Wahatha] to look after" Sionga. Under cross-examination, Cole stated that he did not hear of Sionga's death until the constable arrived at his farm. The Crown Advocate's next question is not recorded, but Cole's answer was revealing: "I didn't report Sionga seriously hurt as I did not wish to go to any further trouble over the matter."

It had been only five years since the Colonial Office had granted Kenyan settlers the right to trial by a jury of their peers. Thus after the defense rested, nine white men, "after a few minutes of deliberation" and without leaving the box, acquitted Cole on both counts.[36] There was little doubt in legal circles that justice had not been served, but there seemed to be no grounds for appeal against the acquittal.[37] Governor Percy Girouard thought the affair concluded. Appointed by London in 1909 to take a firm line against settler carping, Girouard instead proved to be most accommodating to them. He seemed inclined to see things through Cole's eyes, as he informed the Colonial Office that the killing was "due to the prevalence of unrestrained stock theft." London officials saw things rather differently. From the Colonial Office, J. A. Read noted that "In spite of Sir P. Girouard's apologetics it seems to me that murder is murder and that it is out of the question to let the matter slide in the easy manner he appears to contemplate."[38] In late July the trial transcript arrived in the Colonial Office, with Girouard's note that if further action was warranted, he could envision two possibilities: deportation for Cole, or suspending trial by jury.[39] While the men of the Colonial Office would for many years seriously consider revoking settlers' rights to trial by jury,[40] at this point they quickly agreed that deportation would have to be the course pursued. Lord Harcourt, Secretary of State for the Colonies, himself wrote that it was "a very horrible case. . . . Cole must be deported."[41] Girouard equivocated and delayed, but finally, reluctantly, issued the order. The ordinances that had sealed the fates of other unlucky whites could not be employed here. Cole was hardly a vagrant, nor a convicted criminal, nor a madman. The state instead turned to the 1902 Order-in-Council, which permitted the deportation of anyone conducting themselves "so as to be dangerous to peace and good order . . . or is endeavouring to excite enmity between the people of East Africa and His Majesty."[42] Cole's continued presence in Kenya was likely to stir up racial enmity.

During Cole's trial, and especially after his order of deportation became known, settlers rallied around him. Some admitted that his actions had been rash. R. W. Hamilton (who had served as judge in the case) later noted that "though Mr Cole's previous popularity was great and much sympathy for him was aroused by his subsequent deportation, his behaviour was generally condemned."[43] Others, such as Lord Cranworth, believed that it was not the murder itself that was wrong, but Cole's failure to tend to the dying man. "He . . . made an undoubted error of judgement in not reporting the matter to the authorities," he wrote.[44] Nonetheless, "practically every settler in the country was in agreement with the verdict."[45] The musings of Arnold Paice, a famer in Nanyuki, were cruder, but shared the sentiment: "how could they hang the son of the Earl of Enniskillen for blotting out a miserable sheep-stealing nigger?"[46] It "was as cold-blooded a case of murder as one could wish for," he wrote his dear mother in Britain, "But I say what if it was?"[47]

Although Cole seems not to have made any public statements, settlers rushed to his defense. Their arguments against his deportation were tightly intertwined with their ideas about Kenya as their own rightful home. First, and most sound legally, Cole had been acquitted in a properly constituted court. What was this vaunted British justice, they wondered, if a man found not guilty by a jury could be summarily deported by the executive—a punishment the executive shamelessly denied was a punishment, but a mere administrative matter to preserve the peace.[48] As much as Kenya was home, settlers remained part of the empire. Like other settler colonists, they "carr[ied] their sovereignty with them."[49] To have been deported from, say, Russia would have been a rather different situation. There, he could not have expected British laws, British courts, British legal traditions. In Kenya, however, they could insist that they retained their rights as Britons.

At the same time, settlers also insisted that in a savage land, civilized law could not always apply. Police were too far away from isolated farms, while the courts were either overly lenient or paid too much attention to "technicalities" and released obvious criminals. In such circumstances, whites shrugged off the illegality of taking the law into their own hands. This situation was, they argued, common in all pioneering communities.[50] It was the price Britain must pay for the expansion of its colonial empire. Surely all settlers believed in the rule of law. "But in undeveloped countries," Cranworth explained, "and in special circumstances, the Law Courts and the police are powerless to administer justice.

In such circumstances it is not human nature, nor is it right and proper, that citizens should sit still and allow lawlessness to run riot and the efforts of honest toil to become fruitless."[51] That is, citizen Cole had the *duty* to shoot at stock thieves for the betterment of the colony.[52] It was his contribution to developing his new homeland.

To defend Cole was to defend his place in Kenya—why he had a claim to be an integral part of its future. Apologists may have been influenced by Cole's class position, but nowhere in the documents was his birthright noted. Instead, attention was turned to what he had accomplished in East Africa. He was, many commentators noted, a man committed to nothing but selflessly improving Kenya. Residents of Nakuru appealed to the governor to reverse the deportation order against Cole, who "your petitioners would point out . . . is the owner of large flocks of sheep and other property in this Protectorate."[53] They reassured Cole himself that none could question his reputation as a man whose "energies have always been devoted towards the real business of farming, and that practically without exception business, and business only, has taken you away from your farm."[54] A man who had sunk his money into his new home, who had improved the land and the colony, being sent away. Where was the justice in that?

While most settlers understood the deportation of "marginal" whites to be an unfortunate necessity, Cole in no way fell into this category. The *Leader* challenged the government for using an ordinance "passed for the purpose of dealing summarily with dangerous political agitators, or indigents, and employ this to summarily deport one of our most respected and quietest gentlemen setter farmers, a man who is essentially a worker and who has taken no part in the politics of the country."[55] If the government wished to experiment with arbitrary deportation they had selected the wrong subject. For Cole was, the *Leader* wrote, "a man who has been a pattern of industry; who has led a blameless life, and one who has turned this wilderness into a fruitful domain." Any colony needed administrators as a driver of progress, but "equally needed the immigrant or colonist, who literally does the spade work in pioneer development." This, for the *Leader*, gave a special place to the settler: "He is a part of the soul and the body itself. The spirit of the country is in the settler."[56]

That Cole's home was Africa, his defenders continued, was supported by the fact that Africans expressed no desire to see him leave. Of course, in light of the accusation that Cole was "creating enmity" between the races, it made sense to argue the opposite. The killing of Sionga could not excite "racial enmity," Lord Delamere wrote. "The natives in no way view the shooting of a thief as a racial matter," for an African stock owner would have done the same.[57] Far from stirring hatred, Cole had "the confidence of the Masai," he always enjoyed "good understanding and friendly relations" with Africans.[58] According to Lord Cranworth, Cole was "one of the most popular, if not actually *the* most popular, setter with the native population."[59] Cole had so much made Kenya his home that Africans themselves welcomed his presence.

The Colonial Office was unimpressed by settler remonstrances, and Cole went on his way. He spent some time in Australia studying sheep farming, and a short period in German East Africa until he tired of living with Germans.[60] Cole was, he wrote from afar, "like a storm-tossed ship without a helm and so must drift before the wind."[61] He and his supporters repeatedly and unsuccessfully approached Lord Harcourt to permit his return. During the war, Harcourt finally, "in view of the general amnesty to Suffragettes and South African deportees," agreed to end Cole's exile.[62] He quietly returned to his farm in 1916.

But in 1924, Cole was once again forced from Kenya, this time hoping that life in England might help relieve him of debilitating arthritic pain.[63] Yet England was no longer home—there, Eleanor Cole realized, he was "homesick."[64] As Elspeth Huxley writes, drawing on family letters and reminiscences, "Galbraith felt exiled once again and longed for his own land, his sheep, and his servants." "I sit here watching the clock as if I were in prison," Cole sighed. "I want to die where I can hear a zebra barking." The land of his birth was now his exile, his prison. East Africa was home. He and his wife returned to Kenya, his body still failing him. On an October day in 1929, Cole once again shot a man to death. Suicide, this time, rather than homicide.[65]

Conclusion

The deportation of white settlers was about home and belonging, about who threatened the future of white Kenya and who promoted it. A man like Cole could (settlers argued) call Kenya home, for there he labored successfully to produce wealth, to ensure the survival and prosperity of the settler colony. He made Kenya, and made it his home. Vagrants and criminals could assert no such claims. They contributed nothing, and by their very presence they endangered all whites. Kenya (settlers and officials agreed) could never be home for such whites. They belonged elsewhere.

Several decades hence, white settlers were faced with the existential threat of Mau Mau and, later, independence. Although only thirty-two settlers were killed during the Mau Mau rebellion, what so unnerved settlers was that they no longer felt safe at home: home, in terms of their dwellings, where many killings took place, and home in terms of the colony, for a Mau Mau victory would seem to guarantee the obliteration of white rule and white settlement. Mau Mau were asserting their own claims to Kenya as home, one in which all whites—not just the impecunious one—no longer belonged. As independence finally loomed in 1963, settlers had to make a choice: could they envision a home ruled by an African? While many could not, and left for South Africa, Rhodesia, and

Great Britain, others tried to reimagine what home could be. (Later, whites in Zimbabwe and post-Apartheid South Africa would go through the same mental and emotional struggles.)[66] Legally, as citizens, they no longer stood the risk of deportation. Yet this new home was not at all what their ancestors had come to East Africa to build.[67]

Notes

1. Brett L. Shadle, "Patronage, Millennialism and the Serpent God Mumbo in Southwest Kenya, 1912–34," *Africa* 72, no. 1 (2002): 29–54; Kenya National Archive (KNA): Vanga District Annual Report, 1915/16.

2. Harry Thuku, with Kenneth King, *Harry Thuku: an autobiography* (Nairobi: Oxford University Press, 1970); Carl Rosberg and John Nottingham, *The Myth of "Mau Mau"* (New York: Meridian, 1966), chap. 2; W. McGregor Ross, *Kenya from Within* (1927; repr., London: Cass, 1968), chap. 13.

3. Thuku, *Harry Thuku.*

4. KNA: Marsabit District Annual Report, 1930.

5. The following draws on Brett L. Shadle, *The Souls of White Folk: White Settlers in Kenya, 1900s-1920s* (Manchester: Manchester University Press, 2015).

6. Elspeth Huxley, *The Flame Trees of Thika* (New York: Morrow, 1959), 16.

7. See, for example, Ann Laura Stoler, *Carnal Knowledge and Imperial Power: Race and the Intimate in Colonial Rule* (Berkeley: University of California Press, 2002), 34–38.

8. Quoted in Jeremy Seekings, "'Not a Single White Person Should Be Allowed to Go Under': *Swartgevaar* and the Origins of South Africa's Welfare State, 1924–1929," *Journal of African History* 48, no. 3 (2007): 382.

9. Doris Lessing, *The Grass is Singing* (1950; repr., London: Flamingo, 1994), 178.

10. See, for example, Matt Wray, *Not Quite White: White Trash and the Boundaries of Whiteness* (Durham: Duke University Press, 2006); Zine Magubane, "The American Construction of the Poor White Problem in South Africa," *South Atlantic Quarterly* 107, no. 4 (2008): 691–713; Ivan Evans, "Racial Violence and the Origins of Segregation in South Africa," in *Settler Colonialism in the Twentieth Century*, ed. Caroline Elkins and Susan Pedersen (New York: Routledge), 183–202, esp.191–92.

11. *Official Gazette of British East Africa*, II, 6, February 1, 1900. This would seem to have drawn on the Distressed British Subject Act, which operated in much of the empire and permitted the deportation of criminals or the indigent. See W. Robert Foran, *The Kenya Police, 1887–1960* (London: Robert Hale, 1962), 21. See also Mrinalini Sinha, *Colonial Masculinity: The 'manly Englishman' and the 'effeminate Bengali' in the Late Nineteenth Century* (Manchester: Manchester University Press, 1995), 49; Laura Ann Stoler, "Rethinking Colonial Categories: European Communities and the Boundaries of Rule," *Comparative Studies in Society and History* 31, no. 1 (1989): 134–61.

12. See "Town Magistrate's Court," *East Africa and Uganda Mail* (*Mail*), August 23, 1903, 6; October 3, 1903, Supplement; October 10, 1903, 6. Under a 1920 ordinance, vagrants no longer received wages. The costs of deportation would be paid either by government, a previous employer (the military or railway, for example), or friends and relatives. "Vagrancy Laws," *East African Standard* (*EAS*), September 9, 1922, 3.

13. East Africa Order in Council, 1902, para. 24, *Official Gazette of the East Africa and Uganda Protectorates* IV, 70, October 1, 1902, 309.

14. Will Jackson, *Madness and Marginality: The Lives of Kenya's White Insane* (Manchester: Manchester University Press, 2013), 5. Only from the later 1930s did significant numbers of whites actually undergo treatment at Mathare.

15. Shadle, *Souls of White Folk*, 97.

16. "Lowering British Prestige," *Mail*, November 14, 1903, 4. See also "Floreat Britannia," letter to the editor, *Mail*, November 21, 1903, 5.

17. "Local Notes," *Mail*, November 28, 1903, 7.

18. "Restriction of Immigration," *Times of East Africa*, August 25, 1906, 4.

19. Errol Trzebinski, *The Kenya Pioneers* (New York: Norton, 1988), 14–15. This is not to ignore that an unknown number of African women bore the children of white men, but to the best of my knowledge such children remained with their mothers.

20. "Town Magistrate's Court," *Mail*, September 5, 1903, Supplement.

21. Alyse Simpson, *Red Dust of Kenya* (New York: Crowell, 1952), 57. See also Bruce Berman, *Control and Crisis in Colonial Kenya: The Dialectic of Domination* (London: James Curry, 1990), 134–35.

22. Lonsdale points out (apparently referencing the 1930s and later) that "British and Afrikaner schoolboys traded insults but both were Kenyans when dismissing newcomers." "Kenya: Home Country and African Frontier," in *Settlers and Expatriates: Britons over the Seas*, ed. Robert A. Bickers (Oxford: Oxford University Press, 2010), 78–79.

23. As Veracini notes, for settlers "'home' is alternatively (or simultaneously) both the 'old' and the 'new' place." Lorenzo Veracini, *Settler Colonialism: A Theoretical Overview* (Houndmills, Basingstoke: Palgrave Macmillan, 2010), 21.

24. "Settlers' Prospects in British East Africa," *African Standard*, March 12, 1904, 5.

25. "The Racial Perspective," *Leader of British East Africa* (*Leader*), November 25, 1911, 8.

26. Cf. Veracini, *Settler Colonialism*, 41–43.

27. W. S., letter to editor, *EAS*, January 20, 1923, 7. Others argued that Kenya should welcome poorer men, so long as they took to the land, worked hard, and willingly suffered through years of privation, "until the land has been compelled to yield an increase, and wealth and comfort have crowned honest effort, and their children assured a position of responsibility." A. P. T., letter to the editor, *African Standard*, February 27, 1904, 3.

28. Sana Aiyar, *Indians in Kenya: The Politics of Diaspora* (Cambridge: Harvard University Press, 2015).

29. "The Retardation of East Africa and Uganda," *African Standard*, October 3, 1903, 3.

30. "A Plea for the Poor," *Mail*, March 12, 1904, 4.

31. Eleanor Cole, *Random Recollections of a Pioneer Kenya Settler* (privately published, 1975), 34. She spends several pages recounting his early life in Kenya (before they met) but fails to mention the murder or his deportation. As she lived in postcolonial Kenya at the time of her writing, overlooking these events is perhaps understandable.

32. "High Court Sessions," *EAS*, June 6, 1911, 4.

33. Ibid.

34. "Serious Charge against a Leading Settler," *Leader*, May 6, 1911, 11

35. The following draws on "High Court Sessions," *EAS*, June 6, 1911, 5.

36. Ibid.; Bertram Francis Gurdon Cranworth, *A Colony in the Making; or, Sport and Profit in British East Africa* (London: Macmillan, 1912), 56.

37. Reflecting on the case two years later Chief Justice J. W. Barth considered it "a glaring miscarriage of justice." "Notes on Trial by Jury in British East Africa," J. W. Barth, May 19, 1913, enclosure in Governor of Kenya to Secretary of State for the Colonies, May 31, 1913, The British National Archive (TNA): CO 533/118/21531.

38. Quoted in Robert M. Maxon, *The Struggle for Kenya: The Loss and Reassertion of Imperial Initiative, 1912–23* (Hackensack, NJ: Fairleigh Dickinson University Press, 1993), 38. For Cole in the larger context of metropolitan criticism of Kenya, especially the usurping of Maasai land, see Lotte Hughes, *Moving the Maasai: A Colonial Misadventure* (Houndsmill, Basingstoke: Palgrave Macmillan, 2006), 67–71.

39. Maxon, *Struggle for Kenya*, 39. For a detailed review of the correspondence between the CO and Girouard, see Abdullahi Sara, *Kenya at a Crossroads: Administration and Economy under Sir Percy Girouard, 1909–1912* (Lanham, MD: Lexington, 2015), chap. 9.

40. TNA: CO 533/9/36361.

41. Quoted in Maxon, *Struggle for Kenya*, 39.

42. East Africa Order in Council, 1902, para. 25, *Official Gazette of the East Africa and Uganda Protectorates* IV, 70, October 1, 1902, 309.

43. R. W. Hamilton, memorandum, May 25, 1913, enclosure in Governor of Kenya to Secretary of State for the Colonies, May 31, 1913, TNA: CO 533/118/21531.

44. Cranworth, *Colony in the Making*, 56. Ross thought this a general opinion. *Kenya from Within*, 434.

45. Cranworth, *Colony in the Making*, 57. Nine years later, Lord Francis Scott, a new immigrant and soon a leading politician, told his diary that Cole had been "perfectly justified in what he did. . . . He made the one mistake of not reporting the matter at once." Lord Francis Scott Diaries, entry of April 14, 1920, Bodelian Library, Oxford, MSS Brit. Emp. s.349.

46. Quoted in Trzebinski, *Kenya Pioneers*, 159.

47. Quoted in C.J.D. Duder and C.P. Youé, "Paice's Place: Race and Politics in Nanyuki District, Kenya, in the 1920s," *African Affairs* 93 (1994): 272.

48. Cranworth, *Colony in the Making*, 58.

49. Veracini, *Settler Colonialism*, 3.

50. "The Deportation Case," *Leader*, November 18, 1911, reproducing letter from Sir Henry Seton-Karr to *Throne and Country.*

51. Cranworth, *Colony in the Making*, 57.

52. The *Leader* favored "summary punishment" of stock thieves at the hands of settlers, although the paper was careful to note that "We are not here advising shooting." "The Governor's Speech," *Leader*, November 11, 1911, 8.

53. "The Cole Case: Text of the Nakuru Petition," *Leader* November 11, 1911, 8.

54. "The Meeting at Nakuru," *Leader*, October 7, 1911, 13.

55. *Leader*, September 9, 1911. On Cole's lack of involvement in politics, see also Cranworth, *Colony in the Making*, 56; Frank Watkins, letter to the editor, *Leader*, September 23, 1911; "The Meeting at Nakuru," *Leader*, October 7, 1911, 13.

56. "Nakuru, the Cole Case, and cognate happenings," *Leader*, October 7, 1911, 8.

57. "Lord Delamere Protests," *Leader*, October 7, 1911, 9, quoting a letter from Delamere to *Daily Mirror*. See also "The Deportation of Mr. Cole," *Times* September 11, 1911, 3; Cranworth, *Colony in the Making*, 58.

58. Frank Watkins, letter to the editor, *Leader*, September 23, 1911; "The Cole Case: Text of the Nakuru Petition," *Leader* November 11, 1911, 8.

59. Cranworth, *Colony in the Making*, 58. See also "Lord Cranworth Defends Kenya," *East Africa*, October 22, 1925, 90–91.

60. "The Cole Case," *Leader*, December 9, 1911, 7; Elspeth Huxley, *Out in the Midday Sun: My Kenya* (London: Chatoo and Windus, 1985), 96.

61. Quoted in Huxley, *Out in the Midday Sun*, 96.

62. Quoted in Maxon, *Struggle for Kenya*, 80.

63. Cole, *Random Recollections*, 50.

64. Cole, *Random Recollections*, 56.

65. Huxley, *Out in the Midday Sun*, 102–3.

66. See David McDermott Hughes, *Whiteness in Zimbabwe: Race, Landscape, and the Problem of Belonging* (New York: Palgrave Macmillan, 2010); Richard Schroeder, *Africa after Apartheid: South Africa, Race, and Nation in Tanzania* (Bloomington: Indiana University Press, 2012); Melissa E. Steyn, *Whiteness Just Isn't What It Used To Be : White Identity in a Changing South Africa* (Albany: State University of New York Press, 2001).

67. For struggles by contemporary whites to understand their place in Kenya, see Janet McIntosh, *Unsettled: Denial and Belonging Among White Kenyans* (Berkeley: University of California Press, 2016).

Part II
Geographies of Exile

7 In the City of Waiting

Education and Mozambican Liberation Exiles in Dar es Salaam, 1960–1975

Joanna T. Tague

"I'M BEGINNING TO hate money," Janet Mondlane lamented in a letter to her friend, George Houser, in April of 1964. At the time, Mondlane was the Executive Director of the Mozambique Institute, which had only come into being the previous year with the express purpose of educating Mozambican exiles, refugees who had fled the war for liberation with Portugal and had relocated to the Tanzanian capital, Dar es Salaam. Mondlane's letter reveals the profound obstacles faced by those who sought to organize educational programs for such exiles. Money, of course, was a foremost concern: "We have so many things to spend it on, and it is so scarce! The literacy and primary program out at the large refugee camp is developing and becoming more demanding. It is like a baby we gave birth to which is growing more like a horse than a human. But I am beginning to realize that it is one of the most vital aspects of the Institute."[1] As the American wife of Eduardo Mondlane, president of the Mozambique Liberation Front (FRELIMO), Janet Mondlane wielded significant influence in Mozambique's struggle for independence. And though scholars have interpreted Mozambique's war for independence in myriad ways—as a guerrilla insurgency, as an extension of the apartheid state, as yet another corollary to Cold War allegiances—we cannot fully comprehend the complexity of the struggle for liberation unless we examine the education of Mozambican exiles in Dar es Salaam.[2]

After having achieved independence in 1961, Tanzania emerged as a "haven" for African liberation movements that challenged the continuation of white minority rule on the continent.[3] Throughout the 1960s and 1970s, a plethora of liberation movements—all banned in their own colonies—had headquarters in Dar es Salaam: the MPLA of Angola, PAIGC of Guinea-Bissau, FRELIMO of Mozambique, SWAPO of South West Africa (Namibia), and ZAPU of Southern Rhodesia (Zimbabwe). Tanzania's president, Julius Nyerere, and his government facilitated the settlement of these liberation groups in Dar es Salaam, which became a "gathering place" not only for the leaders of these groups but also for the thousands of refugees who followed their leaders to this cosmopolitan city.[4]

In the early 1960s, those arriving in Dar es Salaam were dispersed throughout the city and Mozambican liberation leaders found it extremely difficult—if not impossible—to keep track of their diffuse exile community. Educating this scattered community became a top priority for leaders of the Mozambican liberation movement—indeed, Mondlane's letter tells us that the Institute's educational program was "vital" to the overall success of the liberation movement. As this chapter demonstrates, however, the formation of the Mozambique Institute not only enabled liberation leaders to centralize their exile community; it also allowed them to construct and provide a very particular type of educational experience for those in exile.

To assess this relationship between liberation and education, I use exile as an analytical category. A broad concept that frequently glosses over complex lived realities, the very term "exile" encapsulates a range of experiences, from coercion to free will. Yet we often default to imagining exile as punitive. To that end, this chapter challenges the conflation of exile with punishment by framing exile as opportunity. Exile could offer occasion for (re)creating community, and exiles cultivated such networks in a broad range of spaces—often in imperial centers of political power but just as frequently on the periphery of (or even beyond) the colonial gaze. As such, there is a geography to exile: historically, hubs have emerged where exiles gathered and where they made claims, as Trina Hogg's chapter in this volume examines. Such hubs were essential during African wars for liberation—Dar es Salaam was the preeminent hub for liberation exiles and other activists from across the continent.[5] And yet, the very existence of such gathering places compels us to speak of degrees of exile, as a spectrum in which collectivities of exiles might be more saturated in certain spaces than in others. The saturation point matters because of the inherently Janus-faced nature of exile: though imperial powers could employ exile as a means toward fueling empire, the colonized could also wield exile as a weapon in the dismantlement of empire.[6]

This chapter examines the genesis of and transformations in educational programs for Mozambican refugees in Dar es Salaam. It asks what kinds of communities arise amongst those in exile? More specifically, how can we understand the nature of education in exile? What were the consequences of providing educational training and opportunity to some exiles, but not to others? And finally, what became of those who attended the Mozambique Institute? This chapter argues that the structure of the education Mozambican refugees received during their war for liberation consisted of multiple stages of exile. Ultimately, the ability of Mozambicans in Dar es Salaam to secure educational advancement led to the creation of a group who would, during exile, acquire the knowledge, skills, and connections necessary to run the country at independence. The Mozambique Institute provided education on a shoestring, but the very fact of exile and the education exiles received positioned them as a fortunate community.

Although many students were not "elite" prior to or even during exile, the opportunities offered by the Institute contributed to the making of an intellectual elite, prompting us to consider the ways in which exile has an extraordinary capacity to produce an elite.

Exile and Political Authenticity

What qualities differentiate "exiles" from "refugees"? Part of the ambiguity in distinguishing between the two terms lies in the history of international humanitarianism. Because the 1951 Convention Relating to the Status of Refugees only protected Europeans displaced during World War II, international law did not legally recognize Africans as refugees. Though the 1967 Protocol Relating to the Status of Refugees would remove such geographic and temporal restrictions, we know far too little about the experiences of African refugees prior to the Protocol because they could not be officially categorized as such. Instead, national governments, NGOs, activists, and African liberation leaders used a plethora of terms—refugees, exiles, students, political refugees, terrorists, freedom fighters, or liberation exiles—to refer to the displaced. The distinction between such terms was slippery, and many people occupied multiple categories simultaneously, laying claim in equal measure to being an exile or a refugee.

We also know very little about how African refugees and liberation leaders throughout the 1960s defined and navigated their own exile. Their inability to claim refugee status precluded assistance from the United Nations High Commissioner for Refugees (UNHCR), and lack of substantive UNHCR support often meant that African liberation movements in exile assumed responsibility for refugees from their home territories. Prior to the formation of FRELIMO, however, three groups competed with one another for dominance in the Mozambican liberation movement.[7] Based in Dar es Salaam, UDENAMO, MANU, and UNAMI each depicted their group as the *only* legitimate Mozambican liberation organization and their leaders used such claims of legitimacy to solicit support from international organizations. For instance, in April 1961 UDENAMO representative Jaime Rivaz Sigauke wrote to George Houser, President of the American Committee on Africa (ACOA),

> We are the first and purely African political organization in Mozambique, working under exile in Tanganyika. . . . I was instructed . . . to make two appeals. First, to all American people to back us in our struggle for freedom . . . second to ask you, sir, for financial aid.[8]

Exile generated narratives of purity as well as contamination, even treachery. Sigauke's letter, for instance, showcases the extent to which Mozambican liberation leaders pointed to their own state of exile as evidence of political purity.[9] Each group envisioned themselves as pure and every other group as tainted, fueling distrust between exiles. When Mr. L. M. Millinga, Administrative Secretary of MANU, wrote to Houser, he admitted: "we have no and will never never never have relations with UDENAMO whatsoever may happen to us."[10] According to Millinga, UDENAMO consisted of agents acting on behalf of the Portuguese government in order to collect information about other groups. They were not to be trusted.

The pursuit of education offered exiles common ground. In June 1962, when the three groups unified under FRELIMO, the political leadership came to perceive of exile (and the students' shared educational experience at the Mozambique Institute) as an opportunity to foster unity among communities that previously distrusted one another. After Eduardo Mondlane was elected president of FRELIMO, he and Janet prioritized refugee education. They petitioned the Ford Foundation for a grant and in 1963 they received $100,000 to establish the Mozambique Institute, the nonmilitary arm of FRELIMO dedicated to providing secondary education to the growing number of Mozambican students in the Tanzanian capital.[11] From the beginning, Janet Mondlane served as Executive Director of the Mozambique Institute.[12] In this way, because FRELIMO and the Mozambique Institute came into being in tandem, the very process of moving through the ranks of the Institute unified students around FRELIMO's liberation ethos. The Mozambique Institute, however, was not the first educational program specifically targeted to refugees living in Dar es Salaam. Rather, Project Tanganyika—a program run by the African-American Institute—preceded and heavily influenced curricular and administrative planning at the Mozambique Institute.[13]

Refugee Education: The African-American Institute and Project Tanganyika

In August 1962, the African-American Institute began working in Dar es Salaam. The Institute's primary purpose was to provide education to refugees coming into Tanzania from the various colonies of southern Africa. As such, the African-American Institute attempted to acclimate refugees by placing them in Tanzanian secondary schools, but they faced significant obstacles in doing so. For example, the only European language that Mozambican refugee students knew was Portuguese—though many were not proficient in that language, either. This language barrier meant that Mozambican students could not easily transition into—let alone succeed at—Tanzanian schools, where the medium of instruction was English.

The Institute's very limited success in placing Mozambican refugee students in Tanzanian schools led to the idea of establishing a *separate* institution for refugee education in Dar es Salaam. This illustrates the tensions between immersion in host society and (the sometimes more practical need for) apartness during exile. Staff at the Institute were quite cognizant of the possibility that Mozambican students might be afforded opportunities for study that Tanzanian students might not receive (or that Tanzanians might simply assume Mozambican students had opportunities that they did not). To that end, staff worried that Mozambican students might utilize their educational skills to "compete with students of Tanganyika."[14] This question—the extent to which liberation exiles posed a threat to the educational opportunities of hosts—requires further investigation. One could, however, speculate that Mozambican students were not seen as a significant source of competition amongst their hosts because (as this chapter will later explore) the very purpose of exile was ultimately to leave Tanzania. Indeed, a desire to leave Tanzania was one indication of one's dedication to the liberation movement. Mozambican students never imaged that their stay in Dar es Salaam would be permanent because they did not anticipate that they would acquire permanent jobs or educational posts in the city.

The tendency to place Mozambican students in Tanzanian schools waned when a group of volunteer teachers with Project Tanganyika (a program for undergraduates from the Phillips Brooks House at Harvard University and Radcliffe College for Women) arrived in Dar es Salaam to establish an institution singularly devoted to refugee education. The African-American Institute and Project Tanganyika jointly ran the new school. It was the only educational facility on the African continent set up especially for refugee students, and it was open to them without restriction. When classes began the first week of January 1963, there were five volunteer teachers and one hundred students. Unfortunately, there was no clearly identifiable goal toward which refugee students were studying: the school did not issue certificates, and the staff soon realized that the institution was of "limited academic merit." In part, this was due to the fact that fluctuations in the refugee population were such that most of the students were only at the school for a very brief period of time. The continuous turnover of the student body made systematic teaching and regular academic progress "almost impossible."[15]

One reason for the high degree of fluctuation in the student population was that the various liberation groups in Dar es Salaam were working to secure scholarships for refugee students—either in Africa or abroad. For that reason, many of the students soon came to see the school as "a kind of academic waiting room," where they could pass the time while FRELIMO leaders arranged scholarships for them. John Eldridge, Regional Representative of the African-American Institute in Dar es Salaam, noted that one of the problems refugee students faced was that the "academic waiting room" they encountered in Dar es Salaam followed them abroad. Fortunate to have secured a scholarship to the United States (often at Lincoln University in Philadelphia or Rochester University in New York), many refugees discovered that they were not ready to enter a university—often due to a lack of proficiency in the English language. Students who received scholarships and then left the city of waiting expected that they would begin their university education immediately. They therefore found this academic delay not only disheartening but, according to Eldridge, refugee/students abroad found themselves once again in a position of insecurity.[16] In this way, exile was, as Edward Said observed, a "permanent state," as the multiple layers of exile—the various forms that exile took—followed students geographically.[17] This notion of permanency, however, revolved around their educational advancement; students *hoped* to attain a scholarship abroad and did not fear being physically in exile as much as they feared a stalled education. In this way, the purpose of being in exile was intimately linked with ideas of permanency: one had to have a purpose (and to be serving the liberation movement through that purpose) to avoid being in permanent exile.

Faced with such challenges, in late 1963 the staff at the Institute implemented a series of changes in order to improve the academic rigor of the school. Teachers instituted entrance examinations. Consequently, many of the weaker students were dropped. Next, the school adopted a uniform admissions procedure. For the first time, teachers began to use syllabi prescribed for Tanzanian schools. Through these measures, the school achieved an impressive faculty to student ratio of eleven-to-one. By January 1964, the school had a total student enrollment of one hundred, and was looking to expand.[18] To aid in this expansion, and to keep refugee students from settling throughout the city (i.e., unmonitored and uncontrolled), the Tanzanian government allocated a twenty-acre plot of land where another school, Kurasini, was built. In building Kurasini, refugee students provided all of the labor. By the end of the year, the school had two hundred and fifty students and a total staff of thirteen teachers.[19] John Eldridge believed Kurasini offered a sound, rational approach to refugee education because the school's program helped "convert worthy human beings from a liability to their hosts into an asset for all of Africa."[20] Eldridge's words reveal that, in Dar es Salaam in the 1960s, the ability of an exile to secure an education determined whether their host society conceptualized of their presence as a burden or a boon.

The Education of Exiles and the Mozambique Institute

It is important to understand the history of the African-American Institute—and its associated Project Tanganyika—because they set one example for the ways in which the Mozambique Institute might structure refugee education in Dar es Salaam. There was also considerable overlap between the two institutes: eventually, many refugee students lived at the Mozambique Institute but attended the African-American Institute's Kurasini School. Nonetheless, in its early years the Mozambique Institute was beset with a range of problems, most of which stemmed from linguistic barriers and a lack of funding.

The grant from the Ford Foundation that the Mondlanes received in 1963 provided funding to open and operate the Mozambique Institute in Dar es Salaam for the first year. With the grant, the Mondlanes were able to build a boarding house where young Mozambican refugees could live while they attended local, Tanzanian secondary schools. However, much like the linguistic problems the African-American Institute faced two years earlier, this immediately became problematic. In its first year, the fifty refugee students housed at the boarding school spoke different languages. Students had varying educational backgrounds as well. This was due to the fact that many of the students who arrived at the Institute had attended school (almost always missionary education) prior to leaving Mozambique, while other exiles had not had any formal education prior to leaving. Such varying experiences back in Mozambique often meant that students ranged in age from seven or eight years old to their early twenties. Substantial fluctuations in student demographics stemmed, in part, from Portugal's notorious neglect of African education in colonial Mozambique. In 1962–1963, official statistics estimated 373,978 African students in preprimary school throughout Mozambique, 20,869 in primary school, and 119 in secondary schools. G. Mennen Williams (then Assistant Secretary of State for African Affairs) speculated that this "calculated policy" of denying Africans education had created an "intellectual wasteland" in Portugal's African territories.[21] Unable to attend university in Mozambique, African students had to study abroad—but while in 1962 there were more than one thousand students in the United States from Nigeria alone, there were only five students from *all* of Portuguese Africa (Angola, Guinea-Bissau, and Mozambique).[22]

Competition for a seat at the Mozambique Institute was severe. Those students who arrived without exposure to any formal schooling were often streamlined into the army, to serve as soldiers while in exile rather than students. Conversely, throughout the war FRELIMO soldiers sought out exceptional students still in Mozambique: they then transported students identified as talented to Dar es Salaam (and then, possibly, on to an education abroad). The pursuit of education thus began as exile, but that original exile begat other experiences of separateness. For example, because of the wide disparity in student capabilities, rather than send students to Tanzanian schools, the Mondlanes decided that the Institute itself would be a secondary school, though one that would follow a Mozambican curriculum and use Portuguese as the medium of instruction.[23] Here, then, we see liberation leaders intentionally distancing local hosts from refugee students. That Mozambican students attended their own school, where the curriculum revolved around a language that many Tanzanians did not speak, reveals the varying degrees of apartness in exile: students were initially separated from their homes in Mozambique, then from their hosts in Tanzania, and eventually from one another as they received scholarships abroad.

Student accommodations reflected such apartness. By September 1965, ninety-two students from the Mozambique Institute lived in hostels at the African-American Institute's Kurasini School. The inability of the Mozambique Institute to provide students with accommodation at their own school reveals one of the ways students remained separated not only from the host society but from one another—from the Mozambican exile community—as well. Some refugee students lived at Kurasini, some in the boarding house at the Mozambique Institute, some at the nearby Mgulani refugee camp, and many were scattered throughout the city. Moreover, students and teachers alike were dispersed throughout Dar es Salaam, finding accommodation where they could. While in the city of waiting, exiles found themselves in multiple layers of apartness.

Beyond accommodation, students faced a variety of difficulties. One was simply a change in environment, which was usually more severe if the student had only very recently left Mozambique. Because many of the refugees came from rural Mozambique, one of the teachers at the Mozambique Institute, Ruth Minter, observed that "being in a city at all [was] new. For the others there [was] at least the newness of *this* city."[24] Most refugee students were in their teens. Some came to Dar es Salaam with their parents, some with friends, others came alone. Teachers not only had to educate students, they had to provide a support system for the displaced as well.

Another difficulty facing students was the Institute's expectations of them. Many students had attended schools in Mozambique (mainly mission schools), but the Institute was a very different type of institution. The staff expected students to acquire an education so that, after Mozambique achieved independence, they could fill positions in the new government, teach in the schools, and fill technical positions throughout Mozambique. According to Ruth and Bill Minter, both American teachers at the Institute, students had to be reminded that their school performance was, to some extent, a "measure of their dedication to the movement for liberation."[25] As such, their education-in-exile not only provided an opportunity for students in the present; it could determine future status. Given the inadequacy of their education in Portuguese East Africa, many students found this expectation overwhelming. But it did induce them to study harder: if a student's dedication to the liberation movement could be measured by their academic success, receiving a scholarship abroad would demonstrate ultimate devotion. In this way, both students as well as the political leadership came to see the Mozambique Institute as the educational arm of the military front, FRELIMO.

A third difficulty faced by students and teachers alike was the inadequacy of resources. Several factors contributed to this problem. For one, much like the African-American Institute, the Mozambique Institute largely relied on volunteer teachers. Because of this, the teaching staff became quite cosmopolitan. By October 1966, the staff had become "fairly international:" eight African Mozambicans, three white Mozambicans, a Czech teacher, a German secretary, an Indian business manager, a Swedish tutor, a part-time American English teacher, as well as Ruth and Bill Minter.[26] This cosmopolitan composition meant that donations and supplies tended to be international as well. School supplies consisted of items from many different countries, thus in several different languages. The medium of instruction was Portuguese, but the Institute had very few books in Portuguese. Indeed, half of those books were math and science textbooks—not only quite outdated but usually beyond the academic level of the students as well.[27] There were two children's science kits with instructions and labels in German, which only the German teacher could translate. Ultimately, if a teacher could not translate a particular text, it became an unusable resource.[28] The library had many books in French and Italian, but no one could translate them and so they remained unusable and unused.

Another problem the students faced was that the teaching pool had an exceptionally quick turnover. In part, this high teacher-turnover rate was due to the fact that the Institute used refugee students who were in the "academic waiting room" (i.e., awaiting scholarships abroad) as volunteer teachers. Indeed, many of the teachers were older students waiting for overseas scholarships, who left the Institute after they received them.[29] Many refugee students entered the Institute already having been promised (usually either by FRELIMO or by the Mozambique Institute) that they would receive scholarships for university study abroad. To solidify their scholarship, they would first need to tutor other refugee students.[30] Here we see quite clearly the scaffolding of liberation education: turnover rates in the student body mirrored those in the teacher population because they were one and the same. Refugee education was an exile intentionally perpetuated and extended abroad, often to major hubs of other exiles, as Susan Dabney Pennybacker's chapter in this volume demonstrates. By the end of 1965, there were one hundred thirty Mozambican students enrolled in universities in the United States, the USSR, Hungary, Czechoslovakia, Yugoslavia, Algeria, England, Switzerland, Romania, Belgium, India, and Portugal.[31] Much like the teaching staff, through the Mozambique Institute the refugee student population became exceptionally cosmopolitan.

Student Life at the Mozambique Institute

Compared to the tens of thousands of Mozambicans displaced during the war for independence, those who attended the Institute were by far the more fortunate ones. The Institute provided housing, clothing, and three meals every day to all students. Catholic Relief Services (CRS) continually donated bulk quantities of dry milk and grains, as well as large shipments of medical supplies. Music, sports, and recreation were a substantial part of the Institute's program. Some of the students were members of the Kurasini football team, while the Institute itself had several volleyball teams, which held intra-institute competitions. In her 1965 annual report, Janet Mondlane wrote that she and the staff had "discovered considerable talent among the students" who performed on "the guitar, drums, and penny-whistle."[32] Every Saturday evening, the Institute held film screenings for students.

Despite such amenities, staff at the Mozambique Institute regarded the duration of a student's exile in Dar es Salaam as an opportunity for them to harness certain behaviors, namely those qualities the liberation movement desired as ideal in its future citizens. For example, the Institute instilled discipline and a sense of hierarchy among its students.[33] The staff established a student government in order to instill leadership qualities in the students and to facilitate the discipline and running of the hostels. Here we see the appendages of a government in exile—the building blocks of what would become an independent government. At the beginning of each term, the students elected a Prefect, who was chairman of the student government. They also elected a representative for every ten students. The Prefect and the representatives worked with the staff to supervise all student activities. Both male and female elected representatives were in charge of running the hostels. They delegated the tasks of cleaning the kitchen, dining rooms, and library, and they assigned to each student a quota of chores, which rotated on a weekly basis.[34] At the Institute, regimented discipline undergirded refugee education. By 1968, Janet Mondlane noted that daily life at the Institute had become "more linked with the standards of discipline and government inside Mozambique—as much as possible a piece of Mozambique" in Tanzania.[35] FRELIMO leaders anticipated that students would import the order and obedience honed during exile upon their return to an independent Mozambique. According to Ruth Minter, Mozambicans at the Institute were "among the fortunate, with a sense of purpose—and concrete jobs to do, jobs that contribute to a movement."[36] This complicates the quintessential debate surrounding exile: "Exilium mors est" ("Exile is death") or "Exilium vita est" ("Exile is life").[37] Torn between these two extremes, experiences of exile emerge neither as be-all nor as end-all, but as more nuanced, as gradations along this spectrum.

The academic calendar of the Mozambique Institute also created a hierarchy within the refugee community. During academic breaks, students from the Institute worked at other refugee camps in Tanzania. For example, during the June 1965 holiday, fifty male students from the Mozambique Institute went to the refugee camp at Bagamoyo to teach literacy classes. During that same holiday, the Institute's female students reorganized the library, repaired the linens at both hostels, took sewing and cooking classes, and followed an informal program of independent readings.[38] These vignettes reveal a gendered exile experience. Only male students went to the Bagamoyo refugee camp and only male students taught there. The female students never taught at Bagamoyo; in fact, they remained at the Institute during breaks to take courses in cooking and sewing. This pattern repeated itself every year. Over the five-week December break in 1966, all of the male students went to work at the Bagamoyo refugee camp. They built a new primary school and helped with general repairs. Meanwhile, the female students cleaned and painted the Institute. They helped repair books and they organized the library.[39] Students practiced those behaviors and norms that the liberation movement hoped to export back home at independence. In this way, exile was also a process of (re)formation, an occasion to foster qualities that undergirded the citizenry of an independent African state. And yet, what possibly mattered more was *not* that female students attended to domestic/private tasks while male students taught in public spaces, but rather that the liberation movement (after centuries of educational neglect) enveloped women as integral to the struggle for education.

The Institute employed a hierarchical approach to refugee education, writ large. Students from the main refugee camp at Bagamoyo could pass their examinations and then transfer to the Mozambique Institute in Dar es Salaam, where they would enroll in the tutoring program and join others in the academic waiting room.[40] In this way, there was a strong incentive to study in the refugee camp: do well at Bagamoyo, and one might advance to the Mozambique Institute and, from there, secure a scholarship abroad. Nonetheless, there was a fundamental loophole in this system. Only those students who had obtained a significant level of education *before* arriving in Dar es Salaam (i.e., before leaving Mozambique) could pursue education as refugees. In other words, only the most qualified refugees could become *students*. John Gerhart, who worked in the schools at this time, explained that there were "not enough qualified refugees to fill the scholarships available."[41] This put the Mozambique Institute in a difficult position. FRELIMO soldiers recruited many of the students from inside Mozambique "because of their ability."[42] FRELIMO soldiers knew or learned of promising students, and transported them to the Institute in Dar es Salaam. Once there, the most advanced students could pursue their studies abroad, but those who did not excel would go off for military training.[43] This was problematic because most students did not want to be soldiers in the liberation struggle. Indeed, many hoped to secure scholarships so that they could *avoid* participating in the liberation struggle.[44]

This friction between these two essentialized roles—student *or* soldier—manifest itself in the upper echelons of FRELIMO's political leadership. In July 1963, one year after the various liberation groups unified, Paul J. Bayeke, Deputy Information Secretary for FRELIMO, wrote George Houser, "we have no money in our party. . . . [Would you] help me to get some food and fare from Dar es Salaam to America[?] Will you please find a scholarship for me?"[45] Again, we see the various layers or phases of liberation exile: from Mozambique, to Dar es Salaam, and possibly onward to the United States. But the correspondence between Houser and Bayeke reflects a larger problem that confronted FRELIMO: many members of FRELIMO would rather have attained scholarships so that they did not have to fight in the war for liberation. Eduardo Mondlane was well aware of this. In January 1964, he admitted to Houser, "Some of our best young men prefer to be students than political workers."[46] Indeed, FRELIMO had to ensure that a fine line distinguished soldiers from students. Education could not trump liberation, yet at the same time many exiles hoped that education might enable them to avoid battle.

Transformations in Exile Education

This tension between needing soldiers to carry out a guerrilla war yet desiring to create an educated group who would lead an independent Mozambique irrevocably changed the nature of refugee education.[47] By March 1968, 144 students attended the Institute. At that time, Father Mateus Gwengere, who had arrived in Dar es Salaam from Mozambique in mid-1967, concluded that Eduardo Mondlane was not militant enough. Mondlane was moving too slowly, Gwengere told students at the Institute, which meant the war would be protracted and that many of them would eventually have to fight. Gwengere's speculations spread fear among the students. Hadn't their advanced academic standing insulated them from the possibility of fighting in the war for independence? Violence erupted at the Institute. Many students left Dar es Salaam, and FRELIMO was never able to account for their whereabouts.[48] The Institute closed for two-and-a-half years. By the time it reopened, its ideological foundations had changed substantially. Prior to the revolt, the Institute advocated individual academic achievement. The more advanced students worked as teachers until they received their scholarships and eventually left Dar es Salaam. After the revolt, however, the new school at Bagamoyo privileged self-reliance. The primary objective of the Institute became the creation of a self-sufficient body of students, so much so that, by 1970, the Institute tried to design the school at Bagamoyo so that it reflected the conditions *inside* Mozambique. In effect, the school tried to mimic life in rural Mozambique as much as possible. There was a well with a pump instead of running water. The students grew most of their own food. There was no electricity, bathrooms were outdoors, and students cooked over an open fire. All of this was an attempt to "make it easier to transport the school to Mozambique" at independence. Gone were the days of volleyball competitions, film screenings, and pennywhistle lessons. Despite this ideological revolution, there was still strong demand from students to attend the school. By 1971, there were over two hundred students attending the school at Bagamoyo, with another one hundred waiting to attend.[49] Education had not lost its luster. In fact, it is telling that the school had a larger student body (and longer wait list) when it tried to recreate the conditions of home. Were the initial conditions of exile—the first years of the school—too far removed from the realities of a Mozambique to which they would all return?

Almost fifty years after the war for liberation, it is eye-opening to examine the trajectories of those who graduated from the Mozambique Institute. Their accomplishments reveal the importance of exile education, of the alliances forged during exile, and of the processes involved in creating an educated political elite. Among those who attended the institute were Joaquim Chissano (future president of Mozambique, 1986–2005).[50] Armando Emílio Guebuza, president of Mozambique from 2005–2015, also served as a teacher at the Mozambique Institute. Antonio Palange (who acted as librarian at the Mozambique Institute, tutored students in history and geography, and taught Portuguese at all levels) went on to be a medical doctor. From 1994–1999, Palange served as a member of Parliament.[51] In November 2001, he founded a new political party, the Congresso dos Democratas Unidos, "aimed at promoting national reconciliation and a policy of understanding between the different ethnic and racial groups."[52] João Unyai also went on to become a physician—a profession many students went in to because the country sorely needed doctors at independence. Eduardo José Bacião Koloma worked with Guebuza at the Mozambique Institute. He went on to study at Karl Marx University in Leipzig, Germany, where he received a master's degree and then a doctorate in law in 1981. He returned to Mozambique to work with the Ministry of Foreign Affairs, then served on the United Nations General Assembly Sixth Commission (legal affairs) and was ambassador in Britain.[53] The cumulative trajectories of these men showcase the Institute's ability to use exile as a means to transform the perception of Mozambique as an "intellectual wasteland."

Conclusion

In the 1960s, the Mozambique Institute was the "only one of its kind" on the African continent.[54] A young organization that had no experience in settling or assisting refugees, the Mozambique Institute tried to provide education on a shoestring. But the goal of the Mozambique Institute was the continued education of refugees who were already qualified for secondary and university study. An architect carefully designed the Institute, which was run through a Board of Trustees. Janet Mondlane and the Board carefully selected students from among hundreds of applications, many of whom went on to attend universities in North America and Europe.

In the city of waiting, exile was tenuous: Dar es Salaam was (from the students' perspective) not the final destination within the total experience of exile. Refugee students hoped that they might teach other students until they received a scholarship, which might then send them to another place and through another phase of exile, as though in some way getting further and further away from home (geographically) would enable a faster (temporal) return to a liberated homeland. Such provisions and amenities, of course, were not made for the tens of thousands of refugees who settled in southern Tanzania during Mozambique's war for liberation. As such, the process of educating refugees in Dar es Salaam can be seen as a process of privileging the already privileged, of creating an elite in-exile.[55]

Notes

1. American Committee on Africa (ACOA) files at the Amistad Research Center; Box 142, file 40, "Tanzania Correspondence, January-April, 1964." Letter from Janet Mondlane to George Houser, April 3, 1964.

2. For interpretations of the war as a guerrilla insurgency, see: Thomas Henriksen, *Revolution and Counterrevolution: Mozambique's War of Independence, 1964–1974* (Westport, Connecticut: Greenwood Press, 1983); Barry Munslow, *Mozambique: The Revolution and Its Origins* (London: Longman Group, 1983); on the role of the apartheid state: João M. Cabrita, *Mozambique: The Tortuous Road to Democracy* (New York: Palgrave, 2001); as liberation through a Cold War lens, see: Vladimir Shubin, *The Hot Cold War: The USSR in Southern Africa* (London: Pluto Press, 2008): 119–150.

3. John D. Gerhart. "Dar es Salaam Becomes Center of Refugee Intrigue: Nine Exiled Regimes Have Headquarters in City," *The Crimson*; September 25, 1964. Note: Tanganyika achieved independence from the United Kingdom in December 1961. When Tanganyika merged with Zanzibar in April 1964, the country assumed the new name "Tanzania." For the sake of simplicity, I only use the term "Tanzania" throughout the chapter.

4. Bill Minter, *No Easy Victories: African Liberation and American Activists over a Half Century, 1950–2000* (Trenton: African World Press, 2007), 10.

5. Andrew Ivaska, "Movement Youth in a Global Sixties Hub: The Everyday Lives of Transnational Activists in Postcolonial Dar es Salaam," in *Transnational Histories of Youth in the Twentieth Century*, ed. Richard Ivan Jobs and David M. Pomfret (New York: Palgrave Macmillan Transnational History Series, 2015), 188–210.

6. On this relationship between empire and exile, see the chapters of Ruma Chopra and Aliou Ly, respectively.

7. The União Democrática Nacional de Moçambique (UDENAMO), the Moçambique National African Union (MANU), and the African National Union of Independent Mozambique (UNAMI).

8. ACOA, Box 142, file 35, "Tanzania Correspondence, 1961." Letter from Jaime Rivaz Sigauke, UDENAMO representative, to George Houser, April 24, 1961.

9. For more on the making of myth during exile, see: Liisa H. Malkki, *Purity and Exile: Violence, Memory and National Cosmology among Hutu Refugees in Tanzania* (Chicago: University of Chicago Press, 1995).

10. Letter from L. M. Millinga, MANU Administrative Secretary, to George Houser, July 5, 1961.

11. George Houser, *No One Can Stop the Rain: Glimpses of Africa's Liberation Struggle* (New York: Pilgrim Press, 1989), 183. Though the Mozambique Institute and FRELIMO were ideologically married, they were two separate entities. The Institute had its own budget, as well as its own Board of Trustees.

12. Portugal quickly contested the ethics behind the grant. The Portuguese Foreign Minister, Alberto Franco Nogueira, accused the Ford Foundation of using the grant to secretly finance FRELIMO. Nogueira's strong allegations prompted the Ford Foundation to cancel any further contributions.

13. The African-American Institute (or AAI, predecessor to the Africa-America Institute) was founded in 1953 by two American professors, Horace Mann Bond and William Leo Hansberry. Though the Institute initially sought to provide financial and social support to African students studying in the United States, by the early 1960s AAI had established several schools in newly independent African countries. That Bond was President of Lincoln University, a historically black institution, was one reason why so many students from Africa attended that particular university.

14. British National Archives, file FO317/176933, The African-American Institute Report on the Special Scholarships and Training Program, Dar es Salaam (May 1964), by John Eldridge, Jr. Also see Michael A. Samuels, "The FRELIMO School System," *Africa Today*, 18, no. 3 (July 1971): 69.

15. The African-American Institute Report (May 1964).

16. Ibid.

17. Edward Said. *Power, Politics, and Culture: Interviews with Edward W. Said* (New York, Vintage Press, 2002), 56. Of course, this begs the question whether exile is permanent or "transient;" see Vinay Lal, "Enigmas of Exile: Reflections on Edward Said," *Economic and Political Weekly* 40, no. 1 (Jan. 1–7, 2005): 30.

18. The African-American Institute Report, (May 1964).

19. Gerhart, "Dar es Salaam Becomes Center of Refugee Intrigue."

20. The African-American Institute Report (May 1964).

21. NARA Box 44. File General Reports Mozambique. Confidential memo to Governor Harriman from Mennen Williams, undated, "Education in Mozambique and Consul General Wright's Final Roundup Report—Information Memorandum."

22. Oberlin College Archives. Box 1, Series II, Part 2. Acc. 30/307. Letter to Mr. Lysacht J. M. Mbhalati from Eduardo Mondlane, April 29, 1962.

23. ACOA, Box 92, file 36, "The Mozambique Institute."

24. Register of the US National Student Association, International Commission Records, 1966–1967. Box 283, file "The Mozambique Institute" at the Hoover Archives. Letter from Ruth and Bill Minter, October 1966. Emphasis in the original.

25. Register of the US National Student Association, October 1966.

26. Ibid.

27. Ibid.

28. Ibid.

29. Ibid.

30. ACOA, Box 142, file 44, Memo titled "Report" from the Mozambique Institute, September 1, 1965.

31. Ibid.

32. Ibid.

33. Christian A. Williams elaborates on the ways in which liberation movements relied on such spaces to discipline future citizens in "Ordering the Nation: SWAPO in Zambia, 1974–1976," *Journal of Southern African Studies* 37, no. 4 (December 2011): 693–713. According to Williams, "Repeatedly, camps were the sites where conflicts emerged and through which liberation movement officials, together with host governments, disciplined their members" (712–713).

34. Memo titled "Report" from the Mozambique Institute, September 1, 1965.

35. ACOA, Box 142, file 52, "Tanzania Correspondence January-April, 1968." Letter from Janet Mondlane to George Houser, April 20, 1968.

36. Register of the US National Student Association, October 1966.

37. Banished from Rome by Augustus in 8AD, the poet Ovid declared, "Exilium mors est" ("Exile is death"). By contrast, Victor Hugo found exile "rejuvenating." Lal contends that, unlike Ovid, Hugo may have claimed, "Exilium vita est" ("Exile is life"). From Lal, "Enigmas of Exile," 32.

38. Memo titled "Report" from the Mozambique Institute, September 1, 1965.

39. Register of the US National Student Association, October 1966.

40. Memo titled "Report" from the Mozambique Institute, September 1, 1965.

41. Gerhart. "Dar es Salaam Becomes Center of Refugee Intrigue."

42. Ibid.

43. In particular, they went to military training camps in Algeria, or at several locations in Tanzania.

44. File FO371/176933, "Interview given by Mrs. Mondlane to the Syracuse Herald Journal on the Mozambique Liberation Front," at the British National Archives. Memo from Margaret Bryan.

45. ACOA, Box 142, file 39, "Tanzania Correspondence, July-December 1963." Letter from Paul J. Bayeke to George Houser, July 4, 1963.

46. Letter from Eduardo Mondlane to George Houser, January 16, 1964.

47. Use of the word "desiring" here is highly debatable. Of increasing interest to historians is whether (or the degree to which) African liberation movements wanted intellectuals among their rank and file. See Christian A. Williams. "Ordering the Nation: SWAPO in Zambia, 1974–1976," *Journal of Southern African Studies* 37, no. 4 (December 2011): 693–713. According to Williams, SWAPO leadership told exiles that they were suspicious of intellectuals and that "SWAPO was a movement of illiterate people" (696). Williams found that exiles told SWAPO leadership: "Our wish, in fact our decision, is that each and everybody of us be trained militarily before he/she pursues any ordinary academic studies" (697). The tension between academic study and military training and the ways in which liberation groups managed such tensions requires further research.

48. Michael A. Samuels, "The FRELIMO School System," *Africa Today* 18, no. 3 (July 1971): 70. For more on the student rebellion at the Mozambique Institute, see Michael G. Panzer, "The Pedagogy of Revolution: Youth, Generational Conflict, and Education in the Development of Mozambican Nationalism and the State, 1962–1970," *Journal of South African Studies* 35, no. 4 (December, 2009): 803–820.

49. Houser, *No One Can Stop the Rain*, 193–194.

50. Memo titled "Report" from the Mozambique Institute, September 1, 1965.

51. Mozambique FAST Update 4, September-November 2001 by Roland Dittli, MA: 5; published in Berne by the Swiss Peace Foundation, Institute for Conflict Resolution.

52. João Gomes Cravinho and Markus Scheuermaier, "Mozambique—Recent History," in *Africa South of the Sahara* (London and New York: Routledge, 2002), 705.

53. *Mozambique Political Process Bulletin*, Issue 45, February 1, 2010.

54. Gerhart. "Dar es Salaam Becomes Center of Refugee Intrigue."

55. On this, see Aijaz Ahmad, who is critical of the intellectual in exile, or "refugee intellectuals," who according to Ahmad celebrate postcolonial theory but neglect any mention of class and their status as the privileged, as elites. From Lal, "Enigmas of Exile," 30–34.

8 Amilcar Cabral and the Bissau Revolution in Exile

Women and the Salvation of the Nationalist Organization in Guinea, 1959–1962

Aliou Ly

DEPORTATION AND EXILE are often conventionally viewed as two sides of the same coin, namely the forced removal of local political, social or cultural leaders, or the displacement of entire groups, from their homelands. During the colonial period, European powers employed deportation and exile to silence local political, religious, and sociocultural resistance. The physical stress and mental duress that resulted from these harsh practices led many Africans to associate deportation and exile with punishment. Much of the literature related to deportation and exile focuses on the harsh conditions in which the deported and the exiled lived, and how they died, often alone, in foreign places. Deportation, however, was not universally harsh: for some, the experience of exile delivered (usually unanticipated) political, social, or cultural advantages. As Sana Camara's chapter in this volume notes, Cheikh Ahmadu Bamba, the founder of Mouridism in Senegal, asked his followers to commemorate the day he received his order for deportation to Gabon from the French.[1] A similar story of exile occurred during Portuguese Guinea's struggle for independence.

In colonial Guinea-Bissau or Portuguese Guinea, the Partido Africano da Independencia da Guine e Cabo Verde (PAIGC) and its leader, Amilcar Cabral, hoped that worker strikes would force the Portuguese to begin negotiations toward independence. Instead, with the colonial massacre of strikers at Pidgiguiti in 1959, nationalist Portuguese Guineans and Cape Verdeans realized they needed to change their strategy. They called for self-exile, mirroring the behavior of the Sanwi in Côte d'Ivoire, as described by Thaïs Gendry in this volume, and the Ohori in Dahomey in the early 1900s.[2] And like Kate Skinner's discussion of Togoland nationalists in this volume, in exile they found a louder voice and new resources. The Portuguese Guinean self-exile in the Republic of Guinea was not an isolated case of positive outcome; as Skinner attests in her chapter, the five thousand seven hundred people who left Ghana in the summer of 1960 for Togo because of fear of persecution gained protection and assistance from the Togolese government.

In this chapter, I argue that self-exile in the Republic of Guinea shaped and influenced how the PAIGC conducted itself. The PAIGC benefited from its self-exile in at least three areas. First, at the most basic level, the PAICG leaders avoided arrest and surrender, but they also found a safe place to organize in the neighboring Republic of Guinea or former French Guinea. The Republic of Guinea, its capital Conakry, and its first president Sekou Touré became symbols of African resistance to colonialism. It was also thrust into the center of anticolonial and pan-Africanist mobilization from all over the continent as was from 1957 Kwame Nkrumah's capital, Accra.[3] The Republic of Guinea, after its independence in 1958, became for African nationalists what Britain in the post-World War era was for Afro-Caribbeans, South Asians, and Southern Africans, as demonstrated by Susan Dabney Pennybacker in this volume. Second, their relocation permitted the development of alliances. As a result of these alliances, the Portuguese Guinean nationalists witnessed the importance of women's participation and roles in pre- and postindependence Republic of Guinea. Third, besides joining forces with other nationalist organizations, Cabral also fostered alliances between the PAIGC and the sociocultural organizations of Portuguese Guineans living in neighboring countries. Most of these organizations were less politically oriented and functioned more as avenues through which Portuguese Guineans tried to maintain various social and cultural connections. Francisca Pereira remembered that when she joined the PAIGC as one of the first women members, she joined through their sociocultural organization. A youth without political awareness, she joined the party because her social organization joined forces with the PAIGC. "The only thing I knew was our country was occupied by the Portuguese. It was Cabral's first wife, Maria Helena Vihena Rodrigues, who explained to me and other young Portuguese Guineans whenever we visited her what colonialism was and its implications in our daily lives."[4] Most importantly, not only did self-exile help the PAIGC to survive, it also created the opportunity for women to meaningfully be included in its membership, and even within its leadership. This newly adopted attitude of inclusion of women fostered the evolution of PAIGC to the extent that it was able to prepensely change its future culture and customs towards women.

According to Francisca Pereira, the PAIGC, newly relocated in Conakry, Republic of Guinea, witnessed the ability of Democratic Party of Guinea/African Democratic Rally (PDG/RDA) women to mobilize and decided to add women's mobilization to its own agenda.[5] Guinean women participated in the Guinean independence movement by developing nationalist songs, slogans, uniforms, and symbols. They participated in the PDG/RDA, reinforcing the party structure and challenging gender expectations within the party.[6] The women of the Republic of Guinea played a key role in the 1958 referendum by supporting the country's independence and refusing to let France determine the country's future or political agenda.[7] For a long time, they were the main force behind president Touré's political agenda.[8] For Elizabeth Schmidt, masses of women became really involved in politics only during the RDA/PDG general strike in 1953 where they provided material assistance and community mobilization. Sekou Touré and the RDA/PDG leadership recognized the masses' political potential by 1953 and started to call on them. By 1955, French officials recognized Guinean women's roles.[9] But how precisely was the RDA able to mobilize the masses of women? If the early group of women political participants joined the nationalists because they were married to nationalist leaders, nonelite women joined the nationalist organizations without intending to challenge sociotraditional structures or gender roles.[10] The majority of women identified themselves as proud child-bearers, family caregivers and guardians of the social order. They played a key role in the fight for the independence from the French.

Conakry as a Hub of Anticolonialism and Pan-Africanism

Early in 1958, President Charles De Gaulle, in a desperate attempt to save the French-dominated community, proposed a new constitution. On September 28, 1958, French citizens throughout the empire voted on the new constitution in a referendum. For Africans, a "yes" vote meant remaining in a French-dominated community; a "no" vote indicated a choice for independence and control of their own destiny. Guineans under the leadership of Sekou Touré, the general secretary of the Democratic Party of Guinea/African Democratic Rally overwhelmingly voted "no" by 94 percent.[11] The Guinean response to the referendum was unique among French territories in Africa.

When French Guinea suddenly became independent, Africans from all over the continent and beyond relocated to Conakry for political, economic, or social—even sentimental—reasons. African nationalists and anticolonialists from Asia, the Caribbean, and the Americas moved to Conakry, either to help build the newly independent country or to use Conakry as a hiding place in which to organize their own struggles for independence. The Union of the Peoples of Cameroon organized its rebellion from Conakry after being forced into exile.[12] Exiles from Portuguese Guinea formed social and political organizations with Africans of many political persuasions in the new hub of anticolonial machinations.[13]

As the capital city of one of the first sub-Saharan African countries to gain independence, Conakry played a key role in anticolonial struggles for

African nationalists seeking refuge and a place to organize themselves and receive training.[14] Kwame Nkrumah, who had led the British Gold Coast to independence in 1957, relocated to Conakry after the 1966 military coup. Conakry was not alone in that role. As Jo Tague's chapter in this volume demonstrates, Dar es Salaam became the home to Mozambican revolutionaries fighting against Portuguese rule. Accra, the capital of Ghana—the first sub-Saharan British colony to achieve independence—was also a breeding ground for anticolonial movements and pro-Africa sentiments.[15] Susan Pennybacker affirms that Lusaka, capital city of Zambia, was a second home to many Southern Rhodesians and South Africans during their years of struggle for independence, or a stop off on the way to London.

PDG/RDA Women and the French Guinea Independence Struggle

In Conakry, the PAIGC and Amilcar Cabral witnessed the significant roles Guinean women played during the pre-independence period. Following the creation of the RDA (African Democratic Rally) in 1946 in Bamako (French Soudan), women of Guinea joined the PDG/RDA nationalist movement as mothers and wives before being influenced later by the PDG's political goals and strategies.[16] In Guinea, the widespread mobilization of women begun by Touré's PDG/RDA in 1953 resulted by 1954 in the mobilization in lower Guinea alone of more than six thousand female members.[17] Touré and other African nationalist leaders from French colonies, persons such as Lamine Guèye, had recognized the importance of women's political participation in independence movements, especially as mobilizing agents. In 1953, French Guinean women had, of their own initiative, rallied around the strikers in French West Africa and their families by providing care, food, and militant support. This now legendary participation led Touré and nationalist organizations in French Guinea to see the unavoidable need to mobilize and recruit women into their party. This move was crucial because women's participation led to the legislative victory of the PDG/RDA in 1954 and to Guinea's unique "no" vote on the French referendum of 1958.

The implication of the mass participation of women in political matters was not something new in French colonized territories. Before World War II, under the leadership of Lamine Guèye, the Senegalese contingent of the French Section of the International Workers Organization, affiliated with the French Socialist Party (Section Française de l'Internationale Ouvriére (SFIO)), championed women's emancipation in the colonies in recognition of women's support of Guèye's political career.[18] The Brazzaville Conference followed the creation of the Senegalese contingent of the SFIO in January 1944. During the conference, delegates insisted on the need to protect and implement women's rights, condemned polygyny and child marriage, and recognized women's roles in resistance movements. They also made a proposal for equal rights for women in colonial society, a proposal that led to granting women the right to vote for the first time in metropolitan elections in 1945.[19] In 1945, Fily Dabo Sissoko, a French Soudanese leader of the French-Soviet Union Association/French West Africa Section (Association France-URSS/Section de L'AOF), reiterated the same appeal for the emancipation of women, thereby mirroring changes in France.[20] Throughout French West Africa, women participated actively in nationalist and political struggles and helped organize mass protests. For example, on December 21, 1949 in Côte d'Ivoire, a group of women members of the Democratic Party section of the African Democratic Rally (Party Démocratique de Côte d'Ivoire/Rassemblement Démocratique Africain (PDCI/RDA), under the leadership of Ouezzin Coulibaly, organized a demonstration in Grand Bassam against the arrest of eight of their political leaders. French colonial repression was brutal against these women.[21] Four years later, the French Guinean women showed their aptitude in participating in organized strikes by helping strikers and their families.

A new women's organization formed in 1954 in French Guinea, within the Democratic Party of Guinea/African Democratic Rally. This new organization was peculiar because of the absence of Western-educated women on the board. They were women from the masses. The new president, Mafory Bangoura, was a cloth dyer "without formal schooling."[22] By August 1954, the organization had six thousand female members in lower Guinea, of which four thousand eight hundred resided in Conakry.[23] In October 1954, according to Schmidt, "Sekou Touré proclaimed that 'the women have constituted a vast movement that is worrying our adversaries.' They were the force behind many of the newly created neighborhood and village committees and that expanded membership drives."[24]

Given the PAIGC's pre-exile mentality and ideology, women would most likely never have been recruited. During the pre-exile period, 1956–September 1959, the PAIGC leadership believed for safety reasons women must be left out of the party membership.[25] Thus, exile allowed the PAIGC and Cabral physical safety, made possible new alliances, and, most importantly, gave them new perspectives on the roles and possible contributions of women in the anticolonial fight. In other words, exile created the gendered opportunity for the Portuguese Guinean nationalists to be successful later. To understand how the PAIGC self-exile led to the opening of women's membership in the party, it is important to visit the PAIGC agenda during the 1956–1959 period.

PAIGC The Early Years, 1956–1959: Existing in Bissau (Portuguese Guinea)

In 1956, Africans with Cabo Verdean and Portuguese Guinean origins in Bissau clandestinely organized the *Partido Africano da Independencia da Guine e Cabo Verde*. The party set as its main goals the immediate territorial independence of Portuguese Guinea and the Cape Verde Islands, the democratization and emancipation of African populations, the achievement of rapid economic development, and social and cultural advancement for their peoples.[26] Between 1956–1959, the PAIGC attempted to organize workers into unions and to use those units as leverage to force the Portuguese to negotiate for the independence of the colony. Amilcar Cabral and other nationalists believed the petty bourgeoisie would be the engine of the nationalist movement.[27] The revolutionary movements needed to mobilize the "middle classes" to support its project.[28]

Between 1956–1959, the PAIGC infiltrated the ports and other spaces of state employment in order to organize workers and encourage them to demand better living and working conditions. It was because of these demands that the Pidgiguiti massacre happened.[29] We know a lot about Cabral's ideological orientation because he was a prolific author. From Cabral's perspective, class interests and experiences played a crucial role in politicizing the masses. The foremost achievement of the PAIGC organization was the construction of a working-class base for the party in urban Portuguese Guinea. The PAIGC aided in the creation of a clandestine trade union, the *União Nacional dos Trabalhadores da Guine* (UNTG), which under the influence of the PAIGC organized a series of workers' strikes throughout 1958. These strikes culminated in the Pidgiguiti Massacre of August 3, 1959, in which fifty dockworkers were killed and twenty-one sentenced to five years in prison.[30]

After the massacre, the PAIGC realized that the so-called Portuguese Guinea *petite bourgeoisie* was not a reliable force for the PAIGC as they were more interested in protecting their socioeconomic conditions, and for that reason they were more amenable to making deals with the colonial administration.[31] The tragedies at Pidgiguiti also pushed Cabral and his followers to embark on an armed struggle from September 19, 1959.[32]

When scholar Stephanie Urdang states that the involvement of women was a goal from the very beginning, I interpret that she is referring to the period when the PAIGC decided to give up secrecy and become visible after the 1959 dockworkers massacre.[33] Because when the party was clandestine, it was not mobilizing the masses or sending political mobilizers into the countryside. During the 1956–1959 period before the Pidjiguiti massacre, the PAIGC was a secret political organization and did not advocate women's membership. For example, Carmen Pereira found out about the existence of the PAIGC sometime in 1956–1957. According to her, the PAIGC did not have female members because of the belief that "if you want to keep a secret, you should not tell your secret to a woman because women are talkative."[34] This affirmation corresponds to a stereotype and excuse used to explain the practice of the PAIGC to isolate female members and to continue the discrimination Portuguese Guinean women had been facing within their sociocultural structures and organization. According to Bacar Cassama, the rejection of women's membership stemmed from long-standing beliefs about the place of women in traditional Portuguese Guinean sociocultural beliefs. Portuguese Guinean women should prepare themselves to be housewives and agents of reproduction.[35] This traditional Portuguese Guinean sociocultural belief regarding women as nonpolitical agents would be challenged as soon as the PAIGC relocated to Conakry, Republic of Guinea.

Cabral's Self-Exile and the Reshaping of the PAIGC, 1959–1962

Self-exile saved PAIGC leaders from arrests, allowed the party to develop new alliances with African nationalist organizations, and finally helped the PAIGC to link with the Portuguese Guinean diaspora living outside of Portuguese Guinea. However, most importantly, being in Conakry gave women the opportunity for participation and involvement. The new PAIGC strategy or attitude of inclusion of women allowed the party to see the need to change its old sociocultural views about women.

During the early period of self-exile, 1960–1961, the PAIGC had limited members and recruits in Conakry, and the movement lacked financial resources, weapons, and international support or contacts.[36] For some time the house in which Cabral and his wife lived was the PAIGC headquarters and their resources and income were the party funds. More significantly, none of the party members had had political experience in the countryside and none had any knowledge of armed struggle.[37]

The first group of self-exiles consisted of the PAIGC leadership, Amilcar Cabral, his wife Maria Helena Vihena Rodrigues, and his brother Luiz Cabral, who arrived in Conakry during the last quarter of 1959.[38] Exiles from the early, 1959–1962 period may be divided into several groups. Members of the first group had been in the party since the mid-1950s and had been in charge of nationalist agitation in the Republic of Guinea. They were all from educated middle-class families, and many of them were Cape Verdeans or of Cape Verdean background. The second group included a substantial number of Portuguese Guineans from Portuguese Guinea, "Assimilados [civilized] conscripts," who participated in the Pidgiguiti strikes or deserted from the Portuguese army and made their way to Conakry, Republic of Guinea.

A third group comprised young Portuguese Guineans in their late teens and early twenties from urban centers. Most of them were from indigenous or Portuguese Guinean backgrounds.[39]

> At first [Young Portuguese Guineans] came to urban centers—from that section of the society, which Cabral defined as the *déclassés*. Many of them had only recently migrated to the towns in search of employment and usually lived with relatives. They had little prospect of finding jobs and most of them were involved in petty trade or other marginal occupations that had often led to their harassment by colonial authorities.[40]

During the last quarter of 1959, a handful of members of the PAIGC left Bissau for Conakry. Before the creation of PAIGC, Bacar Cassama was working in a colonial administration farming research institute in Bissau, and Amilcar Cabral had taken a job as an agronomist in Portuguese Guinea in 1952. During Cabral's work at the Bissau farm he met Bacar Cassama in 1954 and convinced him to prepare for a later struggle.[41] The history of the PAIGC during these years and afterwards was tumultuous.

As Patrick Chabral recounts, "in 1960, the PAIGC had no weapons, no financial resources and no international contacts. It had no experience of political mobilization, little knowledge of military matters and only the faintest notion of what the Portuguese Guinean countryside was like."[42] The party's self-exile in Conakry, Republic of Guinea would be a most instructive and enriching period for the party.[43] Conakry allowed the PAIGC to build schools for their political mobilizers and the Portuguese Guineans who joined the movement after 1959. Cabral and the PAIGC had the opportunity to deepen their strategic and theoretical knowledge and build new alliances with émigré Portuguese Guineans exiled in Republic of Guinea, and others from Luso-African territories and former French Guinea.

Beyond the fact that exile allowed the PAIGC to carry out its goals, the party was able to gain strength and deepen its strategic and theoretical knowledge by a newfound ability to build alliances with other organizations. In Conakry, Cabral set up an exile organization, in which the PAIGC brought together exiles from Portuguese Guinea living in Conakry and Dakar, Senegal. In 1962, Cabral estimated that fifty thousand Portuguese Guineans had settled in the neighboring countries. With Henri Labery, leader of the Front for the Liberation of Portuguese Guinea and Cape Verde (FLGC), a political party that included more than thirty thousand Cabo Verdean exiles and émigrés from Portuguese Guinea, Cabral and others formed the FUL (United Front for the Liberation of Guinea and Cape Verde).[44]

In the same way that Cabral tried to unite all exiles and émigrés from Portuguese Guinea and Cape Verde living in neighboring countries, he also attempted to unite all nationalists from Luso-African colonies living in Conakry and elsewhere. He held the belief that all these struggles must be waged together in order to dilute the concentration of the Portuguese colonial army. Cabral's goal was achievable. In Conakry, there already existed the Movement for the Liberation of the Portuguese Colonies in Africa whose members were from Cape Verde, Mozambique, Angola, Portuguese Guinea, and São Tomé and Príncipe.[45] In Casablanca in April 1961, both Mozambique's FRELIMO and Angola's MPLA joined the PAIGC to create the Conference of Nationalist Organizations of the Portuguese Colonies (CONCP). The talks for the creation of the CONCP started in Conakry, and thus Cabral's relocation to Conakry was central.[46] The joining of forces between Luso-African nationalist organizations helped nationalist struggles strategize the anticolonial fight from a continental perspective, allowing almost all Portuguese colonies to open military fronts simultaneously and in a very short period of time. This kept pressure on the Portuguese army on multiple fronts by preventing the possibility of Portuguese forces concentrating in a single field of conflict. Liberation wars started in 1961 in Angola, in 1963 in Portuguese Guinea, and in 1964 in Mozambique.[47]

Thus, in exile, Portuguese Guinean nationalists of the PAIGC first discovered a safe place to organize their future struggles for independence. However, the place became less safe following the Portuguese invasion of 1970 and the Portuguese assassination of Amilcar Cabral in Conakry, Republic of Guinea-Bissau in 1973. The PAIGC party was then able to develop alliances with other nationalist groups and sociocultural organizations and benefited from their capacity for mobilization, experience, and financial organizations as these organizations could not prosper and were not allowed in Portuguese Guinea. These alliances led to the strengthening of the party's theories and strategies, which ultimately led to a fuller inclusion of women in the national liberation struggle.

The Inclusion of Women in the PAIGC's Political Agenda

The inclusion of women in the PAIGC and in the national struggle was one of the turning points in the movement. It occurred when the movement was in exile, after September 1959. Conakry, in the Republic of Guinea, was the first place that the PAIGC accepted female members because women were already members of certain sociocultural organizations and political movements that became allies of the party after 1960. When Francisca Pereira and Lucette Cabral joined the PAIGC headquarter's office as executive aides in 1960, they were merely respected and viewed as office workers who could bring nothing to the political struggles the party was facing because they were women. Pereira stated, "later, the party started to view the Democratic Party of Guinea/African Democratic Rally women's roles and participation in political mobilization and awareness, how women of the Republic of Guinea supported Sekou Touré, who personified the PDG/RDA ruling party and it was then that the PAIGC executive, mostly a male group, started to think about replicating the same model."[48] Then, after involuntarily accepting women who came from different groups from their previous alliances in Conakry, the PAIGC executive bureau, under Amilcar Cabral's leadership, became more and more interested in recruiting more female participation in Portuguese Guinea. Very shortly, Amilcar Cabral and the PAIGC executive organization came to realize that this was a positive move for their nationalist organization, since the first Portuguese Guinean countryside people who came to encounter the PAIGC mobilizers were women. They protected, helped hide, interacted with, and nourished the PAIGC mobilizers sent into the countryside during the early period of mobilization, 1960–1961.[49] As Urdang notes,

> At first few women attended the meetings called by the mobilizers; those who did relayed the message to the women of their village and encouraged them to attend. Attendance by women slowly increased. By the time I visited the country just over a decade later, men and women were attending meetings of the population in equal numbers. Half the speakers that I heard were women, who told me of their participation in the revolution and who spoke with confidence before hundreds of people.[50]

When women of Portuguese Guinea became members of the PAIGC, they had the support of at least Amilcar Cabral and the PAIGC executive bureau. Amilcar Cabral understood it was important to fight simultaneously for national independence and for gender equality. Without freeing women from the traditional sociocultural inequalities that kept them exploited, independence would not be complete.

For Amilcar Cabral political independence within an unequal sociocultural framework in which half of the population were not allowed to work outside of the household, were not independent economic agents, and whose chances of improving their lives was limited did not embody complete independence.[51] Portuguese Guinean women did not have access to land, higher education, or economic decision-making opportunities. Carmen Pereira, the daughter of the first Portuguese Guinean lawyer, said her father believed that when a woman knows how to write she should focus on learning how to run a house not to seek knowledge to get involved in administrative or economic activities that placed her in competition with men.[52] Amilcar Cabral had seen how the women of Guinea had to challenge the gender division that existed within the RDA/PDG in order to gain executive roles during the struggle for Guinean independence even though very few of them ever attained executive positions.[53] Following that model, in 1961 the PAIGC instructed its women members to create the Democratic Union of the Women of Guinea-Bissau (UDEMU), a women's organization committed to raising women's awareness of their conditions and opportunities and fighting for gender equality.[54]

It was very unusual to have a male leadership instructing the women to form a women's organization to fight for gender equality in Portuguese Guinea. The PAIGC benefitted from women's membership and participation in the national liberation struggle; not only did women help to mobilize, but often they also convinced their husbands, sons and brothers to join the fight.[55] Second, after the onset of armed struggle, women participated actively as transporters, carrying baskets full of weapons through the southern territories using market networks. During the war, the women fought, spied, and transported supplies, weapons, and wounded guerilla fighters. In 1966, the PAIGC decided to take women out of direct combat operations. Some women fighters such as Titina Silla refused to put down their guns, though, and continued to join male fighters in the battlefields.[56]

Without the ability to rethink the purpose of the movement, to meet new people, and to explore other possible organizational structures, Amilcar Cabral and the national liberation movement would most likely have followed historical patterns of using men as the main participants in the struggle for independence, relegating women to secondary roles as in Algeria.[57] During exile in Conakry, Amilcar Cabral and the PAIGC were able to reconsider the role women could play in the movement, by their observation of the roles played by PDG/RDA women in the Guinean national struggle for independence, their alliances with Luso-African nationalist groups, and the Conakry sociocultural organizations held by Portuguese Guineans men and women living in the newly independent Republic of Guinea.

The exile period was very beneficial in helping the PAIGC as this would have been impossible on Portuguese Guinean soil because of the harsh conditions imposed by the Portuguese colonial system and lack of financial and material support. Cabral himself taught in the PAIGC pilot school set in Conakry, Republic of Guinea, where he prepared his party political mobilizers before they left for the Portuguese Guinea countryside between 1960–1962 to mobilize peasants.[58] The PAIGC was able to build a secondary school in Conakry where Portuguese Guinean youth started their schooling before being sent to foreign countries for higher education.[59] From Conakry, the PAIGC was able to internationalize their national struggle through participation of women in political activism, which they did, for example, through UDEMU participation in the Pan African Women's Organization.[60]

Conclusion

Given the beneficial ways in which the PAIGC shifted its original policy of national struggle between 1956 and 1959 by choosing exile, Amilcar Cabral and the PAIGC saved and deepened their revolutionary movement. As a counternarrative to the failed nationalist exile movement that relocated to Togo from Ghana narrated by Skinner in this volume, exile for Cabral and the PAIGC created an opportunity for success. In 1956, the party and its founding members excluded women's participation in the unquestioned belief that "women are weak and can't keep a secret."[61] By the end of their exile, they had begun to recognize that "it would be impossible to win the fight without women's participation."[62]

Exile and deportation have heretofore been portrayed as moments of sadness and hardship; however, in the case of the PAIGC, the outcome of exile proved beneficial. Amilcar Cabral and PAIGC saved their lives and their organization, received help from Sekou Touré through his vice president Saifoulaye Diallo, and learned about mass mobilization, in particular, the mobilization of women via those of the RDA/PDG of Guinea. The national struggle for Portuguese Guinean independence might not have succeeded without the PAIGC's self-imposed exile and the resulting participation of women in the revolution. The most beneficial lesson acquired by the PAIGC during its self-exile period was when it created the opportunity for women to meaningfully be included in its membership. The newly adopted attitude fostered the evolution of the PAIGC and ended up being very useful to PAIGC political mobilizers during the early years of the struggle for independence.

Notes

Bissau was the former capital of Portuguese Guinea and is the capital of the Republic of Guinea-Bissau. Portuguese Guinea is also called the Portuguese colony of Guinea-Bissau. Guinea means the Republic of Guinea, which has Conakry as its capital city. The Republic of Guinea was a former French colony that became independent in 1958 under the leadership of Sekou Touré and the Democratic Party of Guinea/African Democratic Rally (PDG/RDA).

1. Cheikh Anta Babou, *Fighting the Greater Jihad; Amadu Bamba and the Founding of the Muridiyya of Senegal, 1853–1913*, (Athens; Ohio University Press, 2007).
2. Marcus Filippello, "Exile and the Kingdom: An African Community's Response to Early French Colonial Policies" (paper presented at the RIT Conable African Studies Symposium, Rochester, New York, April 2–4, 2015).
3. Meredith Terretta, "Cameroonian Nationalists Go Global: From Forest Maquis to Pan-African Accra," *Journal of African History* 51, no. 2 (2010): 189–191.
4. Francisca Pereira, interviews by author, Bissau, August 9 and 16, 2008.
5. Ibid.
6. Ibid.
7. Frederick Cooper, "Possibility and Constraint: African Independence in Historical Perspective," *Journal of African History* 49, no. 2 (2008): 168.
8. Elizabeth Schmidt, *Mobilizing the Masses: Gender, Ethnicity and Class in the Nationalist Movement in Guinea, 1939–1958*, (Portsmouth, NH: Heinemann, 2005). See also Lansiné Kaba, *Le "Non" de la Guinée á de Gaulle*, (Paris: Editions Chaka, 1989), 80–86; Pierre Messmer, *Après tant de batailles: Memoires*, (Paris: Albin Michel, 1992), 234; and Charles De Gaulle, *Memoirs of Hope: Renewal and Endeavor*, trans. Terence Kilmartin (New York: Simon & Schuster, 1972), 55.
9. Schmidt, *Mobilizing the Masses*, 117.
10. Schmidt, *Mobilizing the Masses*.
11. See Ruth Schachter Morgenthau, *Political Parties in French Speaking West Africa* (Oxford: Clarendon Press, 1964), 399; Edward Mortimer, *France and the Africans, 1944–1960: A Political History* (New York: Walker, 1969), 324; Virginia Thompson, "Niger," in *National Unity and Regionalism in Eight African States*, ed. Gwendolen M. Carter (Ithaca: Cornell University Press, 1966), 162; and Elizabeth Schmidt, *Cold War and Decolonization in Guinea, 1946–1958* (Athens: Ohio University Press, 2007), 157.
12. Richard Joseph, *Le mouvement nationaliste au Cameroun: Les origines sociales de l'UPC, 1946–1958* (Paris: Editions Karthala, 2000).

13. June Milne, *Kwame Nkrumah: The Conakry Years: His Life and Letters* (London: Zed Press, 1990).

14. See Meredith Terreta's chapter in this volume.

15. Harcourt Fuller, *Building the Ghanaian Nation-State: Kwame Nkrumah's Symbolic Nationalism* (New York: Palgrave MacMillan, 2014), chap. 7; David Birmingham, *Kwame Nkrumah: The Father of African Nationalism* (Athens: Ohio University Press, 1990).

16. Elizabeth Schmidt, "Cold War in Guinea: The Rassemblement Démocratique Africain and the Struggle over Communism, 1950–1958," *Journal of African* History 48, no. 1 (2007): 95–121.

17. Schmidt, *Mobilizing the Masses*, chap. 5.

18. *Journal de l'Afrique de L'Ouest Française (*Paris, France), April 1, 1939.

19. Morgenthau, *Political Parties,* 40

20. Fily Dabo Sissoko, *Profession de Foi* (Bamako: French Soudan-Imprimerie, 1945).

21. *Climats* Newspaper (Grand Bassam, Ivory Coast), January 19, 1950.

22. Schmidt, *Mobilizing the Masses,* 126.

23. Ibid.

24. Ibid.

25. Francisca Pereira, interviews by the author, Bissau, August 9 and 16, 2008.

26. Amilcar Cabral, *Revolution in Guinea* (London: Stage 1, 1969), 30; Basil Davidson, *The Liberation of Guinea: Aspects of an African Revolution* (Baltimore: Penguin Books, 1969), 32; Richard Gibson, *African Liberation Movements: Contemporary Struggles Against White Minority Rule* (Oxford: Oxford University Press, 1972), 253.

27. Cabral, *Revolution in Guinea,* 62, 64–66. See also Amilcar Cabral, *Return to the Source: Selected Speeches by Amilcar Cabral,* ed. Africa Information Service (New York: Monthly Review Press, 1973).

28. Firoze Manji and B. Fletcher Jr., "Amilcar Cabral and the Struggle of Memory Against Forgetting," in *Claim No Easy Victories: The Legacy of Amilcar Cabral,* ed. Firoze Manji and Bill Fletcher Jr. (Dakar: CODESRIA and Daraja Press, 2013), 6.

29. Bacar Cassama, interview by the author, Bissau, August 14, 2008.

30. Gibson, *African Liberation Movements,* 253.

31. For Amilcar Cabral on "the *petite bourgeoisie,*" see David Birmingham, "The Twenty-Seventh of May: An Historical Note on the Abortive 1977 'Coup' in Angola," *African Affairs* 77, no. 309 (1978): 554–564. See also Patrick Chabal, *Amilcar Cabral: Revolutionary Leadership and People's War* (Cambridge: Cambridge University Press, 1983), 174.

32. Richard Gibson, *African Liberation Movements,* 254; Chabal, *Amilcar Cabral,* 60; Amilcar Cabral, *Alguns Principios Do Partido* (Lisbon: Seara Nova, 1974), 43.

33. Urdang affirms; "Early in the first stage, PAIGC showed a consciousness of the fact that women's liberation had to be fought on two fronts—from above and from below." Stephanie Urdang, *Fighting Two Colonialisms: Women in Guinea Bissau* (New York: Monthly Review Press, 1979), 17.

34. During my interview with Carmen Pereira, she remembered how she found out about the PAIGC. She found documents and a PAIGC flag under the mattress. When she confronted her husband Umaro Djalo, he responded that she should not pursue the issue further and that women should not be aware of political activities because women could not keep secrets.

35. Carmen Pereira, interview by the author, Bissau, August 21, 2008.

36. Chabal, *Amilcar Cabral,* 60–61.

37. Ibid., 61.
38. Francisca Pereira, interviews by the author, Bissau, August 9 and 16, 2008.
39. Patrick Chabal, *Amilcar Cabral,* 61.
40. Ibid. For more interviews of these young militants see Gerard Chaliand, *Armed Struggle in Africa* (New York: Monthly Review Press, 1969), 53–60, 71–82; and Urdang, *Fighting Two Colonialisms,* 85–92, 142–150, 195–197, and chap. 8.
41. Bacar Cassama, interview by the author, Bissau, August 14, 2008.
42. Patrick Chabal, "National Liberation in Portuguese Guinea, 1956–1974," in *African Affairs* 80, no. 318 (1981): 81.
43. Chabal, *Amilcar Cabral,* 67.
44. Gibson, *African Liberation Movements,* 256.
45. Francisca Pereira, interviews by the author, Bissau, August 9 and 16, 2008.
46. Mario Augusto Ramalho Cissokho, interview by the author, Bissau, August 8, 2008.
47. Ibid.
48. Francisca Pereira, interviews by the author, Bissau, August 9 and 16, 2008.
49. Urdang, *Fighting Two Colonialisms,* 37.
50. Ibid., 30.
51. Ibid., "Introduction."
52. Carmen Pereira, interview by the author, Bissau, August 21, 2008.
53. Cooper, "Possibility and Constraint," *Journal of African History* 49, no. 2 (2008): 168; Filomina Chioma Steady, *Women and Leadership in West Africa: Mothering the Nation and Humanizing the State* (New York: Palgrave Macmillan, 2011), chap. 4; Schmidt, *Mobilizing the Masses.*
54. W. O. Maloba, *African Women in Revolution* (Trenton, NJ: Africa World Press, 2007), 95–104; Urdang, *Fighting Two Colonialisms.*
55. Urdang, *Fighting Two Colonialisms,* 119–166.
56. Carmen Pereira, interview by the author, Bissau, August 21, 2008.
57. Marnia Lazeg, "Gender and Politics in Algeria: Unraveling the Religious Paradigm," *Signs* 15, no. 4 (1990): 755–780.
58. Gerard Chaliand and Michel Vale, "Amilcar Cabral," *International Journal of Politics* 7, no. 4 (1977–78): 3–17.
59. Amilcar Cabral, "A Report to Our Friends," *Africa Today* 20, no. 1 (1973): 7–13.
60. Francisca Pereira, interviews by the author, Bissau, August 9 and 16, 2008.
61. Carmen Pereira, interview by the author, Bissau, August 21, 2008.
62. Udé Camara and NDo Mané, interview by the author, Bissau, August 2, 2010.

9 Brothers in the Bush

Exile, Refuge, and Citizenship on the Ghana-Togo Border, 1958–1966

Kate Skinner

In the summer of 1960, Edward Kojo Mfojoh learned that two of his close friends had been summoned for an interview at the police station in Ho (the administrative headquarters of the Volta Region of Ghana). Mfojoh waited to see what would happen. Neither of his friends returned. They were informed on their arrival at the police station that, due to their suspected involvement in acts of conspiracy against the government of Ghana, they and twelve others were subject to a preventive detention order and would be detained for a period of up to five years. Mfojoh and the detainees were members of the same political party. Like them, Mfojoh opposed the Convention People's Party government of Kwame Nkrumah, and was a vocal critic of its stance towards the neighboring Republic of Togo and the peoples of the border area. Fearing that he too would be detained, Mfojoh decided to leave the country. After crossing the border on foot during the night, he arrived in the cocoa-marketing center of Kpalimé, where he contacted fellow goldsmiths and sought to establish a new network of customers for whom he could practice his craft.[1] Mfojoh was just one of approximately five thousand seven hundred people who left Ghana between 1958 and 1961, and resided in exile in French Togoland (from 1960, Republic of Togo) until the coup d'état that toppled the Nkrumah government in 1966.[2]

Recent scholarship on decolonization in Africa has paid attention to the physical movements of political activists across borders, and to the mechanisms by which radical, left-leaning, and anticolonial movements sought support from newly independent nations. While Joanna Tague (this volume) highlights the role of Dar-es-Salaam as a hub for exiles from southern African liberation struggles, Jeffrey Ahlman, Meredith Terretta, and Klaas van Walraven have all pointed to Nkrumah's Ghana as a nodal point in networks of radical activists.[3] The Conference of Independent African States and the All-African Peoples' Conference, both held in Accra in 1958, debated the means by which Ghana and other newly independent states might provide ideological, diplomatic, economic, or logistical

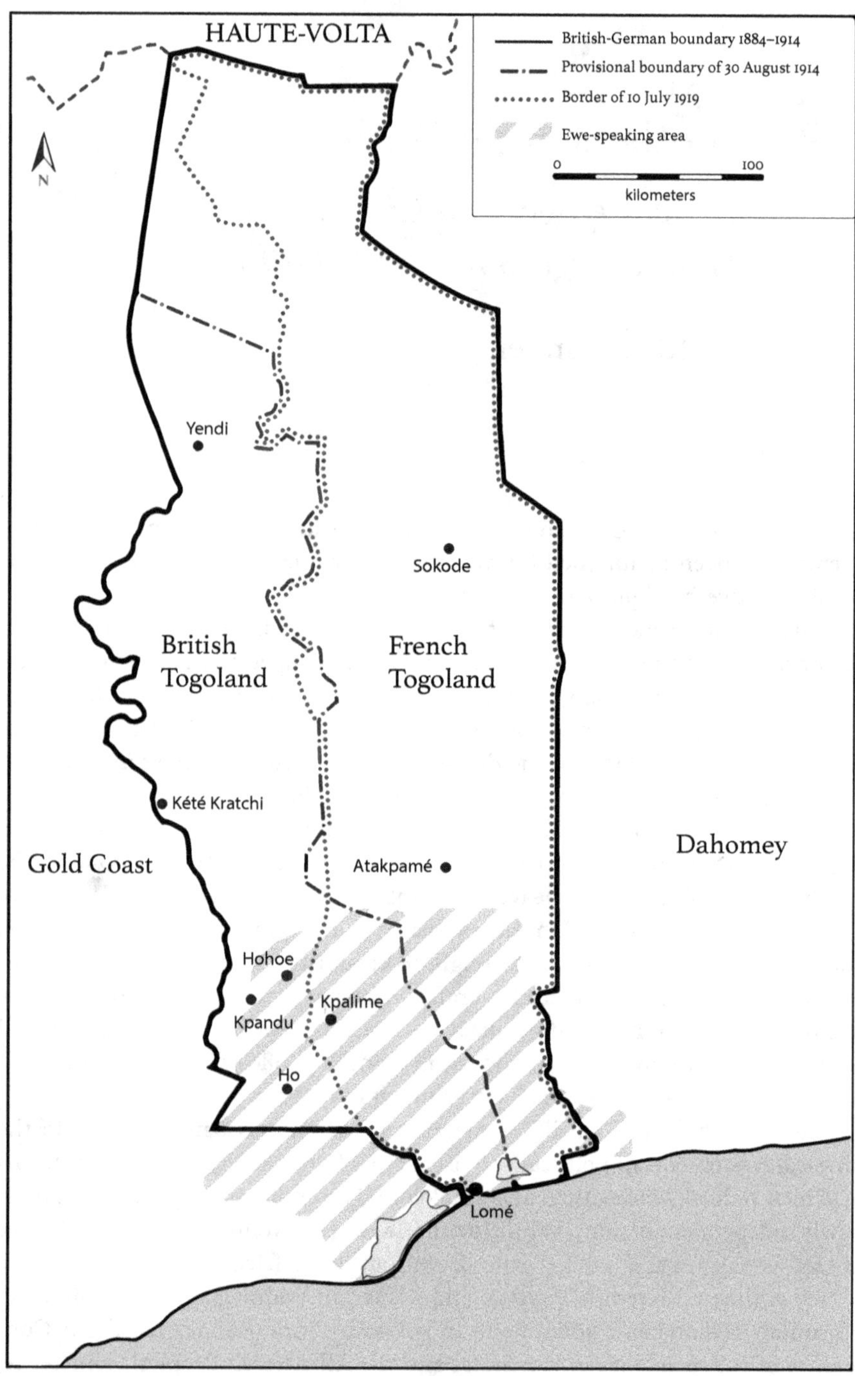

Map 9.1 Ghana-Togo Borderland. (Reproduced with permission from Kate Skinner, *The Fruits of Freedom in British Togoland* [Cambridge University Press, 2015].)

support to anticolonial nationalist movements, and mobilize international opinion against racist settler regimes. The Bureau of African Affairs went on to confirm Accra's position as a hub for numerous exiled freedom fighters fleeing repressive colonial regimes or the puppet governments which replaced them. For Terretta, this movement of radical, left-leaning, and anticolonial activists into Accra, and the projection from Accra of an evolving vision of pan-Africanism, provides evidence that older ideals of solidarity between African peoples were not displaced by territorial nationalism during the 1950s but found new forms and outlets.[4]

This chapter contributes to an "archive of exile" by reminding us that while Accra provided refuge to those whose stance was endorsed by the Nkrumah regime, those with dissenting views were forced out. Whereas Nathan Carpenter—for French Guinea—and Trina Hogg—for British Sierra Leone—examine in this volume the legal foundations of exile and its direct application to African subjects by nascent or insecure colonial regimes, this chapter will outline how flight across borders became a logical response to postcolonial legislation which aimed to ease the anxieties of emergent states by suppressing domestic political opposition.

The status of people like Edward Kojo Mfojoh was heavily contested. Article 14 of the 1948 Universal Declaration of Human Rights indicated that all individuals had the right "to seek and enjoy in other countries asylum from persecution" unless they were attempting to avoid prosecution for "non-political crimes" or for "acts contrary to the purposes and principles of the United Nations."[5] The 1951 Geneva Convention on the Status of Refugees, however, was restricted to people in Europe who had been displaced by events of the Second World War and its immediate aftermath. Africans who fled their countries of origin as a result of political struggles could therefore claim the right to seek asylum, but, as Tague also notes, they did not qualify as refugees within the terms of the Convention until its temporal and geographical restrictions were lifted by protocol in 1967.[6]

From the perspective of the Togolese government, the five thousand seven hundred people who crossed Ghana's eastern border to seek refuge in Togo did so due to a well-founded fear of persecution, and were thus, for all intents and purposes, refugees in need of protection and assistance. Through the Preventive Detention Act of July 1958, the Ghanaian government had allowed for the arrest of individuals and their detention without trial for a period of up to five years.[7] By issuing preventive detention orders against its political opponents, the government had demonstrated that it was prepared to apply this legislation in practice. Thus individuals who were themselves the subject of a preventive detention order, or were members of the same political opinion as other individuals who were the subject of such an order, had a well-founded fear that they would be arrested and detained without access to a fair trial. In defining Mfojoh and the five thousand seven hundred other new arrivals as refugees, the Togolese government adopted new international language to highlight the oppressive stance adopted by the Nkrumah regime towards its political opponents and particularly towards those people who lived close to the Ghana-Togo border and were critical of the manner in which disputes over the border had been resolved in 1956–57.

From the perspective of the Nkrumah government, however, those individuals who were subject to preventive detention orders had either engaged in acts of conspiracy against an elected government or were likely to do so, and were being detained in the public interest, as a matter of safety. According to this logic, no Ghanaian national who respected the territorial integrity of Ghana and the sovereignty of its government could have a well-grounded fear of persecution, and thus the majority of the five thousand seven hundred people who had left for Togo could not be described or treated as refugees.

In examining these different perspectives on the movement of individuals across the Ghana/Togo border, this chapter argues that, despite the wider context of anticolonialism and calls for pan-African unity, both of the new governments insisted upon their preferred versions of what Liisa Malkki has termed "the national order of things."[8] In confronting displacement, both governments responded by insisting on the primacy of territorial integrity and national sovereignty. But they did not agree on how people living in the Ghana-Togo border area could be induced to respect the territorial integrity of either state or the sovereignty of either government, or what this implied for the status of individuals who crossed the border.

The Togolese government regarded "the refugee problem" as a direct consequence of the questionable manner in which the Ghana-Togo border question had been settled in 1956–57: if the wishes of the people had been accurately assessed and acted upon, there would not be so much opposition to the border, the Ghanaian government would not find it necessary to use preventive detention to suppress its opponents in the area, and people from the Ghana side of the disputed border would not find it necessary to seek refuge in Togo.[9] From the perspective of the Ghanaian government, the majority of the five thousand seven hundred arrivals in Togo were living in self-imposed exile, and the host government was exaggerating the extent of popular opposition to the border in order to undermine the legitimacy of the 1956/7 settlement in the eyes of the international community, and thereby reopen the border question with a view to aggrandizing its own national territory. Paradoxically, the disputed nature of the border and the ambiguous status of those who crossed it actually strengthened politicians' commitment to "a national order of things" even as their rhetoric of pan-African unity intensified.

This effect can also be seen more widely, beyond the corridors of power. Oral histories and local-language sources suggest that, despite their dispersal amongst

Togolese host communities, and despite their belief in an enlarged Togolese homeland, the refugees and their hosts insisted on the temporariness and hardship of their dislocation. In describing refugees as "brothers" who had been "driven into the bush," the local-language press deployed metaphors which, like those in the Cape Verdean poems discussed by Marina Berthet in this volume, emphasized the rootedness of human cultures in the soil and espoused a territorialized version of identity. In stressing the aberrant nature of their displaced condition, the refugees and their hosts questioned the character and values of the leader of the government which had imposed it upon them. From this perspective, Nkrumah was not a pan-African hero, but a person unfit to be the father of a family of African nations. In recalling the sufferings associated with their period in Togo, the refugees insisted not upon the falsity of any national order of things, but upon the illegitimacy of the particular order which had displaced them, for when the Nkrumah regime was toppled in 1966, almost all of them returned "home" to Ghana.

The Struggle for the Nation

In May 1956, a plebiscite was held in the United Nations trust territory of British Togoland. Voters were asked to choose between "union" with, or "separation" from, the neighboring British colony of the Gold Coast, which was soon to achieve its independence as Ghana. The wording of the plebiscite question was vague in two respects. First, the nature of a "union" could not really be understood outside of the wider, and as yet unresolved, debate about the type of constitution to be adopted by an independent Gold Coast/Ghana. The Convention People's Party (CPP), led by Nkrumah, sought a unitary constitution with a unicameral legislature, whilst their political opponents preferred a federal structure with some form of upper chamber, and requested a bill of rights. Thus the precise nature of the independent government which would preside over a "union" of British Togoland and the Gold Coast had not been clarified for voters in the plebiscite.

The term "separation," however, was equally vague, for it did not specify the option that was favored by Nkrumah's key opponents in the trust territory: S. G. Antor and the Togoland Congress argued not simply for "separation" from the Gold Coast, but for the reunification of the British trust territory with its French-administered counterpart to the east in order to form an enlarged independent Togoland nation. They thus envisaged that all of the people living in the two United Nations trust territories would become citizens of a single independent state, which could then choose at some point in the future whether it wished to join in a federation with Ghana (perhaps alongside other West African states). Those who favored "separation" further objected to the role of the British administration in organizing the vote, because the British openly favored "union."[10]

The results of this plebiscite in effect fixed Ghana's eastern border, but they were also heavily contested. Voters in the northern section of the trust territory indicated an overwhelming preference for "union," whilst those in the southern section favored "separation" but by a smaller majority. In view of the longstanding British practice of administering separately the southern and northern sections of the trust territory, it seemed plausible to Togoland Congress leaders that the plebiscite result could lead to a "union" of the northern section with the Gold Coast, and the "separation" of the southern section. The United Nations, however, was persuaded by the British government's view that the partition of the trust territory was inadvisable, and that the narrow overall majority for "union" must prevail.

Togoland Congress leaders still expected that the nature of the "union" would be determined at a roundtable conference between themselves and their Gold Coast counterparts.[11] This expectation was also to be disappointed, because the victory of Nkrumah and the CPP in the Gold Coast elections of July 1956 was interpreted as an endorsement of the proposals for a unitary constitution. The United Nations thus agreed to terminate the trusteeship agreement for British Togoland, paving the way for the northern and southern sections of the trust territory to be integrated with the Gold Coast under a unitary constitution. At the moment of Ghanaian Independence in March 1957, the Togoland Congress had been thoroughly defeated, and it seemed that the pursuit of an independent reunified Togoland nation was a lost cause.

A year later, however, things were looking rather different. Across the border, the nationalists in French Togoland won the critical elections of April 27, 1958. The Comité de l'Unité Togolaise (CUT) and its allied movement, Juvento, took 61.1 percent of the valid votes, and 29 of 46 seats in the new legislative assembly.[12] The CUT leader, Sylvanus Olympio, became prime minister with a clear mandate to reject the limited autonomy that France had offered in 1956, and to hold out instead for a fuller measure of self-government. His party was also committed to the reunification of British and French Togoland.

The electoral success of Olympio and the CUT thereby raised the possibility that an independent government of French Togoland would seek to "reclaim" the former British Togoland from Ghana. This was a welcome development for Togoland Congress activists, for they now had a powerful ally across the border. But it posed a challenge to the Ghanaian government's plans to generate hydroelectric power by damming the river Volta, and it thereby jeopardized a core element in Nkrumah's strategy for modernization.[13] This was the context in which the CPP government began to close the net around its opponents, in the former British Togoland and indeed elsewhere in Ghana.

In early 1960, as the Independence of French Togoland approached, the police presence was doubled in the former British trust territory area.[14] Preventive detention orders (which allowed for arrest and detention without trial for a period of up to five years) were issued against individuals who were suspected of cultivating subversive links with French Togoland and plotting disturbances aimed at a revision of the border settlement of 1956–57.[15] Further preventive detention orders were issued through the spring and summer of 1960, prompting an exodus of activists who feared that they would also be arrested. The use of preventive detention within Ghana, however, did not eliminate political opposition to the Nkrumah regime. Rather, it resulted in the formation of communities of opponents in exile, particularly amongst the clusters of Togoland Congress activists and supporters who gathered across the border in the areas of Kpalimé, Atakpamé, and Badou.

Neocolonialism and National Sovereignty Reconfigured

The negotiations over the nature and terms of French Togoland's independence took place between 1958 and 1960 in the context of a wider debate about the future status of France's African colonies and President Charles de Gaulle's proposals for a French Community.[16] The French certainly preferred the more malleable African politicians, and had no affection for those whom they deemed too energetic in their quest for greater political and economic autonomy from metropolitan France.[17] The legendary French animosity towards Olympio, however, was tempered by a more pressing threat from Accra; for, in his concern to stave off any future attempts to reclaim British Togoland from Ghana, Nkrumah was making the case for French Togoland to follow its British counterpart into a "union" with Ghana.

France's permanent representative at the United Nations complained formally to the secretary-general in March 1960 about Ghana's annexationist intentions towards French Togoland.[18] At the independence celebrations on April 27, 1960, a Ghanaian military intervention in French Togoland did not materialize, but once the celebrations were over, Ghanaian ambitions in Togo manifested themselves in the Ghana-Togo Union Movement. The French ambassador in Accra explained that the explicit aim of this movement was to remove the artificial border and to encourage the formation of an economic and political union between the two states. He added, however, that the movement had been formed "at the instigation of the CPP and the Bureau of African Affairs," and that it intended to mobilize support by forming branches within Togo as well as within Ghana.[19] The ambassador regarded this as a deliberate provocation, and linked it to an editorial in the *Ghanaian Times* on July 13, 1961, which challenged Olympio to hold a referendum and allow the inhabitants of Togo to decide whether they wanted to unite with Ghana.[20]

The CUT (known from 1960 as "Unité Togolaise") mounted a two-pronged response. First, within Togo's own borders, it sought to demonstrate the strength of domestic support not simply for the survival of Togo as a separate sovereign nation-state, but also for its historic claim to reunification with the former British Togoland.[21] The second prong of Togo's response was directed outwards, to the international community. In October 1961, Paulin Freitas, Togo's minister for foreign affairs, broached at the United Nations General Assembly in New York the exodus of Ghanaian citizens to Togo as refugees. The French embassy in Lomé sent a telegram to Paris to warn the government of Freitas' intentions: under the cover of a social and humanitarian appeal, Freitas would draw attention to the political dimension of the exile problem and thereby seek to reopen the Togoland question.[22] The following day, the French ambassador in Lomé received a telegram reporting what had transpired at the General Assembly in New York. Freitas' agenda, according to the French representative, was scarcely hidden: he had spoken directly about the problems that stemmed from the manner in which the former British Togoland had been integrated into Ghana.

Freitas argued more specifically that, contrary to the modalities implemented in Cameroon, the United Nations had approved the integration of British Togoland with Ghana on the basis of the overall majority achieved in the plebiscite of May 1956. Had the United Nations accepted the need to count the votes of the northern and southern sections of British Togoland separately, the southern section could have been reunited with French Togoland, as the majority there had clearly wished. Freitas concluded that it was this misguided approval of a single counting zone that had encouraged the Ghanaian leadership in thinking that it would be possible for them to annex the remainder of Togo after independence. While Freitas indicated that it was the sheer volume of refugees entering Togo that had prompted him to ask the United Nations for assistance, the Ghanaian representative wanted to know why Freitas had not brought this matter directly to Accra.[23] The French ambassador to Togo, Henri-François Mazoyer, concluded that the refugee question had provided Olympio with a perfect opportunity to internationalize his quarrel with Nkrumah.[24]

Despite their misgivings about the African politicians who had succeeded them, both the British and the French governments prioritized the territorial integrity of their former colonies above other interests. Contrary to the French ambassador's anxiety about an expansionist Anglo-Saxon conspiracy, in the Togo Annual Review for 1960 British diplomats had been emphatic in their support both for Olympio's leadership and for the survival of Togo as a separate country.[25] In 1961, however, the British were perturbed by the Togolese government's decision to bring the refugee question to the United Nations, and therefore suggested that while the "good offices" of the High Commissioner for Refugees could be used to ease the situation, there was a question mark over the "status of many of the so-called 'refugees.' Our own information was that the majority were in fact people, mainly Ewes, who moved at the time of the plebiscite in 1956–57, preferring to live in what was then French Togoland rather than remain in the Gold Coast, and others who left Ghana for Togo after Togo's Independence in April 1960."[26]

This disingenuous representation of the exile community in Togo was probably related to the British government's desire to minimize friction with Nkrumah in the run-up to the Queen's visit to Ghana in November 1961, and to avoid giving Nkrumah a pretext whereby he could withdraw Ghana from the Commonwealth.[27] By February 1962, the Foreign Office was prepared to concede that those arriving in Lomé in the wake of the Sekondi-Takoradi workers' strike were bona fide political refugees, but argued that as "their number is very small . . . it may be difficult to justify helping them out on a purely refugee basis." Their preferred alternative was that "assistance to the Togolese should be given under some other umbrella."[28] The British were worried by Nkrumah's shift to the left, and they regarded Olympio as a valuable counterweight, who would provide a "link between the moderate Nigerian leaders and the French-speaking States."[29] But the Foreign Office could not bring itself to support Olympio or his government in any move that might ultimately lead to the reopening of the border question. This would have entailed an implicit admission that their insistence on a single counting zone in interpreting the results of the 1956 plebiscite had been a mistake.

The French ambassador to Togo, on the other hand, disliked Olympio intensely. But while the French government may have had little interest in preserving a Unité Togolaise government led by Olympio, they certainly wished to maintain Togo as a separate country and resist what they perceived as Nkrumah's annexationist intentions. Olympio's own anxieties about Nkrumah may also explain why he was ready to enter a defense pact with France. Mazoyer was skeptical about the amount of assistance that would actually reach the refugees, and believed that the Olympio regime was using them primarily for political capital at the United Nations, but he also reminded the French foreign minister that "for political reasons, which have lost none of their significance" it was in the French interest to support the Ghanaian refugees in Togo. Mazoyer therefore recommended expenditure of approximately six million francs for the provision of tools and equipment to those who could support themselves as artisans.[30]

The refugees do not appear to have benefitted from any large-scale concerted assistance from the Togolese government between their mass arrival in 1960 and their departure in 1966. The United Nations High Commissioner for Refugees did not bring his final report to the General Assembly until April 1963, by which point most of the refugees had been in Togo for two to three years.[31] In July 1962, the UNHCR representative, M. E. Ettmueller, produced a preliminary report and made recommendations as to how the exiled refugees should be assisted.[32] Much of the implementation, however, was left to La Ligue des Sociétés de la Croix Rouge (later renamed as the International Federation of the Red Cross). In August 1963, concerns were expressed about the small amount of piecemeal assistance that the refugees had actually received.[33] And as late as 1965, the Western Togo Refugees' Union petitioned the Togo government on a variety of matters regarding their material welfare.[34]

The Paradox of Uprootedness

The "western Togo refugees" bear little resemblance to the "modern, postwar refugee" who emerged as a "knowable and nameable figure" and an "object of social-scientific knowledge" through the spatial concentration and bureaucratic processes that became key features of the camps of post-war Europe.[35] Many exiles were treading the paths of their parents during World War II, and of their grandparents from the turn of the century.[36] The refugees were not pathologized by the aid industry or its experts, for the engagement of external agencies was not sufficiently intensive or sustained to significantly reshape either the self-understandings of refugees or local perceptions of them. Rather than being concentrated in camps, targeted by experts, or forced into dependency on aid agencies, the western Togo exiles were relatively easily dispersed into host communities which treated them as "social persons." Family networks extended across the border and could be called upon to provide accommodation to new arrivals and advise them on potential means of earning a living in a new place; several key social institutions—including the Roman Catholic and Presbyterian churches—operated in both Ghana and Togo; the same language of everyday interaction (Ewe) was used on either side of the border; and travel around the border region for the purposes of trade, training, paid work, weddings, and funerals had been commonplace for decades. At the level of political imagination, the refugees were hardly in a "foreign" country at all: they had simply moved from the western to the eastern part of the reunified Togoland that had long been the object of their own political struggle and that of their host communities.

My point here is not that the refugees had things easy. Those who were commercial cocoa growers found themselves living at distances that made it difficult or impossible for them to manage their farms.[37] Those who had invested in education or training for white collar jobs found that a shift from an Anglophone to a Francophone literate environment rendered them unemployable in their chosen profession—a problem similar to that experienced by Lusophone Mozambican refugees in Dar-es-Salaam and described by Tague.[38] And although traders and artisans, like Edward Kojo Mfojoh, could rely on the Ewe language for their interactions, it still took time to build up new networks of clients and suppliers.[39] The experience of exile may not have transformed the refugees into "naked unaccommodated men," but they certainly experienced disruption to their livelihoods and dislocation from

Fig. 9.2 Daniel Awumey on far right, pictured with three sons of chief Gustav Amedome of Kuma-Apoti, who hosted Daniel Awumey during his time of exile in Togo. (Courtesy of William Awumey.)

their households; almost all of them returned to Ghana after the coup that overthrew Nkrumah in 1966, and later in life they looked back on their years in Togo as a time of trial.[40]

This desire and propensity of refugees to return "home" resonates with understandings which associate ancestral and familial belonging, and the right to access land, with a very specific place. The peoples of the Ghana/Togo border area combined considerable experience of migration (and the accumulation of property, marital partners, and professional or social networks in different places) with a normative emphasis on the individual as a "citizen" (*dumetɔ*) of his/her own "hometown," in which key family relationships and material interests (particularly claims to land) were located. The dilemmas of citizenship in the new nation, however, added a new and distinctive layer to these older ideas of belonging, because individuals envisaged a "greater Togoland" as their homeland, and yet emphasized their sense of displacement and uprootedness within it.

A brief examination of the depiction of refugees in the local-language press will provide some insight into this paradox and connect it to the exile idioms in which issues of citizenship, territorial integrity, national sovereignty, and pan-African relations were discussed. In particular, the Ewe-language newspaper *Ablɔɖe Safui* (the Key to Freedom) followed the Ghana-Togo border question and the refugee predicament through the early years of independence.[41] The

Fig. 9.3 People of the Gbi villages gathering at the Leklebi-Dafor border post to welcome home the refugees who were returning from Togo to Ghana in 1967. Daniel Awumey is the shorter man in white clothing, in the middle of the photograph. On the far right, wearing a wig, is A. K. P. Kludze, then a practicing lawyer and later a professor of law and a justice of the supreme court. On the far left, wearing an academic gown, is Mr. Gedzeve of Gbi-Hohoe. Also in academic garb, near the middle, is Professor Azziz Akator of Gbi-Kpeme. Togbe Gabusu IV, paramount chief of Gbi-Hohoe, wears all white and a head cover. (Courtesy of William Awumey.)

owner-editor, Holiday Komedja, began by emphasizing the depths of human suffering inflicted on those who had dared to oppose Nkrumah's CPP government. Referring to events in the town of Kpandu-Aloi in Ghana in the summer of 1960, *Ablɔɖe Safui* described the CPP "thugs," dressed as "general police," who had assaulted Togoland Congress supporters, including one Kwame Kuma, who was beaten so badly that "he defecated on himself and blood oozed from his nostrils."[42] In emphasizing the pitiful state to which the Nkrumah regime was prepared to reduce its opponents, Komedja sought to stimulate sympathy for those who fled across the border into Togo, and particularly to the Kpalimé area where his newspaper was based. He also reported favorably on acts of solidarity on the part of host communities towards the refugees.

> On Tuesday, March 15, 1960 the council of Klutoflime chiefs called the supporters of *Ablɔɖe* from B.M.T. [*Ablɔɖe*! had been the slogan of both the Togoland Congress and the Comité de l'Unité Togolaise during the later 1950s; B. M. T. refers to British Mandated Togoland—i.e., the former British trust territory] and their leaders whom the C.P.P. government had driven into the

> bush, to get to know them and to sympathize with them as was the case with we French Togolese some time ago. [This refers to the fact that chiefs and activists who had opposed the French administration in their part of Togoland had also suffered persecution and had sometimes sought refuge across the border in the British zone, particularly in and around Hohoe.] The paramount chief Pebi IV of Agu-Nyogbo who was the president of the council of chiefs, spoke. But let me conclude simply for you that the name of the brave lasts forever if he perseveres in suffering. . . . Afterwards the council of chiefs donated 10,000 francs to be used for the upkeep of those people who had been driven into the bush. . . . The program ended with a prayer. Freedom![43]

Komedja considered that, in sympathizing with the refugees as fellow human beings, and by helping to rescue them from the indignity of being driven out of culture and into the "bush" (*gbeme*), host communities and local leaders in Togo were demonstrating their own humanity (*amenyenye*) and the dignity that came from their status as persons residing freely in their own homeland (*denyigba*). This in turn invited a contrast with the CPP regime, which, he claimed, espoused socialist equality (*sɔsɔminasoe*) but had abandoned basic social values. *Ablɔḍe Safui* thus set out to challenge the rhetoric of the Nkrumah regime, and particularly to expose its use of metaphors of the family to gain support for its preferred version of Ghana-Togo relations.

Komedja explained to his readers that, during the Togolese independence celebrations of April 27, 1960, an article on Ghana-Togo relations had appeared in the CPP's *Evening News*. Paraphrasing this article, Komedja pinpointed its assertion that "Togo and Ghana have been siblings (*nɔviwo*) since time immemorial. . . . *The Evening News* went on to explain that they will see this brotherliness (*nɔvinyenye*)." *Ablɔḍe Safui*, however, wanted to know whether Nkrumah had understood what brotherliness really meant. For if so, would he still "be driving B.M.T.'s *Ablɔḍe* people into the bush, and arresting and imprisoning . . . and maltreating them[?]" "Has Dr K. Nkrumah freed the *Ablɔḍe* people whom he arrested? Has he allowed to return home those whom he drove into the bush? In what behavior does Dr. K. Nkrumah demonstrate this brotherliness?"[44]

Recognizing the efforts of the Nkrumah regime to undermine Olympio's domestic support and thereby force the smaller republic of Togo into closer political relationship with its larger neighbor, Komedja continued to warn the readers of *Ablɔḍe Safui* about the implications of "brotherliness" in a Ghana-Togo "union" (*habɔbɔ*). The Ghana-Togo Union Movement, he explained, claimed that its "objective is . . . to do away with obstacles and old animosities (*nyadzɔdzɔ vɔwo*—lit. bad matters) between the two countries so that complete brotherliness will bind them all as one." But how could they remove old animosities "if K. Nkrumah does not take his hands off B. M. T. but just pays lip service"?[45] According to Komedja, then, "unity" (*dekawɔwɔ*) between independent African nations could only be achieved by demonstrations of brotherliness which led to a free choice for union.

The latter could not be commanded by the larger states and imposed on their smaller counterparts, in the manner of expansionist colonization. In view of the region's history, he argued, true "unity" between Ghana and Togo now required Ghana's recognition of Togo's national sovereignty, Nkrumah's recognition of Olympio as his equal, and a willingness to revisit the border settlement of 1956/7.

In 1961 Komedja predicted that, one day, the tables would be turned and Nkrumah himself would become a refugee.[46] Four years later, Komedja sensed that he was about to be vindicated.[47] Explaining how Nkrumah had ended up "broke and floundering between white countries looking for loans," Komedja acknowledged the economic challenges associated with the falling world price for cocoa. But he concluded that the real problem lay in Nkrumah's quest "to rule over the whole of Africa" and his pathological inability to respect the territorial integrity of other nations and the sovereignty of their governments. Far from producing unity or providing leadership to a family of African nations, Nkrumah had rather transformed Ghana into a country of "evil-doers and destroyers of African governments," and made Accra into "a place of refuge" for all manner of fugitives who were then trained to make trouble in other nations.[48]

Pan-Africanism was a key ideological and strategic component of many of Africa's anticolonial struggles, but the ambivalence of governmental and popular responses to exile and displacement in the period of decolonization and into independence points to a powerful and widespread attachment to a "national order of things." Nkrumah's opponents—exiled from the former British Togoland, refugees in the new Republic of Togo—criticized his pan-African ambitions by emphasizing the naturalness of territorialized identities and the primacy of national sovereignty for countries emerging from colonial rule. Refugees from the former British Togoland had suffered the human indignity of being driven into the bush, but they were not pathologized, for whilst their predicament provided evidence of the oppressive nature of the Nkrumah regime, the refugees themselves could be incorporated within an imagined greater Togolese citizenship. Their displacement, then, served to reinforce an alternative "national order of things" because, in an imagined greater Togo, refugees belonging to this particular category were not forced to live outside of "the supposedly normal condition of being attached to a territorial polity and an identifiable people."[49] The Togolese thus celebrated their own hospitality to those who were driven out of Ghana, but regarded with skepticism the "freedom fighters" whom Nkrumah had chosen to shelter.

Conclusion

The newly independent government of Ghana passed the Preventive Detention Act in order to contain its domestic opponents and detach them from sources of local and transnational support. Kwame Nkrumah's expectation that this suppression of opposition at home would enable a clearer focus on pan-African foreign policy was confounded for two reasons. Firstly, word-of-mouth reached grassroots political activists more rapidly than the infrastructure of repression. Tipped off by friends and relatives, thousands of men like Edward Kojo Mfojoh ignored the roads and bridges that were designed to transport agricultural exports southwards, to the coast, and instead made their way eastwards, by night, along the bush paths which led to the Republic of Togo. The geography of the border region worked against state attempts to imprison cohorts of political opponents.

Secondly, as demonstrated throughout this volume, the experience of exile could be generative. Small Togolese market towns and administrative centers such as Kpalimé were different from the "hubs of exile" identified in this volume, like London as described by Susan Pennybacker or Paris by Terretta, but they were still spaces in which individuals could build new solidarities as well as reactivate and draw support from older familial and social ties. The struggles of making a living as an exile in the Republic of Togo tested individuals' ideals of "the Greater Togo" which had formed the object of their political ambitions since the mid-1950s; but participation in a community of exiles helped to sustain grievances over the 1956/7 border settlement, placed these grievances within the unfolding dilemmas of the Olympio regime, and contributed to a growing wave of West African resistance to the form of pan-Africanism pursued by Kwame Nkrumah. This chapter therefore extends the patterns of exile outlined by Carpenter and Hogg for French and British West African colonies, and reveals how activists in the independence era could cross international borders and establish in frontier zones new political spaces from which they could challenge the authority of postcolonial states.

Finally, this examination of African-language idioms of citizenship in the era of new nationhood reveals anxieties over the aberrance of displacement and an insistence on the naturalness of territorialized identities. For the owner-editor of *Ablɔḍe Safui*, belonging in the nation-state followed from belonging in a "hometown;" the forced exile of individuals from their hometowns, and their reduction to the status of refugees, was thus a form of state tyranny. Research on recent "autochthony struggles" in Africa has suggested a connection between the intensification of claims to belonging and the relative weakening (or at least, the reconfiguration) of the state, through "processes of intensifying globalization," decentralization, and donors' "by-passing" of the state via increased support to civil society and non-governmental organizations.[50] This chapter, on the other hand, points to the possibility that further research on local-language idioms of citizenship, belonging, and exile in the era of state-building and new nationhood will open up new perspectives on autochthony discourses in Africa.[51]

Notes

1. E. K. Mfojoh, interviews by the author, Sokode-Gbagble, Volta Region, June 2, 1999 and July 19, 2000. The author and editors are grateful to Cambridge University Press for permission to reprint in this chapter a very small amount of material from pages 170, 173–74

and 200–206 of Kate Skinner, *The Fruits of Freedom in British Togoland: Literacy, Politics and Nationalism, 1914–2014* (Cambridge University Press, 2015).

2. To give the reader a sense of the relative size of the refugee community: the population of Togo was approximately 1.58 million in 1960, and the population of Ghana was approximately 6.65 million. World Bank data, accessed January 16, 2017, http://data.worldbank.org/country/ghana and http://data.worldbank.org/country/togo.

3. Jeffrey Ahlman, "The Algerian Question in Nkrumah's Ghana, 1958–1960: Debating 'Violence' and 'Nonviolence' in African Decolonization," *Africa Today* 57, no. 2 (2010): 66–84, and Ahlman, "Road to Ghana: Nkrumah, Southern Africa and the Eclipse of a Decolonizing Africa," *Kronos* 37, no. 1 (2011): 23–40; Meredith Terretta, "Cameroonian Nationalists Go Global: From Forest *Maquis* to Pan-African Accra," *Journal of African History* 51, no. 2 (2010): 189–212; Klaas van Walraven, *Yearning for Relief: A History of the Sawaba Movement in Niger* (Leiden: Brill, 2013).

4. Terretta, "Cameroonian Nationalists Go Global," 204.

5. United Nations, "Universal Declaration of Human Rights," 1948, accessed January 16, 2017, http://www.un.org/en/documents/udhr/index.shtml#a14.

6. Office of the United Nations High Commissioner for Refugees, "Convention and Protocol Relating to the Status of Refugees," 1951, 1967, accessed January 16, 2017, http://www.unhcr.org/3b66c2aa10.html.

7. This was later extended to ten years.

8. Liisa Malkki, "Refugees and Exiles: From "Refugee Studies" to the National Order of Things," *Annual Review of Anthropology* 24 (1995): 495–523.

9. The making of the border is well explained in Paul Nugent, *Smugglers, Secessionists and Loyal Citizens on the Ghana-Togo Frontier: The Lie of the Borderlands Since 1914* (Athens, OH: Ohio University Press, 2002). Opposition to the 1956/7 settlement is explored in Skinner, *The Fruits of Freedom*.

10. United Nations Trusteeship Council, "Report of the United Nations Plebiscite Commissioner for the Trust Territory of Togoland Under British Administration" (T/1258, June 19, 1956).

11. Kosi Kedem, *How Britain Subverted and Betrayed British Togoland* (Accra: Governance and Electoral Systems Agency, on behalf of Kosi Kedem, 2010).

12. D. E. K. Amenumey, *The Ewe Unification Movement: A Political History* (Accra: Ghana Universities Press, 1989), 319–20.

13. Stephan Miescher, "No One Should Be Worse Off: The Akosombo Dam, Modernization, and the Experience of Resettlement in Ghana," in *Modernization as Spectacle in Africa*, ed. Peter Bloom, Stephan Miescher, and Takyiwaa Manuh (Bloomington, IN: Indiana University Press, 2014), 184–204.

14. Dennis Austin, *Politics in Ghana 1946–60* (London: Oxford University Press, 1964), 319.

15. A copy of the text of the detention order to Moses Kofi Asase of Ho-Dome is in the author's possession.

16. Frederick Cooper, *Citizenship between Empire and Nation: Remaking France and French Africa, 1945–1960* (Princeton NJ: Princeton University Press, 2014).

17. Godwin Tétévi-Adjalogo, *Histoire du Togo: le regime et l'assassinat de Sylvanus Olympio, vol. 3.* (Paris: NM7 Editions, 2002); François-Xavier Verschave, *La Françafrique: le plus long scandale de la République* (Paris: Stock, 1998).

18. Centre des Archives Diplomatiques, Nantes (hereafter CADN). Accra Ambassade 61: Armani Bérard, French ambassador and permanent representative at the United Nations, to Dag Hammarskjold, United Nations secretary-general, March 12, 1960.

19. CADN, Accra Ambassade 61: Ambassade de France au Ghana, Accra, to Ministre des affaires étrangères, Paris, July 14, 1961.

20. Public Records and Archives Administration Department, Accra. SC/BAA/434 Bureau of African Affairs. Correspondence between Nkrumah, Ako-Adjei and Dei-Anang in 1961/2 confirms their distrust of Olympio and their desire to undercut his support within Togo in order to generate popular pressure in favour of a Ghana-Togo Union.

21. CADN, Accra Ambassade 61: Secretary-general of Unité Togolaise to Ambassade de France, Lomé, September 23, 1961. Similarly, the national assembly, which, after 1958, was dominated by Unité Togolaise, continued to pass motions in favour of reunification. The National Archives, Kew, UK. DO 195/75 Ghana-Togo Relations: doc. 24, Corbett, British Embassy, Lomé, to British embassy, Dakar; UK High Commission, Accra and Lagos; and Foreign Office, London; June 7, 1961.

22. CADN, Lomé Ambassade 59: C. Mantel, Ambassade de France au Togo, Lomé, to Diplomatie, Paris, October 6, 1961.

23. CADN, Lomé Ambassade 59: Diplomatie, Paris, to Ambassade de France au Togo, October 7, 1961.

24. CADN, Accra Ambassade 61: H. F. Mazoyer, Ambassade de France au Togo, Lomé, to Ministre des affaires étrangères, Paris, December 6, 1961, "Les relations avec le Ghana depuis la levée de tutelle."

25. The National Archives, Kew (hereafter TNA). DO 195/75 Ghana-Togo Relations: Togo Annual Review for 1960, J. H. A. Watson, Dakar, to Foreign Office, London, January 23, 1961.

26. TNA, DO 195/75: G. T. P. Marshall, Foreign Office, London, to D. M. Edward, UK mission to the United Nations, Geneva, February 23, 1962.

27. The British High Commissioner in Accra was concerned by the hostility towards Nkrumah that was being displayed in the British press in October 1961. TNA, Kew, DO 195/39 Preventive Detention in Ghana: UK High Commissioner, Accra, to Commonwealth Relations Office and Cabinet, London, November 7, 1961.

28. TNA, DO 195/75: G. T. P. Marshall, Foreign Office, London, to D. M. Edward, UK mission to the United Nations, Geneva, February 28, 1962.

29. TNA, DO 195/75: Togo Annual Review for 1960, J. H. A. Watson, Dakar, to Foreign Office, London, January 23, 1961.

30. CADN, Lomé Ambassade 59: H. F. Mazoyer, Ambassade de France au Togo, Lomé, to Ministre des affaires etrangères, Paris, August 8, 1962 (for quotation) and May 9, 1963 (for Mazoyer's comments on the refugee situation in the aftermath of Olympio's assassination).

31. CADN, Lomé Ambassade 59: High Commission for Refugees, Rapport final sur l'assistance aux refugies au Togo, April 9, 1963, intended for the United Nations General Assembly, original in English.

32. CADN, Lomé Ambassade 59: M. E. Ettmueller, chargé de mission, Lomé, to the High Commissioner for Refugees, July 12, 1962.

33. CADN, Lomé Ambasaade 135: Petition for Review of Attitudes of UNHCR, Lomé, June 16, 1963.

34. Archives Nationales Togolaises, Lomé, Series: Klouto, Dossier 110, Affaires Politiques: Western Togo Refugees' Union, Kpalimé, to Ministre de l'intérieur, October 26, 1965; petition from the Western Togo Refugees' Union, Kpalimé to the President of the Republic, Lomé, August 11, 1965; and W. K. Prempeh, Secretary of the Committee of the Youths for the Refugees, Kpalimé, to Adjoint Commandant, Cercle de Klouto, Kpalimé, n.d.

35. Malkki, "Refugees and Exiles," 498.

36. Benjamin Lawrance, *Locality, Mobility, and "Nation": Peri-Urban Colonialism in Togo's Eweland 1900–1960* (Rochester NY: Rochester University Press, 2007); Donna Maier, "Slave Labor and Wage Labor in German Togo, 1885–1915" in *Germans in the Tropics: Essays in German Colonial History*, ed. Arthur Knoll and Lewis Gann (New York: Greenwood Press, 1987), 73–92.

37. Emmanuel Dzeletsu, interview by the author, Dzolo-Gbogame, June 12, 2010. Emmanuel's father, Manfred, had been separated from his cocoa farm in British Togoland during his period of exile in French Togoland. This created financial problems for the family and Emmanuel was forced to leave his secondary school in Accra in order to pursue training as a teacher.

38. Bernice Ametowobla, interview by the author, Ho, August 12, 2000. Bernice's husband, the Rev. Francis Ametowobla, was not able to continue in his profession as a graduate teacher due to his difficulties with the French language, and eventually the family moved on to Liberia.

39. Edward Kojo Mfojoh, interviews by the author, Sokode-Gbagble, June 2, 1999 and July 19, 2000. Daniel Awumey was among the group of refugees who fled from Hohoe in the spring of 1960 and remained in French Togoland until 1966. He opened the first convenience store in Kuma Apoti, and, according to his son William, became quite prosperous by the standards of the day. William Awumey, correspondence with the author, November 14, 2014.

40. Liisa Malkki, "National Geographic: The Rooting of Peoples and the Territorialisation of National Identity among Scholars and Refugees," *Cultural Anthropology* 7, no. 1 (1992): 24–44 at 34. Here Malkki is referring to Victor Turner, *The Forest of Symbols: Aspects of Ndembu Ritual* (Cornell University Press, 1967). In the chapter 'Betwixt and Between: the Liminal Period *in Rites de Passage*,' Turner drew from the work of Arnold Van Gennep and Mary Douglas to develop the concept of interstructural liminality. He described those in a liminal position as "naked, unaccommodated man"—a phrase which he had borrowed from Shakespeare's King Lear. In Malkki's view, experts who stress the aberrance of displacement also indirectly reinforce the perceived naturalness and normalcy of territorialized national identities. Nugent's interviews also led him to believe that the Ghana/Togo refugees were "awaiting the day when they could return to their homes." *Smugglers, Secessionists and Loyal Citizens*, 216.

41. I am currently working with Wilson Yayoh on translations of, and a commentary on, this newspaper.

42. *Ablɔḍe Safui*, 28, July 13, 1960, translation by Edem Adotey and Wilson Yayoh.

43. *Ablɔḍe Safui*, 24, March 23, 1960, translation by Edem Adotey and Wilson Yayoh.

44. *Ablɔḍe Safui*, 26, May 26, 1960, translation by Edem Adotey and Wilson Yayoh.

45. *Ablɔḍe Safui*, 36, n.d., but judging by contents, October 1961.

46. Ibid.

47. *Ablɔḍe Safui*, 49, May 12, 1965, translation by Tina Dugbazah and Wilson Yayoh.

48. Ibid.

49. Malkki, "Refugees and Exiles," 516.

50. Peter Geschiere and Stephen Jackson, "Autochthony and the Crisis of Citizenship: Democratization, Decentralization, and the Politics of Belonging," *African Studies Review* 49, no. 2 (2006): 1–7, quotation from pages 1 and 4.

51. This perspective has begun to emerge from the project that Wilson Yayoh and I have undertaken, with the support of the British Academy's International Partnership and Mobility scheme.

10 A Cold War Geography

South African Anti-Apartheid Refuge and Exile in London, 1945–1994

Susan Dabney Pennybacker

The global war that formally ended in 1945 and the events of its immediate aftermath—Nuremberg, the brutal repression of anticolonial risings in the French empire, Indian independence and partition, the 1948 Middle East war, the promulgation of South African apartheid that year, and the subsequent British aerial bombing of Malaya—formed a protracted conjuncture in which Europe's cities, many now in stages of physical ruin, felt the refracted pulse of events that forever altered their demographies. In postwar London, the confluence of the Cold War and the events of "decolonization" were hardly separable, and political exile from these theaters of conflict was prevalent.

This chapter explores individual South African exile testimonies about the period from the 1950s to 1994, when each informant discussed below passed some time in London.[1] Their testimonies were taken by two South African interlocutors Hilda Bernstein (1915–2006), and Wolfie Kodesh (1918–2006), leading anti-apartheid activists of Communist backgrounds who both had been exiles in Britain. Bernstein and Kodesh spoke with their subjects proximate to Nelson Mandela's 1991 release from prison and his 1994 election as president. Bernstein was a Russian Jewish immigrant to South Africa from Britain at age eighteen, from a Soviet diplomat's Bolshevik family. She served in the Johannesburg City Council from 1943 and was engaged in labor and women's organizing efforts—all as a South African Communist Party (SACP) member, though the SACP's forerunner, the Communist Party of South Africa (CPSA), was declared illegal in 1950. After her husband and fellow Communist, the architect Lionel "Rusty" Bernstein, faced house arrest and each had endured other forms of repression, they fled to Botswana in 1963, and on to London, returning to South Africa in 1994. Kodesh was the son of Jewish pogrom-era migrants to South Africa, where he grew up in Cape Town's legendary District Six and fought in the Ethiopian campaign against the Italian invasion of the 1930s. A journalist and underground activist who had hidden Mandela in his Johannesburg flat, Kodesh was a CPSA/SACP member from 1938 and, like Bernstein, faced banning as well as detention. In 1963, he also fled to London, and later to Lusaka, returning to South Africa in 1991. Bernstein's and Kodesh's interviews took place in exile locales that included Britain and in some instances South Africa, after a subject's return; Bernstein used her interviews in part toward the publication of *The Rift* (1994), and both sets of testimonies came to constitute archival collections. The refugee, émigré, visitor, and exile presences articulated within are cases drawn from a wider project in which this author treats the interrelated histories of postwar activist networks running between and among Delhi, Port-of-Spain, southern Africa, various points in Europe, and London.[2]

The Metropole as Exile Hub

Britain, and especially London, had received exiles throughout the earlier twentieth century, the post-Versailles transfers of populations dwarfing previous immigration. While London did not emerge from the 1914–1918 war as a full-blown "multiracial" and "multicultural" center, remaining predominantly white and largely Protestant, interwar era racial politics reflected the centrality of seaward movement. The lascars and descendants of Afro-Caribbean and American slaves, Africans and Asians who worked on the lower decks, as well as prominent colonial intellectual activists, came to live and work in London, bound up in the patterns of political organization that dominated the European capitals, but subject to a wider geopolitics.

Communists, Second International socialists and social-democrats, anarchists, and the advocates of liberalism and labourism who arose in the parliamentary framework at Westminster and beyond, increasingly engaged these new demographic and political layers as the empire sustained the increasingly pervasive economic slump. Interwar era antiracism and anticolonialism encompassed early critiques of labor conditions in the South African mines, on some issues adopting a language that took inspiration from the circles of Comintern (Communist International) agents and visitors.

The numbers of exiles, immigrants, and refugees in Britain, still predominantly white, had come to encompass many Jews (300,000 by 1914, as compared with roughly 20–30,000 persons of African and Asian descent), and other Europeans who came in the wake of Hitler's 1933 ascent to power and the subsequent political repression, racial laws, and depredations of his regime—the vast majority of whom were centered in London. The fallout from postwar anti-imperial activism and the accompanying social and economic movements of imperial implosion thrust thousands more toward London in waves of better-off émigrés, working-class migrants, "asylum-seekers," and the diplomatic corps of the newly independent states.

Before the repressive British Nationalities Acts of the postwar era began to limit the numbers of those who could meet the legal standard of entry into Britain, labor recruitment swelled the Afro-Caribbean presence in West and South London. South Asians came to form the largest postwar communities, complemented by continued in and out-migrants from Ireland, the Dominions, and the African continent, including significant numbers from the former British southern Africa, as conditions worsened economically and the calculus of white political and personal safety became more deeply affected by conflict. African students were joined in London by working class African immigrants, some of them war veterans remaining after demobilization.

Arrivals benefitted from many measures of the British welfare state, its public provision enhanced by the needs of war devastation and by the competition with both Europe and the Soviets. Yet they also confronted a suspicious and often hostile racial environment. Racial progress and racial panic coexisted in Britain during the postwar administrations and into the years of Margaret Thatcher's and John Major's governments, punctuated by serious acts of violence and systematic discrimination, and even more often by private prejudice. The liberal democracy that claimed inalienable rights to safe haven for so many, was at the same time the weak surviving pivot of an exploitative empire that fostered unresolved relationships at home. Tens of thousands of South Africans, some defying death and imprisonment for their opposition to the regime at home, made their way to points in southern Africa, Europe, the US, Israel, and Britain after the War. Joanne Tague's portrait of Dar es Salaam in this volume, offers one instance. Those in London were not the only South Africans to leave; people of all political persuasions who possessed resources or contacts to do so fled the National Party's government, and the violence, economic dislocation, and political repression that grew in their homeland.

Britain allowed entry to those who were defined as British subjects, and admitted many others on temporary visas and permits, in an elaborate system of conventions. These persons were not political dissenters in many instances, and most were not political activists. But for the committed few thousand South Africans who continued actively to oppose apartheid from abroad, London served both as a critical center of operations for the public propaganda campaign of the growing international anti-apartheid movement, and as one command center for the underground armed struggle against the South African government that ensued after the early 1960s—the latter engendering full Soviet support until 1989. This double existence—as a peaceful, antiracist, broadly based, global "human rights" movement in one guise, and as a paramilitary, ideologically orthodox, communist-engaged, black-dominated and secret underground movement in another—characterized one kind of an anti-apartheid urban-centered Cold War geography.[3]

Exiles from South Africa

Many exiles were banned from returning to South Africa. Events at home brought intensified repression, the episodes of the Sharpeville Massacre of 1960, and the Soweto Uprising and shootings of 1976, marking off two of the periods of the

Fig. 10.1 Carol Brickley, British "convenor" of the City of London Anti-Apartheid Group, speaks at a protest against MI5 surveillance of activists, London, 1985. (Courtesy archives of the CLAAG, and *Non-Stop Against Apartheid*.)

greatest flight abroad, as militants and their families daringly challenged the security forces (BOSS) and army at their heels. Though the British government allowed entry rights, and in many cases allowed visas and permits to be extended, it also allowed the South African security forces to use London as an arena for surveillance in which to extend the regime of repression at home. Some exiles simply attempted to blend anonymously into life in Britain to avoid further scrutiny.

A surreal conflict between being welcomed and being followed, between being celebrated and of being arrested or deported, was a prominent feature of anti-apartheid exile, as it was in the Parisian context described by Meredith Terretta in this volume. Many persons simply fell out of sight and left no testimony. Some South African exiles lived long enough to return to Africa. South Africans from a multiplicity of racial and ethnic backgrounds found themselves and their families in contradictory and opposite circumstances, now residing in a country with a sizable *white* majority beset with many racial problems, and most of them in what was a massive, spatially segregated urban agglomeration. Londoners were divided by race and ethnicity to a significant extent, and especially by socioeconomic difference, the communities of color almost entirely subsumed in poor, predominantly white areas until much later in the city's demographic evolution.

South African exiles were not a homogeneous mass of people. Those of all class backgrounds were among the arrivals in London, though black Africans were most likely to remain on the African continent in states of refuge, especially in postindependence Zambia, Mozambique, and Tanzania—Tague's study a case in point. Many whites arriving were of British ancestry and did not face the kinds of restrictions that had so deeply affected Jewish and Central European entrants to Britain between 1933 and 1939; the latter had been legal aliens, *not* British subjects.[4] Interwar policy had catered to the more educated, the employable, and those with connections, while the South African exodus spanned a more inclusive social hierarchy. Jewish activists were highly represented among the political dissenters, and in some instances were descendants of British subjects who had been transmigrants, though most acquired tentative rights as political exiles after arrival.

The "archive" of London South African political exile is a multitudinous one. As South African President Frederik Willem de Klerk began to move toward a *rapprochement* between Mandela and the key players in the West, leading members of the activist community seized the moment to begin a process of communal debriefing. "Exile archives" grew in the late 1980s and early 90s; many of their interviewees were on the cusp of returning to South Africa, some after decades abroad, others after exile for a much shorter period.[5]

PH's family left South Africa because of his parents' Liberal party political activity in the Pretoria area; both parents were placed under banning orders in 1960. They had harbored the family of the white teacher John Harris, who was charged with planting a station bomb in 1964 in Johannesburg leading to an episode in which an elderly passerby was killed—a crime for which Harris was executed when PH's family left. PH was sixteen when he and his siblings came to England. He told Hilda Bernstein, "there's a whole interesting phenomenon . . . about the impact on children which you probably will be looking at . . . the number of nervous breakdowns that there are . . . that transition can be very, very dramatic and difficult to family life."

In interviewing him Bernstein (also a southern England exile at that time), stated "We whites are immediately acceptable because we're white and the others are immediately identified as strangers. And treated as such." PH replied:

> And subject to racism in Britain as well, which is still very, very powerful. And I think of the black families who are in exile . . . I think of visiting . . . [a black exiled family's] house in Finchley [North London] . . . a fairly run-down house . . . of seeing a situation of cold rainy weather and [of their] somehow just looking totally out of place in it. And a kind of depression about that kind of existence which . . . for blacks it's just enormous. Whites, you can try and escape from that in one way or another.[6]

In 1993, Communist activist and interviewer Wolfie Kodesh spoke in Johannesburg, with HL, the son of Edwardian missionaries to East Africa.[7] Despite his engagement in "terrorist" activities as a young South African Liberal Party cadre, HL possessed the patrial right of abode in Britain. Because of the illness of his mother, he was able to obtain a British passport and to travel there after his release from a South African prison in 1971: "There were a large number of people I knew . . . a large number of other exiles . . . people whom I had been in jail with . . . my whole culture was . . . English . . . my parents were English . . . England certainly wasn't my home but a very easy comfortable place to live in." (Here, HL's remarks call forth Shadle's description in this volume of the earlier generation of Kenyan white settlers.) Kodesh asked HL about the racial context he had witnessed in England; other South Africans had reported seeing "black people and white people doing a 'black man's job.'" HL replied: "I think my vision . . . fairly soon—was how insidious the British society was . . . all these appearances but in fact if you ever wanted to change anything 'I can't. . . .' The system worked very, very effectively and very strongly. It was a highly sophisticated, very conservative society." In 1981, HL went to work on a newspaper in Salisbury, in newly independent Zimbabwe and then managed to get back to South Africa, where he reflected on his return: "If you're white, you're privileged. And I think that we do, we still suffer. . . . But when I think of the other people, particularly black South Africans, and the ways that their lives have been totally destroyed, that's what still makes me very, very angry."

London's spatial and social segregation replicated divisions only too familiar to South Africans; metropolitan racial inequities came as bitter revelations. Yet many also reveled in the freedoms of London, attaching themselves to persons whom they met there and to social movements and activist circles, and living political and personal lives of complexity, in patterns common to exile in other locations—as seen elsewhere in this volume, Cape Verdeans, Congolese, and Mozambicans all experienced features of this complexity in otherwise very different contexts. Their place of origin and commitment to anti-apartheid politics (in the cases of the exiles whose words appear here) drew them to partake of metropolitan culture, to contribute to it, and continually to assess it as outsiders and as interlopers, as Londoners in one guise and as birds of passage in others.

RA, a white woman South African, came to the UK to do an MA degree, and remained there in part because she felt that she and her Sri Lankan husband could not live in South Africa after the passage of the prohibitive Mixed Marriages Act. In 1958–1959, she became involved with the Movement for Colonial Freedom that had a strong "feed-in" from the Communist Party and the Labour Party. She met her spouse in the circles of the West African Students' Union and the Nigerian Students' Association. "That was what we were here for . . . to make contact and live the kind of life you could not live in South Africa." She recalled for Bernstein their meeting houses in London, the physical structures so emblematic of mobilization. She said to Bernstein "they were there [in London] as activists, we all were, to do our job and we were also there because it was a place where you got emotional excitement. . . . I think it is important to stress the African base of this thing and people who tell the story too often forget it. To say nothing of the women . . . their energies come out of the conflict between what you've left and where you are." Metropolitan life fostered many relationships and tore others apart.

The legal freedoms of exile did not extend to the possibility of remaining free under apartheid. JG, a black journalist, left South Africa under protest, through Botswana. From there he went to write in (what was still) Tanganyika, then Kenya, then the USA, studying at Harvard, working in New York City, and then departing for eleven years' work in London. JG described for Bernstein, the fear that underlay many of his life's problems: "I fell in love with this woman who was a photographer from England, now you start thinking we love each other, we get married, how the hell do I take her home? Live with her where there are a myriad of laws that are blocking that woman? No way, you can't do it. . . . Exile is frustrating. Totally frustrating."

The experience of domestic strife and discord is recorded in many of the interviews with South Africans. MB, a black South African woman was married to a black South African literary figure who achieved celebrity status in the human rights movement while they were in exile in London with their children. She described the Finchley neighborhood schoolyard chatter directed at her sons and her antipathy toward her husband:

> I said, "You know, it seems like *you* . . . *you're* the champion of women's rights except for me." And I think he was just taken aback. . . . We never really looked after our children, and in the meantime, I would be struggling, he'd been to China, he's been all over the place. . . . Whether I was in England or in America, there was still no support and it's only much later I realize that, well here's a man who's really running away. . . . I remember the first things . . . my young sons . . . they came back and they said, what's a wog? . . . And the girls have told me later on, when they needed a father, it's coming back again to this man, but there were times that they needed [him], and he just wasn't there for them.

Even if the home realm was recalled as emotionally secure and sustaining, any family or couple or individual could have come up against the walls of English class and racial exclusion.

JM, a black journalist and actor, left South Africa with his parents for London shortly after the Sharpeville shootings, when he was starting school. His father composed the score for an important traveling South African theater production that had a celebrated London run. His parents used the money from the success of the opening performances in South Africa to finance the trip abroad, and used their tourist passports to stay for what they thought would be a short time. JM explained his father's motives for leaving South Africa to Bernstein: "I think the assumption was . . . moving into a bigger pool where things were freer . . . my father thought he would be able to develop as a composer and a writer and found lots of doors closed to him in a country where who you know and what you know is very important and what your educational certificates say, and so on. . . . He didn't have anything that was relevant to that, nor in fact did my mother . . . and they were not prepared to go back to South Africa until serious change had occurred."

They went on to independent Zambia in 1964. But JM's mother separately (and differently) explained to Bernstein, that his father's first BBC job had ended because her husband went on a trip with an African National Congress group to Algeria for its independence celebrations, a visit discovered by the BBC. He had gone to Algeria even though both parents had been active only as sympathetic supporters of the ANC while abroad. JM said he himself did not feel that he had roots in the UK: "It's a lot to do with the racialism, it's a lot to do with an anger at the nature of the society which is you know, repressive in the most dangerous ways . . . in unseen ways, in ways which the natives actually, I think, to a large extent, don't perceive anymore. It goes very far back, deep into their historic roots, and it leads to . . . more constrained forms of expression than most societies that I know in a way. And that frightens me. Also the weather's not very pleasant. . . . I feel happier when I am living in an African country . . . doing [films] in Kenya . . . and . . . Zimbabwe."

VB, a black South African woman, left her country at age three and a half with her parents, both politically motivated, to come to Botswana, Zambia, and finally to England, arriving when she was seven. VB first visited South Africa at eighteen, and several times thereafter, telling Bernstein: "I spent a couple of months in a rural area, which was quite a shock to the system. I'd never lived in a hut. I'd never used a Primus stove. . . . I'd never used an outside latrine . . . not in my conscious years. . . . You pick it up and you fit in, you know. But I don't think a lot of people, out of choice, would go and live in the countryside on that basis." BV could not see herself returning, even to Johannesburg. She felt there was a loss of privacy and reserve in South Africa: "and that can be a culture shock. It is something you actually have to get used to." Her testimony challenges any presumption that black African exile in London was uniformly undesirable, except as a measure of temporary refuge. It was harder to assimilate at an older age, and indeed, some white exiles found British reserve suffocating, alienating, and unfamiliar if they were without income or family, especially as they endured London's rough and unremitting labor markets, stripped of racial privilege, subject to legal constraints, and often dependent upon state welfare bureaucracies.

The ambivalence in the testimonies taken as a whole was not always as present in the words of a given individual, but the bifurcated world of the apartheid state and the "free" state—the urban worlds and the rural and shire worlds of South African and Britain, comingled with the images of past and future that guided many in the reconstruction of their lives undertaken for their listeners. These led to the positing of a future that would relinquish such ambivalence, that could be more decisively chosen, even as many acknowledged that the future, once witnessed, was disappointing, or at best, uncharted. Though not a post-Stalinist state, apartheid South Africa functioned on the basis of violent coercion and repressive, bureaucratic regulation and control. The exiled South African

Communist Party (SACP) also enforced the discipline of its membership living globally; the British welfare state and government, police, and Foreign Office officials represented other points on a spectrum of invasive authority. In these instances, the slippery divisions of the Cold War absorbed and accommodated the contradictions of living not in one of the two superpowers, but of living in their interstices—reflections of the global order that shimmered in distinctive ways.

GC was among a large group of white exiles who came to Britain to avoid military service. He left South Africa in 1976 when he was on active duty call up for the war in Angola, first stopping in Botswana, in a pattern that bespoke the impact of another theater of the Cold War on the outcomes for the apartheid state. GC told Bernstein of finding shelter with ANC supporters in London, working "off the books" for a Left employer, being granted the immigration services' "exceptional leave to remain," and four years' later, acquiring refugee status. He was trailed by BOSS; in an interrogation session with security officers, a colleague was shown photos of his meeting her in an Oxford Street pub in Central London. GC spoke with Kodesh:

> I found the attitude of British people very unfriendly. . . . There was very little support from any of the British people I met, and very little understanding. . . . It was very hard to make a living in those days, because we weren't allowed to work while we were waiting for our asylum application, one could go on the dole [unemployment benefit] but it was very, very low. And I ended up squatting in a very run-down old house in the East End. And living . . . in conditions of poverty, which of course I wasn't accustomed to, being a white South African. And of course, the weather and the dreariness of London became very psychologically oppressive and I think the only thing that really kept me going, was my commitment to the South African struggle and the support I got from my comrades.

In his time in London, he helped to lead the war resisters' movement, but became determined to join the underground organization in the front line states, *Umkhonto we Sizwe*, and to return to Africa for training. He went to the Soviet Union for seven months after his first stint in Africa, then back to Lusaka, and returned to the UK for the birth of his daughter. His journeys bespoke the Cold War context of the militarized armed struggle in Africa, the relative freedom of travel that obtained in the middle zones that lay between African states of varying political allegiances, the lesser power that Britain now was, and the magnanimity of the Soviet state in its South African project. The USSR was a competing base of support to that offered by Britain, involving different kinds of political means testing. GC and others cruised between these points; Havana was also on the map for some young South Africans in long-term exile and training, as was the German Democratic Republic and other points in the former Eastern Europe.

When he again returned to Botswana, GC played a central role in the movement based there: "our role . . . was to oversee and implement all the underground activities of the ANC from Botswana." GC preferred his *Umkhonto we Sizwe* experience to the London years: "In London . . . the city is so big and vast, that you can't physically have that kind of community [a close, communal group of politically involved people, as he had before leaving South Africa]—one comrade is this side of London, it takes you an hour and costs you almost a pound to get there and back. . . . The external social life is so far removed from the realities with which you are concerned . . . too big, too dreary, too expensive a place to live." GC elevated his inspirational time in the African resistance movement over metropolitan exile, insisting on its revelatory role for his cohort of white radicals, engaged with their black counterparts. He said, of Botswana refuge:

> [This was] my first extended period in any black African country. . . . As a white South African, even a politicized white South African, I had a lot of hang-ups, especially of my generation who had never had the chance to work politically with or socialize with black people. So that type of experience was quite strange in that sense. . . . I felt very strongly that I should join *Umkhonto we Sizwe*. . . . That period in *Umkhonto we Sizwe* was . . . the greatest time in the movement that I've ever had. . . . And if you weren't there, you've missed a lot. . . . Now [in postapartheid South Africa] we have a lot of white *Umkhonto we Sizwe* comrades inside the country . . . having been trained with black comrades. . . . It's not just that this is a symbolic white participant . . . they went to the same training, the same hardships . . . slept in dugouts or tents or whatever it is, together . . . ate lousy food, got malaria together. This was the experience of the '76 generation, of black comrades, and we've had to share it . . . we have to continue sharing it. . . . For me, that is the most important aspect of my generation of exiles, of white exiles.

Umkhonto we Sizwe's military activity in Africa was complemented both by an "above-ground," British-led, and visible movement in London, and by illicit activities launched inside of apartheid South Africa.[8] Those in South Africa began to rely on the London operations for more and more information with which to fuel work in a censorious and repressive environment at home, using advances in communications technology to link the disparate urban infrastructures. One participant in these exchanges of vital data, testified:

> So you know, the geographical separation has been a nominal thing at many levels. Of course it has been very important and an inhibiting thing at other [points]. . . . But now that they can pick up phones and faxes and telexes without fear of any kind of reprisals, talking to a banned organization, we're on the hotline all the time, I mean we're feeding information in . . . feeding our books in for the first time! That's been so gratifying to actually reach that market, although our brief is international, and had to be because we were raising international consciousness, it's been so marvelous to have people openly clamoring for our stuff inside South Africa.

These remarks portray another freedom represented by London, anticipating the discourses on information technology of our own era, sharply distinct from the culture of surveillance that GC recalled above. In this version of London's role, information flowed from the British metropole assisting activism in the far more repressive South African context.

In 1993, Kodesh interviewed a close relation of one of the leading members of the ANC, the black male activist MM, in Johannesburg. MM came from a small town in the Transkei, and from a leading African political family that fled to Lesotho in 1957 and for a few years traveled freely in and out of South Africa, as no passports were required. This changed after 1962 when his father went underground. After Mandela's 1963 arrest, his father and others were seized at Arthur Goldreich's Liliesleaf Farm, outside of Johannesburg and imprisoned. MM then obtained a Lesotho passport and crossed South Africa into Botswana in 1964, and through the channels of the ANC, went to Lusaka, Dar es Salaam and finally, on an ANC-purchased air ticket, flew to London in 1965: "Myself personally, I wanted to join *Umkhonto we sizwe* but a scholarship had been arranged for me in England so it was decided that I should go to school. . . . Most students were processed in Dar es Salaam in those days." This journey was welcome: "I thought it was a wonderful adventure to see Africa because as you know in South Africa we are so isolated."[9] Tague describes the cosmopolitanism and elite educational training offered to some of those arriving in Dar es Salaam.

In England, MM went to a South African students' house in suburban Surrey, set up by a fellow exile, and for several months of 1965 had a chance to "look around . . . although you know English from school, it's not a spoken language as such. . . . I think the first thing is to get used to speaking English as a normal spoken language . . . and it was still quite very cold when I first got there in April." MM joined the Labour Party's youth section, the Young Socialists, and found his new comrades already engaged on many issues of South African anti-apartheid, and all else:

> In fact the shock to me was how little I knew about the rest of the world, so I found the . . . months before I started college very useful because I finally had the time to catch up on, to try to catch up on, reading about South Africa. . . . I didn't know anything about Vietnam, but I went to demonstrations . . . and had to quickly learn . . . and . . . about the Cold War as well. I mean the whole world was totally a closed book to us from South Africa . . . and there were lots of debates in the Young Socialists . . . for example, on Stalin's role in the Spanish Civil War and I didn't even know there was a Spanish Civil War . . . because before I'd just been [in] South Africa and Lesotho; that has been, that was, my world.

After completing a series of college courses in London, MM became a trainee engineer on the flyover project behind Paddington Station and, in 1968, a site engineer on a shopping center in the Wood Green neighborhood and in the building of a housing estate in Chelsea. He married an Englishwoman whom he met in the anti-apartheid movement, and visited Algiers in 1972 where he met exiles from the ANC. His trip affords another example of the travel between the British metropole and one of the capitals of the Non-Aligned movement.[10] In 1973, MM left the UK with his family to work in Tanzania, and returned to England after three years to undertake further education that led to his career as a journalist. His exile was a refuge, a chance to grow.

Wolfie Kodesh spoke with DG in August of 1993, in London—a male, Jewish South African, who was a defendant in one of the key trials of South African history. Spared the death sentence, DG spent twenty-two years in prison for treason while his wife, who had been held in more limited detention, left the country with their children to live in London; he joined them there after a negotiated release. DG spoke to Kodesh of the political conundrum of the South African Communist Party, its adherents, and followers, and commented upon the bewilderment of life as he found it in exile:

> I came out and found myself in a world where the issues are not as stark and as simple as they are to South Africans involved in the progressive movement. Where we know quite simply that racism is apartheid, apartheid is part of capitalism, is part of imperialism and this was accepted throughout the ANC and the liberation movement ever since I've known [of it]—and not just amongst communists as such. For African people when I was growing up, they knew from the advertisements and where they worked who their employers were and that the capital was British and American, General Motors, Ford, General Electric. . . . But when you get to Europe . . . in the climactic period of the Cold War, all these things got blurred in the kind of "Oh we are democratic in Britain. We have a great human rights record." And when you know what the British state through its armies and so on, and colonial administration had done in Africa and Asia and Latin America and the Americans had done and were doing and the British were supporting it [what the US was] doing and benefitting from [it]. And there's a kind of ideological falsity about Europe and its politics. And yet the mass of people seem[s] to accept it. And so it was exciting actually to see this.

Here, London is displayed in both the hubris and depth of its cosmopolitanism.

DG finally spoke at length about the 1989 breakup of the Soviet Union, and of communists who had been unwilling to admit to its "weakness of theory and practice. . . . Perhaps terror and authoritarianism can sap the will of people to take initiatives and fight back." He acknowledged what he had seen as "the need to defend the Soviet Union" in the Cold War era, though the demise of [the Soviet presence in] Africa had, in his view, brought about a "freer Southern African region. . . . It's an odd contradictory element." Kodesh's interviews often display a redemptive quality—the subject recounts an activist's life story for posterity, settling scores, and often evoking high drama. At the heart of this kind of testimony is the sense of motion, both in geographic terms, and in the movement of ideas—a realignment of perception through experience. The latter was often traumatic. London became the setting for private realignment, personal discord, and marital and family reckoning.

Conclusion

While kindness and curiosity surely populate many anecdotes, a will for revenge against the British or a sense of the implacable perception of difference that is never overcome, seemed to propel a majority whose testimonies fuel this project, to depart London once more or to enjoy it where affordable as tourists and as infrequent guests in the years after those of their most intense metropolitan residence and engagement. Even long time expatriates, residents, and those who are now citizens can seek an existential return to their precious points of origin that may never come in lived experience. This metropolitan imaginary has its own demise embedded within it—a will to depart, bound up with the perceptions of possibilities and very often with political developments in South Africa and elsewhere on the African Continent.

In considering these imaginaries, the private lives and plights of individuals only recently deceased or still living engage an important, necessary, and urgent layer of inquiry, pursuing another act of appropriation in which the private realm actually informs a deeper understanding of political narrative. The glances at the problems of sexuality, marital plight, and cults of masculinity exposed within the fragments gathered here form an interface with the entangled issues of racial politics, racial etiquette, and racial antagonism that the testimonies also display. The occasion of motion, the occurrence of movement from one highly provocative zone of global conflict to an historic center of exile in London, and in some cases early repatriation, provided interviewers the opportunities of inquiry.

As London's global metropolitan role shifted back and forth across a revealing political limelight, the world of the exile often merged with that of the global political activist and the visitor. Information technology altered space and time distances and disguised the constraints of borders, the most recent closing years of the anti-apartheid struggle a spectacular case in point. Contemporary London thrives on the political tourism of a vast array of communities in transition back and forth, and increasingly confronts its real and presumed dangers; the most recent fraught discourses surrounding the recruitment of British-born youth to "radical Islam," and the key role that immigration debate played in the lead up to the election of 2014, as well as in the 2016 European Union debates and "Brexit," offer contemporary cases in point. This essay takes the London exile experience as a basis from which to offer suggestive commentary on these wider issues, demonstrating that the lives of individuals in motion and their reflections upon them upend both "urban" and "Cold War" paradigms for the postwar era. It not only makes the ties of each to a broad history of "decolonization" more transparent, but identifies a location in metropolitan, democratic culture on the trail of the ostensible Cold War opponent—in the person of the London-based cosmopolitan, antiracist radical, someone with roots in the former British empire, possessing wavering rights to enter and reside in the great metropolis, who became both its emblem and its outcast: bearer of the twin burdens of refuge and exile.

Notes

1. I am grateful to audiences in the UK and the US who have commented upon this work in recent years. Leslie Witz, Jan Gross, Lynn Lees, Seth Koven, Jonathan Hyslop, Judy Ann Seidman, David Robb, and the late James A. Miller, all provided trenchant criticisms of iterations of its wider project and in some cases, first-hand knowledge of the issues governing the material-in-progress. I am especially grateful to Stanley Sello and other present and former members of the staff of the Mayibuye Archive of University of the Western Cape/ Robben Island Museum, for assistance with access to the oral history collections cited within, and to the staffs of the South African Historical Archive, and the Wits Historical Collections at the University of the Witwatersrand, for help in the use of related material. Initials are used to protect copyright. My former colleagues at the University of the Western Cape, and at WISER (Wits Institute for Social and Economic Research), University of the Witwatersrand, provided the best possible contexts for developing this project in its early stages. I am grateful for past support for this work rendered by the Shelby Cullom Davis Endowment of the Department of History, Princeton University, and by the Office of the Dean and the Trustees of Trinity College, Hartford, Connecticut.

2. See Hilda Bernstein, *The Rift: The Exile Experience of South Africans* (London: J. Cape, 1994). The book-in-progress which treats material in this essay, is entitled *Fire By Night, Cloud By Day: Refuge and Exile in Postwar London.*

3. Seventy thousand people born in South Africa resided in the UK in 1991, though not all 'exiles' were native-born South Africans. See Mark Israel, *South African Political Exile in the United Kingdom* (London: Palgrave Macmillan, 1999), 1, 92–101 on the changing legal conditions of entry. Essential narratives of the era are: Roger Fieldhouse, *Anti-Apartheid: A History of the Movement in Britain* (London: Merlin, 2005); Stephen Ellis and Tsepo Sechaba (the latter a pseudonym), *Comrades Against Apartheid: the ANC and the South African Communist Party in Exile* (Bloomington: Indiana University Press, 1992); and Stephen Ellis, *External Mission: the ANC in Exile, 1960–1990* (Oxford: Oxford University Press, 2013). On London, see esp. Mark Gevisser, *A Legacy of Liberation: Thabo Mbeki and the Future of the South African Dream* (London: St. Martin's Press, 2010); and Lynn Carneson, *Red in the Rainbow: The Life and Times of Fred and Sarah Carneson* (Cape Town: Zebra Press, 2010). On the armed struggle organization called *Umkhonto we Sizwe*, "Spear of the Nation" or MK, see James Ngculu, *The Honour to Serve: Recollections of an Umkhonto Soldier (*Claremont: David Philip, 2009). On anti-apartheid, see, David Everatt, *The Origins of Non-Racialism: White Opposition to Apartheid in the 1950s* (Johannesburg: Wits University Press, 2009); and Rob Skinner, *The Foundations of Anti-Apartheid: Liberal Humanitarians and the Transnational Activists in Britain and the United States, c. 1919–64* (New York: Palgrave Macmillan, 2010);

and Elizabeth M. Williams, *The Politics of Race in Britain and South Africa* (London: I. B. Tauris, 2015).

4. For a larger discussion of refugee issues of the interwar era, and the historical literature that engages it, see Susan Pennybacker, *From Scottsboro to Munich: Race and Political Culture in 1930s Britain* (Princeton: Princeton University Press, 2009).

5. The archived interviews are subject to all the qualifying conditions of ethnographic study: the interviewers' political biases and personal connections to their interviewees, the racial complexion of the interviewing sessions and the temporal locales in which they were conducted, the stated purposes to which they were dedicated (subsequent publication and perhaps the stated intent of generating an *archive*), the access issues that lay in the future (who would read these, when?), and the ages, gender, and a multiple of *other* "identities" of a person that varied greatly in the testimonies. The two important collections of interviews sampled here are those conducted between 1989–91, by Bernstein, (University of the Western Cape, Mayibuye Center, *Hilda and Rusty Bernstein Papers, 1931–2011,* "Transcripts and Tapes of Interviews," B41.2.2); and the longer group of interviews conducted from 1992–95 by Wolfie Kodesh, who spoke with persons in South Africa.(University of the Western Cape, Mayibuye Center, *The Wolfie Kodesh Collection: historical papers and oral history of exile interviews,* Z6616.K59, 016.968). My own interviews conducted in South Africa between 2006 and 2010 and not excerpted here also inform this essay. Underlying this part of my inquiry are profound problems: the retrospective rendering of one's political affiliations and actions in the face of unpredicted modes of change and outcomes, and the violation of the sanctities of privacy and the subliminal domains of the exiles. These engage in turn the problems of representativeness that hound the ethnographer, and the problems of hindsight that beset the historian.

6. See, the *Hilda and Rusty Bernstein Papers,* B4 1.2.2, as cited above. All subsequent excerpts from interviews with Bernstein are taken from this collection.

7. See, the *Wolfie Kodesh Collection,* Z6616.K59,016.968, as cited above. All subsequent excerpts from interviews with Kodesh are taken from this collection.

8. For the best account to date of Britain's 'official' antiapartheid movement, linked to the global 'human rights' campaign and efforts like those supporting divestment and consumer sports and goods boycotts, see Rob Skinner, *The Foundations of Anti-Apartheid.* The book self-evidently does not encompass the history of the Left, or of the SACP. See, also, the British Anti-Apartheid Movement's archives site, http://www.aamarchives.org/.

9. He found Tanzania exciting. The ANC leader Oliver Tambo was there at that time as well as Moses Katane, the activist who had represented South Africa in the anticolonial circles of the Comintern in Europe in the 1930s.

10. Others in Algeria included Black Panther Party leaders Eldridge and Kathleen Cleaver, members of the Palestinian, Tunisian, and Asian liberation fronts, and Vietnamese from the NLF (National Liberation Front). At the University in Dar Es Salaam were the Guyanese Walter Rodney and the Brazilian exile Milton Santos. Ruth First and Harold Wolpe, both South African communist exiles, came as lecturers to the University. In 1982, First was assassinated in her university office in Maputo by an exploding letter bomb. Wolpe and AnnMarie Wolpe taught at the University of Essex, UK. See Tague's essay in this volume for a larger narrative of Dar es Salaam.

11 The French Trials of Cléophas Kamitatu

Immigration Politics, Leftist Activism, and Françafrique in 1970s Paris

Meredith Terretta

CLÉOPHAS KAMITATU WAS thirty-nine years old when he fled Mobutu's Congo with his wife and his child. They entered France on September 9, 1970 at which time they were issued a residence permit, renewable every four months.[1] During the Kamitatu family's first two years, everything went well. Kamitatu was admitted to the doctoral program at the Institute d'Études Politiques de Paris (popularly known as Sciences-Po) and finished his first two years at the top of the class.[2] His eldest child was enrolled in school and his second child was born in Paris in December 1971.[3]

In 1971, a few weeks before the first official visit to Paris of Mobutu Sese Seko, President of the Democratic Republic of Congo, Kamitatu published a book entitled *La grande mystification du Congo Kinshasa: Les crimes de Mobutu* with François Maspero press.[4] It recounts the events that led him and others to oppose what he described as Mobutu's reign of terror against high level politicians who had served in Congo's previous governments. Kamitatu, who had previously served as Minister of the Interior, Minister of Economic Planning and Coordination, and Minster of Foreign Affairs, was among those Mobutu targeted. Among other things, the book recounts how soon after Mobutu seized power on November 25, 1965, Kamitatu was sentenced to five years in prison and four other politicians were publicly hanged for their alleged involvement in a plot to take power.[5] After his release from prison, Kamitatu escaped Congo and sought refuge in France, most likely in order to avoid coerced cooptation into the Mobutu regime.

When Maspero published *La grande mystification du Congo*, the Mobutu regime took action. Kamitatu's family members and friends were arrested in Kinshasa. The Congolese ambassador in Paris asked the French government to launch judicial proceedings against Kamitatu and his French editor, François Maspero.[6] The French government banned the book on June 30, 1971 and charged

Kamitatu and Maspero with public offense to a foreign head of state.[7] They were convicted by the Criminal Court of Paris, and filed an appeal.[8]

In February 1972, Kamitatu applied for political refugee status in France, which he eventually obtained on October 6, 1972.[9] Yet despite his refugee status, from September 1972 to September 1973, the Minister of the Interior, Raymond Marcellin, at the orders of French president Georges Pompidou, attempted to compel Kamitatu to leave French territory. Third Worldist activist lawyer Jean-Jacques de Félice defended him from deportation on every front ranging from the local prefect of Seine-Saint-Denis, where Kamitatu resided, to the State Council, France's highest court.[10] During the months spent facing expulsion, Kamitatu penned no fewer than fourteen letters, petitions, appeals, and memoranda to the Administrative Court of Paris, the Refugee Appeals Commission, and the State Council. De Félice pled his case in three hearings. During this period, Kamitatu had no legal right to work in France and had difficulty finding lodging for his family. His wife became ill and his older child anxious. All the while, Kamitatu continued to pursue his doctoral study at Sciences-Po. The courts eventually protected Kamitatu's refugee status. He remained in France, completed his doctorate, and published another scathing critique of the Mobutu regime: *Zaïre: Pouvoir à la portée du peuple*, with L'Harmattan press in 1977.

This chapter uses the Kamitatu case to analyze two political currents, each characterized by entangled transregional networks of French and African state and non-state actors in early 1970s France. First, Kamitatu's case fell in the crosshairs of the emergence of immigration as arguably *the* political issue facing France and its population—immigrant or not—in 1972. Secondly, through the figure of Kamitatu as a political refugee and his advocates in France, this chapter scrutinizes the Africa policies of the French government as the powerful Gaullist trio—President Georges Pompidou, Prime Minister Pierre Messmer, and Jacques Foccart, Chief of Staff for African and Malagasy Affairs from 1958 to 1974—collaborated to shape them from the summer of 1972 to the spring of 1974. In enabling an examination of the ways that French politics of immigration intersected with Franco-African foreign relations during Foccart's final years as *Monsieur Afrique*, the Kamitatu case brings something new to our understanding of *Françafrique*—a term describing the postcolonial intensification of France's bilateral relationships with the independent African states it had formerly ruled as well as those it sought to bring into its sphere of influence, such as Mobutu's Zaïre.[11] Contra a vein of mostly Anglo-American scholarship that has called the usefulness of Françafrique as an analytical category into question, this chapter views Françafrique operating as a contingent conceptual shorthand through the latter half of the twentieth-century that African and French state and nonstate actors alike invoked to achieve specific political ends.[12] The chapter analyzes Kamitatu's legal case to argue that a Gaullist Africa policy intersected with and influenced the politics and legislation of immigration and censorship within France itself in the early 1970s.

The chapter begins with a discussion of France's political context in the early 1970s through a focus on immigration and censorship in the service of France's Africa policy under the Pompidou-Messmer government, the late Gaullist years. In this respect, it operates as a parallel to others studies of exile hubs in this volume, notably those by Susan Pennybacker, Aliou Ly, and Joanne Tague. It then investigates and analyses the legal strategies utilized by French officialdom seeking to expel Kamitatu and by the Leftist advocates working to keep him in France. It concludes by considering France's foreign relations with postcolonial African heads of state as a proxy for political confrontations over immigration, governance, and liberal democracy within France itself.

Do Exiles Have Legal Rights?

In September 1972, two circulars, one signed by the Raymond Marcellin, Minister of the Interior, and the other, by Joseph Fontanet, Minister of Labor, Employment, and Population, were applied in September 1972 under Prime Minister Pierre Messmer. The Marcellin-Fonatanet circulars signaled the French government's increased control of immigration and launched immigration as a leading political issue in France.[13] The circulars irregularized the status of thousands of immigrants in France by making the issuance of residence permits contingent upon the immigrant's possession of a work contract and "decent lodging," and by putting an end to automatic regularization procedures for workers and automatic renewals. The immediate result was to strip immigrants of their legal status in France as their residence permits and/or work contracts expired. The circulars placed local prefects and police stations in charge of issuing both the required status documents and orders of expulsion for those who could not legally obtain them and made administrative courts responsible for the implementation of immigration policies. Kamitatu's order of expulsion, issued in September 1972, the very month the Marcellin-Fontanet circulars came into application, thus coincided with France's first *en masse* measures of expulsion.

As the Marcellin-Fontanet circulars inaugurated the French government's control of immigration, so too they signaled a turn in French perceptions of immigrants. On the extreme Right, Jean-Marie Le Pen's National Front and the New Order depicted immigrant workers as criminals causing unemployment and created new phrases to discuss immigrants including "threshold of tolerance," "*immigration sauvage*" (usually glossed as illegal or uncontrolled immigration), and "clandestine migrants."[14] The French Left took up immigration as a political cause, perhaps most effectively through the creation of a Group of Information and Support for Immigrant Workers (GISTI), an association of lawyers, magistrates, students of law, and other legal activists including de Félice, Kamitatu's lawyer.[15] GISTI launched a movement that comprised public awareness campaigns, provided legal advice and support to immigrants, coordinated literacy and social integration initiatives with social workers in the suburbs, joined with other associations to organize hunger strikes protesting immigrant conditions including lodging and employment, and launched investigations of housing conditions.[16] In facilitating public debates about immigration and exposing governmental measures taken to control it, GISTI's end goal was to bridge a growing divide between immigrant and nonimmigrant workers.[17] Throughout the 1970s, as the French government attempted to codify immigration by decree or circular rather than through parliamentary legislation, GISTI continued to file appeals with the State Council as part of their campaign to politicize legal questions of immigration, such as follow-to-join rights for the families of immigrants and refugees.

GISTI's support for intellectual immigrants such as Kamitatu afforded another kind of visibility to the association's goals. GISTI lawyers' advocacy for exiled intellectuals—known as oppositionists in their countries of origin—fit a mode of politically engaged legal activism that the association undertook in the 1970s and maintains to this day. Jean-Jacques de Félice—Kamitatu's lawyer—and Georges Pinet—who represented Mongo Beti, the Cameroonian French writer whose book, *Main basse sur le Cameroun: Autopsie d'une décolonisation* was banned in France in 1972 and who was also threatened with expulsion—were among the active founders of GISTI.

The Effects of Françafrique on Immigration and Censorship in France

The political, economic and cultural effects of France's ongoing relationships with postcolonial francophone African governments in the 1960s and 1970s have been well examined.[18] French Third Worldists and African oppositionists at the time labeled these relationships *neocolonialist* in their ensemble while the successive Fifth Republic French governments and the African leadership they supported referred to them as Franco-African "cooperation." More recently, postcolonial Franco-African relations have been portrayed as formative of Françafrique—a term used to characterize what historian Jean-Pierre Bat describes as the "official illegality," secret police and unofficial personal networks that successive French Gaullist governments, primarily through the figure of Jacques Foccart, set in motion in the independent African states it had formerly ruled.[19] The censorship of Kamitatu's book and the government's efforts to expulse him from French territory are symptomatic of the effects of Françafrique on judicial and political processes within France itself.

The publications that Raymond Marcellin banned as Minister of the Interior numbered 680 from May 1968 to the summer of 1974 when Michel Poniatowski replaced him.[20] All but twelve of those on the list were pornographic in nature and published outside of France. The dozen non-erotic works included the Cuban and French editions of *Tricontinental*, the official magazine of the Organization of African, Asian, and Latin American Peoples' Solidarity, Jean-Claude Garot's *Le Point*, a call to revolution published in Belgium, the *Petit Livre Rouge des écoliers et lycéens*, a student's guide to Maoism published in Switzerland in 1971 and in France in 1972, and *The Anarchist Cookbook* and *The Cultivator's Handbook of Marijuana* published in the US. The remaining political works that Marcellin banned were critical of African postcolonial regimes. Three, including Kamitatu's, issued from Congolese authors and one from Mongo Beti.[21] All four were published in France, three with Maspero press. The Minister of the Interior legitimized the censorship of these works with the decree of August 27, 1939, permitting the French government to ban literature "de provenance étrangère" (lit. of foreign origin). Why would the French government ban African-authored works critical of the regimes that, at the very same time, French journalists disparagingly critiqued in the pages of French newspapers?[22] It did so at the request of Ahmadou Ahidjo and Mobutu Sese Seko, respectively presidents of Cameroon and Congo-Zaire, as a way of silencing the literary critiques of oppositionists who had taken refuge in France. At the same time, it was a part of an ongoing harassment of François Maspero, in the sights of Minister of the Interior Raymond Marcellin since he took over the ministry with the objective of "restoring order" following the events of May 1968.[23] In other words, the aims of Ahidjo, Mobutu, and Pompidou aligned in the early 1970s to censor the free speech of their most troublesome and vocal critics.

Scrambling for a toehold in Congo-Zaïre in the early 1970s, the French were eager to count Mobutu among the African heads of state who were "friends of France."[24] Mobutu invited Foccart to Congo-Zaïre in March 1970. When he visited it for the first time, Foccart's impression of Congo-Zaïre was that it was "an underdeveloped country with fantastic potential" for the exploitation of resources unsurpassed elsewhere in Francophone Africa.[25] After Foccart's tour, Mobutu expressed his desire to "do great things with France," to open the country to French investors, and his hope that, in return, "he would henceforth be treated as the other francophones."[26]

Mobutu made a first official visit to France in March 1971, during which Pompidou seduced him—if Foccart's memory is to be believed—and he returned to Zaïre with a greater than anticipated loan from the French Aid and Cooperation Fund, commitments to technical assistance, and the French Company of Insurance for Exterior Commerce's promise to underwrite French investment, a pledge that Foccart himself negotiated.[27] Yet Foccart soon realized that Mobutu was leveraging France's courtship to gain the upper hand in his relations with Belgium.[28] It was during the Pompidou regime's carefully orchestrated dance of seduction, a time when Mobutu "blew alternately hot and cold," that Kamitatu's book was published.[29] Although it was banned on June 30, 1971, merely six weeks after its publication, censorship did not satisfy Mobutu. He called for Kamitatu's expulsion. On November 2, 1971, Foccart asked the Minister of the Interior to keep Kamitatu under close surveillance as though awaiting reason to arrest and/or deport him.[30] Foccart referred to the book's publication and its aftermath as the "non-event that poisoned Franco-Zairean relations for 18 months."[31]

In April 1972, Zaïre withdrew from the Joint Afro-Malagasy Organization (OCAM), the Francophone African economic community formed in 1965, and Mobutu worked actively for its demise. Despite, or perhaps because of this, the French government was prepared to go to great lengths not to alienate the self-proclaimed *Maréchal* by appearing to provide a safe haven to his political enemies.[32] In sum, the Kamitatu affair presented the French government with an opportunity to curry favor with Mobutu at a time when France wanted it—an opportunity Foccart did not miss. Foccart increased surveillance of Kamitatu over the summer, and in June, on Foccart's advice, Pompidou ordered Marcellin to "distance" him from France.[33] However, as demonstrated below, politics, judicial processes, and international refugee protocols rendered his expulsion impossible, or, as Foccart surmised over twenty years later, made Marcellin unwilling to follow through.[34]

De Félice, Kamitatu, and his advocates would argue that the French government privileged its relationship with African heads of state over the civil liberties of French citizens and African oppositionists seeking refuge in France. In July 1972, Maspero had penned an opinion piece for *Le Monde* entitled "Of Foreign Origin" in which he discussed the Minister of the Interior's abuse of censorship laws, particularly Article 14 of the Law of the Press enabling the ban of any work "of foreign origin." He highlighted the successive bans of "two books on Africa," Kamitatu's and Beti's, and the fact that Marcellin cited "diplomatic reasons" when asked why he ordered their censorship. He then exposed a causal relationship between the censorship of these particular books and France's "interests" in Africa, which were "more than 'diplomatic.' The government must prevent any cause for reproach from its francophone African allies. From whence the necessity to discourage, by any means, potential oppositionists from coming to France to express themselves."[35] Driving straight to the center of France's politico-cultural memory of censorship, Maspero recalled the ban, on the basis of exceptional legislation, of two books condemning torture in Algeria, *La Question* and *La Gangrène*, published by Editions de Minuit under the directorship of Jérôme Lindon who had insisted at the time: "put us on trial and condemn us if we are guilty of lies and defamation." Maspero explained, "We learned later on . . . why the trials never took place. There were neither lies nor defamation,"[36] thus suggesting, through comparison, the accuracy of Kamitatu's portrayal of Mobutu.

Maspero's opinion piece followed the current strategy of French associations, on the extreme Left, like GISTI, to use the law and the press as modes of political action. Through publicly visible contestation in the courts, together with timely press releases and opinion pieces, French activists and lawyers instrumentalized the government's censorship of books authored by Francophone Africans to raise awareness and shape public opinion about French officialdom's peculiar relationship with African heads of state.

Kamitatu's advocates leveraged international refugee law with perhaps even greater utility than they did public opinion. As Kamitatu's case unfolded, the French government became more familiar with the judicial strictures and implications of having recently ratified the 1967 Protocol on the Geneva Convention relating to the Status of Refugees.

Refusing Residency to a Refugee

Only in 1971 did France ratify the 1967 Protocol removing the Convention's geographical and temporal restriction to refugees from Europe who fled events that had taken place prior to 1951. From 1951 to 1972, 98 percent of those accorded refugee status in France were of European origin.[37] A year after France ratified the 1967 Protocol, in February 1972, Kamitatu was among the first Africans to apply for the status of political refugee through the French Office of Protection of Refugees (OFPRA). Not having received a reply within three months, on June 20, 1972, Kamitatu, represented by Jean-Jacques de Félice, filed an appeal to nullify an implicit rejection of refugee status with the Refugee Appeals Commission of the State Council. Before the Commission could rule on the appeal, the Minister of the Interior took steps to deport Kamitatu. On September 4, 1972, five days before Kamitatu had achieved the two years of residency on French soil required to become a permanent resident, the local prefect summoned him to his local police station where he was served with a refusal of residency from the Minister of the Interior, and granted eight days to leave French territory.[38] The reason given for nonrenewal was that "his presence in the territory constitutes a threat to public order."[39] An intricate legal battle—in which jurists, ministers, and lawyers contested France's immigration politics and Africa policies in French courts—ensued between the French government and Kamitatu.

On September 6, 1972, de Félice sought help from the office of the Minister of Foreign Affairs, Maurice Schumann, who had previously shown his disapproval of Foccart's networked orchestration of Franco-African relations.[40] In the Kamitatu case, Schumann worked to prevent Foccart's efforts to have the oppositionist expelled from France on Mobutu's demand. On September 11, de Félice also wrote to Prime Minister Messmer, Pompidou, and Minister of Justice, René Pleven, declaring Kamitatu's expulsion to be illegitimate and indicating that he was appealing the decision.[41] On September 12, Kamitatu filed for the nullification of the refusal of residency with the Administrative Court of Paris.[42] On the same day, the UN High Commissioner of Refugees intervened in Kamitatu's favor with the French Ministry of Foreign Affairs.[43] On September 15, Foccart followed up with Marcellin to ask that "the precise date of the actual departure of Mr. Kamitatu" be made known to him.[44] On September 18, René Pleven, the Minister of Justice, informed de Félice that, although the Refugee Appeal Commission would soon issue its ruling, the Minister of the Interior would not "envisage deferring his decision."[45] Kamitatu would have to leave French territory with the appeal pending in the Administrative Court and would only be able to return if a favorable decision was reached.[46]

At the hearing before the Refugee Appeals Commission on September 28, the State Council officially granted the status of political refugee to Kamitatu.[47] On October 9, de Félice issued a press release recounting the decision. "Having abstained from all political activity," wrote de Félice, "Kamitatu is—as the State Council rapporteur recognized—the very personification of a political refugee fearing death in his own country and in search of asylum."[48] With this statement, de Félice portrayed Kamitatu as a legitimate refugee. He then added a final sentence suggestive of Marcellin's role in mortgaging France's civil liberties to an African president: "The Minister of the Interior gave no reason for his decision [to order Kamitatu's expulsion]—however, the motive might well be 'friendly response to foreign head of state's pressing intervention'—how disquieting to find ourselves here."[49]

Despite Kamitatu's newly granted refugee status, the Minister of the Interior intensified procedures to have him expelled. Marcellin addressed a letter to the Refugee Appeals Commission on November 8, 1972 stipulating that the measure against Kamitatu on September 4, 1972 was not an expulsion order, but merely a refusal to renew his temporary residence permit.[50] Since "the competent authorities viewed it as inopportune to authorize this foreigner, who has since been qualified a refugee, to prolong his stay in our territory where, by his political activity, he severely compromises France's relations with a foreign state," Kamitatu's residence permit would not be renewed, nor would he be issued a work permit.[51]

Although Kamitatu was not politically active in France per se, the French government viewed his book—which made no mention of France at all—as signaling a degree of political activity that the Minister of the Interior deemed threatening to public order. It was a position that recalled the late 1950s era of decolonization, when the Ministry of the Interior infiltrated African student groups to keep communists and anti-French nationalists connected with political parties in French African territories under surveillance.[52] Building on interrelationships forged in previous decades, by the 1970s, French Third Worldism intersected with African opposition politics in a Franco-African nexus of political activism.

On November 22, 1972, Kamitatu sent a letter to the President of the Refugee Appeals Commission denying any involvement in political activity compromising France's relations with a foreign state.[53] Spelling out what he perceived as the

French government's effort to stifle his freedom of speech in order to appease Mobutu, Kamitatu wrote:

> If the expression of a free opinion opposed to that of the current government of my country is considered sufficient motive to have me expelled . . . then I fear that prosecutions in France are designed to sanction, not the threat to public order in France, but the very essence of opposition to the regime in power in my country, for no other reason than said regime maintains good relations with France.[54]

At the end of the letter Kamitatu argued that it was unfitting for a country claiming to uphold the Geneva Convention to order him to leave "the French territory which I chose as a land of asylum and from which I have undertaken no violent or subversive action against the regime in power, despite my fundamental disagreement with any and all forms of dictatorship."[55] The ambiguity in the last sentence as to which regime in power—France's or Zaïre's—was a form of dictatorship, was surely intentional.

On December 5, 1972, Kamitatu filed a claim with the State Council to nullify the September 4 refusal of residency.[56] Nine days later, Schumann sent a personal letter to Foccart strongly suggesting the pursuit of Kamitatu's expulsion had gone too far. Because Kamitatu had committed in writing to refraining from political activity while in French territory, "we have fulfilled, to say the least, our duty vis-à-vis Mobutu. In asking us to violate our laws and ethics, he would be guilty of trampling our sovereignty . . . something, I know, you would be the last to subscribe to."[57]

On December 21, 1972, the Minister of the Interior withdrew the decision to refuse Kamitatu residency and filed a brief with the Administrative Court of Paris indicating that he would be authorized to stay in France.[58] This is most likely the act which Foccart later remembered as Marcellin having "refused to proceed" with Kamitatu's expulsion, a refusal in which he was "supported by [the Minister of Foreign Affairs] Schumann."[59] "Try to get Mobutu to understand that the President of the French Republic lacks the capacity to expel a foreigner!" reminisced Foccart, who deplored Pompidou's lack of understanding of the degree to which Kamitatu's continued presence in France soured Franco-Zairean relations.[60]

The State Council did not rule on Kamitatu's appeal when it came before it in April 1973, citing the ministerial repeal of December 21, 1972.[61] Yet even this was not the end: the following year, on September 7, 1973, Kamitatu was summoned to the local police station a second time where he was again served with an eight-day expulsion notice. The reason given was "public offense to a foreign head of state," contrary to Article 36 of the press law of July 29, 1881.[62] It was a criminal charge of which he and Maspero had been convicted and fined for his banned book, and which was under appeal in the higher courts. Citing as evidence the criminal conviction and the refusal of residency dating to September 4, 1972, the Minister of the Interior's expulsion order stipulated that Kamitatu's presence in French territory posed a threat to public order. It was the only legal basis on which a refugee might be expelled. According to Articles 32 and 33 of the Geneva Convention on the Status of Refugees, codified in French law by the Law of July 25, 1952 and its Decree of Application from May 2, 1953, a refugee could be expelled for "reasons of national security and public order." However, no signatory state could expulse a refugee if so doing put his life or liberty in danger.

Foccart's account of the second attempt to expulse Kamitatu deviates notably from the archival record. He recalled that Pompidou summoned Marcellin a week before Mobutu's official visit to Paris, which took place in October 1973, and asked him to "distance" Kamitatu, the thorn in the side of Franco-Zairean relations. In Foccart's account, Marcellin refused unless Pompidou ordered him to do so in writing and added that an expulsion order would certainly be nullified in the State Council, which would allow Kamitatu to return to France in triumph.[63] It is difficult to know why Foccart, who kept meticulous notes on conversations and negotiations—official and unofficial—would blame what he referred to vaguely as Marcellin's "juridical arguments" for thwarting the French government's attempt to have Kamitatu removed in time to accommodate Mobutu's visit. In reality, Kamitatu remained in France because de Félice's legal defense, coupled with the advice and behind-the-scenes intervention from the Ministry of Foreign Affairs, defeated the second ministerial order of expulsion in the courts.

Beginning on September 11, 1973, de Félice assisted Kamitatu in preparing his legal defense before the Administrative Court, where Kamitatu filed to nullify the decision of September 4, 1972, upon which the expulsion order was based.[64] Kamitatu prepared a statement of defense which he filed two days before the hearing. Invoking the Soviet dissenters best known to the West in the 1970s, Aleksandr Solzhenitsyn and Andrei Sakharov, Kamitatu wrote:

> I suppose that the Minister of the Interior does not consider it "an especially serious" crime or misdemeanor to make a claim for democracy and freedom in one's country if it is governed by military dictatorship. Does my approach as a writer differ from that of Sakharov or of Soljenitsyne [*sic*] except that they are from the European continent and I, from a State whose head is overly sensitive? . . . Could you restore to France her image as safe haven for those who seek to defend democracy, law and justice by ensuring the respect of rights and law?[65]

The same day that Kamitatu filed his statement of defense, Henri LeClerc, an activist lawyer with GISTI and member of the League of the Rights of Man (LDH) wrote to inform Kamitatu that: "your conflict with Mobutu will be heard before the 11th Chamber of the Paris Court of Appeals on Wednesday, the 12th of December."[66] Of course Mobutu's name did not figure anywhere on the case docket—LeClerc's implication was that the French government represented the Zairean *Maréchal*'s legal and political interests, and hence, that it prosecuted Kamitatu on his behalf.

On October 3, de Félice made a comprehensive legal argument before the Administrative Court demanding the nullification, on the basis of excess of power, of the Minister of the Interior's refusal of residency decision of September 4, 1972, upon which the order of expulsion of September 7, 1973 was based. It was a contentious appeal against an administrative act that de Félice alleged violated the law. He argued four juridical means for the nullification.[67] First, the order of expulsion was based upon a manifest error of assessment of Kamitatu's threat to public order, given the Refugee Appeals Commission's portrayal of him as politically reserved and compliant with French law, and since the Administrative Tribunal, despite its power to do so, had not independently investigated the seriousness of the threat he allegedly posed. Second, the expulsion was ordered while Kamitatu's conviction was under review in the Appellate Court of Paris, thus anticipating a conviction that had not yet been definitively issued. Third, de Félice argued that the ministerial decision constituted a misuse of power since the Minister of the Interior began a new expulsion procedure after having withdrawn the previous one in order to escape a contentious nullification before the State Council: allowing the Ministry to begin a new procedure of expulsion would expose his client to judicial insecurity. Finally, the ministerial decision was "particularly ill-founded in law" because it cited the refusal of residency on September 4, 1972 as "proof" that Kamitatu threatened public order, and presented the "effect" (nonrenewal of residence permit in 1972) as the "cause" of Kamitatu's 1973 order of expulsion.

Kamitatu's case files end after the hearing before the Administrative Court. The Administrative Court refused to rule since the ministerial decision to refuse residency had already been withdrawn. Correspondence with Maspero indicates that de Félice worked mostly pro bono on staying the second expulsion in 1973.[68] Although the precise judicial outcome to the case is thus unknown, when Mobutu arrived in Paris for a private visit on October 11, 1973, Kamitatu was still in France awaiting his December 12 hearing before the Court of Appeals on the criminal charge of "public offense to a foreign head of state." The week before that hearing was to take place, a member of the staff of the weekly French satirical muckraking newspaper, *Le Canard Enchainé*, discovered men who were in fact agents of the Direction de la Surveillance du Territoire (DST) under Marcellin's direction attempting to bug the paper's offices.[69] The newspaper sued the French government, French journalists were scandalized by what they characterized as an attack on the freedom of the press and on democratic liberty, and Marcellin was reassigned to the Ministry of Agriculture and Rural Development and replaced with Jacques Chirac.[70]

Before vacating the Ministry of the Interior, in early 1974, Marcellin banned a last book published with Maspero press in early 1974: *L'Ascension de Mobutu, du sergent Joseph Désiré au general Sese Seko*, written by Jules Chomé, a Belgian lawyer of Zairean origin who had defended Kamitatu at trial in Leopoldville (Kinshasa) in 1966.[71] The Belgian government did not ban Chomé's book, resulting in Mobutu's public repudiation of Zaïre's former colonial power.

Pompidou's death, Marcellin's transfer, and Foccart's departure closed the chapter of France's censorship of African-authored works. In 1976, after a brief visit to Zaïre in 1975 following Mobutu's amnesty of all political exiles in 1975, Kamitatu completed his doctoral thesis and took his PhD. He published *Zaïre: Pouvoir à la portée du peuple* with L'Harmattan press in 1977. Unlike his previous memoir, a polemic against the Mobutu regime as he personally experienced it, his second work was based on empirical data illustrating the state's kleptocratic rule, mismanagement of economic resources and bilateral aid, and patrimonial nepotism as a mode of governance. In the preface he weighed his options as a political exile. He could join the regime in power as he had been invited to do since 1975; settle comfortably in a western country and find a high-paying job; or remain in the exiled opposition. At the time he penned his preface, he opted for the third choice. But in 1980, he decided to return to Zaïre where Mobutu awarded him a ministerial portfolio. The first option he described in his preface—making due with "the new situation" where, with "a little skill, I could, under the patronage of the guide, exercise one or more functions of responsibility"—became the one he ultimately pursued.[72]

Conclusions

Mobutu's exaction of France's censorship of Zaïrean oppositionist writing unmasked Foccart's unbridled attempts to obtain France's access to the "unsurpassed resources" of the Francophone giant of Central Africa. Foccart cared little about whether French civil liberties and even less whether international refugee protections were mortgaged during Zaïre's integration into the *pré carré* of Françafrique. In his recollection of the Kamitatu incident that so "poisoned" Franco-Zairean relations in the early 1970s, Foccart described the "arguments of the jurists of the Ministries of the Interior and Foreign Affairs" as "*mesquin devant la raison d'Etat.*" *Raison d'Etat,* "a purely political reason for action on the part of a ruler or government, especially where a departure from openness, justice, or honesty is involved," was a mode of governance which Mobutu typically employed.[73] *Mesquin*, as Foccart used it, referred to the small-mindedness of those ministers and jurists at the highest echelons of the French government who could not see, as he so clearly did, that the rule of law, and the protections of civil liberties and of political refugees were of no great matter in France's pursuit of Mobutu's Zaïre.

Foccart's inability to have his point of view prevail indicates his waning power as the Gaullist political era ceded to the center-right in early 1974.[74] Moreover, Foccart's inability to accommodate Mobutu on the Kamitatu issue demonstrates that in the view of some French officials in Messmer's government, certainly in Foreign Minister Schumann's, Foccart's Africa policy compromised French sovereignty to an unacceptable degree. Schumann's letter to Foccart, coupled with Pompidou's unwillingness to "distance" Kamitatu, sheds light on the unease with which some Gaullists who carried the Resistance in their political memories witnessed the French government's bolstering of autocratic African regimes at the expense of their vision of France's "republican tradition."

Beyond revealing how the French government instrumentalized French judicial processes to maintain and expand Françafrique, the Kamitatu case also shows how the French Left used the censorship trials of French publisher François Maspero and African authors—just as immigration became a politicized and hotly debated issue throughout France—to bring Françafrique's very existence into the public eye. In Kamitatu's expulsion orders and in the activists who mobilized to keep him in Paris, we can chart networked interrelationships between French and African nonstate actors who, together, shaped the French Left in the 1970s. Kamitatu's expulsion orders, chronologically situated between the application of the controversial Marcellin-Fontanet circulars in September 1972 and the Chilean coup d'état of September 11, 1973 that brought Augusto Pinochet to power and displaced thousands of Latin Americans, many of whom gained refuge in France, foregrounded ongoing battles in the politics of immigration in France. The Kamitatu case reveals the degree of imbrication, along the political spectrum from right to left, of French and Francophone African politics in the 1970s.

Notes

The author would like to thank Benjamin Lawrance, Nathan Carpenter, and participants in the Conable Conference of February 2015 for feedback on early drafts of this chapter, as well as Sylvie Thénault, Liora Israël, and Bassirou Barry for facilitating access to the Jean-Jacques de Félice archives housed at the Bibliothèque de documentation international contemporaine. Research funding was provided by the Social Science and Humanities Research Council of Canada and the Louise and John Steffens Founders' Circle of the Institute for Advanced Study in Princeton, NJ.

1. Bibliothèque de documentation internationale contemporaine (BDIC), Fonds de Félice, Dossier Kamitatu-Massamba, Cléophas Kamitatu-Massamba to Monsieur le Président de la Commission des Recours des Réfugiés et Apatrides, Recours contre décision du refus de reconnaître la qualité de réfugié, June 16, 1972.
2. Dossier Kamitatu-Massamba, G. de Löys, Direction, Institut d'Etudes politiques de Paris, October 6, 1971 ; R. Henry-Gréard, Direction, Institut d'Etudes politiques de Paris, June 28, 1972 and July 18, 1972.
3. Dossier Kamitatu-Massamba, Cléophas Kamitatu-Massamba to Monsieur le Président de la Commission des Recours des Réfugiés et Apatrides, a/s Recours contre décision du refus de reconnaître la qualité de réfugié, June 16, 1972.
4. Mobutu's official visit began on March 29, 1971. Mobutu would change the country's name to Zaïre on October 27, 1971 as part of "authenticité."

5. Evariste Kimba, Emmanuel Bamba, Jérôme Anany, and Alexandre Mahamba. On the so-called Pentecostal Plot, see Georges Nzongola-Ntalaja, "The Continuing Struggle for National Liberation in Zaïre," *The Journal of Modern African Studies* 17, no. 4 (1979): 609.

6. BDIC, Fonds de Félice, Dossier Kamitatu-Massamba, Cléophas Kamitatu-Massamba to Monsieur le Président de la Commission des Recours des Réfugiés et Apatrides, a/s Recours contre décision du refus de reconnaître la qualité de réfugié, June 16, 1972.

7. *Journal official*, p. 6304, June 30, 1971. The order to ban the book designated it as a foreign work (ouvrage de provenance étrangère) and rested upon a decree the French government passed in 1939 enabling it to censure and seize any work of foreign origin. C. Kemedjio, *Mongo Beti: Le combattant fatigué* (Berlin: Lit, 2013), 388.

8. See François Maspero, "Provenance étrangère," *Le Monde*, July 18, 1972. On the censorship, criminal charges, and fines Maspero faced from 1968 to 1974 in France, see Bruno Guichard, Alain Léger, and Julien Hage, eds. *François Maspero et les paysages humains* (Paris: Broché, 2009).

9. BDIC, Fonds de Félice, Dossier Kamitatu-Massamba, République française, Commission de Recours des Réfugiés au nom du people français, No. 7365, M. François Bernard, Rapporteur, September 28, 1972.

10. On Third Worldism in France, see Kristin Ross, *May '68 and its Afterlives* (Chicago: University of Chicago Press, 2002), 158–169. On de Félice see Barry Bassirou, Israël Liora, and Thénault Sylvie, "Jean-Jacques de Félice, avocat militant des droits de l'homme," *Matériaux pour l'histoire de notre temps* 115–116, no. 1 (2015): 1–96.

11. Mongo Beti and French journalist François-Xavier Verschave popularized its pejorative use, which President Félix Houphouët-Boigny first used positively in 1963 to refer to Côte d'Ivoire's continuing economic and political relationship with France. See Mongo Beti, *La France contre l'Afrique* (Paris: La Découverte, 1993) and François-Xavier Verschave, *Françafrique: Le plus long scandale de la République* (1998; repr. Paris: Stock, 2003). For historical studies of France's special relationship with Africa, see, among others, Tony Chafer, "Franco-African Relations: No Longer So Exceptional?" *African Affairs* 101 no. 404 (2002): 343–63; Gordon Cumming, "Transposing the 'Republican' Model? A Critical Appraisal of France's Historic Mission in Africa," *Journal of Contemporary African Studies* 23, no. 2 (2005): 233–52; Jean-François Médard, "France-Africa: Within the Family," in *Democracy and Corruption in Europe*, ed. Yves Mény and Donatella Della Porta (London: Pinter, 1997), 22–34. For Jacques Foccart's role, see Frédéric Turpin, *De Gaulle, Pompidou et l'Afrique (1958–1974)* (Paris: Les Indes savants, 2010) and Jean-Pierre Bat, *Le syndrome Foccart: La politique française en Afrique, de 1959 à nos jours* (Paris: Folio, 2012).

12. These critics argue variously that France's privileged sphere of influence extended beyond the territories it administered, and that France's policies and bilateral relations with postcolonial African states were not everywhere the same throughout the continent, but rather depended on its geopolitical interests as well as the nature of the regime in power. For an overview, see Tony Chafer, "Hollande and Africa Policy," *Modern and Contemporary France* 22, no. 4 (2014): 513–31.

13. On the Marcellin-Fontanet circulars, see Michelle Zancarini-Fournel, "La construction d'un 'problème national': L'immigration 1973, un tournant?" *Cahiers de la Méditerranée* 61 (2000): 147–157; Liora Israël, "Faire émerger le droit des étrangers en le contestant, ou l'histoire paradoxale des premières années du GISTI." *Politix* 16, no. 62 (2003): 115–143.

14. Zancarini-Fournel, "La construction d'un 'problème national,'" 147–157, 148.
15. GISTI stands for Groupe d'information et de soutien aux travailleurs immigrés. Israël, "Faire émerger,"115–143.
16. Israël, "Faire émerger."
17. Zancarini-Fournel, "La construction d'un problem national."
18. See above, footnote 12.
19. Bat, *Le syndrome Foccart*, 333.
20. A complete historical list of publications censored in France is available at https://fr.wikipedia.org/wiki/Liste_de_livres_censurés_en_France.
21. The other two titles censored were Ntite Mukendi-Mampaka, *Enterrons les zombies. Essai de remise en question de la politique nationale* (Paris: Impr. France-Ouest, 1969) and Jules Chomé, *L'Ascension de Mobutu, du sergent Joseph Désiré au général Sese Seko* (Paris: Editions Maspero, 1974).
22. See, as one example of press coverage concurrent with the Kamitatu case, "Zaïre: Corruption et népotisme," *Le Figaro*, October 12, 1972.
23. Guichard, Léger, and Hage, *François Maspero.*
24. Bat, *Le syndrome Foccart*, 276–287.
25. Jacques Foccart and Philippe Gaillard, *Foccart Parle*, Vol. 2 (Paris: Fayard/Jeune Afrique, 1997), 184.
26. Ibid.
27. Ibid., 185.
28. Ibid., 186.
29. Ibid.
30. Frédéric Turpin, *Jacques Foccart: Dans l'ombre du pouvoir* (Paris: CNRS, 2015), 286.
31. Foccart and Gaillard, *Foccart Parle*, 187.
32. Bat, *Le syndrome Foccart*, 388.
33. Turpin, *Jacques Foccart*, 287.
34. Foccart and Gaillard, *Foccart Parle*, 187.
35. François Maspero, "De provenance étrangere," Libre opinion, *Le Monde*, July 18, 1972.
36. Ibid.
37. Luc Legoux, *La crise de l'asile politique en France* (Paris: CEPED, 1995).
38. BDIC, Fonds de Félice, Dossier Kamitatu-Massamba, Procès Verbal, September 5, 1972, Commissariat de Sécurité Publique, Bobigny ; Bulletin de notification d'une procédure d'expulsion, Kamitatu-Massamba Cléophas, Préfecture du Val d'Oise, September 7, 1973.
39. BDIC, Fonds de Félice, Dossier Kamitatu-Massamba, Mémoire du Ministre de l'Intérieur, October 16, 1972, as quoted in Séance du 22 novembre 1972 au nom du peuple français, le tribunal administratif de Paris, Sieur Kamitatu-Massamba contre Ministre de l'Intérieur.
40. Turpin, *Jacques Foccart*, 279–287. Bernard Magniny, technical advisor to the Minister of Foreign Affairs, began to provide assistance to Kamitatu's legal team even before the ministerial decision to refuse residency was issued in September. See BDIC, Fonds de Félice, Dossier Kamitatu-Massamba, Cléophas Kamitatu-Massamba to Mr. Maurice Schumann, Minister of Foreign Affairs, June 17, 1972.
41. BDIC, Fonds de Félice, Dossier Kamitatu-Massamba, De Félice to Georges Pompidou, President of the Republic, September 11, 1972; De Félice to Pierre Messmer, Prime Minister, September 11, 1972; De Félice to René Pleven, September 11, 1972; De Félice to Maurice Schumann, Ministre des affaires étrangères, September 12, 1972.

42. BDIC, Fonds de Félice, Dossier Kamitatu-Massamba, Cléophas Kamitatu-Massamba to President of the Administrative Court of Paris, September 12, 1972.
43. Turpin, *Jacques Foccart*, 287.
44. Ibid.
45. BDIC, Fonds de Félice, Dossier Kamitatu-Massamba, René Pleven to De Félice, September 18, 1972.
46. Ibid.
47. BDIC, Fonds de Félice, Dossier Kamitatu-Massamba, République française, Commission de Recours des Réfugiés au nom du people français, No. 7365, M. François Bernard, Rapporteur, September 18, 1972.
48. BDIC, Fonds de Félice, Dossier Kamitatu-Massamba, République française, press release drafted by De Félice, n.d., apparently October 1972.
49. Ibid.
50. BDIC, Fonds de Félice, Dossier Kamitatu-Massamba, Minister of the Interior to Refugee Appeals Commission (copy), Reg./5 No. 77 11—S, November 8, 1972.
51. Ibid.
52. See Françoise Blum, "L'indépendance sera révolutionnaire ou ne sera pas. Etudiants africains en France contre l'ordre colonial," *Cahiers d'Histoire: Revue d'Histoire Critique* 126 (2015): 119–38.
53. BDIC, Fonds de Félice, Dossier Kamitatu-Massamba, Cléophas Kamitatu-Massamba to President of the "Section Contentieux" of the State Council, November 30, 1972.
54. Ibid.
55. Ibid.
56. BDIC, Fonds de Félice, Dossier Kamitatu-Massamba, Séance du 31 oct 1973 au nom du peuple français, le Tribunal administratif de Paris, Mr. Kamitatu-Massamba vs. Minister of the Interior, No. 1995 of 1972, No need to rule.
57. Personal letter from Maurice Schumann to Jacques Foccart, Paris, December 14, 1972, as quoted in Turpin, *Jacques Foccart*, 287.
58. BDIC, Fonds de Félice, Dossier Kamitatu-Massamba, Séance du 31 oct 1973 au nom du peuple français, le Tribunal administratif de Paris, Mr. Kamitatu-Massamba vs. Minister of the Interior, No. 1995 of 1972, No need to rule.
59. Foccart and Gaillard, *Foccart Parle*, 187.
60. Ibid., 187. Kamitatu's refugee status figures nowhere in Foccart's recollection of the events.
61. BDIC, Fonds de Félice, Dossier Kamitatu-Massamba, Notification d'une décision, Secrétaire du contentieux du Conseil d'Etat à M. Cléophas Kamitatu-Massamba, July 23, 1973.
62. BDIC, Fonds de Félice, Dossier Kamitatu-Massamba, République française, Préfecture de Val d'Oise, Bulletin de Notification d'une procedure d'expulsion, Mr. Kamitatu-Massamba, Cléophas, September 7, 1973.
63. Foccart and Gaillard, *Foccart Parle*, 188.
64. BDIC, Fonds de Félice, Dossier Kamitatu-Massamba, De Félice to Kamitatu, September 12, 1973.
65. BDIC, Fonds de Félice, Dossier Kamitatu-Massamba, Mémoire de défense contre procédure d'expulsion, Montmorency, September 11, 1973.
66. LeClerc to Kamitatu, October 1, 1973.
67. The argument is recapitulated in BDIC, Fonds de Félice, Dossier Kamitatu-Massamba, Séance du 31 oct 1973 au nom du peuple français, le Tribunal administratif de Paris, Mr.

Kamitatu-Massamba vs. Minister of the Interior, No. 1995 of 1972, No need to rule ; and appears in De Félice's notes on the file.

68. BDIC, Fonds de Félice, Dossier Kamitatu-Massamba, De Félice to Maspero, 8 Oct 1973; Maspero to De Félice, October 9, 1973.

69. See reports in *Le Monde* on December 12 and 13, 1973.

70. Foccart and Gaillard, *Foccart Parle*, 221–222.

71. Julien Hage, "Les littératures francophones d'Afrique noire à la conquête de l'édition française (1914–1974)," *Gradhiva* 10 (2009): 81–105.

72. Cléophas Kamitatu-Massamba, *Zaïre: Le pouvoir à la portée du people* (Paris: L'Harmattan, 1977), 7.

73. Oxford Dictionaries, "raison d'etat," accessed December 7, 2017, http://www.oxforddictionaries.com/us/definition/english/raison-d'etat.

74. See Turpin, *Jacques Foccart*, 279.

Part III

Remembering and Performing Exile

12 Forced Labor and Migration in São Tomé and Príncipe

Cape Verdean Exile in Poetry and Song

Marina Berthet

THE THEME OF exile, as visited in the arts, has led researchers to critique concepts such as "point of departure" and "point of arrival," "visas," "traffic," "nation," "identity," "culture," and "space," and thus to criticize the concept of migration and the very actions of migrants themselves.[1] Previously often perceived as an individual who relocates through economic necessity, and who loses identity or culture in order to integrate into a host society, the migrant has come to be considered an individual with choices, and one possessing the agency of decision-making imbued with innumerable reasons to travel, migrate, emigrate, or immigrate. Through artistic expression in particular, the migrant repositions him or herself between political and sentimental policies, empowered, as Patrick Chamoiseau and Édouard Glissant indicate, to choose the "place" of "homelands" and to engage affective languages, such as desire.[2] Art, in a most general sense, has become a means to translate the voices of migrants in different ways, and a means of expressing the most profound sentiments of exile.

This chapter discusses migrants from Cape Verde (located all over the world) who have produced a dense literary, theatrical, poetic, musical, and cinematic repertoire on exile in general and, more specifically, about workers contracted for forced labor on cocoa plantations (called *roças*) in São Tomé and Príncipe during the late nineteenth and early twentieth centuries. Written and practiced expressions, that sing, tell, or give meaning and sense to the act of forced labor in exile, are part of the corpus that I use here to reflect on the artistic expressions created by Cape Verdeans in order to interpret forced migration. Based on my analysis of poems by Eugénio de Paula Tavares (1867–1930) and Gabriel Mariano (1928–2002), and songs by Kodé di Dona (1940–2010), Orlando Pantera (1967–2001), and Ntóni Denti D'Oro (b.1926), I search for meaning in the aesthetic expressions that left indelible imprints on the imagination of the archipelago concerning the subject of the migrant labor experience—those often referred to as *serviçais* or *contratados*—in São Tomé and Príncipe. Cape Verdeans, even today, share in this artistic repertoire that has at its heart the subject of migration to São Tomé and Príncipe, and which has established a shared common exile imaginary and memory of this tragic episode.

The history of colonialism in Cape Verde and forced labor on plantations in São Tomé and Príncipe has been well documented.[3] But the administrative sources and statistical reports that undergird this history are incapable of conveying the experience or memory of the histories of migration, labor, and loss for Cape Verdeans. By contrast, songs and poems are a rich archive for understanding how migrants and the Cape Verdean society itself experienced, remembered, and represented forced migration and labor in São Tomé and Príncipe and how this history has been folded into a shared imaginary of this period held by Cape Verdeans around the world. The expressive practices, communicative spaces, and the expression of feelings held in common unite scattered Cape Verdeans across what Édouard Glissant called *Tout-Monde*, and connect the Cape Verdean diaspora.[4]

Performances offered opportunities for resistance. Poems and songs were instruments of criticism used against the colonial Portuguese government and a means of political struggle. These poems and songs are significant elements of a way of being, of travelling, of expression, and a source of research for the social sciences. Cécile Canut and Catherine Mazauric have addressed the intertwining of art and mobility and contend that this relation cannot be reduced to an artistic "theme." Art and mobility are intrinsic to social dynamics and therefore are considered powerful engines of aesthetic movements. They are the creators of symbols and semiotic elements that represent the polyphony of the migrants, constructing a new form of life through travel. In the case of São Tomé and Príncipe, forced migration or deportation is the inspiring element of these artistic creations and of the political reasons in Cape Verde for protest against the sending of a workforce to São Tomé and Príncipe.[5]

Forced Migration and Labor on São Tomé and Príncipe

As Nathan Carpenter states in his chapter in this volume, "colonial regimes had myriad ways of dealing with individuals who proved to be difficult, dangerous, or unwanted."[6] In the cases analyzed here, those who were not wanted in Cape Verde were people from low socioeconomic conditions, who died of hunger when crops could not grow because of drought. Historian Antonio Carreira places the beginning of this migration in the second half of the nineteenth century. This corresponds to a time of food crisis in Cape Verde brought on in part by devastating drought conditions. In a decree from March 1864, the colonial government, in response to the terrible famine, gave free passage on its boats to all individuals who wanted to emigrate to the island of São Tomé or to Luanda, Angola, taking them from the ports of Praia and São Vicente.[7]

The "free trip" obviously raised suspicions among Cape Verdeans at the time, and among those who have examined this history from a distance. Free transportation represented a political strategy and an effective means of persuasion. As well as offering transport, the government at the time insisted on the fact that the choice to leave Cape Verde was voluntary by directing the decree at everybody who *wanted* to emigrate. In other words, the migrants were cast as volunteers and—taking advantage of the food crisis on the Cape Verde islands—the authorities thus induced the most vulnerable to emigrate in search of a better life.

According to Carreira, the journey to São Tomé and Príncipe was presented—through official colonial discourse—as the only solution that guaranteed the survival of Cape Verdeans impacted by famine and drought. This "false solution" consisted of a summary departure carried out by the colonial authorities.[8] To have kept these people in Cape Verde would have meant the colonial government would have needed to develop strategies and policies of aid. By sending the Cape Verdeans to São Tomé and Príncipe, responsibility for looking after the workers passed to the owners of the *roças*.

While colonial officials certainly presented this as a voluntary migration, Cape Verdeans viewed the movement as a deportation, as a forced labor migration, and as a condemnation to exile. It was a punishment for which no crime was committed, unlike the long history of penal labor exiles (*degradados*) throughout the Portuguese empire that continued into 1950s under the regime of António de Oliveira Salazar (1889–1970), particularly to Angola.[9] In the eyes of later intellectuals like Carreira, the argument of hunger and drought was but an excuse employed by the colonial government to construct a political discourse that legitimated forced migration to the cocoa islands. Indeed, from the earliest days, the migration of Cape Verdeans towards the *roças* was presented as a solution for the Portuguese colonial government, in order to ensure the necessary manpower for the development of cacao monoculture in São Tomé and Príncipe, which was also a Portuguese colony. Historian Augusto Nascimento, among others, suggests that the history of migration to São Tomé and Príncipe at this time was one of induced migration.[10] He posits an administrative intervention that influenced people to migrate to certain destinations and suggests that ultimately the decision to move belonged to the individual. However, this is not how many Cape Verdeans themselves describe this history.

The great cultural production of poems, articles, songs, and accusations on the subject of migration to São Tomé and Príncipe suggests a "great unanimity" among Cape Verdean artists, journalists, and researchers.[11] Eugénio Tavares, Baltasar Lopes da Silva (1907–1989), Antônio Carreira (1905–1988), the *Claridosos*, the poets of *Certeza* and *Suplemento Cultural*, and the writers from *Nova Lagarda* and from the 1960s are unanimous in their description and representation of migration to the islands.[12] This is not a portrayal of a "voluntary" movement or a "solution" to famine, but of a period of immense suffering.[13] These representations cross generational boundaries; the current generation of artists—who themselves may not have experienced the labor regimes in São Tomé and Príncipe—sustain this view. But all are part of the Cape Verdean diaspora; from cherished artists like Cesária Évora (1941–2011) to poets like Baltasar Lopes, all were or are migrants.[14]

Undoubtedly, it is important to focus carefully on the period chosen for analysis and also to underline the complexity of the phenomenon to understand that the definition of migration also has an ideological character. The movement of Cape Verdeans to São Tomé and Príncipe lasted for nearly a century. Reasons for departure, treatment on plantations, and communities engaged in this history changed over time. Conditions on the plantations changed after the 1940s, for example, and international campaigns including that sponsored by the League of Nations tried to mobilize public opinion on the living conditions of migrant workers who were confined to São Tomé and Príncipe. Thus, we should not homogenize the experience of migration and a history that lasted a century. But in the late-nineteenth and early-twentieth centuries, emigration progressively became an (illusory) alternative to hunger. This was one of many attempts by the colonial government to try to influence the population of the Cape Verde islands to tread the path to other colonial holdings such as São Tomé and Príncipe or Angola.[15]

Over the period of Cape Verdean migration to São Tomé and Príncipe from the late nineteenth to mid-twentieth century, many intellectual and artistic movements stood up against this phenomenon. This migration was referred to as forced by Cape Verdeans who, since the beginning of the migration, denounced the treatment received by migrants, whether at the moment of recruitment, in the crossing by boat, upon arrival in São Tomé, or during temporary or prolonged life on the plantations.[16] One of the first to denounce the colonial facts and the migration to São Tomé and Príncipe was Luis Loff de Vasconcellos in his 1903 pamphlet *O Extermínio de Cabo Verde*, published in Lisbon, in which he derided the attitude of Portuguese authorities in relation to Cape Verdean migration.[17] The issue was subsequently addressed in many literary and artistic currents, but also by the local media in Cape Verde, showing how this phenomenon worried intellectuals, artists, and journalists and became a political leitmotif with which to criticize the actions of the colonial Portuguese government. The following from a 1912 publication is illustrative: "The system of the plantations was characterized by forced and unhuman labor. The workers on the plantations (servants) were little more than serfs. The 'emigration' of Cape Verdean workers to the plantations wasn't just big business: it was a genuine crime."[18]

Discussion of the nature of forced migration and the working conditions in São Tomé and Príncipe occupied the intellectual space of Cape Verde.

Furthermore, in literary studies, the theme of migration-mobility on the archipelago sparked new forms and concepts, particularly in poetry and prose including the concepts of *evasionismo* (evasion) and *hora di bai* (a faraway or distant land). Such concepts served to characterize or idealize Cape Verdeans as fundamentally itinerant. Migration was seen as a characteristic inherent to the archipelago. Later, in the 1940s, other poems would rebel against the idea of the Cape Verdean as a natural-born migrant, alleging the importance of nailing one's feet to the homeland and creating contrary concepts such as *anti-evasionismo* (anti-evasion) and *antiterralongismo* (lit. anti-faraway land).[19]

One of the most important critiques of the conditions in São Tomé and Príncipe came in the form of *Romanceiro de São Tomé*, created, according to Alfredo Margarido, by Osvaldo Alcântara (1907–1989).[20] It was a vehement protest against the conditions of Cape Verdean workers in São Tomé and Príncipe and against the attitudes and discourses of the colonial government.[21] Among the other movements that stood out from this social and political protest, positioning themselves against the contracting of Cape Verdean agricultural workers heading to São Tomé and Príncipe, we can mention poets and writers, starting from the first decade of the twentieth century, the *Claridosos* generation, the *Nova Largada* group, *Suplemento Cultural* and the *Independência Africana* generation.[22] These groups set new standards for literary aesthetics and language, abandoning European literary conflicts, such as that between Portuguese Romanticism and New Realism. Their founders aimed to free Cape Verdean writers from Portuguese traditions, to awaken Cape Verdean collective conscience, and to recover local cultural elements long suppressed by Portuguese colonialism, such as the Cape Verdean Creole. Nélida Maria Tavares Rocha noted that along with the production of articles, reports, and poems on the subject of forced labor in São Tomé and Príncipe, "great unanimity" was created among journalists, researchers, writers, and artists of different generations dealing with this issue: "If there was a convergent theme in poetry created by Cape Verdean poets, this convergence is fully achieved in the poems that address the issue of the *contratado* to São Tomé and Príncipe."[23]

Poetry as Critique and the Creation of a Shared Affective Memory

The poets Eugénio Tavares, Pedro Corsino de Azevedo (1905–1942), Jorge Barbosa (1902–1971), Osvaldo Alcântara (1907–1989), Gabriel Mariano (born José Gabriel Lopes da Silva), Ovídio Martins (1928–1999), and Onésimo Silveira (b. 1923) denounced the colonial government's manipulation of policy to favor immigration to the cocoa islands. Cape Verdean poetry, as well as songs and novels, represent a means of political struggle against, resistance to, and criticism of the colonial system, as Leroy Vail and Landeg White argued decades ago.[24] The poets chronicle, and imagine, the travel conditions, the experience of crossing by sea, and the day-to-day life of Cape Verdeans in exile. This kind of description and denouncement can be compared to Sana Camara's analysis, in this volume, of *Poems of the Seaway* by Ahmadu Bamba, who also denounced the injustices and atrocities endured during French colonial oppression. What garners my attention most in Camara's work and that permeates my research is the concept of compassion and that which the author identifies as "an organic bond with his people even in exile, as he is spiritually committed to their cause."[25] In their poems or songs, the authors speak directly to the emigrants, expressing solidarity, considering their brothers and sisters who had no choice but to go to São Tomé and Príncipe, and expressing the need to maintain ties with them.

In 1912, Eugénio Tavares wrote the poem "Emigration (The purpose of emigration to S. Tomé)" which deals directly with emigration to São Tomé. In this poem, Tavares addresses the migrants, saying "you." To the poet, São Tomé is a "friendly land" but "gaunt, sad, depleted and a cursed land of exile." Therefore, to emigrate to São Tomé means to die, not only in symbolic terms, but also from the dreaded African sleeping sickness. Moreover, emigration is associated with different feelings such as "pain" and "suffering." Throughout the poem, Tavares remembers the terrible conditions of the trip during which the migrants represent a "herded" homogenous mass. The poem asks questions of the migrant, inquiring: "why are you going to São Tomé"? Tavares seeks the reasons that made his countrymen choose São Tomé and Príncipe as a destination.[26] Probably inspired by his own experience of migration, Tavares also suggests that the emigrants choose a new route, towards the United States: "The land of work and freedom."[27] Eugenio Tavares associated the contract in São Tomé with: "eating from wooden bowls, the bread of slavery that the devil kneads—of this slavery dressed as liberty, which is an insult to human dignity."[28]

The manner in which the migrants were treated on the ships is a recurring element in many of the poems and songs. Tavares understands the migration project as a necessary experience, "something of youth," a rite of passage. From his experience, the author adheres to this "community of feelings and senses," but does not travel for the same reasons or under the same conditions and cannot own the experience in the same way. What they share is an experience, their memories and feelings linked to migration. Arjun Appadurai—with his notion of community of feelings—considers both the local and the global, not in terms of boundaries between spaces, but as a continuity of spaces that are not separate.[29] The vision proposed by Appadurai can be understood as familiar and intimate; that is, it is not defined by a geographical perspective, but by an existential one. When appropriating Appadurai's reflections, I consider migration to be—far more than the experience of recreating a local community—an "engine" that provides building blocks for a new membership and a new experience that precedes life in the local community. An assumption here is that migration does not separate those who remain on the islands from those who travel. It is through artistic expressions and the expressive practices that the historic subjects find and strengthen existing social links beyond the frequented spaces and places, both near and far. The sense of inseparability of people and spaces is created through aesthetics and art.

Another poem written more than forty years later falls within a fierce and evident political struggle. "Comissário ad hoc" by Gabriel Mariano, written at the beginning of 1950 and published at the start of the 1960s, stands out for its open criticism of the plight of the exiled Cape Verdeans.[30] Mariano is regarded as a militant poet who engaged with the political and cultural resistance of the archipelago against the colonial system. His cultural activity brought him to the attention of Portuguese colonial authorities and he was deported to Mozambique.[31] Probably influenced by his legal training, Mariano not only denounced the painful experience of being contracted for a regime of forced labor, but also pondered the legal legitimacy of the procedures used by the local authorities.[32] Unlike the majority of poems that address forced labor from the perspective of the contracted, the poet chose to deal with the same issue and the travel conditions of the migrants, but directing himself at the "foreman of the slaves," a Cape Verdean who, master on board, takes his countrymen to the plantations on São Tomé and Príncipe. This "foreman" is called the "ad hoc Commissioner."[33]

While Tavares directs himself at the emigrant and proposes another more successful emigration, Mariano directly attacks the agents of the system, as well as the Portuguese colonial system itself, which he experienced in his last decades. This poem stands alone for its open and violent critique of the agents whom Mariano describes as traitors. The contractors were paid "per head" for those who emigrated. They are the people who appear in various songs and books in which the candidate for contraction decides to go to the *roças* and asks to put their name on the list.[34] In these songs the commissioner does not travel, he stays at the port, he organizes the departure. Were the foremen or commissioners ("contratadores") all Cape Verdeans? It is difficult to answer this question as there are few existing studies on the subject. It is outside the scope of this chapter to present hypotheses about the role of these agents in the history of migration. The virulent, accusatory tone of the poem centers on the role of these agents or commissioners and leaves no room for compromise.

The significance of the poem resides in the fact that Mariano raises a crucial point in understanding the organization of the taking of migrants to the dreaded islands, as well as strategic issues of certain Cape Verdean political actors who opted to work for the Portuguese, and who were considered "traitors." The power of the "ad hoc Commissioner" lies in the control he has over his brothers (who, nonetheless, have "equal blood" to the foreman) and the use of privileged spaces. "'Him' in a fine cabin and 'them' in the hold." The first stanza presents the commissioner, but in the second it is the "emigrant slave" that becomes the main character through the use of the word "them."[35]

The cry of the poet is this same criticism of the travel conditions of the contracted. He blames the "commissioner" for his political choice and for taking his brothers to a land of exile. The direct and fearless tone of Mariano draws attention to the power dynamics of colonialism during a period of Portuguese dictatorship and heavy government censorship. A state of revolt runs through the entire poem, associated with "syncopated repetition."[36] As Rocha explains in her analysis, Mariano makes sure to stress the comparison "like you," showing that nothing separates the commissioner from his contemporaries: "They are men of flesh like you, brother. Of flesh and nerves like you, brother."[37] The poet then uses this contrast to highlight the position of the traitor, the captor of slaves—to whom this poem is directed—distant both socially and physically from the contracted, by focusing on the singular for the important individual and the plural for the mass of unnamed workers.

Both Tavares and Mariano wrote *mornas*. The *morna* is a lento tempo monotonic music and dance genre from Cape Verde, with complex origins in the eighteenth and early nineteenth century, today considered the national musical form.[38] The lyrics are usually in Cape Verdean kriol, and instrumentation often includes *cavaquinho* (a small guitar-like instrument), clarinet, accordion, violin, piano, and guitar. According to Margarido, Mariano was bilingual and always wrote *mornas* in kriol, the shared language of affection, and which showed the originality of the islands.[39] However, he chose Portuguese for his poems, probably for the same reasons as Tavares, as a more direct form of attacking the colonial authorities and the elite, along with the Cape Verdean migrant workers who rejected kriol and insisted on speaking only the colonial language, the so-called *contratados*.[40]

I observe the intrinsic relationship between *morna* and poems, between music and poetry, and how this influences the artists—and Gabriel Mariano—in their form of production. Poems can become *mornas*—for instance, Eugénio Tavares created the "Hora di Bai"—because rhythm and cadence are present in the poems. The spirit of music appears within them. The *morna* genre is replete with iconic songs that run back and forth between migrants and nonmigrants constituting an "engine" in itself, of reconstructed memories and inspired melodies. One *morna* that became a national symbol, an emblem for generations of migrant workers in São Tomé and Príncipe is "Sodade," written in the 1950s by a migrant from the island of São Nicolau, Armando Zeferino Soares (1920–2007). Soares stated that he wrote "Sodade" on the occasion of a *dispidida* (farewell) of a group of friends who went to labor in São Tomé and Príncipe.[41]

The *morna*, and its companion, *funaná*, explained below, are styles of music that are in constant dialogue with the literature of migration. It is possible to encounter in them a direct relationship with work-themed poems though words, sounds, and gestures. If poetry and literature were the means chosen by many Cape Verdean writers to speak about the contracted exile, I venture that it was the songs that made this phenomenon better known outside of Cape Verde. Some of the most emblematic songs of contemporary Cape Verdean music can be highlighted here. Through music and rhythm, bonds are created between the migrants, independent of the place of destination, and the relationship between music and poetry is intrinsic to the theme of migration.

From Literature to Popular Song

Our musical narrative begins with the song "Fomi 47," in *funaná* style by Kodé di Dona.[42] *Funaná* is a musical style marked by the presence of two key instruments—a Cape Verdean accordion known as the *gaita* and an idiophone known as the *ferrinho*. Farmhands appropriated these instruments to compose songs to express their daily difficulties—their anguish, their social criticism, their love. Political criticism is part of the *funaná* repertoire—known for its festive/sensual dance—which is played on the accordion. In "Fomi 47," sung in *badiu*, the singer Kodé di Dona points to hunger as a motive that led the hopeless Cape Verdean farmer to choose to embark for São Tomé. "Discouraged with my life, I saw the boat and I decided go to Sao Tomé."[43] The singer even describes the ease with which he is contracted (in 1959) and turned into a number. "I went to Santa Maria beach, to Fernando's office, I told him my name, he wrote it and he gave me a number 37."[44] Kodé Di Dona chooses to describe the crossing of the migrant and their suffering.

The singer—and composer—talks about forced migration, using the first person "I" to tell his story. Asserting his empathy with the *contratados* because he decided to migrate to São Tomé and Príncipe too, he conveys a sense of shared suffering. "Discouraged with my life . . . I went to Santa Maria beach, to the office of di Fernando di Sousa, to leave my name." The singer underlines the despair with which he (like many other men and women) was signing his name to the dreaded list of *contratados* to board the ships. The clerk (foreman) wrote down a name and the individual became a number. It is suffering sung with a dynamic voice and spurred on by the *ferrinho* played by one of the most representative voices of *funaná*; it is an almost harrowing, repetitive song that gets under the skin with the electricity of the national musical repertoire.

Another relevant song that has been widely interpreted by Cape Verdean singers (such as Lura (b. 1975) and Mayra Andrade (b. 1985), for example) is "Tunuka" by Orlando Monteiro Barreto, better known as Orlando Pantera, and Ildo Lobo (1953–2004). In the song, the singer dialogues with Tunuka, his companion on the trip. He describes the departure and the migratory movement between Cape Verde and São Tomé and Príncipe. Tunuka is probably the name of a lover. In

"Tunuka," the singer/interpreter crosses the Atlantic towards São Tomé and Príncipe. Fernando Arenas considers that Pantera exalts the courage of Tunuka, as well as the unity of Cape Verde.[45] Tunuka represents those who left, those who came, and those who stayed.[46] "Tunuka" talks about those who were forced to cross the sea to work in Sao Tomé. As in other compositions, the conditions encountered during the crossing are roundly denounced. The poem refers to the close ties maintained between the two characters despite the difficult living conditions, helping each other out in order to survive.[47] The rhythmic tone is from the same musical instruments used in the other song "Hunger in 47" ("Fomi 47") by Kodé di Dona; it is one of denouncement. Yet again, we have here a composer who has opted to describe the departure, the terrible crossing at sea, and the way that the contracted were treated. A new aspect that appears in this song is the solidarity between the migrants who share the same experience of the suffering journey.

If in the songs we hear many emotional descriptions of the sea crossing towards São Tomé, the most remarkable (of what I observed during my fieldwork) is the comings and goings of the contracted workers travelling between Cape Verde and São Tomé and Príncipe. Sometimes the migrants, having fulfilled their contracts, returned to Cape Verde; but given the lack of opportunities, they chose to agree to a new contract in São Tomé and Príncipe. Pantera's methods of production are associated with his experiences, his sensibilities, and his life story, intertwined with childhood trips to Angola or imagination and inspiration. An unnamed journalist uses two devices—creative palpitations and *mundivivência*—to convey the composer's journey and his process of poetic and musical subjectivity. Pantera has creative palpitations and is defined by *mundivivência* (a mixture of the Portuguese words for *world* and *experience*) in his thinking. The author explains that this sophisticated musical production involving this *mundivivência* combined with traditional universal rhythms allows the artist to infect his audience with his creativity.[48]

I close my analysis of poetic and musical journeys with another artist from the island of Santiago, Cape Verde. Ntóni Denti D'Oro, also known by the name António Vaz Cabral, like so many others travelled to Portugal during the colonial period in search of a more economically stable life, but returned to Cape Verde shortly after, in 1974. The musical style that governs his artistic expression is the *batuque*—a musical style rooted in the oral tradition of the islands, especially Santiago.[49] *Batuque* (*batuku* in Kriol) is both a Cape Verdean musical genre and a dance form, and possibly the oldest from the islands. Compared with other musical genres from Cape Verde, the *batuque* is the only genre that is polyrhythmic. Denti D'Oro was, according to Domingos Silva, one of the only male members of the celebrated band Batuque e Finaçon.

One song on their 1998 album "Cape Verde Batuque Et Finacon," called "Sambuna e finaçon," is a long song improvised by Denti D'Oro. Starting from the lament "my mother, my mother" (oia, oia, *nha mai, nha mai*), Denti D'Oro talks about the migrations to São Tomé and Príncipe in the 1940s. He sings about the store where the *contratado* gave his name to the foreman.[50] The destination of the workers is the South (São Tomé, "*Pan bá sul*") and hunger is the reason for choosing the contract.[51] These are elements contained in both this song and in "Hunger in 47" ("Fomi 47") by Kodé Di Dona. The composition is improvised and "full of repetition," which does not always give a logical sequence to the verses.[52] He rants, cries out, and sings about the tragic fate of those who went to São Tomé and Príncipe.

Denti D'Oro recounts, with emotions laid bare, the conditions of workers in the *roças* (plantations) and their vulnerability in the face of colonial violence and evil. In this song, we have access to a description of the cruelty exercised by the Portuguese bosses and references and criticisms from the poet about "life in the South" on the plantation, elements that are missing in the other compositions and poems presented. He tells the story of a woman, the victim of physical and sexual violence at the hands of her boss ("*Patron dja txoman na si kasa*") and of a situation over which she has no choice. With no justice in the South, it impossible for the contracted to complain to the General Curator of the Indigenous.[53]

It should be emphasized that Denti D'Oro frequently mentions Cape Verdean women in his songs, highlighting many day-to-day themes that they experience. It is rare to hear a song that transmits the cruelty of the colonizer and the suffering that was experienced by contracted women. Although the artists mentioned in this text are men, there is also extensive literature written by female authors talking about the theme of migration in general and some texts deal with this, specifically about migration to the South.[54]

Conclusion

So what then do the songs and poems presented have in common? Can the content of the compositions be used to better understand migration as a heterogeneous, dense, and polysemic phenomenon? What is the link that connects these artistic creations? Returning to the start of this chapter, my main suggestion is to think of each of these expressive practices as part of a dense artistic *corpus* and work of art that inscribes itself in Cape Verdean thought and imagination. At the same time they emphasize the compassion and experience of migration as something capable of uniting several time-spaces of the archipelago of Cape Verde and its migrants, nomads, workers in São Tomé and Príncipe, exiles and wanderers circulating in *Tout-Monde*.

A sense of inseparability of people and spaces is created through aesthetics and art. It is the sharing of sensitivities that consolidates social bonds among the *Kriol* community of feelings. To be *Kriolo* is to belong to a particular (imagined) community of feelings, senses, and shared intimacy among migrants and nonmigrants.[55] The notion of *Kriol*, much more than the concept of national identity, helps us to think of migration as an ontological experience, from which individuals who migrate, and those who remain in the archipelago, interpret, explain, and give meaning to their existence and their historical episodes.

If a sense of "departure" is inherent to the conceptualization of the exile experience in many African societies, as the introduction and other chapters in this volume suggest, it seems even more foundational in the social practices of insular societies, such as those of Cape Verde. In the academic sphere, the historian Antonio Carreira came across "the wide exit door" (in his own terms) of Cape Verdeans and in several works he analyzed Cape Verdean emigration.[56] The "leaving" began to be described through different sources. In the arts and in literature, emigration to São Tomé was rapidly associated with slave labor, and artists and authors drew a musical and poetic journey, describing the situation of the contracted Cape Verdean in the cacao islands.

Cape Verdean poets, artists, and journalists led, through their writing and music, the denunciation of the Cape Verdean contract system and the forced labor imposed on migrants to the dreaded equatorial islands. In general, many writers, with poems and prose, created a literature of protest against the contracting of Cape Verdeans for São Tomé and Príncipe, which they considered to be a deportation, a forced exile from which the contracted would never return.[57] The songs are sung with varying Cape Verdean rhythms (including *funaná* and *morna* styles) and they are loaded with emotions and feelings of compassion. It is through artistic expressions and the expressive practices that the historical subjects find and strengthen existing social links beyond the frequented spaces and places, both near and far.

Notes

1. Nadia Kiwan and Ulrike Hanna Meinhof, "Music and Migration: A Transnational Approach," *Music and Arts in Action* 3, no. 3 (2011): 1–18; Cécile Canut and Alioune Sow, "Les voix de la migration: Discours, récits et productions artistiques," *Cahiers d'Études Africaines* 213–214, no. 1–2 (2014): 9–25; Rui Cidra, "Produzindo a música de cabo verde na diáspora: redes transnacionais, world music e múltiplas formações crioulas," in *Comunidades Cabo-Verdianas: as múltiplas faces da imigração Cabo-Verdiana*, ed. Pedro Góis (Lisboa: Acidi, 2008).

2. Édouard Glissant and Patrick Chamoiseau, *Quand les murs tombent: L'identité nationale hors-la-loi?* (Paris: Éditions Galaade, 2007), 16–17.

3. Catherine Higgs, *Chocolate Islands: Cocoa, Slavery, and Colonial Africa* (Athens: Ohio University Press, 2012); Augusto Nascimento, "As fronteiras da nação e das raças em São Tomé e Príncipe. São-tomenses, Europeus e Angolas nos primeiros decênios de Novecentos," *Varia Historia* 29, no. 51 (2013): 721–743.

4. Édouard Glissant, *Traité du Tout-Monde* (Paris: Gallimard, 1997).

5. Cécile Canut and Catherine Mazauric. *La migration prise aux mots: Mise en récits et en images des migrations* (Paris: Le Cavalier Bleu, 2014), 10.

6. Nathan Carpenter in this volume.

7. Manuel Brito-Semedo, *A construção da identidade nacional: análise da imprensa entre 1877 e 1975* (Praia: Instituto da Biblioteca Nacional e do Livro, 2006); n° 250, de 19 de Dezembro de 1863, publicado no B.O n.3 Praia Janeiro de 1864 na portaria apud; Nélida Maria Tavares Rocha, "O contratado na poesia Cabo-Verdiana," Licenciatura em estudos Cabo-verdianos e Portugueses. Universidade de Cabo Verde (2010), 15, accessed March 4, 2017, http://portaldoconhecimento.gov.cv/bitstream/10961/2076/1/monog%20impri.pdf; Antonio Carreira, *Migrações nas Ilhas de Cabo Verde*, 2nd ed. (Mira Sintra: Instituto Cabo Verdiano do Livro, 1983), 28.

8. Carreira, *Migrações*, 149.

9. Timothy J. Coates, *Convict Labor in the Portuguese Empire, 1740–1932: Redefining the Empire with Forced Labor and New Imperialism* (Leiden: Brill, 2013), 4–8; José Beleza dos Santos, "O degredo e a sua execução em Angola," *Boletim da Sociedade de Geografia* 50, 1–12 (1932): 151–182.

10. Rocha, "O contratado na poesia," 6; Augusto Nascimento, *O sul da diáspora : cabo-verdianos em plantações de S. Tomé e Príncipe e de Moçambique (Praia*: Edição da Presidência da República de Cabo Verde, 2003).

11. Rocha, "O contratado na poesia," 38.

12. Rocha, "O contratado na poesia," 14.

13. For further discussion, see Maria do Carmo Cardoso Mendes, "Exílio e diáspora em Cabo Verde," *Revista Diacrítica* 29, no. 2 (2015): 167–183.

14. Alberto de Cavalho, "Sobre diáspora e emigração cabo-verdianas," *Via Atlantica* 10 (2006): 11–31.

15. Nardi Sousa delivered an interesting conference paper about contemporary Cape Verdean migration from São Tomé and Príncipe to Angola and the reverse, at a conference held in Praia, February 2012, with the title "Um diálogo sobre a identidade do ex-colonizado: Angolanos e Cabo-verdianos em Angola" May 13, 2012, accessed March 6, 2017, https://cidadeseglobalizacao.wordpress.com/2012/05/13/um-dialogo-sobre-a-identidade-do-ex-colonizado-angolanos-e-cabo-verdianos-em-angola/. See also, Portal de Angola, "Cabo-verdianos em situação 'indigna e degradante' em São Tomé e Príncipe," September 9, 2014, accessed March 6, 2017, http://www.portaldeangola.com/2014/09/cabo-verdianos-em-situacao-indigna-e-degradante-em-sao-tome-e-principe/.

16. Luiz Andrade Silva, "Os exílios na literatura caboverdiana," July 5, 2006, accessed March 6, 2017, http://www.islasdecaboverde.com.ar/islas_de_cabo_verde/noticias/os%20exilios_na_literatura_caboverdiana.htm.

17. Luís Loff de Vasconcellos, *O Extermínio de Cabo Verde: pavorosas revelações* (Lisboa: Livraria Editora Guimarães, Libanio & Co., 1903); also, Cristiano José de Sena Barcelos, *Alguns apontamentos sobre as fomes em Cabo Verde desde 1719 a 1904* (Lisboa: Tipografia da Cooperativa Militar, 1904), 66–67, 82–85; See also, Luiz Andrade Silva, *Crónicas da terra longe* (Lisboa: Chiado Editora, 2015).

18. Quoted in and translated by Lisa Åkesson, "Making a Life: Meanings of Migration in Cape Verde," Gothenburg, University of Gothenburg, Ph.D. dissertation, 2004, fn.17; Lisa Åkesson, "Narrating São Tomé: Cape Verdean Memories of Contract Labour in the Portuguese Empire," *Etnográfica* 20, no. 1 (2016): 57–76; Elisa Silva Andrade, *As ilhas de Cabo Verde da "Descoberta" à independência Nacional (1460–1975)* (Paris: l'Harmattan, 1996);

António Carreira, *Cabo Verde: aspectos sociais: secas e fomes do século XX* (Lisbon: Ulmeiro, 1984); Augusto Nascimento, *Poderes e quotidiano nas roças de S. Tomé e Príncipe de finais de Oitocentos a meados de Novecentos* (Lousã: Tipografia Lousanense, 2002).

19. Concepts which refer to a movement against the "distant land" movement (distant land is a translation of *terra longe*), against the exile of Cape Verdean people, against the forced migration, against the evasion of Cape Verde. For further information, see Juliana Braz Dias, "Projetos migratórios e relações familiares em Cabo Verde," *Revista Interdisciplinar da Mobilidade Humana* 14, no. 26/27 (2006): 23–54; and, Dante Mariano, "Terra longe e diáspora," *Latitudes* 12 (2001): 22–25.

20. See Mario de Andrade, *Antologia tematica de posia africana, 1: na noite gravida dos punhais* (Lisboa: Editora Sa da Costa, 1977), 230.

21. Alfredo Margarido, *Estudos sobre literaturas das nações africanas de língua portuguesa* (Lisbon: A Regra do Jo, 1980), 562.

22. Rocha, "O contratado na poesie," 14.

23. Rocha, "O contratado na poesie," 12.

24. Leroy Vail and Landeg White, "Forms of Resistance: Songs and Perceptions of Power in Colonial Mozambique," *The American Historical Review* 88, no. 4 (1983): 883–919.

2. Sana Camara this volume.

26. All translations are mine. Tavares' poem is called "Emigration." E. Tavares, *Poesia conto e teatro* (Praia: Instituto Caboverdiano do Livro e do Disco, 1996).

27. Rocha, "O contratado na poesie" 20.

28. Tavares first published (under the pseudonym Orion) the poem in a journal called *O Independente* n.35. See: Rocha, "O contratado da poesia," 12.

29. Arjun Appadurai, *Après le colonialisme. Les conséquences culturelles de la globalisation* (Paris: Payot, 2000).

30. Rocha, "O contratado na poesia," 21.

31. See Ebenezer Adedeji Omoteso, "*Contratado*: Forced Relations in Lusophone African Literature," *Journal of the African Literature Association* 3, no. 2 (2009): 144–167.

32. Rocha, "O contratado na poesia," 21.

33. Rocha, "O contratado na poesia," 21.

34. M. Fernandes, "Por uma leitura antropológica da literatura caboverdiana de ficção," *Ecos* 3 (2005): 55–63.

35. Rocha, "O contratado na poesia," 23.

36. Rocha, "O contratado na poesia," 23.

37. Rocha, "O contratado na poesia," 23.

38. Margarida Brito, "Breves apontamentos sobre as formas musicais existentes em Cabo Verde," in *Os Instrumentos Musicais em Cabo Verde* (Praia, Mindelo: Ed. Centro Cultural Português, 1998), 13–25.

39. Alfredo Margarido, "Do nativismo ao mundo que o mulato criou," *Latitudes* 16 (2002): 61.

40. Margarido, "Do Nativismo," 62; for *contratados*, see Marzia Grassi and Iolanda Évora, eds., *Género e migrações Cabo-Verdianas,* estudos e investigações, 43 (Lisboa: Imprensa de Ciências Sociais, 2007).

41. It may be reasonably translated as "farewell" or more literally as "departure."

42. It is very difficult to know exactly when this song was written. Some claim it was written in 1959, others at the end of the 1980s. From what I could ascertain, the song was recorded for the first time in 1987.

43. "Desanimado nha bida, d'djobi barco, Pa'n ba santumé."

44. "N'ba praia Santa Maria, Na scritori di Fernand di Sousa, N'dal nomi e pom na papel, El dam numero 37." Brito, "Breves apontamentos," 6.

45. Fernando Arenas, *Lusophone Africa: Beyond Independence* (Minneapolis: University of Minnesota Press, 2011), 95.

46. *"Tunuka é nós ki bai/É nos ki bem/é nos ki fika li-mé."*

47. *"Sukuru ka da-l kudádu, . . . Nu mára nós kondom, nós limária nu dexâ-l La/ É nós ki mbárka pa Sam Tomé, Injuriádu marádu pé/." /"Mi ku bo ki stába la me/Tudu m-dádu m-da-u també/Na nós pom di kada diâ, oxi dretu manham mariádu/Ramediádu ka tem midjor.*

48. A mix of two words: *world* and *experience.*

49. Margarido, "Do nativismo" 56–62.

50. *"n'fla ô homi / nhu Mostran / Pan bá santa nomi na papel."*

51. *"Pamó nós tera ka teni nada."*

52. Domingas da Costa de Pina, "Ntóni Denti D'Oro - O Rei do Batuque," Licenciatura em estudos cabo-verdianos e portugueses. Instituto superior de educação palmarejo, Santiago, Cabo Verde, 2007.

53. Da Costa de Pina, "Ntóni Denti D'Oro," 41.

54. For more information on the migration of women see Monteiro Pedro Manoel "Caminhos da ficção cabo-verdiana produzida por mulheres: Orlanda Amarilis, Ivone Aida e Fátima Bettencourt," Faculdade de Filosofia, letras e Ciências Humanas, Universidade de São Paulo, 2013.

55. For further discussion, see Eurídice Furtado Monteiro, "Crioulidade, colonialidade e género: as representações de Cabo Verde," Revista Estudos Feministas 24, no. 3 (2016): 983–996.

56. Antonio Carreira, *Migrações nas Ilhas de Cabo Verde*, 1st ed., (Lisboa: Editora Área das Ciências Humanas e Sociais – Universidade Nova de Lisboa, 1977), 147.

57. Abílio Duarte, Amílcar Cabral, Artur Vieira, Daniel Conceição, Dante Mariano, Felisberto Vieira, Lopes Luís Romano, Mário Fonseca, Francisco Fragoso, Manuel Duarte, Nelson Cabral, Osvaldo Osório are some of the names of Cape Verdean authors engaged in resistance against Portuguese colonialism.

13 Sheikh Ahmadu Bamba and the Poetics of Exile

Sana Camara

In the nineteenth century al-Hajj 'Umar al-Fūti (1793–1864) embarked on a *jihād* of the sword (*jihād al-sayf*) to fight European intrusion and the so-called infidels (*kāfirūn*) of Islam in the Haut-Sénégal-Niger region.[1] He was defeated in the battle of Massina by Ahmad al-Bakkā'ī al-Kuntī (1803–1865), the son of Muḥammad al-Kuntī (d. 1825).[2] Al-Hajj 'Umar al-Fūti's failed *jihād* slowed the revival of Islam in the states he attempted to conquer.[3] However, other *jihād* movements based on new peaceful models to consolidate the practice of Islam in Senegal were ultimately undertaken by emerging clerics. A key figure was Sheikh Ahmadu Bamba (1853–1927), the scion of an influential and literary family, who sparked the fire of Muslim culture in Senegal, strongly influencing the thought and daily activities of its people. Bamba "showed no interest in the *jihād* of the sword, but only in the *jihād* of the soul."[4]

Sheikh Ahmadu Bamba was a productive scholar whose ideology of passive resistance found full expression in his poetic compositions and treatises drawing upon the Prophet Muḥammad's directive to the Muslim community to fight in the path of God (*jihād fi sabīl Allāh*) against the carnal soul, namely against the ego. This is known in Ṣūfī circles as the greater *jihād* (*jihād al-akbar*), commanding the good and forbidding the bad, and withdrawing verbal and physical support from all acts forbidden by *sharī'a*, or Islamic law.[5]

Bamba also illustrated the beauty of the Arabic language in his exquisite lyrics. The accepted name for the kind of poem he composed is the *qaṣīda* (ode), which proceeds from the careful craftsmanship of verse (*bayt*), rhyme, and meter that work in harmony to transport the soul to excitement and delight. Readers experienced in rhyme and rhythms will find that Bamba greatly enriched his *qaṣā'id* (poems) with various metrical forms and elaborate rhyme schemes, allowing him to lift his poetry to a higher artistic level.[6] In addition to the craftsmanship of the poems, Bamba's poetry is also rich in religious content and social commentary. This chapter reflects on the narrative of resistance embedded in the poetry of Sheikh Ahmadu Bamba while he lived in exile in Gabon (1895–1902). It examines how Bamba became an exile and focuses on a few poems in which he interprets the impact of his exile. I offer a parallel narrative to Marina Berthet's discussion of Cape Verdean poetry and song, and reflect on the meaning of exile for the exiled, through a lens of creative or politicized artistic production.

Ahmadu Bamba, the Murīdiyya, and Exile

Sheikh Ahmadu Bamba Mbàkke was born in 1853 in Mbàkke Bawol, the village founded 145 km northeast of Dakar by his great-grandfather Maam Maaram (ca. 1703–1802) in the kingdom of Bawol, which was located in the west-central part of Senegal, southwest of the kingdom of Kajoor and northwest of the kingdoms of Siin and Saalum. Maam Bàlla Aysa, the immediate grandfather of Sheikh Ahmadu Bamba, became the third successor of Maam Maaram in the village of Mbàkke Bawol. But the majority of the village adherents opposed his leadership, and he decided to move from Mbàkke Bawol and migrate to Saalum on the north bank of the Gambia, which was ruled by the *jihādist* Màbba Diakhou Ba (1809–1867). The French who had invested their fortunes in Senegal were concerned about safeguarding their interests in the face of Màbba Diakhou Ba's growing power. Thus they began to draw the local rulers into war.

In 1854, General Louis Faidherbe (1818–1889), the French governor of Senegal until 1861, and again from 1863 to 1865, began his military conquest of new territories, establishing fortified trading in the interests of French commercial policy. For the ensuing one hundred years or so the French colonial administrators were able to realize their political and economic programs in Senegal and the interior. Governor Faidherbe and his successors found it necessary to proceed with their wars of conquest against the Senegambian states, where resistance began to emerge, in order to consolidate their strategic positions.

Most sovereigns of Wolof states, like Alburi Njaay (d. 1902) of Jolof, Makoddu Kumba Faal (d. 1863), and Lat Joor Jóob (1842–1886) of Kajoor, were ousted by the French authorities. Momar Ànta Sali, Sheikh Ahmadu Bamba's father, was then Lat Joor Jóob's *qāḍi* or legal consultant. Before his death in 1883, he entrusted Sheikh Ahmadu Bamba with the care and protection of his entire family.[7] It now fell to Sheikh Ahmadu Bamba, said to be the perfect man (*al-insān al-kāmil*), to serve the cause of the Mbàkke family's lineage, but also to show the ideological content of his creative work, which would be consonant with his own conduct founded upon the example of the Prophet Muḥammad. His faithful demeanor is best described by Coulon: "A zealous follower of the Muslim style of mysticism (*taṣawwuf*), Ahmad Bamba's religious style was never that of either a fanatic or a demagogue. He was rather known for his deep piety, passing most of his time in prayer or religious retreats (*khalwa*), living according to the classic *Ṣūfi* ethic of withdrawal from the affairs of the world. He was utterly without political ambition."[8]

While Bamba's fame and stature were extending throughout the Wolof states of Senegambia in the late nineteenth century, French political and military initiatives shook Senegal to its foundations, displacing or dismantling most of the local rulers named above. In search of new ways, many of the rulers' subjects, whether Muslim or *ceddo* (people following indigenous beliefs), eschewed the prevailing ethos of the French cultural order and took shelter with the prestigious cleric.[9] Both *ceddo* and Muslims were disenchanted with the moral authority of both the local and colonial rulers; they began to feel, given Bamba's high moral disposition, that he was the repository of the esoteric knowledge bestowed upon renowned *Ṣūfī* saints. They gathered around him in the religious city of Touba, which he founded, and he initiated them in the order known as the *Murīdiyya*.

The early development of the *Murīdiyya* did not alarm the French colonial authorities as it seemingly posed no immediate threat to their political hegemony over much of the country. Opposition to the expansion of the order first came from local chiefs and clerics, who felt that Bamba was exploiting their subjects and depleting their economic resources. Some of these leaders lodged their complaints with the French administration under false pretenses and warned of an Islamic holy war looming on the horizon, threatening the very foundation of colonial power.[10] The French saw no alternative but to keep close watch on Bamba's activities. On August 10, 1895, Senegal's governor, Martial Merlin (1860–1935), gave the order for the arrest of Bamba in an attempt to undermine his moral authority and spiritual legitimacy. In September 1895, the French authorities exiled Bamba and Sàmba Lawbe Njaay, the *Buurba* or ruler of Jolof, to Gabon.[11]

Bamba's exile was part of a wider French policy of suppression of African leaders in all areas of French colonial Africa. There were multiple exiles in Gabon in the nineteenth century. As early as 1844, Governor Louis Édouard Bouët-Willaumez (1808–1871) arrested Mukhtār Sīdi, an emir of Brakna in southwest Mauritania, and exiled him to Gabon.[12] In 1892, Colonel Alfred-Amédée Dodds (1842–1922), commander of the French colonial soldiers, invaded Dahomey (present-day Benin) and deposed King Béhanzin (1844–1906), who was sent into exile to Martinique and later died in Algeria. In 1894, the French appointed his brother Prince Goutchile, also known as Agoli-Agbo, to succeed Béhanzin as the next king of Dahomey. He too was removed and exiled to Gabon in 1900.[13] Samori Touré (1830–1900), the emperor of the Wasulu, which included the Mande-speaking states of Guinea highlands and Niger river tributaries, was opposed to colonial expansion and fought the French as early as 1883. After long years of resistance, Samori Touré was finally captured in a surprise attack by the forces of Captain Gouraud on the upper reaches of the Cavalla River on September 29, 1898 and sent into exile to Gabon, where he died of pneumonia in 1900.[14] Gabon was thus foregrounded by the French administration as the locus of alienation and psychological trauma.[15]

Samori Touré's capture is still described as one of "the longest series of campaigns against a single enemy in the history of French Soudanese conquest."[16] Samori Touré is all the more interesting insofar as it is believed by contemporary

Murīds, the disciples of Sheikh Ahmadu Bamba's order, that he not only died on the outskirts of Mayumba, on the Atlantic Ocean coast of Gabon, but that he pledged allegiance to Bamba before his death. He did so in the arms of Bamba, who then offered appropriate prayers and rites, and even composed an ode on behalf of Samori Touré as Mūsā Ka writes:

> He [Bamba] journeyed on to Brazzaville, and then to São Tome
> That is where he met Samory, and people were shouting "Well, what!"
> That is when Demba Njaay met Samory
> In the company of Biraan Siise, resembling the people of the trench.
> They visited Sheikh Bamba and gathered their souls
> Which, while in big tears they entrusted to Bamba.
> That same day Samory entrusted his son to Bamba;
> His name is Ahmadu Samory, together with his mother.
> Saranke is the name of his mother; she met with Bamba.
> Their tombs are still there on the outskirts of Mayumba.[17]

In contrast to Samori Touré's deadly sickness, Mūsā Ka suggests in the lines above, and in another poem (*Nattu*), that Samori Touré and Biraan Siise were burnt in a firing-oven in the same manner as the people of the trench (*aṣḥāb al-ukhdūd*), mentioned in the Qur'ān.[18] According to Muslim commentators, the *aṣḥāb al-ukhdūd,* also known as the "Martyrs of Najrān," were burnt in the ditches only because of their belief in God.[19] Stories about Bamba's bond with Samori Touré explain why one sometimes sees Samori's portrait in contemporary graffiti in Dakar.

Sūfism, Ṣūfī Poetry and the Influences of Bamba

Once announced, the decision to exile Bamba incited great dissatisfaction among the Murīd disciples. They feared that their *Ṣūfī* master would not make it back home. So they recommended that he resort to the sword and gun in order to establish the truth and superiority of his religion. Bamba not only wished for his exile to take place as expressed in one of his poems entitled *Muqaddimāt'al-khidma*, but he had a vision of his return from exile.[20] He anticipated his exile in the *qaṣīda* entitled *Asīru ma'a l-Abrāri*, composed in the very year of his expatriation:

> The enemies of Allāh believed, during the moment of
> My solitude, that I was their prisoner.
> They were all wrong.
> They are all unbelievers, prisoners of Satan
> And of their own pleasure. As for me, I walk towards Allāh,
> Possessor of the Heavenly Seat, the Most Grand.
> (vv. 47–8)

To better understand the poetry of Bamba, one needs to accept first and foremost the centrality of the sacred text of the Qur'ān and the Arabic language to his poetry, and to *Ṣūfī* poetry in general. According to Philip Hitti:

> [The Qur'ān is] not only the basis of the religion, the canon of ethical and moral life, but also the textbook in which the Muslim begins his study of language, science, theology and jurisprudence. Its literary influence has been incalculable and enduring. The first prose book in Arabic, it set the style for future products. It kept the language uniform.[21]

Despite a diversity of ideologies, *Ṣūfī* poetry cannot be dissociated from the religion since its guiding principles and moral values are informed by the Qur'ān.[22] Besides implementing the will of God known as *sharī'a*, or the exoteric path of Islam, Sūfism adds an esoteric path leading to the intimate knowledge and devotional love of God.[23] William Stoddart observes:

> Sūfism is the spirituality of the religion of Islam. Mysticism makes its appearance as an inward dimension in every religion, and to attempt to separate the mystical element from the religion which is its outward support is an arbitrary act of violence which cannot but be fatal to the mysticism, or spiritual path, concerned.[24]

Bamba's *qaṣā'id* are the reenactment of the prescriptions of the Holy Book in the image of the Prophet Muḥammad. Endowed with some measure of light and mental energy, the poet always expressed his intentions to fully apply himself in the service of the Prophet.[25] This is the origin of his sobriquet, *Khādim'ur-Rasūl*, the Servant of the Messenger.[26]

Bamba's Exile Poetry

The *qaṣā'id,* known to the Murīd collective consciousness as the "Poems of the Seaway" (*Yoonu géej gi* in Wolof), reflect the spiritual warfare Bamba undertook to fight the French cultural control of the Senegalese community. In most of these poems written during his exile in Gabon, Bamba denounced the injustices and atrocities he endured under colonial oppression. Yet it is hard to find verses in which the poet describes in detail the numerous incidences of coercion or physical and mental suffering that the French colonial administration inflicted on him in an attempt to compel him to yield information or make a confession favorable to their sociopolitical objectives. In all of his poetic enterprise, Bamba's panegyrics are devoted to praising the Prophet Muḥammad, but they ultimately invoke their greatest authority in the name of Allāh.

In appropriating the esoteric language of the Qur'ān to his mystic experience, Bamba distances himself from graphic descriptions and concrete evocations of events. His *qaṣā'id* register a series of personal experiences often expressed in a metaphorical language that is beyond ordinary human perception. This discursive

Fig. 13.1 Tafaa Seck Baye Fall, "Bamba and the Gabon Experience." (Private collection of Baye Omar Keinde, Touba. Reproduced with the permission of Tafaa Seck Baye Fall.)

feature of allusive and symbolic expressionism, it seems, is notable in the writings of all *Ṣūfī* poets, as Trimingham points out: "The mystic speaks the imaginative language of vision, symbol, and myth, through which he can express truths beyond the reach of formal theology."[27] In *Rasā'il Ibnul-'Arabī*, the Arab Andalusian Ibn al-'Arabī warns his readers that "this kind of spiritual insight and knowledge must be hidden from the majority of men by reason of its sublimity. For its depths are far reaching and the dangers involved great."[28] Thus, it is no surprise that the *qaṣā'id* of Bamba operate within a gnostic system of reference, clothing his thoughts in cryptic language in which the use of words is predominantly metaphoric.

In some of the *qaṣā'id* written before and during exile, Bamba makes cursory references to the vicious procedures that were conducted in dungeons or secret places and involved corporal punishments, hunger, sleepless nights, and other brutal treatments aimed at breaking him psychologically. Yet, in spite of his affliction, he stood resolute against adversity and found solace in writing about divine protection against the insidious measures of mankind:

> May the one who illuminated my country facilitate my rapport
> With Islam during my exile in the islands!
> May the light of the Arabic language and of the Book inundate me

During the time of my service to the Prophet
Despite the presence of the colonizers!
May the Revelation of the Certainty made by Allāh
For the Intercessor serve as my shield
Against the persecutors and the cannons!
(*Jāwartu*, vv. 26–28)

Bamba accepted the ordeal of exile and confinement imposed upon him by French officials stoically. This acceptance allowed the scholar-ascetic to maintain his retreat (*khalwa*) and asceticism (*zuhd*) in the interest of reaching greater enlightenment. This is evidenced by his creative production on the island of Mayumba (Gabon), where he produced an abundant body of writing unveiling his insights into the mystic path leading to his love of and proximity to God. The writings were later made available to his disciples.[29]

Berthet's study of Cape Verdean forced migration to São Tomé and Príncipe is valuable in its emphasis on the social and cultural bonds between the exiles and the homeland community, which continued despite the attempt by the totalitarian rulers to obliterate these connections. She argues that "through the artistic expressions and the expressive practices the historic subjects find and strengthen existing social links beyond the frequented spaces and places, both near and far. The sense of inseparability of people and spaces is created through aesthetics and art."[30] Similarly, in his poetry, Bamba assumes the leading role of protector and executor of the religious precepts of his disciples. He enthusiastically carries the burden of their tribulations and moral discomfort. With a prophetic vision he presides over their fate and rids them of the corruption and imperfections of the social order. Murīd faithful for example look to Bamba's enlightened teachings and examples of courage, even after his death and indeed into the present, as they face the rigors of their own, often perilously difficult, lives.[31] Mamadou Diouf observes that,

> The miracles that accompanied the exiles (of Bamba), in particular the exile in Gabon and the sojourn in Mayumba, constitute the library on which Murīds draw in order to make sense of their project of accumulation, the difficulties involved in their travel through the world, and their promised success.[32]

While in exile Bamba dedicated himself to the performance of the remembrance and invocation (*zikr*) of God's names and attributes and those of His beloved Prophet.

Qaṣā'id, like *Aṣ-Ṣindīdi*, *Tuḥfatu l-Mutaḍarri'īna*, and *Maṭlabu sh-Shifā'i*, instruct Murīd disciples in the principles of praying, remembering, and abandoning themselves to God. They seek Allāh's blessings on all believers who faithfully adhere to the fundamentals of Islam:

Make my tongue and heart in faith utter Your name when I
Die, O my Lord!

Solidly rivet my faith in my heart without anguish until I
Truly wish to meet You, O my Lord!
Make my death a source of rest and joy that alienate me from any
Evil and any compelling calamity, O my Lord!
Watch over my body when my soul leaves me. And in the tomb,
Never subject it to any test, O my Lord!
Be my help and companion when they have buried my body
And when I am alone, O my Lord!
Do not shroud me with whatever could frighten me. Rather,
Protect me from whatever I shall fear, O my Lord!
Save me, save all Muslims! Save my mother! Amen!
O My Lord!
Forgive us, as well as her! Hide our vices. Be Kind to
Us and to her when we go astray, O my Lord!
(*Aṣ-Ṣindīdi*, vv. 36–43)

The process of Bamba's renunciation of external and internal pleasures concluded in his triumph of exile and reintegration into Murīd society:

I repent to Allāh and promise myself to abide by the pact
In hopes of receiving his grace. Thus He has given
Me eternal and unlimited blessings.
I have been taken over by happiness born from the thanks
That I give to Allāh. May Allāh thank the Prophet,
Honor him and eternally love him.
I hide in my heart favors that I have gotten
By divine grace. I'll be jealous and avaricious in
Making them known, for the soul is a cemetery and can keep secrets.
(*Asīru ma'a l-Abrāri*, vv. 18–20)

Bamba implicitly revealed his gratification in his search for spiritual and mystical powers gained through asceticism. He ultimately takes for himself the title of the perfect man in whom one finds the conflation of divine and human attributes.

The *Ṣūfī* concept of the perfect man was initially found expressed in the writings of Muhyī'd-Dīn Ibn al-'Arabī's theosophical manual, *Fusūsu'l-hikam* (Bezels of Wisdom), and further expounded in 'Abd al-Karīm al-Jīlī's *al-Insān al-kāmil*, which served as a powerful commendation of *Ṣūfī* activity.[33] In al-Jīlī's theology, the perfect man is one who, after craving for the greatest knowledge, comes to know God and His actions, and subsequently mirrors from within the divine attributes—of essence, beauty, majesty, and perfection—in order to achieve his oneness with God. Following the pattern of the creation of 'Ādam in the image and with the attributes of God, as narrated in the Qur'ān and the *ḥadīth*, al-Jīlī (1365–1406) envisions the prophets and the chosen saints (*awliyā'*) as having developed the full potentialities of divine reality (*al-Ḥaqq*). Prophets and mystics are all celestial intermediaries empowered by God to transmit His blessings and assistance. Yet, al-Jīlī emphasizes substantial differences between the two groups in the way they receive illumination (*ilhām*) and their insight into the nature of God. In doing so, he has identified the Prophet Muḥammad as the paramount perfect man, for having said among other things: "He who has seen me has seen Allāh." Saints or mystics are first and foremost an outward manifestation of the essence of the most excellent in mankind; Muḥammad who revealed the truths of the Qur'ān and the *ḥadīth*, whether symbolically or allegorically, therefore stands in a privileged position to inhere in the divine essence (*dhāt*). Thus Muḥammad's truthfulness connects all other creatures to divine reality. Since Muḥammad himself is a created being, the mystic first takes on his physical nature before absorbing his inner essences, but neither the prophets nor the saints can be identified with God absolutely.[34]

There are analogous references in Bamba's *qaṣā'id* that induce the reader to accept that he met with the Prophet, who then manifested himself through him and enjoined him to perform a spiritual *jihād* by way of the purification of his *nafs* (lower soul, ego):

> My only companions are the Book of Allāh and
> The Messenger of Allāh. And they were my only companions
> At sea when I was in exile.
> I converse in my poems with the Prophet,
> While he is lying down in al-Madīnah and I live together with
> Him in al-Madīnah and I bow down to him.
> (*Asīru ma'a l-Abrāri*, vv. 26–27)

Spiritual purification would be conducive to the faithful guidance of his people on the right path to divine truth. The word *nafs* has been used alternatively to express ego, soul, self, or person. In the Qur'ān, it occurs in several passages in the sense of the human body and soul: "O mankind! fear / your Guardian Lord, / Who created you / from a single person (*nafs*), / created, out of it, / his mate, and from them twain / scattered (like seeds) / countless men and women; / fear Allāh, through Whom / you demand your mutual (rights), / and be heedful of the wombs / (that bore you): for Allāh / ever watches over you."[35]

Sūfīs often ascribe to the *nafs* a negative connotation and render it as the lower self that is inhabited by a host of passionate appetites or sensual desires. Thus the *nafs* represents best the animal nature in mankind that incites it to succumb to physical debaucheries. The Qur'ān emphasizes three stages of the nafs: *nafs al-ammāra* (the inciting nafs), (*nafs al-lawwāma*) (the self-blaming nafs), and *nafs al-muṭma'inna* (the nafs at peace). The *nafs al-ammāra* controls man's impulses, lower desires, and worldly satisfactions and cultivates in him the commission of evil. This is the very *nafs* that the Prophet Yūsuf condemned strongly when Zulaikhā, the wife of 'Azīz, king of Egypt, attempted to entice him with her blind passion.[36] Because such a *nafs* is prone to evil, it can never become one with God. The *nafs al-lawwāma* reproaches itself for being carried away by its ego and not controlling its evil conduct. Ultimately the guilty person begins to struggle with his own soul.[37] He is awakened by the consciousness to resist temptations and equally repent to the ever-forgiving God in order to return to perfection.[38] The *nafs al-muṭma'inna* (the soul in tranquility) occurs when the heart and soul of man become pure and unsullied. His self-knowledge has reached the level of enlightenment in which he now coalesces with divine reality. This is the ideal stage at which God is pleased with the soul that has undergone transmutation from worldly desires and trials to spiritual cohabitation with Muḥammad. That is when man is promised entry into heaven, where he will rest in peace. In *Ṣūfī* language, however, the stages of purification are sevenfold and culminate in the absolute purification of the soul that the aspirants designate as *nafs al-kāmila* (the perfect soul).[39]

The *qaṣā'id* of Bamba synthesize the attributes described above that enabled him to conquer the imperfections of the *nafs* and subvert the delusions of the colonial order. These attributes manifest themselves as the embodiment of the logos (*quṭb*) of Muḥammad. In this intermediate position, they build faith in the holy texts and exhort and illustrate by example the virtues of devoting oneself to the worship of Allāh.

Bamba's *qaṣā'id* thus proceed from an apprehension of an impelling force intent on directing the primordial values of his community toward a superior spiritual order. In the dialectical tension that opposes the colonial ideology to Bamba's spiritual insights, there seems to be little room for mutual concessions. The poet continuously argues against the manifest inadequacies of a doctrine whose propositions are marked by perversity and grounded in evil. Bamba expresses contempt for the theory of the degradation of mankind and offers in its place a transcendental order in accordance with the cardinal virtues of faith and love.

It is interesting to note in this regard that the *jihād al-nafs* (against the soul, self-will) that Bamba is performing is not an attempt to absolve himself from sin and guilt. He only assumes the stance of the perfect man described above and stands up against the satanic powers that are engulfing his people in the realms of darkness, and are inciting them to acts of evil. To achieve victory, the poet intimates a divine order for the acquisition of sublime attributes and powers to conquer the forces of evil:

> My happiness in the two abodes was granted to me
> Thanks to the songs that I compose for the Prophet's benefit,
> Through poems and songs. This happiness is real

And profitable to me.
My seeds are the Book of Allāh and the Traditions of
The Prophet. And I have used them as a shield against
This futile happiness of which others take advantage.
My abodes are empty and I am separated from my family
Because of my solitude when I dedicate to writing
My poems in honor of the Prophet.
The temptations from humans have deceived the Whites in
Their attempts against me. They were nourishing
The hope of killing me and their hope was let down.
. . .
I repented to Allāh about the look that I could have directed
Towards someone other than Him. For I have signed with Him
A pact that I intend to honor.
(*Asīru ma'a l-Abrāri*, vv. 12–17)

In all his *qaṣā'id*, Bamba remains constant in his resolution to fight the flaws of mankind, and offers the alternative proposition to devote the entire self to the recollection of Allāh.

Bamba fully submitted to Allāh and to the Prophet Muḥammad and was, by virtue of his conduct, consecrated by the Prophet Muḥammad the *Quṭb zamānihi* (Axis of his age), to whom no favor is denied: "Thanks to the Qur'ān, I have come close to the Lord / I have gained control of my soul, thus I have alienated the Cursed One" (*Jāwartu*, v. 1). Thus, by way of compensation to service well rendered, God, according to poet Mūsā Ka, assigned Bamba the erection of two mosques as signs of His overflowing grace:

You will build two mosques in your country
Very soon you will return to energize the congregation
You will build a great mosque in Jurbel
No one will uproot it, no one will pray faltering
You will build a great mosque in Touba
Very soon you will return to Daaru Salaam and Touba.[40]

In 1902, at the request of Sheikh Sīdiyya Bāba (who in the 1880s provided sanctuary for Bamba in Boutilimit, which is situated about 150 km southeast of Mauritania's capital), Sheikh Ibra Faal, Bamba's most respected disciple, and Deputy François Carpot, the French administration released and returned Sheikh Ahmadu Bamba to Senegal.[41] In June 1903, Bamba was arrested again and exiled to Souet-el-Ma in the Trarza region, which extends from areas north and east of Mauritania's capital, southward to the border with Senegal. The French decision to send Bamba to Mauritania was based on the assumption that Sheikh Sīdiyya Bāba would "provide him with an example of the benefits of collaboration with

French authorities."[42] In 1907, the administration gave authorization for Bamba to return to Senegal but made sure he lived under surveillance in the village of Céyeen Jolof (Luga Region). Finally, in January 1912, Bamba was allowed to return to his native land of Bawol (Jurbel), but was still under the close watch of the colonial administration until his death in 1927.[43]

Bamba's return from his seven-year exile was enthusiastically received by the Murīd faithful as the ultimate coronation of suffering. Bamba broke through the tyranny of opinion with the strength of his moral character and the eminence of his thoughts. Thus his body of poetic work was read as a paean to injustice. A steady light of glory continues to shine over him as Murīds recognize him far and wide as their charismatic Sheikh, endowed with a prophetic aura.[44] A *Grand Màggal* (a pilgrimage) is held annually on the eighteenth day of the month of Safar by the Murīd community in the holy city of Touba in celebration of the date Bamba departed for Gabon. This commemorative date was decided by the second Murīd Caliph, Fallou M'Bàkke, asking the Murīds to remember the weight of suppression bearing down upon Bamba's shoulders during his exile in Gabon for the redemption of his people.[45] Bamba himself illustrated this pain of isolation for the spiritual redemption of his people in a statement made to his family before he was invited to leave his homeland: "For you will ascend in delight to Allāh's heavens / You will be amid those high in Allāh's heavens / As for me Bamba, in solitude, trials and tribulations / And pains I will ascend; I am going to Galwa (Gabon)."[46] Thus Bamba's exile is celebrated by the Murīds as a triumph of love in the image of the prophets who substituted themselves voluntarily as victims in order to restore the divine life of their peoples. Under the weight of his burden, Bamba taught the Murīds the strength to bear their trials with self-restraint. The *Grand Màggal* then is the moment when Murīd faithful around the world congregate around the Great Mosque of Touba and rejoice over the triumph of their order. It is compulsory that the faithful make a visitation (*ziyāra*) to Bamba's blessed tomb. There, they often make offerings, seeking Bamba's intercession on Judgment Day. Most will then visit the other *lieux de mémoire*, such as the cemetery and the mausolea of the Caliphs.[47] "The *Màggal*," as Mamadou Diouf puts it, "repeats the community's memory and actualizes its mission, rejecting permanent establishment elsewhere as improbable."[48]

While Bamba was under surveillance in Jurbel (1912–1927), the Governor General of French West Africa, Joost van Vollenhoven (1877–1918), gave authorization for the building of the mosque facing Bamba's compound known as *Kër gu mag* (great house). The mosque was built between 1916 and 1926 in line with the great tradition of Ottoman architecture, with its central massive dome, four corner minarets, and its vast inner spaces in perfect harmony with the outer space.[49] Murīd traditions report that Bamba could hardly conceal his pride and joy at seeing the finished mosque. This stands in stark contrast to an incident in Gabon, where colonial officials would vehemently deny him prayer rights, let alone erect even a small mosque.[50]

Fig. 13.2 The Great Mosque of Touba, Touba Senegal. (Photo by the author.)

Bamba's Return from Exile and the Development of Touba

Cheikh Guèye and Eric Ross have produced a comprehensive study of the progressive expansion of the village of Touba into a metropolitan area, now the second largest city in Senegal with over five hundred thousand people and growing at 15 percent annually.[51] Though the holy city's management was left in the hands of the Caliphs, who became the supreme leaders of the order after the death of their father Bamba, Touba in Ross's analysis "is a collective work, the result of a multiplicity of acts of will and of inhabitation undertaken within the overarching social and spiritual project bequeathed by its founder."[52]

The central area of Touba was designated for the building of the Great Mosque. In anticipation of growth of settling communities and pilgrims who make it to the *Grand Màggal*, the second Caliph Sëriñ Fallou Mbàkke designed "a homogenizing grid of straight wide streets, and radiating arteries, which converged on the central shrine complex."[53] The Great Mosque of Touba was officially inaugurated by President Léopold Sédar Senghor in 1963, and has since been undergoing major restoration work with funds collected among generous Murīd disciples responding to the needs of the place of congregation. The Great Mosque stands majestically in the middle of the holy city as a major symbol (*mithāl*) of Islamic triumph, resembling in stature the Great Mosques of Isfahān in Iran, of al-Zaytuna in Tunis, and of Damascus in Syria.[54] The mosque faces the Sacred Mosque (*Masjid al-Ḥarām*) built around the Kaʿba of Mecca and is admired for its five minarets and three green domes. Connected to the mosque is an elaborate mausoleum richly ornamented with gold that holds Bamba's remains.

In measuring the construction of the Great Mosque to its epic proportion, Cleo Cantone has come to this conclusion: "Not only does this prophecy add an 'epic' quality to Touba, but it goes further to entrench seemingly marginal Murīd discourse into mainstream Muslim *ḥadīth* that report the Prophet Muḥammad to have said: '*Whoever builds a masjid, seeking the pleasure of Allāh, Allāh will build a house for him in Paradise* [Bukhāri].'"[55]

Across from the mosque, one finds the modern *Khādim'ur-Rasūl* library, also known as *Daaray Kaamil*. The third Murīd Caliph, Abdul Ahad Mbàkke (1914–1989), fostered the development of a culture of scholarly inquiry in the holy city when he founded and designed the library for the practical needs of making Bamba's writings publicly available. The catalog of acquired materials, mostly written in Arabic and indexed according to the Dewey decimal system, includes about sixty-four thousand copies authored by Bamba and fifty-five thousand copies of the Qur'ān. Among the most notable acquisitions are a collection of fifty thousand dealing with Islamic religion and sciences.[56]

According to Murīd traditions, these copies of the entire Qur'ān were written by hand from memory alone, as evidence of the remarkable place of literacy in Murīd life. The library with its collections and scholars is testament to the place of Senegal in the world of Islam and Touba as an important cultural/intellectual/theological site. Bamba's last surviving daughter, Soxna Maymuna Mbàkke (1925–2002), is remembered for her ability to transcribe the Qur'ān by memory and for her founding of libraries.[57] It would seem that the city of Touba displays a mosaic of symbols that correlate with the inspired life experience of the Prophet Muḥammad. Eric Ross writes, "Touba expresses the idea that there need not be disjunction between cosmological outlook and existence in the modern world and that life can still be experienced as one coherent totality—as an expression of the Oneness of God."[58]

Conclusion: The Significance of Bamba's Return and the Development of Touba

In 1895 Bamba was cut off from his homeland and his people because it was claimed that he was calling for jihād against the emerging colonial order, and he was forced to dwell in total isolation and alienation, "where his fanatic preaching would have no effect."[59] Part of the Murīd community at the time felt hopeless about Bamba's imminent or possible return as they believed that his existential transition from this geographic shift would be consonant with the end of their Sheikh and the Murīd path. But the exiled poet, grounded in the metaphysical circumstances that gave rise to his poetry, anticipated his own deliverance and return homeward grounded on the metaphysical circumstances. Bamba's discourse took on a religious aspect mixing pain and desire in his quest for the divine truth. Though many of his *qaṣā'id* were grounded in painful experiences at the hands of oppressive French colonial officials, the poet often invoked for inspiration the revelations in the Qur'ān and in the *ḥadīth*, as if his poetic creation should be taken as divine utterance.

As a visionary poet, Bamba instantiated the ideals of resilience and truthfulness, pivotal to the cultural and religious transformation of the large population known as the Murīds of Senegal; they continue to express their vigorous enthusiasm for him and to treat his works with deep respect. Most of the poems mentioned in this chapter were conceived and written when Bamba was at the height of his creative powers while in exile in Gabon. They demonstrate a unifying poetic purpose and exemplify *Ṣūfī* literary traditions in subject matter, form, and versification. They reconcile the poet's private experience of French colonial repression with his unfaltering religious beliefs during moments of trial. In their complex forms of expression, they explore the deepest regions of mysticism in search of the divine truth.

Bamba's seven-year exile in Gabon remains paramount in the calendar of Murīd commemorations. Upon his return from exile Bamba's scathing condemnation and perilous experiences at the hands of colonial officials underwent immediate transmutations as Murīd disciples witnessed his pain tranformed into pleasure by divine intervention. Bamba's written accounts also had an overpowering effect on his people who felt he had avenged their disgrace and humiliation. They helped initiate a new mode of spiritual consciousness to a people thus far subjugated both by host and foreign culture.

Bamba's poetics of exile continue to pervade the Murīds who make it their duty in the image of their saint to visit the four corners of the world in a quest for better financial conditions despite adversity. Yet, the majority often return to make the pilgrimage to Touba as a religious duty. Mūsā Ka summed up the celebration of exile in the following lines: "That is why whosoever celebrated his day of exile / Would have performed *jihād*, the *Umrah* pilgrimage with all wishes granted."[60] Hence, according to Mamadou Diouf, "the *Màggal* repeats the community's memory and actualizes its mission, rejecting permanent establishment elsewhere as improbable."[61]

Notes

1. John R. Willis, "Jihād fī Sabīl Allāh: its Doctrinal Basis in Islam and some Aspects of its Evolution in Nineteenth-Century West Africa," *Journal of African History* 8, no. 3 (1967): 395–415.
2. See David Robinson, *Paths of Accomodations: Muslim Societies and French Colonial Authorities in Senegal and Mauritania, 1880–1920* (Athens: Ohio University Press, 2000), 143–150.
3. See Nehemia Levtzion and Randall Pouwells, eds., *The History of Islam in Africa* (Athens: Ohio University Press, 2000).
4. David Robinson, "Beyond Resistance and Collaboration: Amadu Bamba and the Murīds of Senegal," *Journal of Religion in Africa* 21, no. 2 (1991): 167.

5. Willis, "Jihād fī Sabīl Allāh." There is a vast literature on the subject of Bamba's *jihād*. See: Cheikh Anta Babou, *Fighting the Greater Jihād. Amadu Bamba and the Founding of the Murīdiyya of Senegal, 1853–1913* (Athens: Ohio University Press, 2007).

6. Bachir Mbacké, *Les bienfaits de l'eternel, ou, la biographie de Cheikh Ahmad Bamba Mbacké*, trans. and annot. by Khadim Mbacké (Dakar: IFAN, Université Cheikh Anta Diop, 1995).

7. Robinson, *Paths of Accommodations*, 212.

8. See Christian Coulon, "The Grand Magal in Touba: A Religious Festival of the Mouride Brotherhood in Senegal," *African Affairs* 98, no. 391 (1998): 197.

9. See Michael Crowder, *Senegal: A Study of French Assimilation Policy* (London: Methuen, 1967).

10. Robinson, *Paths of Accommodation*, 214.

11. Babou, *Fighting the Greater Jihād*, 76.

12. David Robinson, Philip Curtin, and James Johnson, "A Tentative Chronology of Futa Toro from the Sixteenth through the Nineteenth Centuries," *Cahiers d'Études Africaines* 12, no. 48 (1972): 586.

13. See David Ross, "Dahomey," in *West African Resistance: The Military Response to Colonial Occupation*, ed. Michael Crowder (London: Hutchinson, 1971): 144–169.

14. See Elizabeth Isichei, *History of West Africa since 1800* (New York: Africana Publishing Company, 1977), 189; Mbaye Guèye and A. Adu Boahen, *General History of Africa* (Berkeley: University of California Press, 1985), 7:123–127.

15. Jeremy Rich "Where Every Language Is Heard: Atlantic Commerce, West African and Asian Migrants, and Town Society in Libreville, ca. 1860–1914," in *African Urban Spaces in Historical Perspective*, ed. Steven Salm and Toyin Falola (Rochester, NY: University of Rochester Press, 2005).

16. Guèye and Boahen, *General History of Africa*, 7:127 (citing T. C. Weiskel).

17. Mūsā Ka, ed. Sana Kamara, *Sëriñ Muusaa Ka: Melokaani Roytéef* (Dakar: Editions Papyrus Afrique, 2008), 60.

18. Qur'ān, 85 (*Al-Burūj*): 4.

19. See David Cook, "The Ashāb Al-Ukhdūd: History and Hadith in a Martyrological Sequence," *Jerusalem Studies in Arabic and Islam* 34 (2008): 125–148.

20. Bachir Mbacké, *Les bienfaits de l'eternel*, 73.

21. Philip K. Hitti, *Islam: A Way of Life* (New York: Henry Regnery, 1971), 27.

22. See John Esposito, *Islam: The Straight Path* (New York: Oxford University Press, 1998), 22–23; Khadim Mbacké, *Sufism and Religious Brotherhoods in Senegal*, ed. John Hunwick, trans. Eric Ross (Princeton: Marcus Wiener, 2005), 57.

23. Esposito, *Islam: The Straight Path*, 100–101.

24. William Stoddart, *Sufism: The Mysitical Doctrines and Methods of Islam* (New York: Paragon House, 1986), 19.

25. Cheikh A. Dièye, *Touba: signes et symboles* (Paris: Éditions Deggel, 1997), 22–26.

26. Babou, *Fighting the Greater Jihad*. The worthiest reward Sheikh Ahmadu Bamba could ask from the Prophet was to canonize him as his servant (*Khādim'ur-Rasūl, Khalīfat'ur-Rasūl*) for having dedicated his entire life to the teaching and protection of the Qur'an and the *ḥadīth*. Sheikh Ahmadu Bamba wrote two books, *Muqaddimāt'al-khidma* (Prelude to Service) and *Bidāyat'ul-khidma* (Initiation into Service), in which he described how he earned the honorable title "the Messenger" bestowed upon him as a person of consequence.

According to Cheikh Dièye, *Touba: signes et symboles*, in *Muhammadiyya'l-habīb*, Bamba proclaimed himself the best Servant of the Messenger (*Asnal Khadīm*).

27. J. Spencer Trimingham, *The Sufi Orders in Islam* (Oxford: Oxford University Press, 1998), 138.

28. Quoted in Ralph Austin, Introduction to *The Bezels of Wisdom*, by Ibn al-'Arabī, trans. Ralph Austin (Mahwah, NJ: Paulist Press, 1980), 24.

29. Popular culture affirms that Bamba's works were numerous—he was said to have written "seven [metric] tons of verse," so remarkably much that only the ocean is large enough to hold it all.

30. See Marina Berthet, this volume.

31. See Mamadou Diouf, "The Senegalese Murid Trade Diaspora and the Making of a Vernacular Cosmopolitanism," trans. Steven Rendall, *Public Culture* 12, no. 3 (2000): 679–702; Allen F. Roberts and Mary N. Roberts, *A Saint in the City: Sufi Art and Urban Senegal* (Seattle: University of Washington Press, 2003).

32. Mamadou Diouf, "The Senegalese Murid Trade Diaspora," 699.

33. Among the vast literature on the subject, see Arthur Jeffery, "Ibn Al'Arabi's Shajarat al'Kawn," *Studia Islamica* 10: 43–77; no. 11: 113–160; Trimingham, *The Sufi Orders in Islam*, 161–63; Reynold Nicholson, *Studies in Islamic Mysticism* (Cambridge: Cambridge University Press, 1921).

34. See Nicholson, *Studies in Islamic Mysticism*.

35. Qur'ān, 4 (*An-Nisāa*): 1.

36. Qur'ān, 12 (Yūsuf): 53.

37. See Stoddart, *Sufism: The Mystical Doctrines and Methods of Islam*, 32.

38. See Qur'ān, 75 (*Al-Qiyāmat*): 2.

39. Trimimgham, *Sufi Orders in Islam*, 154–57.

40. Mūsā Ka, ed. Kamara, *Sëriñ Muusaa Ka: Melokaani Roytéef*, 62.

41. Robinson, "Beyond Resistance and Collaboration," 164.

42. Robinson, *Paths of Accommodations*, 218.

43. See Babou, *Fighting the Greater Jihad*.

44. See Coulon, "The Grand Magal in Touba," 198.

45. Coulon, "The Grand Magal in Touba."

46. Mūsā Ka, ed. Kamara, *Sëriñ Muusaa Ka: Melokaani Roytéef*, 81.

47. Eric Ross, *Sufi City: Urban Design and Archetype in Touba* (Rochester: University of Rochester Press, 2006), 76.

48. Mamadou Diouf, "The Senegalese Murid Trade Diaspora," 695.

49. Babou, *Fighting the Greater Jihād*, 257; Cleo Cantone, *Making and Remaking Mosques in Senegal* (Leiden: Brill, 2012), 174.

50. Mūsā Ka, ed. Kamara, *Sëriñ Muusaa Ka: Melokaani Roytéef*, 61–62.

51. Cheikh Guèye, *Touba: la capitale des mourides* (Paris: Karthala, 2002), 15.

52. Ross, *Sufi City*, 66.

53. Ross, *Sufi City*, 85.

54. See Esposito, *Islam: The Straight Path*; Cheikh Dièye, *Touba: signes et symboles*, 117–122.

55. Cantone, *Making and Remaking Mosques*, 249.

56. Guèye, *Touba*, 196.

57. "Sokhna Maïmounatou Mbacké Koubrâ Bintou Khadimou-R-Rassoul," 2014, accessed March 13, 2017, http://htcom.sn/sokhna-maimounatou-mbacke-koubra-bintou-khadimou-r-rassoul.html.

58. Eric Ross, "Touba: A Spritual Metropolis in the Modern World," *Canadian Journal of African Studies* 29, no. 2 (1995): 256.

59. Martial Merlin, French director of political affairs, 1890s, quoted in Robinson, *Paths of Accommodation*, 216.

60. Mūsā Ka, ed. Kamara, *Sëriñ Muusaa Ka: Melokaani Roytéef*, 50.

61. Mamadou Diouf, "The Senegalese Murid Trade Diaspora," 695.

14 The Legacy of Exile

Terrorism in and outside Africa from Osama bin Laden to al-Shabaab

Kris Inman

In 1991 the Kingdom of Saudi Arabia banished a citizen, Osama Bin Laden, as punishment for his political activities, and he took up residence in exile in the Republic of the Sudan. The exile of this individual sparked a complex chain reaction that forced a wider chasm in Islamic identity globally. The legacy of Osama Bin Laden's exile from the Arabian Peninsula and his relocation to the Horn of Africa is profound, and includes the radicalization of certain East African Muslims and the inspiration of new entities such as Harakat al-Shabaab al-Mujahideen (a.k.a. al-Shabaab). By comparing the statements attributed to Osama bin Laden with public declarations from al-Shabaab, a line may be drawn linking the experiences of exile to violent episodes in the region. Furthermore, violence along the Swahili coast today, much of it the direct result of al-Shabaab action or provocation, reverberates deeply with patterns of conflict between the United States and al-Qaeda (meaning "the base").

This chapter demonstrates that exile often provides space for social, political, cultural, and economic change that may not have been possible if the exiled person or community had stayed in their territory of origin.[1] We have seen elsewhere in this volume that such instances have lasting effects on the host country, the home country, and beyond. As Nathan Carpenter shows, exile is often used as a tool to wield power over difficult, dangerous, or unwanted people. Yet, this tool often backfires and can actually advance the very motives that the state power sought to silence or erase by imposing exile. From Aliou Ly's account of Amilcar Cabral's independence movement against Portuguese colonizers, to Sana Camara's account of the influences from exile of the poet and Muslim leader, Sheikh Ahmadu Bamba, on Senegalese Muslim identity, exile spaces often afford the exile new contexts within which to further their cause. In the cases of Cabral and Bamba, the cause—colonial resistance—was undoubtedly noble. But exiled spaces can also afford the exile a context within which to advance pernicious motives. Exile can allow these motives to mature into real actions that have reverberating consequences through time and space.

The story in this chapter is one of the legacies that may be traced to the exile by a state—Saudi Arabia—that wished to discard from its borders a dangerous and difficult person—the now infamous Osama bin Laden (Bin Laden). This decision backfired in ways that continue to reveal repercussions even today. Terrorist activity in East Africa is illustrative in this regard. Kenya is the prime target of this threat but, to date, counterterrorist efforts have been relatively unsuccessful; some say national responses may fuel the radicals.[2] Extant explanations of Kenya as a target draw incomplete implications and inadequate recommendations, which perhaps explains why Kenya continues to be a target of al-Shabaab.

The purpose of this chapter is to offer a different explanation of why al-Shabaab targets Kenya more than any other neighbor and to discuss subsequent implications of this explanation based on the lessons from the history of Bin Laden and his exile. It was during his time as an exile in Sudan that Bin Laden helped transform al-Qaeda from a group fighting to institute an Islamic government in Afghanistan into a group ostensibly waging global jihad against the West. In the permissive environment of exile in Sudan, Bin Laden cultivated a large coalition of like-minded groups with similar goals: to seek revenge against the US for its policies and activities in Muslim countries.[3] As I show below, in a classic display of "jujitsu politics," Bin Laden used the attacks on September 11, 2001 to bait the US into a military invasion of Afghanistan.[4] Since then—and according to Bin Laden's strategic objectives—as the US and its allies have accelerated and intensified the "War on Terror" (through, for example, the use of drones), Bin Laden and al-Qaeda have used these developments to unify the base and cultivate new affiliates and recruits.

One such affiliate—the subject of this chapter—is the Somali-based al-Shabaab (literal translation: "the youth"). By comparing Bin Laden's public statements inciting Muslims to jihad to al-Shabaab's public statements that explain why it attacks foreign targets on foreign soil, this chapter takes an interdisciplinary approach to show how Bin Laden's legacy of exile continues to inspire al-Shabaab's strategies and tactics. Further, this comparison shows that al-Shabaab has entered into a cycle of violence with Kenya that mirrors the cycle of violence between the US and al-Qaeda, albeit on a smaller scale. Even its name, "the youth," can be traced back to Bin Laden's original "Declaration of Jihad against the Americans," in which he explicitly appealed to Muslim youth, whom he deemed more courageous in and important to jihad than elders.[5]

This chapter begins with a discussion of the current state of terrorism in East Africa. I then review prevailing theories as to why al-Shabaab targets Kenya. I show that, compared to other African Union Mission in Somalia (AMISOM) contributors—especially Ethiopia and Uganda—these explanations fail to fully account for al-Shabaab's focus on Kenya. A puzzle is thus revealed: why does al-Shabaab focus its foreign terrorism on Kenya? To answer this question, I turn to an examination of al-Shabaab's self-justification. As I show below, al-Shabaab's own words are also unsatisfactory to solving our puzzle. Together, the extant explanations fail to fully explain al-Shabaab's preoccupation with Kenya. Because we lack a full understanding of al-Shabaab's motives in Kenya, we misinterpret the implications of current events and Kenya may be making decisions that are counterproductive to a counter-al-Shabaab strategy.

As an alternative explanation, I argue that Bin Laden's exile in Sudan allowed him to lay the groundwork for a network and exchange of ideas in East Africa. If we look to the lessons that al-Shabaab draws from Bin Laden's ideology and strategy for al-Qaeda developed in exile, it appears that al-Shabaab is targeting Kenya because of its position in African geopolitics. Travelling back in time to explore Bin Laden's Sudan exile, when al-Qaeda transitioned from an anti-Soviet Afghanistan liberation movement to a global antiwestern insurgent movement, suggests that if al-Shabaab is following this model, then Kenya is an obvious target. Indeed, in some respects, Kenya is a "softer target," not because of the reasons advanced in the scholarly literature, but rather because al-Shabaab—taking its lessons from al-Qaeda—has engaged the most strategically important country in the region in a cycle of jujitsu politics. In Bin Ladenesque parlance, if Kenya is defeated, the bicycle will stop working and the terrorists will win.

The Current Threat Context in East Africa

Bin Laden-inspired terrorism in East Africa dates back to the early 1990s, when al-Qaeda was active in the region. Among the most violent incidents were the coordinated attacks on US embassies in Nairobi and Dar es Salaam in 1998. But in 2006, a new terrorist threat, al-Shabaab, emerged in Somalia. Though initially it focused on Somali issues, over time al-Shabaab diversified its "terror portfolio" to foreign attacks.[6] The first mass-casualty al-Shabaab attack on foreign soil occurred in the summer of 2010. On July 10, al-Shabaab suicide bombers detonated explosives simultaneously in Kampala, Uganda at a restaurant called Ethiopian Village and in the Kyadondo Rugby Club, where people had gathered to watch the FIFA World Cup. Al-Shabaab claimed responsibility for the attacks soon after, and 74 people were killed and over 100 wounded. The second mass-casualty attack took place on September 21, 2013 at the Westgate Mall in Nairobi, Kenya.[7] At least 67 people died and hundreds more were wounded.[8] Then on April 2, 2015, it launched another mass-casualty attack on University students in Garissa, killing at least 147.[9]

According to the Global Terrorism Database, al-Shabaab has been implicated in, or claimed responsibility for, 340 attacks outside of Somalia. Its terror actions on foreign land have been almost exclusively focused on Kenya, especially after 2011 (although, as table 1 shows, Kenya had nearly twice as many attacks prior to 2011 as all other foreign attacks combined). Of these 340 foreign attacks, 328, or 96 percent, have been in Kenya, with most of the attacks being focused on six cities: Nairobi, Garissa, Mandera, Mombassa, Wajir, and Dadaab.[10]

Al-Shabaab publicly claims that its attacks in Kenya since 2011 are in retaliation for Kenya's October 15, 2011 Operation Linda Nchi (OLN, Kiswahili for "protect the nation"), which al-Shabaab characterizes as an "invasion." The operation involved deploying Kenyan troops to Somalia, with the primary goal being to create a one hundred-kilometer buffer zone on the Somali side of the Kenyan-Somali border in order to prevent al-Shabaab from entering Kenya.[11] In a press release in 2011, Kenyan Defense Minister Yusuf Haji and Internal Security Minister George Saitoti stated that OLN was a response to provocations by al-Shabaab.[12] Later, government officials clarified that the invasion was necessary because al-Shabaab was hindering Kenya's long-term development plans; in fact, the plans for Kenya to invade Somalia had been in the works for some time.[13]

However, Kenya was not the first country to unilaterally invade Somalia militarily. Ethiopia invaded and occupied central Somalia from approximately December 2006 to January 2009. Yet, al-Shabaab has executed a total of only six attacks on Ethiopian territory between 2007 and 2014 (half of these were attacks on the Ethiopian military, not so-called "soft" or civilian targets, which have comprised the majority of Kenyan attacks).[14] Further, al-Shabaab typically characterizes *any* military presence in Somalia as "invasion," applying strong rhetoric against all contributing members of the AMISOM peacekeeping force.[15] Thus, a question arises: if the military "invasion" of Somalia through ONL is the reason for these attacks, then why has al-Shabaab not also attacked Ethiopia and AMISOM-contributing countries in the same way and to the same extent?

Explaining al-Shabaab Attacks on Kenya

Kenya's unilateral OLN coincided with a marked increase in al-Shabaab activity on Kenyan soil, as Table 1 demonstrates.[16] Prior to October 2011, al-Shabaab had only executed one large-casualty attack on foreign soil, in Uganda. Al-Shabaab claimed responsibility for this attack, saying that it was in retaliation for Uganda's military support to AMISOM.[17] Although al-Shabaab did execute several kidnappings and smaller scale attacks prior to the beginning of the operation, after OLN commenced, activities escalated, culminating in the first mass-casualty attack on Westgate Mall in Kenya in 2013. Scholars and analysts offer various hypotheses about the pattern of attacks, and the most prevalent explanation is that Kenya is a "soft target." A 2015 Institute for Security Studies analysis is representative of the factors that commentators frequently attribute to explain Kenya's "vulnerability." The primary reasons are "deep-seated structural state weaknesses and challenges" such as "unemployment, land distribution, marginalization, corruption and the integration of marginalized communities into the national fabric."[18] The implication of this explanation is that if Kenya corrected structural problems, it would be less vulnerable to al-Shabaab. In some respects, this is a truism insofar as targeting poor and marginalized persons is a widespread tactic of terrorist recruitment.[19] Yet if these were truly representative of the factors contributing to the root causes of Kenya's insecurity and al-Shabaab's successful recruitment and attacks on Kenyan soil, then surely al-Shabaab would have a similar reason to recruit and attack Ethiopia and Uganda, countries which demonstrate similar, if not worse, structural vulnerabilities?[20]

A brief comparison of the contexts of Kenya, Uganda, and Ethiopia demonstrates that structural vulnerability is an inadequate explanation. Whereas comparatively Kenya has the highest unemployment rate (9.2%, compared to 5.7% in Ethiopia and 3.8% in Uganda in 2013), this has been consistently high for the past ten years.[21] It is difficult to establish a causal link between unemployment and the spike in attacks on Kenya. Other domestic economic and development indicators demonstrate that Kenya is equal to, or well above, its neighbors. For example, Kenya's Human Development Index (HDI), measured on a scale from 0 to 1 (with higher values indicating better development), has been consistently 0.5 since 2008, compared to Ethiopia and Uganda, which both fall at 0.4.[22] Kenya also has a larger economy, with GDP at $60.9 billion in 2014, compared to Uganda (GDP = $26.3 billion) and Ethiopia (GDP = $54.8 billion); all three domestic economies have grown tremendously over the past ten years.[23]

Sociopolitical data reveal that Kenya is similar to her neighbors in other respects. None of the countries rank as "Free and Fair" according to Freedom House: Kenya is ranked as "Partly Free," whereas both Uganda and Ethiopia are rated as "Not Free."[24] Kenya has the smallest Muslim population (11.1%, compared to 12.1% in Uganda and 33.9% in Ethiopia).[25] All three host numerous ethnic groups, with no one group comprising a majority of the population. Kenya's and Uganda's literacy rates are both 78%, while Ethiopia's is 49%.[26] All three countries have "Minorities at Risk" (MAR) populations; the Somali ethnic group is an MAR in both Kenya and Ethiopia.[27]

Geographically, Kenya may be an easy target because it is contiguous to Somalia and hosts many Somali refugees and Kenyans of Somali descent. However, Ethiopia is also a contiguous country, but is not attacked like Kenya. And al-Shabaab has targeted noncontiguous countries before (e.g., Uganda), so it has the capability to extend force. While proximity may be a factor, it clearly cannot alone explain the frequency of al-Shabaab's attacks on Kenya.

In short, when comparing systemic geographic, social, and economic factors analysts routinely use to explain why al-Shabaab attacks Kenya disproportionately, Kenya, Ethiopia, and Uganda appear remarkably similar. Yet, Kenya is by far the biggest al-Shabaab target outside of Somalia. To understand why, we need to look elsewhere. Perhaps the answer lies in the justifications al-Shabaab provides for its attacks outside of Somalia.

In al-Shabaab's Own Words

For its part, al-Shabaab's justification for attacks in Kenya follows a consistent message: it justifies its actions in terms of "defending" itself, or in "retaliation" of Kenya's military incursion into Somalia. The day after OLN commenced, al-Shabaab released the following to the Kenyan public:

> The recent incursion of Kenyan troops into Somali territory . . . not only highlights Kenya's imprudence in sending her non combat-tested troops to become entangled in Somalia's intricate web of war, but also a wilful [*sic*] negligence towards her citizens.
>
> The Kenyan public must understand that the impetuous decision by their troops to cross the border into Somalia will not be without severe repercussions. The bloody battles that will ensue as a result of this incursion will most likely disrupt the social equilibrium and imperil the lives of hundreds of thousands of civilians; and with war consequently comes a significant loss of lives, instability, destruction to the local economy and a critical lack of security.
>
> Therefore, we call upon the Kenya [*sic*] public to think about their safety and their livelihoods and urge their government to immediately withdraw their troops from Somalia. . . . Do not entrust your fate and the fate of your country to a few sabre-rattling politicians. It is your government and the choice is in your hands.[28]

In the years since 2011, al-Shabaab has repeatedly returned to the two themes evident in this excerpt—retaliation for military occupation, and punishing civilians who elected the leaders who sent troops to Somalia—in its public statements explaining why it attacks Kenya. Over time the statements have changed subtly, from warning the Kenyan people to blaming them for allowing their elected leaders to continue the military campaign in Somalia. Al-Shabaab also draws on historical grievances between the Kenyan state and Muslims living in Kenya. This evolution is starkly observable in the April 4, 2015 statement released by al-Shabaab after the Garrisa University attack, in which the group justified the attack on the basis of Kenyan attacks against Somalis in Somalia. The press release went further, though, citing the murder of thousands of Somalis by Kenyan security forces in the 1984 Wagalla massacre, as well as "mass detention, torture and extra-judicial killings of Muslims" in Kenya, as justification for its actions. The authors of the press release then shifted blame to Kenyan citizens:

> We have repeatedly warned you that the actions of your government will not be without retaliation. Choices have consequences; you chose your government out of your own volition so endure the consequences of your actions for you will bear the full brunt of its follies. Not only are you condoning your government's oppressive policies by failing to speak out against them but are reinforcing their policies by electing them. You will, therefore, pay the price with your blood.[29]

In this text, al-Shabaab continues utilizing the motif of OLN as military invasion, but adds historical grievances that Muslims have endured in Kenya, including war with Somalia (Shifta War, 1964–1967) and atrocities toward Somali Muslims living in Kenya (especially the Bulla Karatasi Massacre of 1980 and the Wagalla Massacre of 1984).[30] By invoking these historic atrocities against Muslims, al-Shabaab brings its rhetoric even closer to that of al-Qaeda, as discussed below.

As with the conventional wisdom, analyzing al-Shabaab's own statements does not resolve the puzzle. If military invasion and historical grievances between Somalia and her neighbors are the reason al-Shabaab attacks Kenya, then why not also attack Ethiopia? Ethiopia was the first to invade Somalia and is credited with radicalizing al-Shabaab.[31] Furthermore, Ethiopia also has a history of committing atrocities against Muslims.[32] If geographic proximity is an explanation, then al-Shabaab should have attacked Ethiopia like it has Kenya.

Al-Shabaab frequently identifies Ethiopia, Uganda, and Kenya as members of the West's "conspiracy" against Muslims. This motif is stark in the statements by al-Shabaab's leader, Sheikh Mukhtar Abu al-Zubair (a.k.a. Godane). Godane, who trained and fought in Afghanistan, brought al-Shabaab into partnership with al-Qaeda, despite dissent from other leaders in al-Shabaab, notably, Hassan Aweys and Omar Hammami.[33] As Godane solidified al-Shabaab's ties to al-Qaeda, the strategy and tactics also came into alignment. He mentions Ethiopia and Kenya repeatedly as "invaders," and says that Uganda's peacekeeping force is a "cover for invasion." He says the countries want to control Somalia and oppress Muslims. Due to this, Godane incites Muslims to "attack them [Kenya, Ethiopia, and AMISOM contributors] successively and continue your raids, prevent them from rest, storm their headquarters, target their routes, eradicate them by explosives, terrorize them by martyrdom, and do not be concerned of their numbers."[34] By its own rhetoric, then, al-Shabaab advocates attacking all three countries; but it continues to focus only on Kenya. So we are still left without a solution to the puzzle. Bin Laden and al-Qaeda laid roots in Somalia throughout the 1990s and Godane, with experience fighting in Afghanistan, brought al-Shabaab into alignment with al-Qaeda. Perhaps the solution lies in the lessons it has learned for waging jihad, dating back to Bin Laden's exile in Sudan.

"The Base" in East Africa

Bin Laden's extremism did not begin in exile; rather, he was exiled from his home country of Saudi Arabia because of growing extremist views that developed after his return from fighting the Soviet Union with the Mujahedeen in Afghanistan. Volumes have been written about the evolution in his thinking and behavior from a man who was supported by Saudi Arabia, the US, and Pakistan in the fight against the Soviet Union invasion of Afghanistan to a man who rose to "public enemy number one" in the US; rather than reworking what others have written, I wish to focus on how his time in Sudan laid the foundations for al-Shabaab's strategy and tactics.[35]

After fighting the Soviet invasion of Afghanistan, Bin Laden returned to Saudi Arabia where he began to see the Kingdom as corrupt, incompetent, and hypocritical. He was particularly impacted by two geopolitical decisions made by the Saudi Royal Family. First, he disapproved of the Royal Family's refusal to intervene in Yemen, while they supported intervention in Afghanistan.[36] Second, he was convinced that Saddam Hussein would invade Saudi Arabia, and when Saddam invaded Kuwait in August 1990, he believed his fears were coming true. He presented a plan to deal with Saddam to the Saudi royal family, but was turned down. Instead, Saudi Arabia aligned with the US, which spearheaded the coalition that invaded Iraq. With the blessings of Saudi religious leaders, the US brought its "infidel" military to the Arabian Peninsula, home to the sacred Muslim cities of Mecca and Medina, in 1990. This development had a lasting impact on his ideology and he never forgot what he perceived as King Fahd's grievous betrayal of Muslims.[37] He came to believe the US was unprincipled and would do anything to advance its interests. These experiences impressed upon him the need to maintain wartime unity amongst Muslim holy fighters in order to create a viable postwar government.[38]

Bin Laden went into exile in Sudan from 1991 to 1996. These five years left an indelible mark on Bin Laden's ideology and strategic thinking. From Sudan, Bin Laden began laying the groundwork to expand al-Qaeda's raison d'être from a local effort focused on Afghanistan to a global war on the US. This transition is evidenced by several observations: from 1992 to 1994, he sent al-Qaeda operatives to support anti-US forces in Somalia; he engaged in several business endeavors in order to build a personal reserve of funds for coming conflicts; through these business endeavors, he supported al-Qaeda members and their families; he sent al-Qaeda lieutenants to the Horn of Africa to expand its global operations and plan for future attacks; he honed his skills as commander of al-Qaeda; and he developed a closer friendship with the Egyptian extremist Ayman al-Zawahiri. Living in Sudan, he also developed a more keen sense of the diversity of Islam around the world, far more than he would have in Saudi Arabia or Afghanistan.[39] These lessons would prove to be useful for future groups, such as al-Shabaab, which also seek to unite Muslims from diverse backgrounds in order to achieve their particular objectives.

Before he left Sudan, Bin Laden succeeded in planting the seeds of his terrorist movement in East Africa and Somalia. He placed training camps in southern Somalia to combat the 1993 US mission to capture aides to Somali warlord General Mohamed Farah Aidid, which resulted in the killing of eighteen American soldiers.[40] In 1992, he sent Khalid Fawwaz (a close friend and Afghan veteran) to Nairobi to build a Kenyan network that would eventually execute the 1998 Embassy bombings.[41] His lieutenants also worked with Sudan's military and intelligence services to collect intelligence in Africa, especially in Somalia. From the US activity in Somalia between 1993 and 1994, he came to believe that while the US had weapons, it did not have the men or the resolve to achieve its military objectives against Muslims.[42] His communiques during this time demonstrate that Bin Laden deliberately decided not to "run Al-Qaeda strictly as a traditional terrorist group, one that by definition is a lethal nuisance to its foes but not a national security threat" but rather, as a global insurgency against America and its allies.[43] This is a crucial point, for combatting insurgencies is a different matter to combatting terrorism—if al-Shabaab is also following this model, it has implications for countering al-Shabaab.

In 1996, under the pressure of US sanctions and the international community, the Sudanese government asked Bin Laden to leave. He went into exile again on May 18, 1996, this time to Afghanistan. He took several lessons with him, lessons which al-Shabaab appears to draw on, as we can see in its rhetoric and actions. Bin Laden came to believe that the Mujahedeen defeated the Soviet Union by bleeding dry its economy and that it would defeat the US in the same way. In his "Declaration of Jihad against the Americans," written just a few months after leaving Sudan, he advises Muslims not to buy American goods because they "are transformed into bullets and used against our brothers in Palestine. By buying these goods we are strengthening their economy while our position and poverty increase."[44] This document reveals what has become a common recipe for justifying the actions of terrorist groups and for recruitment. Specifically, it directs Muslims to join the "war" because: America and its allies are "occupying" Muslim lands and committing massacres against Muslims; the West is propping up corrupt and incompetent governments in Muslim lands, which is detrimental to economies and causes the masses to suffer; governments in Muslim countries refuse to address the grievances of the masses, therefore violence is their only recourse; the West is trying to foment internal war between Muslims in order to destroy them all.

Bin Laden issued a second fatwa in 1998, "Jihad against Jews and Crusaders," where these motifs are sharpened and reiterated: he uses the language of "invasion," "occupation," "massacres," and support for Israel (the ultimate occupier and killer of Muslims) as reasons that Muslims should join the cause.[45] In this way, Bin Laden laid the groundwork for the tactics that groups like al-Shabaab continue to employ today in strategy, recruiting new members, and keeping their base unified to a common cause.

Beyond these recruitment tactics, Bin Laden engaged in jujitsu politics as an explicit strategy. In 1996, Bin Laden told Abdel Bari Atwan that he would "bring the US to fight on Muslim soil."[46] This would achieve three major objectives: first, bringing an "infidel invader" to Muslim land would activate historical grievances, which would in turn assist with recruitment, funding, and unifying the Muslim world against a common enemy; second, it would be easier to kill US soldiers in Afghanistan and Bin Laden thought that this devastation would foment an American public backlash and help to destroy the American government; and third, if al-Qaeda could draw American forces to Afghanistan, it would leave Israel and the Arab regimes unprotected and, therefore, easier to defeat.[47] He believed the 1998 Embassy bombings in Kenya and Tanzania and, later, the 2000 *USS Cole* attack, would incite the US to come to Afghanistan, but they did not. But on September 11, 2001, his wish was granted. The reason Bin Laden focused on the US rather than Israel is illustrated in the following metaphor that he shared with his son:

> Omar, try to imagine a two-wheeled bicycle. One wheel is made of steel. The other wheel is made of wood. . . . America and Israel are one bicycle with two wheels. The wooden wheel represents the United States. The steel wheel represents Israel. Does a general attack the strongest line when in battle? No, he concentrates on the weakest part of the line. The Americans are [the wooden wheel, without which the steel wheel will automatically fail]. . . . First we obliterate America. By that I don't mean militarily. We can destroy America from within by making it economically weak, until its markets collapse. When that happens, they will have no interest in supplying Israel with arms, for they will not have extra funds to do so. At that time, the steel wheel will corrode and be destroyed by lack of attention. That's what we [Muslims] did to the Russians. . . . The Russians spent all of their wealth on the war in Afghanistan. When they could no longer finance the war, they fled. After fleeing their whole system collapsed.[48]

As with so many other stories in this volume, it was through his exile to Sudan that he was able to develop a deeper understanding of the varieties of Islam, hone his skills at messaging to diverse groups, and amass more wealth, power, and influence than he could have obtained had he stayed in Saudi Arabia, where he undoubtedly would have been under constant surveillance and oppression by the government. He also inserted al-Qaeda into East Africa, particularly in Somalia. He laid the groundwork to successfully launch attacks against the US. And he eventually engaged the US in Afghanistan as part of his overall strategy for beating the "Infidels" and their armies.

Bin Laden's Legacy in East Africa

Bin Laden was a known supporter of al-Shabaab until his death in 2011 and al-Shabaab has received substantial support from al-Qaeda over the years.[49] Al-Shabaab grew out of the militant Salafi group, al-Ittihad al-Islami (AIAI, or "Unity of Islam"), which was active in Somalia in the 1990s after the collapse of the Siad Barre regime. AIAI was partly funded and armed by Bin Laden, and many of its members, including current al-Shabaab commanders, followed Bin Laden to Afghanistan in the late 1990s.[50] AIAI gained popularity in the Ogadani region, which had been a source of conflict between Somalia and Ethiopia in the 1970s.[51] This popularity worried Ethiopia. In 2003, AIAI splintered and the hardliners joined the Islamic Courts Union (ICU), an alliance of shari'a courts in Somalia, as its youth militia.[52] The ICU, which formed around 2000 and filled the social service vacuum left by the collapsed state, was popular in Somalia.[53]

By 2006, the ICU gained control of the capital, spreading fear that its youth militia, al-Shabaab, would attempt violent jihad in Ethiopia. This led Ethiopia to invade Somalia in December 2006, at the request of the Somali Transitional Federal Government (TFG). While Ethiopia easily overthrew the ICU, analysts attribute this event to radicalizing al-Shabaab: "Throughout 2007 and 2008, using hit-and-run attacks, improvised explosive devices (IEDs), assassinations, and bombings, Al-Shabaab stymied the Ethiopian advance into the south. This success emboldened Al-Shabaab. . . . Calling for an expulsion of the Ethiopians and the formation of an Islamic state in Somalia, Al-Shabaab rallied considerable support for its cause among the south/central population, transforming itself into a major military movement."[54] Given that Ethiopia was the first Somali neighbor to invade, that Ethiopia and Somalia had a history of conflict, and the invasion is attributed to radicalizing al-Shabaab's ideology, strategy, and tactics, it is puzzling that al-Shabaab has executed so few attacks on Ethiopian soil. Instead, the vast majority of attacks have occurred in Kenya.

An Alternative Explanation for al-Shabaab's Foreign Targeting Strategy

Today, al-Shabaab is one of the most active terrorist organizations in the world. The Study of Terrorism and Responses to Terrorism (START) estimates that it has carried out over two thousand six hundred attacks and killed thousands since its inception. The number of attacks has increased from fewer than six in 2007 to more than eight hundred in 2014 and the majority of these attacks have occurred in Somalia, but foreign attacks have increased steadily since 2011 (see table 14.1).

The influence of Bin Laden's recruitment and unifying tactics is evident in al-Shabaab's rhetoric. al-Shabaab draws on the same motifs that Bin Laden developed during the 1990s: appeal to historical maltreatment of Muslims by non-Muslims; characterize military engagement as "occupation" and "invasion;" and cast the enemy as a member in a global western "conspiracy" to eradicate Islam. However, I argue that there are two other lessons al-Shabaab has learned from Bin Laden: one lesson—degrading the enemy's economy—is evident in primary documents; the other lesson—jujitsu politics as a strategy—is not. To employ jujitsu politics, al-Shabaab could have engaged any of its neighbors, but it chose Kenya. I now provide a possible reason for why.

As discussed above, Kenya's top security personnel justified OLN as a response to "provocations" from al-Shabaab. Thus, al-Shabaab successfully baited Kenya into a military campaign in a Muslim land, just as Bin Laden did with the US in Afghanistan in 2001. This began the cycle of jujitsu politics. Using Bin Laden's bicycle metaphor helps clue us in to Kenya as the target for this cycle.

The choice of which enemy to engage in jujitsu politics is a strategic decision based on taking out the lynchpin. Kenya is not the steel wheel when it comes to

Table 14.1. Al-Shabaab Attacks by Country/Year[1]

Year	Somalia	Kenya	Ethiopia	Uganda	Djibouti	Total
2007	5		1			6
2008	24	1	1			26
2009	55	1		1		57
2010	61	8		2		71
2011	130	32				162
2012	179	53				232
2013	279	37	3			319
2014	782	82	1		1	866
2015	329	56		1		386
2016	498	58		1		557
Total	2,342	328	6	5	1	2,682

1. National Consortium for the Study of Terrorism and Responses to Terrorism (START), 2016, Global Terrorism Database, accessed December 17, 2017, https://www.start.umd.edu/gtd.

military strength: it ranks 77th out of 133 countries, versus Ethiopia (which ranks 41st) which has a much stronger military (but neither is it the weakest of the East African countries; for example, Uganda is ranked 92nd).[55] Thus, Kenya is an easier target, but this is not what makes it an ideal target. Kenya is an ideal target because of its economic position on the African continent. It is this geopolitical economic position that draws al-Shabaab's wrath, not its structural domestic deficiencies or geographic proximity. Nairobi is the business and financial hub for East Africa and Kenyans are prolific businessman across the continent.[56] Kenya also derives major revenue from the tourism industry and Kenya has by far the most tourists per year, compared to Uganda and Ethiopia.[57] Following Bin Laden's logic, if al-Shabaab were to paralyze Kenya, it would have reverberating economic and financial effects across Africa. For Bin Laden, if you destroy your enemy's economy, you win. This lesson is seen in al-Shabaab rhetoric: Godane advocates for "political and economic sabotage."[58] In this way, just as Bin Laden succeeded in drawing the US, the global economic superpower, into an unending war in Afghanistan, al-Shabaab has done the same with East Africa's regional economic superpower, Kenya.

Conclusion

Viewing al-Shabaab's attacks in Kenya through the lens of jujitsu politics implies a different response than what the common wisdom suggests. First, bleeding the enemy dry economically by forcing him to divert more resources to armed forces is a specific terrorist strategy. To date, Kenya's military spending has held at consistent levels (between 8 and 9 percent of government expenditures) since 2005.[59] Kenya should keep military spending steady. Second, al-Shabaab thrives when Kenya responds militarily. Regardless of the facts, al-Shabaab casts its war rhetoric in terms of oppression toward Muslims. Kenyan military action creates a perception of hostility toward Islam that has proven to be a powerful unifying factor and recruitment tool (perpetuating the cycle of violence). To counter this rhetoric, Kenya might work with its Muslim leadership to provide a unified counterpoint to al-Shabaab, one that is based on a moderate and orthodox interpretation of holy Muslim texts. To counter any Islamophobic tendencies within the non-Muslim Kenyan population, Kenya could engage the interfaith community. A council of religions who work with marginalized communities to bring social services and education would provide a much stronger antidote to al-Shabaab than a military response.

Were Kenya to commence a public relations campaign, it could detail the atrocities committed by al-Shabaab. The organization frequently kills Muslims during its attacks in Kenya. For example, many of the people that the al-Shabaab militants murdered at Westgate were Muslims. Many of the surviving Muslim victims struggled to understand how adherents to their faith, the name of which means "Peace," could perpetrate such a heinous attack on innocents and innocence.[60] Scholars have cataloged the killing of Muslims as reasons people have defected from al-Shabaab.[61] Therefore, if the government or civil society provided these details in a systematic way and targeted Muslim communities, it would likely go a long way in countering al-Shabaab recruitment and sympathy. Most importantly, these nonmilitaristic responses would break the cycle of jujitsu politics in which al-Shabaab currently has Kenya engaged.

Notes

1. Analysis or opinions expressed in this paper are those of the author and do not reflect the official policy or position of the US Government, National Intelligence University, the Department of Defense, or any of its components.

2. Andrews Atta-Asamoah and Emmanuel Kisiangani, "Implications of Kenya's Military Offensive Against Al-Shabaab," Institute for Security Studies, October 25, 2011.

3. "A Biography of Osama bin Laden," Frontline, 2014, accessed December 17, 2017, http://www.pbs.org/wgbh/pages/frontline/shows/binladen/who/bio.html.

4. "Jujitsu Politics" is a term used to describe a situation in which one group purposefully evokes a harsh response, usually from a state, in order to recruit members and build solidarity amongst existing members. Psychologists describe it as follows: "Mass radicalization by external attack is so reliable that it can be used as a strategy. Some terrorists have explicitly sought to elicit a state response that will carry far beyond the terrorists to strike terrorist sympathizers who have not yet been mobilized to action. The predictable result is to mobilize terrorist sympathizers far beyond what the terrorists can accomplish alone. We call this strategy jujitsu politics: using the enemy's strength against him." Clark McCauley and Sophia Moskalenko, "Mechanisms of Political Radicalization: Pathways toward Terrorism," *Terrorism and Political Violence*, 20 (2008): 427.

5. Osama bin Laden, "Declaration of Jihad against the Americans Occupying the Land of the Two Holiest Sites," terrorismfiles.org, August 23, 1996, accessed December 17, 2017, http://www.terrorismfiles.org/individuals/declaration_of_jihad1.html.

6. See Jason C. Mueller, "The Evolution of Political Violence: The Case of Somalia's Al-Shabaab" *Terrorism and Political Violence* (May 2016): 1–26.

7. *Terror at the Mall*, directed by Dan Reed (HBO Documentary, 2014).

8. Daniel Howden, "Terror in Westgate Mall: The Full Story of the Attacks that Devastated Kenya," *The Guardian*, October 4, 2013.

9. "Kenya: At Least 147 Dead in Heinous Garissa Attack," Human Rights Watch, April 3, 2015.

10. Global Terrorism Database, University of Maryland, Study of Terrorism and Response to Terrorism (START), 2017, accessed December 17, 2017, http://www.start.umd.edu/gtd/.

11. Atta-Asamoah and Kisiangani, "Implications of Kenya's Military Offensive."

12. "Operation 'Linda Nchi': Kenya Goes to War in Somalia," Kenya Forum, October 9, 2011. The list of provocations includes: attacks on security posts in 2009 and 2010, planting landmines at the border in 2011, raids on the border, and kidnappings.

13. Micah Zenko, "What's Wrong with Kenya's Invasion of Somalia," *The Atlantic*, October 28, 2011, accessed January 16, 2017, http://www.theatlantic.com/international/archive/2011/10/whats-wrong-with-kenyas-invasion-of-somalia/247517/; David M. Anderson and Jacob McKnight, "Kenya at War: Al-Shabaab and Its Enemies in Eastern Africa," *African Affairs* 114, no. 454 (2014): 1–27.

14. Global Terrorism Database.

15. The AMISOM force includes troops from Burundi, Djibouti, Ethiopia, Kenya, Sierra Leone, and Uganda, as well as Ghana and Nigeria who contribute to the police force, AMISOM, 2017, accessed December 17, 2017, http://amisom-au.org/.

16. Anderson and McKnight, "Kenya at War."

17. "Statement Regarding the Blessed Kampala Operations from the Leaders of Harakat Shabaab Al-Mujahideen," Al-Kataib, July 14, 2010, accessed December 17, 2017, https://azelin.files.wordpress.com/2010/07/statement-regarding-the-blessed-kampala-operations.pdf.

18. Andrews Atta-Asamoah, "East Africa Report: Responses to Insecurity in Kenya. Too Much, Too Little, Too Late?" *Institute for Security Studies*, 3 (April 2015): 12.

19. E.g. Tore Bjorgo, ed., *Root Causes of Terrorism: Myths, Reality and Ways Forward* (London, UK: Routledge, 2005); Fernando Reinares, "Radicalisation Processes Leading to Acts of Terrorism: A Concise Report Prepared by the European Commission's Expert Group on Violent Radicalisation," (European Commission, 2008).

20. For comparative data on a host of economic and social factors, see World Bank Indicators, accessed January 20, 2017, http://data.worldbank.org/indicator/.

21. Unemployment is a World Bank Indicator, accessed January 20, 2017, http://data.worldbank.org/indicator/SL.UEM.TOTL.ZS.

22. The Human Development Index is a United Nations Development Program dataset, accessed January 20, 2017, http://hdr.undp.org/en/content/table-2-human-development-index-trends-1980-2013#a

23. Gross Domestic Product is a World Bank Indicator, accessed January 20, 2017, http://data.worldbank.org/indicator/NY.GDP.MKTP.CD/countries/ET?page=1&display=default

24. Freedom in the World, *Freedom House*, accessed December 17, 2017, https://freedomhouse.org/country/kenya; https://freedomhouse.org/country/ethiopia; https://freedomhouse.org/country/uganda.

25. Religious and ethnic identity, *CIA World Factbook*, available for each country as follows: Ethiopia, 2007, accessed January 20, 2017, https://www.cia.gov/library/publications/the-world-factbook/geos/et.html; Kenya, 2009, accessed January 20, 2017, https://www.cia.gov/library/publications/the-world-factbook/geos/ke.html; Uganda, 2002, accessed January 20, 2017, https://www.cia.gov/library/publications/the-world-factbook/geos/ug.html.

26. Literacy Rates, *CIA World Factbook*, accessed January 20, 2017, https://www.cia.gov/library/publications/the-world-factbook/fields/2103.html.

27. The Minorities at Risk, University of Maryland, http://www.cidcm.umd.edu/mar/assessments.asp?regionId=6.

28. "The Kenyan Public Must Think About Their Safety and Security and Urge Their Government to Immediately Withdraw Their Troops from Somalia," *Al-Shabaab Press Release*, October 17, 2011, accessed January 20, 2017, http://somaliwarmonitor.com/2011/10/17/Alshabaab-press-release-the-kenyan-public-must-think-about-their-safety-and-security-and-urge-their-government-to-immediately-withdraw-their-troops-from-somalia/.

29. "Garissa Attack: Burying Kenya's Hopes," *Al-Shabaab Press Release*, April 4, 2015, accessed December 17, 2017, https://www.washingtonpost.com/world/africa/al-shabab-statement-on-deadly-campus-assault-in-kenya/2015/04/04/4577ce52-dad9-11e4-8103-fa84725dbf9d_story.html?utm_term=.55353c786c5c.

30. These massacres are documented in the Kenyan Truth, Justice, and Reconciliation Report, May 3, 3013, accessed December 17, 2017, http://www.icla.up.ac.za/images/un/commissionsofinquiries/files/TJRC_report_Volume_4%20(1)%20Kenya.pdf.

31. Ken Menkhaus, "After the Kenyan Intervention in Somalia," Enough Project, January 2012, accessed December 17, 2017, https://enoughproject.org/files/MenkhausKenyaninterventionSomalia.pdf; Jonathan Masters and Mohammed Al-y Sergie, "Al-Shabab," *Council on Foreign Relations Backgrounder*, March 13, 2015.

32. E.g., Johan Ripas, "Ethiopia: A Wave of Atrocities against Villages in Ogaden," *Somaliland Press*, September 26, 2012; "Ethiopia: Government Continues to Target Peaceful Muslim Protest Movement," Amnesty International Public Statement, November 2, 2012, accessed January 20, 2017, file:///E:/My%20Files(20259)/Native/C/Documents%20and%20Settings/Administrator/My%20Documents/Downloads/afr250162012en.pdf; "Genocide Emergency: Ethiopia—The Ogaden Massacres," Genocide Watch.

33. Mueller, "The Evolution of Political Violence."

34. Sheikh Mukhtar Abu al-Zubair, "Amir of the Harakat Al-Shabaab Al-Mujahideen about the recent developments in the country," April 2012, accessed December 17, 2017, https://azelin.files.wordpress.com/2012/04/shaykh-mukhtar-abc5ab-al-zubayr-22about-the-situation-in-the-country22-en.pdf; Sheikh Mukhtar Abu al-Zubair, "Amir of Harakat Al-Shabab Mujahideen regarding the second London Conference and the situation of the Somali government," May 2013, accessed December 17, 2017, https://azelin.files.wordpress.com/2013/05/shaykh-mukhtar-abc5ab-al-zubayr-22regarding-the-second-london-conference-and-the-situation-of-the-somali-government22-en.pdf.

35. Some of the notable volumes about Bin Laden include: Peter Bergen, *The Longest War: The Enduring Conflict between America and Al-Qaeda* (New York: Free Press, 2011); Jonathan Randal, *Osama: The Making of a Terrorist* (London: Vintage, 2004); Steve Coll, *The Bin Ladens: An Arabian Family in the American Century* (New York: Penguin Press, 2008); Peter L. Bergen, *Holy War, Inc.: Inside the Secret World of Osama bin Laden* (New York: Free Press, 2001); Michael Scheuer, *Osama bin Laden* (Oxford: Oxford University Press, 2011); Lawrence Wright, *The Looming Tower: Al-Qaeda and the Road to 9/11* (London: Vintage, 2006); Seth G. Jones, *In the Graveyard of Empires: America's War in Afghanistan* (New York: W. W. Norton & Company, 2009); and Steve Coll, *Ghost Wars: The Secret History of the CIA, Afghanistan, and bin Laden, from the Soviet Invasion to September 10, 2001* (New York: Penguin Press, 2004).

36. Scheuer, *Osama bin Laden*, 97.

37. Scheuer, *Osama bin Laden*, chap. 4.

38. Scheuer, *Osama bin Laden*; Lawrance Freedman, *A Choice of Enemies: America Confronts the Middle East* (New York: Public Affairs, 2008).

39. Scheuer, *Osama bin Laden*, chap. 4.

40. Freedman, *A Choice of Enemies.*

41. Scheuer, *Osama bin Laden*, 90.

42. Ibid.; Freedman, *A Choice of Enemies.*

43. Scheuer, *Osama bin Laden*, 94.

44. Osama bin Laden, "Declaration of Jihad against the Americans Occupying the Land of the Two Holiest Sites," August 23, 1996, accessed December 17, 2017, https://ctc.usma.edu/wp-content/uploads/2013/10/Declaration-of-Jihad-against-the-Americans-Occupying-the-Land-of-the-Two-Holiest-Sites-Translation.pdf.

45. Osama bin Laden, "Jihad against Jews and Crusaders," February 23, 1998, accessed December 17, 2017, https://fas.org/irp/world/para/docs/980223-fatwa.htm.

46. Abdel Bari Atwan, *The Secret History of Al-Qaeda* (Berkeley: University of California Press, 2008), 221.

47. Scheuer, *Osama bin Laden*, chap. 5; see also, Michael Vlahos, *Terror's Mask: Insurgency within Islam* (Laurel, MD: Johns Hopkins University/Applied Physics Laboratory, November 2002).

48. Omar Bin Laden and Najwa bin Laden, *Growing Up bin Laden: Osama's Wife and Son Take Us inside Their World* (New York: St. Martin's Press, 2009), 177.

49. "Al-Shabaab," National Counterterrorism Center, March 2016, accessed December 17, 2017, https://web.archive.org/web/20160304131514/http://www.nctc.gov:80/site/groups/al_shabaab.html.

50. Masters and Sergie, "Al-Shabab."

51. Mueller, "The Evolution of Political Violence."

52. Masters and Sergie, "Al-Shabab;" Mueller "The Evolution of Political Violence."

53. Mueller, "The Evolution of Political Violence."

54. Bob Wise, "Al-Shabaab," *AQAM Futures Project Case Studies Series* 2 (July 2011), Center for Strategic and International Studies.

55. Military Strength data are from Global Firepower, 2017, accessed December 17, 2017, www.globalfirepower.com.

56. Jeff Otieno, "East Africa: Nairobi termed 'Hub of Impact Investment' as Region Attracts US $9 Billion," *The East African*, August 8, 2015.

57. Tourism data are a World Bank Indicator, accessed January 20, 2017, http://data.worldbank.org/indicator/ST.INT.ARVL.

58. Sheikh Al-Zubair, "The recent developments in the country."

59. Military expenditure data are a World Bank Indicator, http://data.worldbank.org/indicator/MS.MIL.XPND.ZS/countries/KE-ET-UG?display=graph.

60. The events in Kampala, Uganda, and Nairobi, Kenya that are described here are well documented in the international media, so I do not provide copious citations here.

61. John C. Amble, and Alexander Meleagrou-Hitchens, "Jihadist Radicalization in East Africa: Two Case Studies." *Studies in Conflict & Terrorism* 37 (2014): 523–40.

15 Reconstructing Slavery in Ohioan Exile

Mauritanian Refugees in the United States

E. Ann McDougall

"Bakary" is an escaped slave living in northern Cincinnati, so too is "Marieme." Saidou Wane is a surveyor for the city. Across the Ohio River, El Hassen is a middle-class restaurant owner in Erlanger, Kentucky; Yacoub Cheikh is his friend. All are Mauritanian refugees in America's "Greater Cincinnati." The four thousand or so living in exile here are referred to as a "community." But there is more than a river dividing it.[1]

Refugees seeking asylum in the United States from West Africa's Islamic Republic of Mauritania belong to very distinct ethnic, cultural, and social groups; they live in exile for very different reasons. Some are black freed slaves like Bakary and Marieme (*haratine*), others are "white" (*bidan*) freemen like El Hassen and Cheikh; the former are considered Africans who share the Arab-Berber culture and language of the latter. The majority, however, are black, free Mauritanians (African Mauritanians) like Wane, mostly of the Halpulaar ethnicity, with their own language (Pulaar) and culture.

Historically, social tensions between these groups extended to enslavement (haratine enslaved by bidan) and genocide (Halpulaar having been forced from Mauritania by bidan and haratine between 1989–1991). Since the mid-1980s, African Mauritanians have opposed the Mauritanian government; over the past decade, many African Mauritanians expelled to Senegal (or who fled to Mali to avoid expulsion) have returned and tried to reclaim family property. They face ongoing resistance from bidan and haratine who have long since appropriated their land and animals. Most remain "stateless," lacking the required papers to claim citizenship. To assume, therefore, that "country of origin" provides a collective identity strong enough to create a unified—or even identifiable—Mauritanian "community" would be unrealistic.[2]

Ohio's Mauritanians also face an additional challenge, however, namely the reputation of their country. From the late 1980s through the early 2000s,

Mauritania entered the edges of American public awareness as a racist slave society that only officially abolished slavery in 1980–81. Since then, international concern with various forms of forced and/or child labor, trafficking of domestics and entrapment of prostitutes—labeled as "modern-day slavery"—has brought Mauritania back into American consciousness. In 2012, CNN spotlighted Mauritania as "Slavery's Last Stronghold," its inaugural lead story in what has become the ongoing "Freedom Project" series.[3] Its investigative reporter, John Sutter and his videographer "secretly" spoke with and filmed slaves and abolitionists in Mauritania. They then brought the issue home by tracking two Mauritanian refugees who also happened to be escaped slaves, to the Ohio community: Bakary and Marieme.[4] The Freedom Project continues, embracing many global situations; as of December 2017, it was still highlighting Mauritanian developments and resurrecting the 2012 material that so closely ties the "legacies of slavery" in Africa to "ethnicity in exile" in America.[5]

Drawing largely on the case study of these "Ohio Mauritanians," this chapter explores the interplay between their own self-perceptions and strategies to forge "community" and "identity," and the perceptions of "others" as publically articulated in various media (especially CNN), over time. Mirroring Benjamin Lawrance's chapter in this volume exploring how different ideas of nation unfold within exiled communities abroad, I highlight two processes: one, the gradual "erasure" of Halpulaar history and identity in the face of America's embracing of a Mauritanian "black-white" narrative that resonates with its own slave history; and two, the corresponding feminization of that slavery as rape, kidnapping, and infanticide by male masters as perpetrated against women and girls. The latter increasingly constitutes what has been called elsewhere, "the country narrative."[6] In concluding, I reflect on scholarly research on identity in exile.

A History of Racism and Slavery: Myth and Reality

Mauritania officially abolished slavery in 1980. Although not the first time in the region's history (the French colony declared slaving illegal in 1905, the newly independent state enshrined "equality" in its 1961 Constitution), this decree attracted unprecedented international attention. Subsequently, Mauritania enjoyed the incessant scrutiny of global human rights and antislavery groups. Beginning with the 1980 London-based Anti-Slavery Society report (by John Mercer) also used by the UN, the verdict was that the Mauritanian government failed miserably in implementing abolition; shamefully, the government's own members led in slave-ownership. Mercer's influential, twice-published report reduced Mauritania's complex race, ethnic, and class relations to a static "black and white" snapshot. Couched in a discourse of "slavery and freedom," those who were not "free" were black and either slave or "half-slave"; those who were "free" were white and (implicitly) slave masters. Those who were black but also free—African Mauritanians, the Halpulaar, Soninke, and Wolof, the dominant populations in the southern regions—were marginalized in the scenario. Henceforth, international discussion focused on slavery, sidestepping African Mauritanians' historical role as slave owners and their more contemporary experience as victims of bidan discrimination.[7]

In Mauritania itself, however, African Mauritanians (especially Halpulaar), were politically active. In 1986, the *Front de Libération des Africains de Mauritanie* (FLAM, founded 1983), famously published a manifesto accusing Mauritania's government of "Apartheid" policies; in 1987, it was implicated in a failed coup d'état. The situation escalated: from the summer of 1988, Halpulaar were purged from the army and civil service; between 1989 and 1991, upwards of seventy-five thousand (mostly Halpulaar) were forcibly expelled to Senegal.[8] The army and police in charge (frequently beating, robbing, and raping their prisoners, as well as destroying their identity papers) were overwhelmingly haratine. Alongside their bidan *patrons*, they were also the principle beneficiaries of abandoned Halpulaar property.[9]

To the extent that this human crisis was covered by Western media, it was as an extension of the "Apartheid-Slavery" discourse. Attempting to acquire international aid for the refugees, FLAM exploited the already recognized image of Mauritania that resonated so well with American audiences—the refugees were characterized as "Blacks fleeing Mauritanian Slavery." The results of this strategy, ironically, only rendered African Mauritanians less visible as the tragedy unfolded.

In the US, the crisis fed into a renewed campaign against Mauritanian slavery; those in Senegal's refugee camps were largely forgotten. Between 1995 and 2000, the efforts of African American journalist Samuel Cotton and formerly enslaved Mauritanian Moctar Teyeb brought Mauritanian slavery into both a political and a public limelight. In 1995, Cotton founded the Coalition Against Slavery in Mauritania and Sudan (CASMAS) on whose now-defunct website he posted his own articles (among others); in 1996, he testified before a specially convened Washington committee; and in 1998, he published *Silent Terror: A Journey into Contemporary African Slavery.*[10] Teyeb was interviewed several times, most dramatically by *The New Yorker.* A striking photograph of him in a flowing, blue traditional gown undoubtedly helped etch Mauritanian slavery into its readers' consciousness.[11]

Teyeb's experience of "growing up a slave" dated to the late 1960s, early 1970s; he left Mauritania in 1978 arriving in the United States in 1995.[12] Cotton wrote his articles without leaving New York, and based his book on interviews with African Mauritanian refugees.[13] Teyeb deliberately used the term "freed-slaves" (haratine) interchangeably with "slaves;" Cotton similarly made "slave" synonymous with "black." The final disappearance of African Mauritanians in this discourse went unnoticed.

It was at that time that I began writing affidavits on behalf of Mauritanian asylum claimants. I averaged one or two a year over the next decade; they were almost all victims in some way of 1989–91.[14] Their cases were plausible—supported by descriptions of the horrific atrocities of expulsion—and "fear of return" justified, given that many of the individuals responsible for that treatment were still in positions of authority. Yet, claimants repeatedly alluded to some form of "slavery" in their affidavits. In one case, I was able to compare the claimant's original hand-written statement in French with the lawyer's official court submission (in English). The latter had bowed heavily to public understanding of Mauritania as a "slave society"; Samuel Cotton was cited as "an expert." This case provided a rare glimpse into what I suspected was operative in others, namely, the ways in which media analyses fed into the asylum process and became part of the officially accepted "country narrative." For Mauritania, it was one of enslavement.[15]

"Slavery's Last Stronghold" and the Contemporary Face of Mauritania

In spite of Moctar Teyeb's memorable photo-image, Mauritanian slavery slipped from middle-class American minds in the early 2000s.[16] It was the renewed concern for what is termed "modern-day slavery" that again brought it to the fore.

In 2012, CNN launched the "Freedom Project." Mauritania was its lead story. The power of this publicity, presented in text, interview, and video, far exceeded its predecessors in audience accessibility and impact. Its in-country interviews included former slaves and current abolitionists (one bidan and one hratani, freed-slave). The twenty-two-minute video "Slavery's Last Stronghold" was reposted across the internet; viewer comments ran into the hundreds.[17]

The interviews with Mauritanians in Ohio were presented in two parts.[18] In Part One, the article "Mauritanian Refugees make New Home in Ohio," Bakary, El Hassen, Cheikh and Wane are introduced. It opens with the statement that among the refugees "a few like Bakary [a pseudonym], are from the slave class of Black Moors. If they had stayed in Mauritania, they could have been killed or brought back into slavery." This is followed by a link to "Slavery's Last Stronghold." Directly below it, was the link to Part Two, the video "When Freedom is 4000 Miles Away." This brings readers into the home of escaped slave "Marieme"—like Bakary, a pseudonym.[19] But unlike Bakary, about whom we learned very little, Marieme's horrific "flight to freedom" within Mauritania, then across the Atlantic hidden stowed away, is fully recounted (English subtitles to French interview; English transcript). Also unlike Bakary who left his slave wife behind, Marieme managed to bring her children to the United States. The video shows her settled in a quiet, older, Cincinnati neighborhood.

Sutter's presentation of that community is ambivalent. "In Cincinnati, some 4,000 miles from Mauritania, it might seem ethnic differences and long histories of tension and discrimination would melt away. But some of these barriers have followed Mauritanians all the way to Ohio." He then observes that, "despite the lack of commingling, it's clear these communities are trying to leave the past behind—and it seems hate-filled divisions are not present here." The basis for these mixed observations were El Hassen's and Cheikh's assurances that, "The community is not divided. . . . [We are] trying to be united here—trying to teach people to respect humanity. Who we are today is not who we were a long, long time ago. Here, if you're Mauritanian, you're Mauritanian. Nobody cares [what ethnic group you're from]. You're a brother. You're a friend." Yet, as Sutter points out, he and his friend were unaware that their escaped slave "brothers" lived just across the river. And their community association had no "African Mauritanian" members. The claim that "we are not who we were a long, long time ago" is silently countered by the linked "Slavery's Last Stronghold" video. The impression: these "white Moors" were living in denial.

The conclusion brings readers back to the reason for the story in the first place: slavery. "One thing that does unite Mauritanians in Ohio," Sutter notes, "is a desire to help their home country. An estimated one-fifth of Mauritanians live in slavery. The fight for human rights has become a rallying cry for the community here." Concluding words are then given to Wane and Bakary:

> "I think the biggest problem in Mauritania is the government pitting different groups against each other," said Wane, a member of a recently formed activist group called *Touche Pas* [*à ma nationalité* (Don't Touch my Nationality)], which has members in Mauritania and Ohio. It's the desire of most of these Mauritanian immigrants to go back to their home country when it's safe to do so, he said. "We want to be part of the change."[20] Bakary, the man who works as a butcher in the African market, left his wife behind in Mauritania. She is still a slave, he said, and was forced by her master to remarry. . . . The father said he tells his [American] children about his life as a slave. Even if they can't really understand, it's important for them to know what he went through, he said, and what his family members in Mauritania still endure. "I pray every day: 'God, open the door and change this country.'"

Ostensibly a story about Mauritanian refugees and their "community in exile," Sutter's article with embedded videos about slavery in Mauritania and Marieme's escape from it, was intended to put the slave experience at the center of exile and at the core of community identity. Although the bidan were quoted at length avowing "unity" and "brotherhood," their unawareness of former slaves living so close by marginalized them from the community Sutter saw, the one whose goal was to "change their country." Wane and Bakary but above all Marieme (as we see below) personified "being Mauritanian" because of their ongoing engagement with the issues raised in "Slavery's Last Stronghold." The fact that in Sutter's own words, only "a few" among the four thousand in Ohio were from the "black Moor slave class . . . [and] most [were merely] outcasts of one sort or another," does not deter him from concluding that the community self-defines in terms of overcoming historically rooted, racially based slavery—White Moor masters, Black Moor slaves. This is a community with which Americans, coincidentally, could easily identify.

"In the Eye of the Beholder:" Between Self and Other

In her study of Cambodians in America, Carol Mortland has argued that exile creates ethnicity as "self-perception" developed in the face of "the other." She writes: "Exile creates not only homelessness, thus refugeeness, it creates ethnicity, for it is exile that allows, rather forces, a group . . . to see 'others.'"[21] And Barbara Zeus, in her research on Burmese refugees in Thailand, extends Mortland's identity formation analysis to engage with the "perception of others:" "Identity is conveyed through self-perception but also perception by others, therefore identity can only be experienced in the collective."[22] How accurate a reflection of reality CNN's vision of the exiled Mauritanians was in 2012 remains debatable. Any disconnect between CNN's vision of the Ohio community and its own evolving set of "self-perceptions" is therefore important to identify and explore.

The Erasure of History

The first issue to address is the concept of "evolving" perceptions; we are looking at Mauritanians in exile—and images of Mauritanians in exile—over time. While we are not told when (or how) Bakary arrived in Cincinnati, it had been some time ago as he now had a new family and children of school age. Marieme's several efforts at escape purportedly took place in the late 1990s; she arrived in Baltimore in 1999. Presumably, she went through the asylum process at a time when a "slavery-based country narrative" was firmly entrenched (discussed above). Clearly, I have no way of knowing Marieme's personal circumstances, but seeing her recounting the (by now) familiar narrative brought to mind a question I had pondered in the context of earlier cases: how does telling a tale of enslavement—especially one involving rape—for purposes of the asylum claim, affect the women who felt compelled to do this? While clearly not in the same way(s) as for someone recounting a real memory of physical abuse, nevertheless "reliving" a constructed narrative—as one must do repeatedly throughout the asylum process—equally takes an emotional and psychological toll.

Regardless of how Marieme "lived" slavery (as experience or narrative), the CNN snapshot of her is fixed in undefined time.[23] Seen side-by-side with "Slavery's Last Stronghold," the impression is one of recent experience, of a life shaped by slavery "to this day." The camera rests frequently on a young toddler. But even as the film was shot, Marieme had been in the United States for a dozen years. The child was, like Bakary's children, born in the United States; this new generation is testimony to a life beyond the confines of Marieme's small house.[24] She and her family have, as Sutter put it in describing Bakary, "moved on." But in the CNN story, her past becomes her permanent present—her permanent prison.

Sutter's Mauritanian exiles are curiously without history. "No one CNN spoke to was sure who was the first Mauritanian to move to Ohio," Sutter observes. Perhaps not, but even the life histories of his informants might have provided some sense of a "timeline." An interview elsewhere with Wane, for example, tells us that he arrived in 1997.[25] Refugees' arrivals are usually tied to "why"—another question Sutter seems only to have asked of Bakary and Marieme. A Cambodian Mutual Assistance Association in Columbus, Ohio (two hours away) aided all refugees. Its website (undated and now defunct) reported (c. 2012–13) that Mauritanian asylum-seekers began arriving in central Ohio in the mid-1990s. Most were men who had been "imprisoned and tortured by the Mauritanian government." Some Mauritanians (like Teyeb) spent years elsewhere before coming to the United States; others, like many Halpulaar exiles (including Wane?), took years to escape Senegal. These factors are not only part of the Ohio Mauritanians' history but of the exile community they would/could create. The Columbus men were mostly applying to have their wives and children join them; this, the website noted, would soon result in "rapidly increased numbers and needs for services."[26] Unfortunately, CNN does not provide even this basic insight into the growing Cincinnati-Erlanger community.

A Role for African Mauritanians?

A 2005 study of Mauritanians in Cincinnati and Columbus by "one of their own," Amadou Birane Baro, noted that Mauritanians were experiencing "a variety of social adjustment problems . . . especially with other [American] Blacks and Muslims."[27] Baro's community did not include White Moors. The study is revealing less for these findings per se than for the underpinning assumption that race (secondarily, religion) should have drawn his community into a particular American culture. While African Americans take pride in their African slave heritage, his own African Mauritanian community consciously disassociates itself from slavery and slave culture.[28] Moreover, in Mauritania, African Mauritanians were defined by ethnicity and social status. As in bidan society, neither color nor religion played a role. That they protected cultural and social distinctiveness in Ohio, therefore, is not surprising.

Yet, only a few years later, these same "Afro-Mauritanians" (Sutter's Americanized terminology) are barely visible. Personified in Wane, they appear only to express solidarity with the former-slave community. Sutter announces that Wane is a member of a "recently formed activist group that has members in Mauritania and Ohio," *Touche Pas;* the implication is that this activism tied Ohio Mauritanians to anti-slavery movements at "home."

Touche Pas à ma nationalité, in America, Movement for Justice and Equality in Mauritania (MJEM), was founded in Mauritania by Halpulaar who opposed the controversial national census carried out from 2011. Those under forty-five were required to provide either a birth certificate or a "live parent" in order to register; those over forty-five, either the living parent or his/her death certificate. Only African Mauritanians and haratine were also being asked detailed questions about the Qur'an, Arabic, and other "affairs" involving bidan. As thousands of African Mauritanians returning from exile lacked identity papers or had lost parents in 1989–91 and as Francophone Halpulaar could rarely satisfy the linguistic, religious, and "bidan-culture" oriented questions—the ostensibly neutral census was targeted by *Touche Pas* as a tool to once again "de-nationalize" Halpulaar.[29]

There has been a strong effort in Mauritania to unite *Touche Pas* with haratine antislavery groups but its strongly defined ethnic/historical base remains a hurdle. That a chapter of *Touche Pas* formed in Cincinnati is telling of how the local community identified itself. In fact, Cincinnati's Halpulaar were actively engaged with the struggles of "their people." In 2009, a "Day of our Pulaar Martyrs" that memorialized the events of 1989–91 had as a subtitle "the battle must continue." Videos show a French-language banner announcing "solidarity with the widows and various activist groups (including FLAM)"; on a less visible wall is a detailed chart which appears to say "Genocide Proof."[30] Another short video documents a public demonstration in September 2011 against the Census Registration itself. Judging from this visual evidence, the people involved were almost exclusively Halpulaar.[31]

Wane asserts that "most of these immigrants want to go home and be part of the change as soon as it was safe"; he is clearly referring to his African Mauritanian exiled compatriots.[32] Sutter deflects this reality with his conclusion that the community was trying to "leave its past and hate-filled divisions behind." In fact, as he observes, the "black" and "white" Moors each had their own Community Associations. In spite of the fact that both claimed to welcome members from "all of Mauritania's groups," the Mauritanian Community Association of Ohio (MCA), based in Cincinnati, was entirely "Afro-Mauritanian," while the Mauritanian Community and Friendship Association (MCFA) across the river in Erlanger was "mostly white Moors."[33] Notable was a lack of observable presence of haratine in either.[34]

The "Feminization" of Mauritanian Slavery

A final issue arising from Sutter's assertion that these Mauritanians were defining themselves in relation to Mauritania's own antislavery activities takes us back to Bakary and Marieme, and what appears to be an effort to "feminize" slavery both as an institution and "a cause."[35] When Moctar Teyeb was literally the face of Mauritanian slavery, circa 2000, his was nevertheless a genderless portrayal; the problem was human, a psychological one in which "slavery was a state of mind." This memorable characterization was frequently articulated not only by Teyeb but by others, including Boubacar Messaoud, founder/director of Mauritanian-based SOS Esclaves and also a former slave. SOS Esclaves has long published internationally viewed annual reports of enslaved men, women, and children (in conjunction with Anti-Slavery International). This is why CNN's "Slavery's Last Stronghold" with its complementary texts and videos struck a contrast: the slave experience had become female, children being extensions of mothers.

While the video filmed in Mauritania is introduced by two male abolitionists and we meet one elderly male freed-slave who refuses to accept his freedom (remaining with his master, the bidan abolitionist), the focus is on a former slave woman, Moulkheir Mint Yarba and her daughter, Selekha. Moulkheir's rescue from her masters is dramatically recreated. Mother's and daughter's histories are each punctuated by abuse, rape, and infanticide at the hands of their respective masters.

"Hope" is the final message. The video ends by bringing viewers to a "secret school" in the capital of Nouakchott where Moulkheir, her daughter, and others "like them" were learning to sew and dress hair in traditional fashion. A separate link takes audiences to a video in which CNN iReporters (young people) from around the world send messages of solidarity to these women.[36]

And then there is Marieme. Her story and that of her daughter, a history which had unfolded more than a decade earlier, eerily echoes Moulkheir's and Selekha's, including the atrocious rape, pregnancy, and baby-murder. In the context of the "Freedom Project," Marieme epitomizes Mauritanian blacks who had fled (implied, "and continue to flee") to America, Moulkheir those who had accomplished that escape within Mauritania itself. Marieme's and Moulkheir's daughters represent a "glimpse of the future." These remain powerful stories, passionately told and imaged.

In October 2014, CNN's "Freedom Project" posted the story of Mbeirika Mint M'bareck, a fifteen-year old pregnant girl rescued from slavery only to be accused of having illegal sexual relations outside of marriage.[37] Authored by Sutter, the article begins with links to the 2012 stories, thereby framing the new story with events that date (in Marieme's case) to the mid-1990s. The charges against Mbeirika were dropped a few days later; a short CNN post acknowledges that.[38] But the original piece linking to "Slavery's Last Stronghold" and "When Freedom is 4000 Miles Away" remains.

The way Mbierika's story is presented reinforces the idea that Mauritanian slavery is still about white male masters raping and abusing black females whose bodies reproduce not only their masters' bloodlines but slavery itself. Or so it appears. In this CNN project, it is through women like Marieme and Moulkheir that this problem can be challenged. In their shadow, men like Bakary become victims, unable to rescue family members from perpetual slavery even as they save themselves. Men like the elderly "freed slave" introduced in Mauritania are incapable of any escape. Whether by design or coincidence, this increasingly gendered imaging of both slaves and masters plays into the media image of Mauritanians. If identity is to be understood, at least in part, "in the collective"—defined by how others perceive you[39]—what does it mean to be perceived of as part of a collective defined not only by slavery but by a particularly racialized and gendered form of slavery?

Identity and Ethnicity in Exile: the "Ohio Mauritanians"

The question of self-perception in contrast to being perceived, and the kind of dynamic this has set up within the Ohio exile community remains central and largely unresolved. However, there has been "life" in Greater Cincinnati since CNN's 2011–12 visit, suggestive of a new stage of development.

The MCA (Ohio)'s website was last updated in 2013; from its photographs and links, it is evident that it remained a predominately Halpulaar group.[40] The MCFA (the Erlanger association) never did have an internet presence; whether it still exists is uncertain. But in 2014, a new association called the Mauritanian Friendship Association of Greater Cincinnati (MFAGC—explicitly including Erlanger), announced itself on the internet.[41] Its website is professional, tapping into all the current social media. While photos from its first annual picnic (in Cincinnati) reflect an overwhelmingly African Mauritanian character, it is notable that one black woman was wearing the bidan veil (*melhafa*) and at least two or three black men in white embroidered bidan gowns are identifiable, suggesting some haratine families were present, still few in number but visible.[42] Significantly, the vice-president of the association, a bidan, is photographed standing with both Halpulaar and haratine.[43]

Also notable on the MFAGC website: in addition to *Eid* celebration wishes in Arabic and English, with translations in French and all four African Mauritanian languages, there is an announcement of an Islamic music concert by a famous bidan musician to celebrate the breaking of the Ramadan month-long fast. Notably, whereas the first annual picnic had been in northern Cincinnati, the concert was to take place in Erlanger. There were also announcements of autumn activities—a community dinner in Erlanger, a Thanksgiving sporting event in Cincinnati. And the second annual picnic was held in July 2015, this time in Erlanger. Although there are no photographs posted from these events—it would be interesting to see the audience for the concert, for example—it is clear that the intent of the new association is to bridge more than the river separating the two communities. In addition to the picnic photos exuding fun and family involvement, the languages used for the celebration of *Eid* acknowledge all Mauritanian communities and social classes.[44] That the base website is in English—the language of their new home—is also an important part of the website's public face. The MFAGC self-presents as a community collectivity that—deliberately or not—challenges the one portrayed by CNN.

We gain further insight into the community's struggle to define its own identity through an incident that also occurred in 2014. If we are interpreting the picnic-photos correctly, namely that some haratine and bidan are identifying with African Mauritanians, then a new local "voice" is emerging that no longer (automatically) privileges bidan.[45] The Mauritanian Embassy in Washington did not acknowledge the new association. To add insult to injury, when a visiting dignitary provided an excuse to invite a select group of "American Mauritanians" to Washington, a "white Moor" (said to be a friend of the ambassador) was invited from the Ohio group, rather than the President of the new nationally inclusive MFAGC. This slight generated a furious internet posting (in French) by Hady Anne, a Halpulaar and Director of Cultural Affairs at the time.

Anne wrote (and repeated in a local radio interview) that: "The *Mauritanian Association of Greater Cincinnati* is known to be a model of integration between our *different national communities*. . . . The only thing around which members' dynamism is articulated remains incontestably their attachment to . . . defining *their Mauritanité*."[46] The article's title accused the Mauritanian Ambassador of "playing at dividing us;" its content assured readers that the Association President was "firm" and would not back down.[47] In the Association's second election in March 2015, Anne was himself elected president. His first message posted to the website was a "thank you" to the MFAGC for its active involvement, "unequalled in the history of our community." He went on to acknowledge it as "the best response to internal quarrels and divisions. The campaign was dignified."[48]

This last point is significant. Hady Anne, an African Mauritanian, had run against two influential bidan—and won. The other candidates became vice president (seen at the first annual picnic) and secretary general. In his words, this was a "new departure" in which the association needed to remain united and committed to solving the community's problems. There was, however, no further mention of or elaboration on "*Mauritanité*," leaving open the question of where the Halpulaar followers of *Touche Pas* see themselves in this new environment.

It is difficult to ignore the timing between the CNN 2012 "Freedom Project" with its focus on Ohio Mauritanians that downplayed the presence of Halpulaar African Mauritanians, the lapsing of the most active of the area's community associations in 2013, the largely African Mauritanian MCA (Ohio), and the subsequent creation of the MFAGC in 2014. Appearances suggest that over the past few years, Mauritanians in Ohio/Kentucky not only reviewed their public identity but actively attempted to change it. Today, identity is often announced even before it is realized, using the very visual and influential internet to magnify media impact. In this case, the effort was reinforced by a direct confrontation with the "official" face of Mauritania, the Embassy in Washington.

To the extent that the CNN story may have been some kind of "impetus" to the community's sudden decision to reshape its image, that image and its multiple representations on the MFAGC website now constitute a competing vision of the community. "Ohio Mauritanians" are not living lives directed to the ending of slavery in Mauritania. Nor do they define themselves in those terms. Hady Anne has recently been a spokesperson for the group; this will change as the group enjoys the experience of democracy on a local level. But at present, it seems that the community is challenging the racialism it perceives emanating from Washington as much, as if not more than, addressing its internal schisms. Hady Anne has made this question of divisiveness—not slavery—the "core issue" the community can collectively agree upon. Black or white, African/hratani or bidan, each should be free to decide how they are seen in Washington and elsewhere. Perhaps one day, that will even include CNN.

Conclusion

It is obvious that a study focusing on the exiles themselves needs to be conducted in order to address fully the issues raised here. In particular, the important question about "gendering slavery" needs both better theoretical framing and integration of research from several disciplines. CNN imposed its own agenda upon the community, that of bringing both the reality and the cause of Mauritanian slavery into the heart of America. Inadvertently, in the process, it shed light on several groups whose "country of origin" ostensibly provided a form of shared national identity but which upon closer inspection, revealed internal fissures defying it.

At the outset of the section "In the Eye of the Beholder" (above), I drew attention to comparative studies of exiles in the US. Mortland points out that Cambodians brought with them the social hierarchy they knew in what were often isolated villages; she raises the crucial question, "when moved into an environment where local society does not recognize that definition of identity, where does one look to substitute for it?" She suggests that Cambodians looked back to their "shared losses and struggles" at the hands of the Khmer Rouge and, in so doing, created "myths of the before." "Being Cambodian in America," she explains, "includes participating in the recitations of these ['before'] myths, as tellers, listeners, and interpreters, to one another and to non-Khmer."[49]

Ohio's Mauritanians, many from villages or herding camps often distant (if not truly isolated) from larger urban centers and rooted in an extremely hierarchical, traditional society, faced a comparable challenge. The status subtly conferred by family association in Mauritania, for example, had no significance in America where external markers like color were given priority. Here, the challenge was exacerbated by the existence of an alternative understanding based on America's view of "black-white" Mauritanian slavery that rendered familial, ethnic, and social (apart from "slave") distinctions invisible. We might usefully view their early Associations (the MCA (Ohio), the MCFA) less as simple ethnic or cultural groups and more as attempts to recreate an environment in which shared understanding of social hierarchy allowed for recognition of identity. From this perspective, the newest MFAGC is all the more significant: the optics emphasize the geographical and social "bridging" of Cincinnati and Erlanger. But embedded in this effort is an attempt to establish a changed societal hierarchy as the new norm for "being Mauritanian" in the US.

The struggle, as both Mortland and Zeus note in different ways, involves engaging with "outside perceptions." Mortland emphasizes the role of the "before" myth in giving meaning to being Cambodian. This process is more problematic to create when "shared struggles and losses" cannot be easily identified, as is the case with the Mauritanians. Here, both those who consider themselves victims of injustice and those who were accused of being its perpetrators constitute the same exile community. Drawing on this notion of the "before" myth, however, one might argue that something comparable is created in the asylum process itself, the one that necessitates engaging with the accepted "country narrative." As we have seen, those narratives are the result of a dialogue between the public (stories in the media) and the private (consultancies with so-called experts, asylum lawyers). Moreover, networks are usually set up in any area to which refugees gravitate to help claimants learn the ropes and, most importantly, how to "tell the tale" expected by immigration lawyers and courts.[50] This process in many ways echoes that of "being Cambodian" in that it draws Mauritanian refugees into being "tellers, listeners and interpreters"—both among themselves and to others.[51] But for Mauritania, that process involves a country narrative of slavery that few Mauritanians have truly experienced and with which even fewer want to be publicly or permanently identified. Moreover, this is the narrative on which CNN and other media continue to put a Mauritanian face. At several levels then, the distinction between "self-and-other" perceptions becomes more blurred than some literature assumes.

Mortland's findings about where Cambodian exiles find acknowledgement of social hierarchy might well be followed by Zeus's question among the Burmese: "What are the places and spaces forced migrants derive their identities from once they have stepped outside their own nation-state and not (yet) been assimilated into a new one, *or are new forms of identity, disconnected from places, really emerging?*"[52] The Ohio Mauritanians seem to be struggling to determine just how connected to place they should or can be. El Hassen implies that "being from

Mauritania," the place, is both sufficient and self-explanatory: "If you're Mauritanian, you're Mauritanian." Hady Anne, on the other hand, speaks of "integrating *different national communities*" and of "*defining their Mauritanité*"—suggesting that the process was evolving to a large extent disconnected from place.[53]

What is emerging here is a dynamic very different from identity formed in simple contrast to (or engagement with) "home," but also more complicated than one of "self-versus-other" perception. Zeus explains what she observed with respect to this complexity, as "re-territorialising" identities:

> Contesting the territorialising concepts of identity also implies turning to an alternative understanding of space and place that separates identity from place "to show that though refugees have to move from their places of origin, they do not lose their identity and ability to exercise power" (Brun, 2001:15). This approach calls for . . . *a different view of space as constituted by a multiplicity of social relations.* Place in turn then is *"a particular articulation of those relations, a particular moment in those networks of social relations and understandings"* (Brun, 2001:15).[54]

"Mauritanité" may appear embedded in a geographical space, a "place" called Mauritania. But the difference between assuming that "that is enough" (perhaps easy to assume as a member of society's elite) and arguing publicly for the need to "define it" is significant. That Hady Anne's understanding was the one chosen by the community to lead it in 2014 suggests that at least a majority believe that this "ethnicity in exile" can be achieved by seeking a "particular articulation" of social relations in this "particular moment" that will evolve irrespective of place of origin.

Saidou Wane and the Cincinnati chapter of *Touche Pas* may still speak of "going back" to be part of the change in Mauritania (his last posted interview dates from February 2012, so it is not clear), but it seems that most of his neighbors of "all nationalities" have chosen instead to be part of their own change. Who they are as Mauritanians in Ohio is no longer who they would be "back home" (the more so considering the effect of current haratine politics on that "home"). They are choosing what to remember, what to celebrate, and how to do both ("Martyrs Day," *Eid*), and what to tell children or not (about slavery, about genocide, about "brotherhood"), all the while "defining *Mauritanité*." Ultimately, it will be their children—the new generation, born in the United States, very visible in the photos of the 2014 MFAGC picnic—who decide its future.

Notes

1. John D. Sutter and Edythe McNamee, "Slavery's Last Stronghold," *CNN*, 2012, accessed April 9, 2015, http://www.cnn.com/interactive/2012/03/world/mauritania.slaverys.last.stronghold/; John Sutter, "Mauritanian Refugees Make New Home in Ohio,"

CNN, March 17, 2012, accessed March 19, 2017, http://inamerica.blogs.cnn.com/2012/03/17/mauritanian-refugees-ohio/.

2. E. Ann McDougall, "'The Immigration People Know the Stories. There's One for Each Country': The Case of Mauritania," in *Asylum at a Crossroads: Activism, Expert Testimony and Refugee Rights*, ed. Iris Berger, Tricia Redeker Hepner, Benjamin L. Lawrance, Joanne T. Tague and Meredith Terretta, (Athens: Ohio University Press, 2015), 121–40.

3. Sutter and McNamee, "Slavery's Last Stronghold"; "Freedom Project: Ending Modern Day Slavery," *CNN*, 2012, accessed April 9, 2015, http://www.cnn.com/specials/world/freedom-project.

4. Sutter and McNamee, "Slavery's Last Stronghold;" John D. Sutter, "When Freedom Is 4,000 Miles Away," *CNN*, March 17, 2012, accessed March 19, 2017, http://www.cnn.com/2012/03/17/world/africa/escaped-mauritania-slave-ohio-cincinnati/index.html; Edythe McNamee, "When Freedom is 4,000 Miles Away," March, 2012, accessed April 9, 2015, http://edythemcnamee.com/projects/when-freedom-is-4000-miles-away/.

5. John D. Sutter, "Mauritania: "Where Escaping Slavery can be a Crime," *CNN*, October 20, 2014, accessed March 19, 2017, http://thecnnfreedomproject.blogs.cnn.com/2014/10/20/mauritania-where-escaping-slavery-can-be-a-crime/.

6. See note 2.

7. E. Ann McDougall, Meskerem Brhane, and Urs Peter Ruf, "Legacies of Slavery, Promises of Democracy: Mauritania in the 21st Century," in *Globalizing Africa*, ed. Malinda Smith (Trenton, NJ: Africa World Press, 2003), 67–88. With all the attention being given to the impact of the abolition act on bidan (whose religious clerics 'debated' its legitimacy in 1980), it is usually forgotten that *all* African Mauritanian ethnicities (as 'groups') were also slave-owning societies. Because their slaves were the same color (although never from the same community), they 'blended' into that community and were less visible to outsiders. These same groups (masters and to the extent that their slaves were freed, former slaves) became heavily Francophone during colonialism; upon independence, although the bidan were handed the reins of power, African Mauritanians were ablest to integrate into the emergent modern economy and engage with the international community. These advantages began to disappear as an increasingly 'Arabized' government turned to the Middle East and funding from Saudi Arabia from the late 1960s: French had been an official language at independence; in 1968 it was replaced by Arabic. A decade later, African Mauritanians (especially the Halpulaar) were chafing under restricted opportunities in government and education. The African Liberation Forces of Mauritania (French acronym of FLAM) began actively campaigning against government discrimination and racism in 1983 (more on this below). Olivier Leservoisier, "Contemporary Trajectories of Slavery in Haalpulaar Society (Mauritania)," in *Reconfiguring Slavery: West African Trajectories*, ed. Benedetta Rossi (Liverpool: Liverpool University Press, 2009), 140–51.

8. More than twenty thousand are guessed to have fled to Mali where their refugee status was never recognized.

9. McDougall, "Immigration People Know the Stories."

10. Cotton established the Coalition in spring 1995, followed soon after by an undated (and no longer accessible) CASMAS website, accessed May 5, 2015, http://antislavery.eserver.org/contemporary/coalition_against_slavery.html. It cited Cotton's 1996 film documentary and *was itself cited on a 1997 webpage*, therefore the site must have been created at some time during this period. He first testified in front of a special joint congressional committee in March 1996.

11. William Finnegan, "A Slave in New York," *The New Yorker*, January 24, 2000; Daniel Pipes, "Interview with Moctar Teyeb. 'Slavery is a State of Mind'," *The Middle East Quarterly* 6, no. 4 (December 1999). Accessed May 5, 2015, http://www.danielpipes.org/6334/moctar-teyeb-slavery-is-a-state-of-mind.

12. The intervening years were spent in Morocco and Libya. Pipes, "Interview."

13. Cotton's *City Sun* articles appeared before he did research in December 1995 and January 1996. In total, he spent three weeks in Senegal-Mauritania; of that time only a few days were with antislavery activists in Mauritania, the remainder with FLAM in Senegal's refugee camps.

14. As in Jeremy Dell's discussion in a paper presented at the 2015 Conable Conference, but not in this volume, one sees in this long-term situation the ambiguity of exile: the consequence of "blunt political force"—those "forced" out between 1989–91, and "exalted experience"—those who followed, choosing to leave against the same political forces who subsequently restricted political voice and action.

15. McDougall, "Immigration People Know the Stories".

16. As did Teyeb himself, seemingly having moved to Canada and out of the spotlight; Cotton (b. 1947) died an early death from cancer in 2003.

17. See videos in Sutter and McNamee, "Slavery's Last Stronghold." CNN also posted the full video to YouTube, accessed March 17, 2017, https://youtu.be/5yQlOPD8mNo. See also the linked articles "How to Help End Slavery in Mauritania," *CNN*, March 17, 2012, http://thecnnfreedomproject.blogs.cnn.com/2012/03/17/how-to-help-end-slavery-in-mauritania / and the iReport "Send your messages of hope to a school for escaped slaves in Mauritania," *CNN*, March 12, 2012, http://thecnnfreedomproject.blogs.cnn.com/2012/03/17/send-your-messages-of-hope-to-a-school-for-escaped-slaves-in-mauritania/. See also: "CNN Freedom Project: Messages of Hope for Mauritanian Slaves," *CNN*, June 1, 2012, accessed March 17. 2017, https://www.youtube.com/watch?v=DLGzVRgbU84. This particular juxtaposition of online presence regarding the issue of slavery (in part in the same country), one in 1995 and the other in 2012, is in and of itself a subject worth further attention (thanks to a Reviewer's comment).

18. Sutter, "When Freedom is 4,000 Miles Away;" McNamee, "When Freedom is 4000 Miles Away;" Sutter and McNamee, "Slavery's Last Stronghold."

19. Both claimed to fear retaliation from Mauritania.

20. An important theme in Kate Skinner's contribution in this volume. However, in this instance (see below) it is actually unlikely they will return even though, like the refugees in Skinner's case study, their exile is "self-imposed" and based on their perception of the illegality and/or oppression of the current regime--not their 'national government' in generic terms.

21. Carol A. Mortland, "Cambodian Refugees and Identity in the United States," in *Reconstructing Lives, Recapturing Meaning: Refugee Identity, Gender and Culture Change*, ed. Linda Camino and Ruth Krulfeld (OPA, Taylor & Francis e-Book, 1994), 6, University of Alberta Library, electronic access.

22. Barbara Zeus, *Identities in Exile: De- and Reterritorialising Ethnic Identity and the Case of Burmese Forced Migrants in Thailand*. Südostasien Working Papers No. 34 (Berlin, 2008): 8.

23. I am suggesting the possibility that Marieme, like many other Mauritanian women refugees, tailored her "narrative" to fit expectations which included "rape by her master." My point is that there may have been many reasons why she escaped from Mauritania, including

exactly what she testified to; however, even the perceived need to recount such horrific experiences is surely part of a larger perceptual problem that, in turn, has a permanent and very personal impact.

24. This last point is clear from the video narration; what is not addressed is exactly whose small child this is.

25. Dan La Boz, "The Movement for Justice and Equality in Mauritania [MJEM]: interview with Saidou Wane," New Politics, February 6, 2012, accessed May 17, 2015, http://newpol.org/content/movement-justice-and-equality-mauritania.

26. Cambodian Mutual Assistance Association (CMAA), accessed in 2012–2013, http://www.servintfree.net/cmaa/otherafr.html, no longer functional. Author has an archived copy of original webpage with this information.

27. Amadou Birane Baro, "Cultural Adjustment Issues of Mauritanian Immigrants in Columbus and Cincinnati Ohio," *Capstone Collection,* Paper #270 (2005). Accessed March 17, 2017, digitalcollections.sit.edu/capstones/270. The CMAA report on the Columbus community concluded that "They are noteably [*sic*] averse to being on public benefits."

28. His paper was submitted to an American program: he was undoubtedly required to present his analysis in the framework of American-based frameworks. Only the paper's abstract is accessible.

29. MJEM website, http://mjem.org; see also note 24.

30. "Journée des martyrs noirs mauritaniens: que le combat continue—Cinci 2," December 6, 2009, accessed May 17, 2015, Part 1: https://www.youtube.com/watch?v=CLqyenNAAys; Part 2: https://www.youtube.com/watch?v=gXtgIIQnPac.

31. Only two, maybe three, men who seem to be haratine, appear. The "solidarity" exercised by those in exile might usefully be compared with this theme as explored in Marina Berthet's chapter in this volume in which, however, the personal and political empathy is generated by those who "stayed" for those forced to "leave." The difference lies in where the source/site of oppression lay.

32. Sutter and McNamee, "Slavery's Last Stronghold."

33. Sutter and McNamee, "Slavery's Last Stronghold."

34. As per above, two, perhaps three, men appear to be haratine.

35. Sutter, "How to Help End Slavery;" and iReport, "Send Your Messages of Hope."

36. iReport, "Send Your Messages of Hope."

37. Sexual relations outside of marriage are punishable by stoning in the oldest of interpretations of Islamic law. This has not, however, been enforced in Mauritania.

38. And with reason. My point here is not to underestimate the impact of what happened to Mbeirika.

39. Zeus, *Identities in Exile.*

40. Mauritanian Community Association (of Ohio), website (last updated 2013): http://www.mca-ohio.org/.

41. Mauritanian Friendship Association of Greater Cincinnati, website, created 2014, Accessed March 19, 2017, https://www.facebook.com/MauritaniaCincinnati.

42. It should be noted that those few (and I underscore "few") who chose to wear "western" clothing could well have been either bidan or haratine.

43. Yacoub Ehlou ould Sheikh Sidiya is a member of a highly respected religious clan from southern Mauritania.

44. The use of hassaniyya, Pulaar and Soninke on the site spoke (literally) to bidan and haratine, Halpulaar and Soninke (respectively) ethnic communities. The use of French and

English signaled, generally speaking, "those who were educated:" in Mauritania, the elite bidan and prosperous haratine were educated in French, most Halpulaar and Soninke were also Francophone (from colonial days). Those who speak English in Ohio have had the resources for education; all children, no matter what ethnicity or (Mauritanian) class who attend school, also speak English. The language choices of the website are revealing of more than one might think.

45. These may also be the same people glimpsed in the 2009 and 2011 videos. Is this a growing involvement of haratine? The visual "evidence" is suggestive but far from conclusive.

46. Hady Anne, "Entretien avec Hady Anne à propos le MFAGC," March 18, 2014 [audio file], my translation and emphasis, accessed May 16, 2015, http://fr.maurigc.org/nouvelles/interview-avec-le-president-hady-anne-a-propos-de-la-mfagc.

47. "L'ambassadeur de la Mauritanie aux USA joue à nous diviser," December 12, 2014, accessed May 16, 2015, posted various places, among them: http://fr.alakhbar.info/9757-0-Lambassadeur-de-la-Mauritanie-aux-USA-joue-a-nous-diviser.html.

48. MFAGC website, 2014.

49. Mortland, "Cambodian Refugees," 14.

50. McDougall, "The Immigration People Know the Stories."

51. Mortland, "Cambodian Refugees," 14.

52. Zeus, *Identities in Exile*, 8, my emphasis.

53. An interesting comparison can be drawn with Skinner's chapter in this volume in which the issues of "defining rootedness" and the significance of "[geographical] territory" both played important roles for self-exiled Ghanaian refugees in Togoland. In this case study, it was the contemporary (colonial) media that deliberately shaped this image of exile.

54. Zeus, *Identities in Exile*, 15. My emphasis; references in original text.

16 A Nation Abroad

Desire and Authenticity in Togolese Political Dissidence

Benjamin N. Lawrance

A UNIQUE ARCHIVE OF exile resides in refugee narratives from Africans today dwelling outside their natal homes. Togolese political dissidents who seek asylum in the Global North are usually required to provide detailed accounts of their political persecution, resulting in an oral historical account that would likely be otherwise inaccessible using traditional interview methodologies in Togo. Asylum narratives offer an unparalleled psychosocial entry point to engage the postcolonial and contemporary African historical experience, and in particular to explore political dissidence, persecution, and torture.

In exile, Togolese political dissidents speak frankly to lawyers and judges about their ordeals, cognizant that their quest for refugee protection often depends on full disclosure.[1] But their narratives are both richly instructive and deeply problematic for reconstructing sociopolitical life under the neopatrimonial prebendal dictatorship of Étienne Gnassingbé Eyadéma (1935–2005). Under the watchful gaze of attorneys, exiles recast their experiences for decision-makers highlighting political developments since their departure.[2] They construct tropes and generalizations that disfigure the personal and specific.[3] They dissemble under hostile and suspicious scrutiny by decision-makers.[4] Asylum narratives specifically describing personal experiences of torture reify the imprimatur of the nation-state as the purveyor of persecutory harm. Informed by lawyers, activists, and engaged scholars, Togolese political exile narratives instantiate exiles as national subjects and the state as torturer.

African historians turn to asylum claims, experiences narrated outside Africa, as a creative way to "think more critically and imaginatively" about "Africa's post-colonial archive."[5] Many of the asylum-seeker testimonies I examine contain unique and otherwise inaccessible first-hand accounts of historical persecution and contemporary violence. In this light, I see asylum seeking as a process that may be investigated as an "emergent archival form," a form that provides context for understanding how the strategies employed shape the narratives and their limitations as evidence.[6] Many refugee stories follow meticulous patterns, however, and as petitions asylum narratives are often highly formulaic.[7] Echoing Luise White's analysis of rumor to reconstruct complex historical "truths," attentiveness to asylum-seeking strategies illustrates how asylum texts are structured by the contexts of production giving rise to powerful representations of postcolonial African nationhood and national sovereignty.[8]

This chapter approaches asylum narratives of Togolese exiles residing in the United States and the United Kingdom as comprising an oral historical archive of political persecution. I argue that torture narratives function as a problematic medium for the instantiation of national identity in general, and a narrow brand of Togolese nationality in particular. Just as the term "exile" conjures new iterations of identity and novel senses of belonging, the asylum interview and tribunal process has been revealed to be a site of complex expressions of national power in absentia.[9] As historians explore creative pathways to document the postcolonial African experience, perhaps the asylum archive can provide the highly personalized sociopolitical detail which reveals the concealed history of individual-state interactions. Although forced to relocate abroad, torture survivors appear to embrace a newfound, unfettered freedom to disclose and document a litany of abuses. To what extent individual acts of persecution recast as state acts are emblematic of a national experience, or, alternatively, purposeful expressions of exilic desire, is the central tension in this chapter.

A Present Fraught with History

As Charlie Piot explains, Togo's "dictatorship complex" began to unravel in the 1990s. Within a few years the state was "a whisper of its former self," and Togo's authoritarian, Mobutuesque *authenticité* politics gave way to horizontal transnational power alliances, to rights-based discourses, and to Pentecostal Christianity.[10] Piot sees the political and economic changes in Togo as both a local reflection of "global neoliberal reformation"—scaling back government, liberalizing markets, and eliminating barriers to entrepreneurialism—and a larger rejection of neocolonial tyranny. Drawing on Michel Hardt and Antonio Negri, and others, Piot discerns "more flexible" forms of sovereignty displacing modernist hierarchical nation-state power dynamics in Togo, such as NGOs, churches, and occult imaginaries.[11]

Togo's political dynamics have certainly changed dramatically in recent years, but how to characterize the Eyadéma decades, at least as they were experienced by the general public, is less clear. Eyadéma's Togo certainly "worked" in a fashion, and his successors continue to shape its destiny within ordered disorder.[12] Eyadéma governed in a manner that many political scientists describe as neopatrimonial prebendal nepotism.[13] In the simplest sense, these terms convey three central "embedded" governing "autocratic" principles that deploy the concepts of family, loyalty, and hierarchy in the governance of the country.[14] Generally speaking, the country was governed as if it was a large family, the center of which was Eyadéma, his allies, and friends. Loyalty to this virtual family unit was a central guiding principle that many anthropologists might describe as an awkward iteration of fictional kinship.[15] Rewards, such as wealth, position, and access to business opportunities, were disbursed from the center and based on loyalty to the family and respect for the hierarchy, within the governing party, the Rassemblement du Peuple Togolais.[16] Adherence was established in complex ways, notably by ethnicity, birth location or "right," and by performing authoritarianism—targeting, harassing, detaining, and in some instances, torturing. Thus, anyone within Togo could assert loyalty and membership, yet certain communities had unequal access to membership of a national familial identity.[17]

During the worst decades of the political repression, external indices received sporadic media coverage and scholarly attention. Most political demonstrations were spontaneous, brief affairs as the government rarely authorized protests. They began peacefully but were routinely violently disrupted; the dimensions of the incidents, particularly attacks by paramilitary and mass detentions, were rarely reflected in the press at home or abroad. Low-level opposition activists were frequent targets of brutality because they were responsible for spreading a party's message, canvassing support, and recruiting members. On various occasions, protests were stopped by the deployment of the *gendarmerie* and the military and, on several occasions, tanks and armored personnel carriers quelled urban protests in Lomé and other cities. On several occasions, most famously in the opposition stronghold Bè, in 1993, 1998, 2003, and 2005, and in Atakpamé and Aného in 2005, the gendarmerie and military fired at unarmed crowds killing hundreds.[18] The total number of politically motivated deaths and disappearances during the almost four decades of Eyadéma may be in the tens of thousands.

Internal dynamics of repression remain much more inaccessible, however. Conditions in prisons and militarized detention camps in Togo were extremely inhumane and unsanitary.[19] Prison cells held people in cramped conditions, often thirty to fifty people in a small cell originally designed for three to four people, with no provision for food, medical care, or ablutions. Young men and boys were subject to intimidation, violence, and sexual assault, and women and children of both sexes were sometimes housed with men.[20] Torture and other forms of cruel and inhumane ill-treatment of prisoners and those awaiting trial were widespread in Togo in violation of international law and treaties to which Togo is party. The UN Special Rapporteur responsible for investigating prison conditions and extrajudicial torture, Manfred Nowak, visited Togo in 2008 after Faure Gnassingbé had assumed the reins of power, and his report observed that cases of ill-treatment by gendarmerie and police officers were not isolated. He found continued evidence of ill-treatment. Other accounts—from the Togolese Commission Nationale des Droits de l'Hommes, Human Rights Watch, Amnesty International, and a 2014 UN addendum to the 2008 report—suggest torture continues, but perhaps to lesser extent.[21]

During the peak of Eyadéma's rule, violence and terror in Togo seemed both randomized and organized; it rarely fit neat descriptive categorization. People were generally on the lookout for the arrival of soldiers or police, heralding a possible crackdown in a particular quarter or village. The appearance of police or military personnel at private home was a widely used form of intimidation. Intimidation and violence were particularly directed at political opponents but not limited to those directly involved in the political and economic life of the country. Togolese not politically active also suffered at the hands of police and paramilitaries, as evidenced by the disappearance of approximately three hundred taxi drivers for no obvious political objectives. Chauffeurs were murdered and dumped at sea during the widespread violence that erupted during the 1998 presidential election, their bodies often found entangled in Beninese fishermen's nets.[22]

Any history of postcolonial Togo must account for not only the tenacity of Eyadéma, the chimera of democratization and rights-based rhetoric, and the massive influx of Chinese extractive capital, but also the startling levels of political repression and targeted violence at particular moments in time. Asylum seekers in the US and UK routinely provide nauseatingly lurid and detailed accounts of persecution and violent torture. Documents—such as photographs, an extrajudicial "convocation" (summons), or an "avis de recherche" ("demand for questioning") delivered to homes or places of employment—seemingly substantiate their experiences. Their bodies, bearing the scars of torture, "display the evidence of truth."[23] For expert witnesses or immigration judges, it may be enough to assert that one particular individual's description of persecution is a plausible account and consistent with what is known about the history of political violence in Togo. But scholars have yet to find agreement on a theoretical framework for incorporating and analyzing the violent particular.

Asylum Petitions and the Violent Particular

Asylum seekers disgorge voluminous and shocking detail about torture at the hands of Togolese state agents. But remaking the violent particularities of torture narratives into an archive for a comprehensive analysis of the modalities of Togolese state power or the exile experience writ large necessitates attention to the form of the asylum petition. Ann Laura Stoler may be but the latest in a series of scholars who have directed our gaze at the epistle-like nature of many archival repositories, but her insight into "genres of documentation," "arts of persuasion," and "affective strains" is particularly instructive here.[24] Three particular dimensions of asylum seeking highlight how it functions as an archive.

First, asylum seekers offer a valuable documentation genre for evaluating lived social experiences. Testimonies are multilayered: each time an asylum seeker narrates an experience, or revisits an earlier statement or interview, a contemporary archive of persecution expands. Asylum narratives—and the snowballing of documentation as claims move toward adjudication—provide a window on the changing contexts of persecutory forms. Thus, while asylum narratives are first-person accounts, collectively they are a contemporary oral historical archive of violence.[25]

Second, asylum offers a critical perspective to revisit methodological debates about persecutory histories, such as establishing the basis of complaint.[26] As asylum claims are increasingly supported by expertise, they constitute a category of persuasive art. Reports by historians, and other experts, translate narratives of "personal trauma" into persuasive acts "of political aggression," anchored to Refugee Convention articles.[27] The discipline of history, modes of historical writing, and the methodologies of historicization have powerful explanatory facility. Often a foil to adjudicators, experts evaluate the legal basis for persecution claims and the history of specific persecutory forms.[28] By comparing claims with publicly available evidence about a real or a purported legal remedy, such as "Country of Origin Information," experts provide a hypothetical basis for advancing a claim. Refugee narratives must thus be interpreted within the pool of material assembled to support a claim.

Third, as a tightly regulated formula for affecting empathy, asylum demands engagement with a register of strategies. Asylum seekers, and their advocates, fashion narratives into persuasive concepts and established frameworks. The narrowness of the original postwar language of refugee protection tied tightly to the legacies of Nazi aggression and the political context Soviet expansion gives rise to creative strategies. Disassembling strategies—as they engage, resist, and seek to subvert criticisms of claims—reveal not only the lived experience of the personal and intimate, but also how persecution *and* refugee convention definitions restrain and conceal the lived experience of the intimate. The treatment accorded political persecution claims in asylum courts reveals a particular bias for documented patterns of serious harm and demonstrable state involvement.[29] Asylum narratives constitute personal lived truths, buttressed by fears, hearsay, and rumors. Strategy may be the key to unlocking a vast archive of personal persecution and collective trauma.

Registers and strategies aside, asylum petitions are highly problematic and some question their reliability as evidence of real country conditions. Meredith Terretta observes that certain countries have a reputation for being "particularly adept at filing fake asylum claims." She cites diplomatic cables exposed by the multinational media organization WikiLeaks that suggest US government officials routinely view Cameroonian asylum narratives as "frivolous or fraudulent" and to be treated with "skepticism." Terretta's solution is to embrace the possibility of fraudulence as a sign that "asylum protocols have failed to keep pace with changing political and economic realities."[30] In conversations with scholars, diplomats, lawyers, and migrants—many off the record and not for attribution—it has been suggested that testimonies by many already outside Togo are manufactured by individuals whose visas are approaching expiration, but who desire to remain in their new setting for various reasons. Certain cities and towns have a reputation for being part of a cottage industry; for the right fee, stories can be manufactured in a few hours, newspaper accounts "published" back home locating the claimant at a site of protest, and assistance provided with filing, including identifying sympathetic lawyers or law students, such as the Cameroonian American lawyer Patrick Tzeuton, who worked in Maryland between 2002 and 2005.[31] Four years before his federal conviction for conspiracy, fraud, and obstruction, Tzeuton described "immigration consultancy" as cheaper than a lawyer. "It is no different than going to a pharmacist or a nurse instead of a doctor," he said. A healthy dose of skepticism is thus advisable with asylum narratives generally.

Using *torture* narratives—embedded within asylum petitions supplied to me as an expert—as evidence is itself highly problematic, and for a number of additional reasons. Scholars have documented how some survivors of trauma "remake" the self as they narrate their torture; trauma reveals the self to be relational, and memory to be multiform and in flux.[32] The discursive strategies of torture survivors proscribe the articulation of important details. As I rarely interview asylum seekers directly, these may be irrecoverable.[33] Coupled to these concerns about the impact of being the expert in the room are additional considerations. Some asylum decision makers appear not to want to listen to the details of torture survivors, and this attitude "colludes" with a tendency on the part of some refugees to avoid discussing painful memories; details are omitted, narratives are flattened.[34] And as many exiled torture survivors live in extremely precarious situations, continuous traumatic stress and general mental health factors into the capacity to disclose depth and detail.[35]

Cognizant of how these factors shape and distort the usefulness of torture narratives, I discern the possible existence of two distinct registers within Togolese torture narratives, and offer an explanation of how they come into being. The first operates on the micro level, narrating personal experiences of brutality. Individuals are effectively recounting the "what," and details often correlate to the specific guidance of an attorney. Some testimonies follow a quotidian narration from first detention to last release, whereas others are episodic, meandering and disjointed. Regardless of whether they are sequential and coherent, or episodic and incoherent, narratives may move seamlessly from one form of torture to the next, skipping over details here and there, or dwelling on particularly traumatic episodes.

In contrast, the second register operates on the macro level, as survivors try to make sense of why their particular experience occurred or happened to them. Most Togolese survivors have been informed of the expectations of refugee adjudication rules insofar as the personal experience must be derived from a specific articulation of a "nexus," or as "on account of" their condition as, variously, an opposition supporter or ethnically marked dissident.[36] This second register appears to be more influenced by the awareness of the audience, and in particular, the decision makers. This second register may emerge from a cognizance of the absence of the perpetrator(s). Not only are survivors liberated and free to explain what happened, but they can name particular individuals. They appear unfettered by fears, including the possibility of a failed claim and deportation or forcible return. The tenor of this register echoes acts of defiance or resistance against the Togolese state as torturer by the individuals themselves as Togolese national subjects.

Qualitative data, in the form of personal narratives or structured interviews, addressed to decision makers or tribunals, is available from 147 Togolese political dissidents who fled Togo and relocated to the United States, United Kingdom, Canada, and the Netherlands, a small fraction of the massive millennial spike in Togolese flight documented by Adzele Jones.[37] From these transcripts, I have selected short passages describing specific incidents or events. I was first asked to provide an expert report on a Togolese political dissident in the US in 2002. Since then I have provided reports for over 160 Togolese citizens. The narratives used here are done so with the permission of the applicant, furnished to the author via the legal representative only after the successful conclusion of the application and the granting of permanent residency and refugee protection. Data is entirely pseudonymous, and no identifying details are contained in the excerpts selected. The use of transcript excerpts poses no danger to individuals in any way, nor does it risk retraumatizing asylum seekers.

A brief note on the broader data set demonstrates the general applicability and utility of the qualitative data. Among the 147 transcripts from US and UK cases, 65 percent are male applicants. 80 percent identify ethnically as being members of southern-dwelling groups, most notably the Ewe and related language groups, including Ouatchi/Watchi, Mina, Guin, and Ani. The vast majority were filed within one year of exiting Togo. Applicants range in age from the early twenties to the late fifties, but the vast majority are in their late twenties and early thirties. The majority are married, and with one or multiple children. The exile narratives of Togolese torture survivors operate on at least two significant registers which reflect the attempts by survivors to comprehend their ordeal.

The Personal Register of Torture

The first register discernible in Togolese exile testimony is that of the personal experience and personal self-narration. Asylum seekers narrate what happened to them personally. They foreground individual acts perpetrated against them; they often move swiftly past the names or identities of the torturers. They may mention other detainees, such as those with whom they shared a cell, but it is often only in passing, almost as an echo of their own experience, a faint verification of their own torture. A recurring theme in torture narratives is the sense that individuals are being targeted personally. Torture narratives often center on the individual and routinely occlude any sense of common experience or group persecution. Torture is recounted as personal and isolating, and, often disorienting. As Patrice, a man in his fifties and head of a distinguished political lineage, noted, "I heard people from nearby cells screaming and crying and I was sure they were being tortured," but he himself was blindfolded and could not see them. Later, even without his blindfold, "it was so dark I could not see anything."

Torture in Togo takes a variety of mundane forms; some of the narratives could conceivably come from almost any country. Ehli, an Ewe man in his forties, who delivered his statement in 2005, explained that after a second day detained as part of a group, without charge, in the gendarmerie in Lomé, "two or three military men came into our cell, took all of us out, laid us down face-up, and beat us with military belts and kicked us with their boots." Amouzou, a member of an opposition party in his early twenties, was whipped "fifty times" during his first interrogation. Subsequently, he was "beaten on a table with wooden sticks that resembled baseball bats." Sowaye, a mother of two from Lomé, was arrested with seven other young market women in 2001. She explained that in detention she and the other detainees were made to "get down on our knees and walk on the sharp gravel. After my knees began to hurt very badly, I could not take the pain. I refused to continue. Two soldiers hit me repeatedly with a big belt and stomped my chest with their boots."

Torture and assault was inflicted in private and public, in formal facilities, secret facilities, and even in people's home. Yawa, a Mina hairdresser, in her forties when she was first attacked in Lomé in 2001, described a raid on her home after she had photographed a roadside corpse a day earlier, a man whom she believed was murdered by soldiers. "The chief soldier hit me in the back and I fell face down onto the floor. He stomped violently on me with his foot and told me that I should have minded my own business. My back and spine hurt terribly." Awali, a Kotokoli man in his twenties when detained, described a similar experience. "The soldiers were armed with batons and the blows came from all directions. . . . I received beatings every morning. I was hit with batons on my legs and buttocks. Soldiers know that these kinds of blows weaken the body and the spirit."

Some torture survivors described the use of particular torture devices. Sankey, a reluctant student activist from Lomé in the 1990s, who attained refugee protection in the US in the mid-2000s explained, "I was being severely beaten on the ground as if I were an animal. One of the instruments they used was a *gourdin* (a baton-like club). This had screws attached to the end of it. They kept beating me and beating me until they thought I was dead." Komla, an Ewe man in his fifties, who now resides safely in New York, described, "when I refused to confess, the soldiers blindfolded me and used live wires to administer painful electric shocks to my body. They would stop the electric shocks periodically and ask me to confess. I refused to answer and eventually they returned me to the cell."

Hot chilies became a routine vehicle for subjecting detainees to pain in the 1990s and early 2000s. Torture survivors described incidents involving chili rubbed in the eyes, forced ingestion of chili soup, or whole raw peppers. Amouzou recounted how "the military cut my skin with a knife. My left leg and ankle were cut with a knife and the military then placed hot chili pepper in the wound. The pain was excruciating. . . . The military then cut my genitals and private parts and threatened to put hot chili peppers in the wounds." And for Komla electrification was only the beginning of his ordeal. Toward the end of his hearing he revealed how "they took a tree branch laced with hot pepper paste and sodomized me with it. This was the most unbearable form of torture."

Sexual assault, like Komla's, overlaps with torture in complex ways, and it is often difficult to discern where one ends and other begins. Afua, a market woman arrested in 2003 at a demonstration, was thrown into the back of a truck. She was slapped and beaten, and then a soldier "tore off" her skirt. A group of soldiers groped her and then sexually assaulted her with their hands. After she screamed, the truck drove on and they beat her with a stick on her back, front, and head. They spoke a language she did not know, and they covered her mouth as they raped her with the stick. Sowaye "begged" one of her torturers to spare her life, and as a result her torture descended into a horrific form of sexual enslavement. In response "he said that he would consider letting" her "live" if she became "his girlfriend." She fought hard against the commandant, whom she named in her petition, but although she struggled, "he started touching" her "all over." When she started putting her clothes back on, he overpowered her. He held her hands down as he took off his clothes, and "brutally raped" her. Once she had escaped from the facility, with the help of a sympathetic soldier, the commandant continued to pursue her in her home. She fled to the US after he visited her house several times, leaving threatening messages.

Endurance torture techniques are routine. Ehli was put "in a stress position" against a wall for twenty or thirty minutes, day after day, until he could not "stand it any longer" and "would fall down." Patrice explained in 2004 that he "was made to walk on" his "knees and stare directly into the sun all day." Komla noted that "the soldiers forced me and the other party members to stand outside and stare into the blazing sun for about thirty minutes. They would beat us if we looked down. The soldiers then forced us to kneel on *cailloux* (large stone gravel) while holding up extremely heavy bricks. This continued for about ten minutes. The weight of the bricks, combined with the uneven surface, made it quite painful to continue holding the bricks. When we would drop the bricks, they would beat us." Gaba, a married father in his thirties, was detained several times during the early 2000s. He recounted how he was forced to stand on a chair and grab onto a steel pipe running across the ceiling, knowing full well that sharp palm tree nut shards lay on the ground beneath him. The guards would then remove the chair from under him and hit the bottoms of his feet until the pain was so great that he was forced to let go and fall onto the sharp nut casings beneath him.

Togo is also the site of peculiar and unusual forms of punishment, incidents that mark the experience as Togolese, and hence slippage into the second, national, register. The most commonly cited of these, recounted by several dozen individuals over more than a decade of interactions with asylum seekers, is routinely referred to as "coffee" or "café noir." Ehli explained,

> At approximately 4 o'clock in the morning, a guard approached me and asked me if I wanted coffee. Without understanding the real meaning of what he was saying to me, I told him yes. He laughed and took me to an office where the commandant was, along with three police officers. As soon as we entered the room, he ordered two other guards standing behind him to "serve me a well-sugared morning coffee." They laid me face-down on the bare floor, and the guard who had brought me from the cage, caned me on my behind. They caned me for what seemed like ten minutes. They didn't ask me anything, just starting caning me, I believe as some sort of intimidation. It hurt so badly that I started vomiting blood. I was also bleeding from my mouth because one of the guards kicked me in the face while I was being caned. The commandant was watching the whole thing.

More than a dozen survivors have described receiving various "doses" or "servings" of "coffee."

Any individual narrative of torture can stand alone, exceptional for its horror or brutality. But what is important here is the personal nature of the register, and the language employed by exiles desperate to document what happened while knowing full well they may never understand why. Returning to Patrice's experience brings this enduring trauma into stark relief. He recounted how "one of the guards ordered the other to cut off my hand. The guards commonly referred to cutting off a prisoner's arm as either a 'short sleeve' or 'long sleeve.' The guard ordered a 'long sleeve' for me meaning that my arm should be cut off at the wrist. They put a knife to my wrist cutting me which I still have the scar of to this day. Suddenly, for a reason I do not know, the guard stopped and left my cell." To this day, Patrice, now safely residing in the US, cannot understand how he left the prison alive and intact. After reading the statements and interviews of many asylum seekers, a vivid personal register is palpable.

The National Register as Torturer

The second register I wish to examine here instantiates exiles as national subjects and the state as torturer. This register frames the nation as a highly political place, a space where being apolitical is not an option. The actions of torturers are recast as presidential acts. The president and his family are frequently invoked; individuals claim that Eyadéma targeted them specifically. The register engages the persistent implicit question of "why me?" seemingly embedded in the personal register. And like the first, this register is also informed by lawyers, activists, and engaged scholars, who counsel Togolese political exiles that their narratives must articulate a broader basis for their torture, one that moves beyond the personal. Some survivors adopted concrete language; they described their decision to join an opposition party, attend meetings, or distribute flyers, and educed their predicament as linked specifically to a belief in the democratic process, electoral reform, or opposition to the ruling family. The various iterations of this second register collectively instantiate the Togolese state as torturer, and in so doing, reify the Togolese nationality of the exiles with powerful and provocative language.

Awali, from a village in the center of Togo, granted asylum in the early 2000s in the US, positioned his experience of incarceration and torture as flowing personally from "lists" supposedly maintained by Eyadéma. Awali stated,

> At the beginning of my political life, I helped my father spread the message of the opposition to the people by distributing newspapers. I became more active in the organization as I grew older and entered high school. I was about fifteen when a Kotokoli soldier came and told my father the news that I was on Eyadéma's black list. Being on the black list meant that I had been identified as an enemy of Eyadéma's regime because of my political views and involvement with the opposition movement. This kind of information was pretty easy to get because Kotokoli in the military would warn other Kotokoli when their names were mentioned around the military camps.

In a single narrative, the threat facing him, before he was detained and tortured, emerged from an imagined list Eyadéma himself compiled. No one had seen the "list" but its existence emerges from rumor, not the president personally. Sowaye described how her rapist threatened to put her name on "the list" if she did not respond favorably to his sexual overtures. Lists are invoked frequently, and their origin and authorship is routinely presidential.

Torture survivors frequently described being targeted by Eyadéma, via his apparatchiks. Sankey recast the violence of soldiers as the violence of the leader himself: "Eyadéma's soldiers beat us. Eyadéma's soldiers dumped bodies of opposition members in a lagoon not far from where I lived." All orders, all violent acts, flow from the president. Afua's ambiguous narrative is more circumspect. She recounted that after her husband had mysteriously disappeared, soldiers in khaki uniforms with "blue patches on the shoulders" showed up at her house. She describes the conversation she overheard, thus:

> The uniformed officer spoke into the walkie-talkie saying, "General, he's not here. Should we search the house?" After that, they started to search the house. They slammed doors, threw mattresses on the ground and searched every closet, even places too small for my husband to hide. Then, they got back on the walkie-talkie and said, "General, he's not here." They left without taking anything. When they left, I followed them out the door and saw their car. The car had a license plate with green letters reading RT and FAT, which stand for République Togolaise and Forces Armeé Togolaise. Normally the license plates in Togo have black lettering, but the lettering on all of the government plates is green instead. The body of the car said Gendarmerie, which means 'Military Police.'"

While the reference to "General" may appear ambiguous to an outsider, anyone with knowledge of Togo would reasonably surmise this must refer to a senior party loyalist, a close confidant of Eyadéma.

Another recurring theme in this second register is the sublimation of personal agency to national identity and the will of the president. Patrice described how his torturers employed personal and familial phrases, and repudiated his dissident activities as attacks on their father and patron, and not legitimate acts of political opposition. "After a while, a bright light was turned on and a man in charge of asking questions came into my cell with other soldiers. I was terrified of what might happen to me. They kept yelling at me to leave 'him' alone, referring to President Eyadéma." In this narrative, Eyadéma is as a father, protector, or family friend.

Ritual and performance further instantiate the nation as persecutor. Sowaye, while still detained with other women, was taken to a field by soldiers who "demanded that we sing 'patriotic' songs about President Eyadéma. The soldiers would hit anyone who fell down and ordered them to do it again." She fell down a few times, and the guards hit her with belts and batons. Ehli was forced to sing and dance, as were others, but they did it one by one. He recounted, "They made me sing a song about Eyadéma and they wanted me to repeat after them. They made me sing this song and dance to the song. I was so weak, I couldn't dance, so that's why they beát my toes in order to make me dance. I watched while they did this to the other men who I had been transferred with as well." For Ehli, it was only after singing that he "began to understand the gravity" of his situation.

As torture survivors struggle to characterize their experience, every aspect of Togolese life is rendered into political action. In contrast with what at times seems to be random acts of violence, against taxi drivers for example, the entirety of the public sphere is recast as tensely politicized, and the president as omnipresent and omnipotent. Again, Awali's narrative is illuminating. He noted,

> spreading antigovernment information is dangerous work and Eyadéma's security forces have many ways of discovering people who belong to opposition groups. The University [of Lomé] is crowded and Eyadéma's men don't wear uniforms, so they are able to gather information about opposition members around the campus without being detected. Political discussions and demonstrations happened on campus all the time and it was common for student activists to be taken away from the campus by military men disguised as students.

Yawa anchored her claim for protection with a direct threat from "the vicious, totalitarian regime of President Eyadéma" who beat her, causing "permanent physical pain," detained her, and threatened her and her children.

President Eyadéma looms large in almost every narrative from dissidents fleeing in the 1990s and early 2000s. Further underscoring the metonymy of the president for all political violence, Yawa claimed "the Eyadéma regime" murdered her stepbrother and uncle, tortured her mother's cousin, and "forced" much of her family "into exile." And exile presents an avenue upon which to inform retrospectively. Sankey offered a parallel story to explain why he became the dissident he now was. He stated, "I watched Eyadéma's soldiers beat young kids to a pulp, and leave them to die in the sand. I did not want these children to die in vain." His political consciousness emerged from a realization that everything he had been told was wrong. "In school, I had been taught that Eyadéma was the 'father of our nation.' I never learned about the bloody coup that brought Eyadéma to power or about Eyadéma's role in the murder of our first president Sylvanus Olympio." In this way, all of the president's lackeys carry the Eyadéma name. Historical violence is recast as familial betrayal and deceit, and perpetrators of violence are also obscured.

Just as all activities within Togo are monitored by state agents, so too external movements are tracked, according to survivors. Yawa, who had traveled to the US to visit a friend before she was arrested, was detained upon her return. She was accused of "meeting opponents of the Togolese government" in Washington, DC, and questioned about specific conversations with Togolese exiles during her trip. Under the threat of torture, she explained that she had "met people in the United States" and talked to one man in particular, but that she "did not know that any of them were dissidents." Later, after her release, she learned that he was "an agent of the Eyadéma regime, posing as a dissident." Komla was so terrified when he filed his first petition for asylum because he thought "that Eyadéma's forces would send people here to find" him. Another Ewe man in the forties, Ayao, claimed to have "learned" that members of Rassemblement du Peuple Togolais (Eyadéma's political party) "were trying to locate my exact location in New York" and had "the intention to harm" him.

The overdetermination of the national register is clearest if we return to Awali. Toward the end of his narrative he described an encounter with "Le Baobab" (a massive savanna tree), as Eyadéma was known to many. After being beaten senseless and thrown in the back of the truck, his torturers took him to see "General Eyadéma." Awali described the reception room as

> large and very fancy–it looked like a formal conference room and there was a large table in the middle. Eyadéma was the only person who was seated and there were armed military men standing all around him. Eyadéma was speaking into a microphone when he asked me who I was and if I was the one who was carrying all of the [secret] documents [about political persecution]. I was only allowed to say 'yes' in response to the General's questions. Eyadéma then asked me who wrote the letters. I wanted to answer him but I was told to shut up, that I didn't have the right to speak when Eyadéma was talking. It didn't matter what I would have said because you cannot say 'no' to Eyadéma. After asking this last question Eyadéma left the room.

Conclusion: A Nation in Exile?

Scholars struggle to document the breadth and diversity of African postcolonial history. Traditional archival repositories—postcolonial iterations of colonial-period bureaucratic records—are often nonexistent in contemporary Africa. What does exist is narrow and offers limited insight. Oral historical interviews conducted in-country, foundational for precolonial and colonial history, are similarly problematic. Even when Africans may talk about more recent history, the political upheavals of the contemporary era are often off-limits. In Togo, very few Togolese speak frankly or on the record about the Eyadéma decades, and with good reason. Indeed, as Mustafah Dhada succinctly notes in his review of Lusophone political dissidents from the violence of the Portuguese African empire, "it is not easy to re-craft a life in exile."[38] In the face of such reticence, we need to think creatively to recover the contemporary African oral historical archive.

Asylum petitions and the testimonies supplied in support of refugee claims—stories recounted with the rich depth only possible when the interlocutors feel reasonably safe and no longer fear for their lives—offer a valuable counterpoint to contemporary histories based on media news outlets and government reports. Yet, not all asylum seekers are successful. Far from it. Many fear disgorging details that could exacerbate their persecution in the event they fail. Asylum texts must thus be evaluated carefully with attention to their outcome-oriented rhetoric and petition-like formulae. Political narratives, detailing torture and incarceration, are especially fraught.

Asylum narratives might best be viewed within the entire "asylum apparatus" wherein, for a fee, narratives and documents are churned out, many of which are highly problematic, if not fraudulent. Togolese avidly desire exile, as Piot's exploration of the diversity visa lottery demonstrates.[39] Asylum narratives capture one part of a wider constellation of exile-oriented narratives. Rather than assuming a one-to-one relationship between a claimant's words and the purported truth, it may be advisable to consider the possibility that manufactured narratives exist among personal testimonies. The manufactured narratives may not record personally experienced events pertaining to the individuals in question, but they did happen, to others. In this way, asylum testimonies may operate as an indirect archive. With the right tools, it is possible to reconstruct a contemporary history of persecution through an oral historical archive built from asylum testimonies.

Togo under Eyadéma was exceptionally violent. For many Togolese, the meaning of Togo and the meaning of Togolese is deeply interwoven with the "authentic" national narrative generated by Eyadéma, his family, and his allies. Yet for Togolese exiles—political dissidents who have fled the country and attained refugee protection elsewhere—the essence of Togo-ness is inextricable from their experience of persecution and torture. How might historians account for this incommensurability? How might scholars redress such imbalance? Attention to the registers employed by refugees as they narrate their ordeals may be revealing. Togolese dissidents' personal traumas appear to be in vivid relief when assembled together. Liberated from fears of retribution, refugees in exile instantiate a terrifying and brutal nation under Eyadéma.

Notes

1. Adzele K. Jones, "Togo on My Mind," in *The New African Diaspora*, ed. Isidore Okpewho and Nkiru Nzegwu (Bloomington: Indiana University Press, 2009), 61–77.

2. Benjamin N. Lawrance and Charlotte Walker-Said, "Resisting Patriarchy, Contesting Homophobia: Expert Testimony and the Construction of African Forced Marriage Asylum Claims," in *Marriage by Force? Contestation over Consent and Coercion in Africa*, ed. A. Bunting, B. N. Lawrance, and R. L. Roberts (Athens: Ohio University Press, 2016), 199–224.

3. Benjamin N. Lawrance, "Historicizing as a Legal Trope of Jeopardy in Asylum Narratives and Expert Testimony of Gendered Violence," in *Politics and Policies in Upper Guinea Coast Societies: Change and Continuity*, ed. Jacqueline Knörr, Christian Kordt Højbjerg, and William P. Murphy (New York: Palgrave, 2017).

4. D. Malone, "INS Doubts Detainee's Fears of Torture in Native Togo," *The Dallas Morning News*, January 3, 1999.

5. Jean Allman, "Phantoms of the Archive: Kwame Nkrumah, a Nazi Pilot Named Hanna, and the Contingencies of Postcolonial History-Writing," *American Historical Review* 118, no. 1 (2013): 106.

6. Benjamin N. Lawrance, "Boko Haram, Refugee Mimesis, and the Archive of Contemporary Gender-Based Violence," *Radical History Review*, 126 (2016): 159–170.

7. Natalie Zemon Davis, *Fiction in the Archives: Pardon Tales and Their Tellers in Sixteenth-Century France* (Palo Alto: Stanford University Press, 1987); Benjamin N. Lawrance, Emily L. Osborn, and Richard L. Roberts, eds., *Intermediaries, Interpreters, and Clerks: African Employees in the Making of Colonial Africa* (Madison: University of Wisconsin Press, 2006).

8. Luise White, *Speaking with Vampires: Rumor and History in Colonial Africa* (Berkeley: University of California Press, 2000).

9. E. Ann McDougall, "'The Immigration People Know the Stories. There's One for Each Country': The Case of Mauritania," in *African Asylum at a Crossroads: Activism, Expert Testimony and Refugee Rights*, ed. Iris Berger, Tricia Redeker Hepner, Benjamin L. Lawrance, Joanne T. Tague, and Meredith Terretta, (Athens: Ohio University Press, 2015), 121–40.

10. Charles Piot, *Nostalgia for the Future: West Africa after the Cold War* (Chicago: University of Chicago Press, 2010), 8–11; Richard Joseph, "War, State-Making, and Democracy in Africa," in *Beyond State Crisis? Post-Colonial Africa and Post-Soviet Eurasia in Comparative Perspective*, ed. Mark Beissinger and M. Crawford Young (Washington DC: Woodrow Wilson Center Press, 2002), 254; see also Birgit Meyer, *Translating the Devil: Religion and Modernity among the Ewe of Ghana* (Edinburgh: Edinburgh University Press, 1999).

11. Piot, *Nostalgia for the Future*, 8–11.

12. Patrick Chabal and Jean-Pascal Daloz, *Africa Works: Disorder as Political Instrument* (Bloomington: Indiana University Press, 1999).

13. Anne Pitcher, Mary H. Moran, and Michael Johnston, "Rethinking Patrimonialism and Neopatrimonialism in Africa," *African Studies Review* 52, no. 1 (2009): 125–156.

14. Pierre A. Louis, "Obscure Despotism and Human Rights in Togo," *Columbia Human Rights Law Review* 23 (1991): 133–165.

15. John Heilbrunn, "Togo: Political Repression and Clan Politics," *African Contemporary Record*, 28 (2001–2002), B225–B235.

16. John Heilbrunn, *Markets, Profits and Power: The Politics of Business in Benin and Togo* (Bordeaux: Centre d'Études d'Afrique Noire, Sciences Po-Bordeaux, 1997).

17. See Stephen Ellis, "Rumour and Power in Togo," *Africa: Journal of the International African Institute* 63, no. 4 (1993): 462–476; Tétévi Godwin Tété-Adjalogo, *Le Togo: la vraie/fausse question nord-sud* (Paris: Éditions Haho, 2007); Comi M. Toulabor, *Le Togo sous Eyadéma* (Paris: Karthala, 1986); E.A.B. van Rouveroy van Nieuwaal, *L'état en Afrique face à la chefferie: Le cas du Togo* (Paris: Karthala, 2000).

18. See Louis Lessard, "Repression politique au Togo," *Le Journal des Alternatives*, January 4, 2005, accessed December 19, 2017, http://journal.alternatives.ca/spip.php?article2113.

19. "Disease, Death Stalk Cramped Prisons," IRIN, September 5, 2012, accessed December 14, 2017, http://www.irinnews.org/report/96248/togo-disease-death-stalk-cramped-prisons.

20. UNHCR Rapporteur Manfred Nowak, "Report of the Special Rapporteur on torture and other cruel, inhuman or degrading treatment or punishment, Manfred Nowak, MISSION TO TOGO," January 6, 2008, accessed December 14, 2017, http://www.refworld.org/docid/4795c8b22.html.

21. The UN Special Rapporteur on the Situation of Human Rights Defenders submitted an addendum in April 2014. See, Margaret Sekaggya, "Report of the Special Rapporteur on the Situation of Human Rights Defenders, Addendum: Mission to Togo," A/HRC/25/55/Add.2, April 16, 2014, accessed December 14, 2017, http://www.refworld.org/docid/534e74fa4.html.

22. "Togo: Rule of Terror," Amnesty International, Index number: AFR 57/001/1999, May 4, 1999, accessed March 20, 2017, https://www.amnesty.org/en/documents/afr57/001/1999/en/.

23. Didier Fassin and Estelle D'Halluin, "The Truth from the Body: Medical Certificates as Ultimate Evidence for Asylum Seekers," *American Anthropologist* 107, no. 4 (2005): 597–608.

24. Ann Laura Stoler, *Along the Archival Grain: Epistemic Anxieties and Colonial Common Sense* (Princeton: Princeton University Press, 2009).

25. Benjamin Lawrance, Iris Berger, Tricia Hepner Redeker, Joanna Tague, and Meredith Terretta, "Law, Expertise, and Protean Ideas about African Migrants," in *African Asylum*, ed. Berger, et al., 29–30.

26. Emily Burrill, "Disputing Wife Abuse: Tribunal Narratives of the Corporal Punishment of Wives in Colonial Sikasso, 1930s," *Cahiers d'Études Africaines* 187–188 (2007): 603–22.

27. Amy Shuman and Carol Bohmer, "Representing Trauma: Political Asylum Narrative," *Journal of American Folklore* 117, no. 466 (2004): 396.

28. Benjamin N. Lawrance and Galya B. Ruffer, "Witness to the Persecution? Expertise, Testimony, and Consistency in Asylum Adjudication," in *Adjudicating Refugee and Asylum Status: The Role of Witness, Expertise, and Testimony*, ed. Benjamin N. Lawrance and Galya Ruffer (Cambridge: Cambridge University Press, 2015), 1–24.

29. Alexander Aleinikoff, "The Meaning of 'Persecution' in United States Asylum Law," *International Journal of Refugee Law* 3, no. 1 (1991): 5–29.

30. Meredith Terretta, "Fraudulent Asylum Seeking as Transnational Mobilization," in Berger et al., *African Asylum*, ed. Berger, et al., 59, 61–62, 64.

31. Maryland Briefing, "Lawyer Is Convicted of Fabricating Asylum Files," *The Washington Post*, February 12, 2009, accessed December 14, 2017, http://www.washingtonpost.com/wp-dyn/content/article/2009/02/11/AR2009021104162.html.

32. Susan J. Brison, "Trauma Narratives and the Remaking of the Self," in *Acts of Memory: Cultural Recall in the Present*, ed. Mieke Bal, Jonathan V. Crewe, and Leo Spitzer (Hanover, NH: University of New England Press, 1999): 39–40; Susan J. Brison, *Aftermath: Violence and the Remaking of a Self* (Princeton: Princeton University Press, 2002).

33. Annie Pohlman, "*Testimonio* and Telling Women's Narratives of Genocide, Torture and Political Imprisonment in Post-Suharto Indonesia," *Life Writing* 5, no. 1 (2008): 47–60.

34. Janus Oomen, "Torture Narratives and the Burden of Giving Evidence in the Dutch Asylum Procedure," *Intervention* 5, no. 3 (2007): 250–255.

35. Craig Higson-Smith, "Counseling Torture Survivors in Contexts of Ongoing Threat: Narratives from Sub-Saharan Africa," *Peace and Conflict: Journal of Peace Psychology* 19, no. 2 (2013): 164–179.

36. Tricia Redeker Hepner "The 'Asylum-Advocacy Nexus' in Anthropological Perspective: Agency, Activism, and the Construction of Eritrean Political Identities," in *African Asylum at a Crossroads*, ed. Berger et al., 225–45.

37. Jones, "Togo on My Mind," 70–71.

38. Mustafah Dhada, "Frankly My Dear, We Should Give a Damn!" *Peace Review* 12, no.3 (2000): 457.

39. Piot, *Nostalgia*, 79–91.

Epilogue

From Exile with Love

Baba Galleh Jallow

As I watched Yahya Jammeh leave Gambian soil and step into the plane that carried him into exile, I felt heaviness in my chest and tears pouring uncontrollably down my face. No, they were not tears of joy at the fact that the tyrant who forced me and many other innocent Gambians into exile was himself now being forced into exile. Indeed, I cannot pretend to know why the tears poured out of my eyes and kept doing so for so long. Perhaps it was my sense of the tragic nature of human life; perhaps it was the reaffirmation of my conviction that those who make other people's lives miserable must in the end become miserable themselves—that we indeed do reap what we sow, as Jammeh is now destined to do for the rest of his life. Perhaps it was because, finally, the giant rock of injustice we have been striking for so long has finally crumbled into dust and our dear little country has been given another lease on life.

Living in exile is like living in a desert of the spirit. From day to day, the exiled person longs to return to home, to walk on the earth of his birth, to see the familiar scenes of his home, to visit the places he frequented as a child, to meet old friends and relatives and to revel in the sweetness of being surrounded by his own people, people who appreciate him as a person and who do not define him by the color of his skin. The exiled person watches from afar as his parents succumb to the hand of death and he is not able to go home to witness their burial or to visit their final resting places. He thinks of the longing in the eyes of his mother or his father as they lay on their death beds, wishing they could see their child one last time and knowing how futile that wish is. The exile's siblings and friends and relatives pass away and he is chained to his spot of exile. The parents of dear friends and neighbors—kind elderly men and women who treated him like their own children in his childhood days pass away and he is not able to commiserate with their families. Day after day, he hears of people passing away, some distant relatives, some dear childhood friends, some school mates or respected neighbors, and he is unable to attend their funerals or visit their families. The pain of longing for home grows deeper by the day as the years pass by and he remains stranded in a foreign land. Once in a while, he dreams of home only to wake up

Fig. Epilogue.1 Yahya Jammeh leaves The Gambia for Equatorial Guinea, 22 January 2017. (Jason Florio.)

and realize that he is so far away from home and cannot go home because of a tyrannical regime that has claimed ownership of his country and denies him the right to live and work in his own motherland.

Exile is an intolerable condition but one tolerates exile just because one has to. For some of us, exile from The Gambia was made almost tolerable by the fact that we remained perpetually connected to home. We refused to take our eyes off the reason for our exile and persistently hammered away at the foundation of the evil that was the regime of Yahya Jammeh. We insisted on spiritually and emotionally living at home and having our say in the affairs of our country—the say which Jammeh sought but failed to deny us. We insisted on our freedom to participate in the discourse on the future and destiny of our dear country that Jammeh sought but failed to deny us. We insisted that tyrannical regimes like Jammeh's could force us into exile, but they could never force us to remain silent and therefore be accessories to the ritual political murder of our country that he repeatedly committed through his unbridled and mindless despotism. For us, *physically* going into exile did not translate into *mental* exile. While physically we lived in a faraway and often hostile land, our hearts and minds spent every single day and night, every minute and hour on the soils of our dear Smiling Coast, tending to the wounds that the Jammeh regime continuously inflicted on our dear motherland. Silence was never an option for us and hesitation or compromise on matters of truth and justice as far as they affected the future and destiny of our country was never an option. We were determined to keep calling out Jammeh and vigorously chipping away at the seemingly stout trunk of despotism he represented until it collapsed under the weight of its own blunders, crimes, and sins against humanity and against itself. We were encouraged by the firm knowledge that while despotism often thinks of itself as indomitable and invincible, it is always engaged in a process of perpetual self-destruction that will eventually claim its life. Jammeh's tragic fate is living testimony and a reaffirmation of this natural truth. Perhaps the tears flowed down our eyes at the beauty of the truth of natural justice manifesting right before us.

People go into exile for many reasons; exiles, however, fall into two groups. There are those who become exiles because of their insistence on respect for natural justice and the sanctity of human dignity; and they do so for the right reasons. And there are those who become exiles because of their disrespect for natural justice and their trampling on the sanctity of human dignity; such an exile is entirely for wrongheaded reasons. Jammeh belongs in the latter group. He did not go into exile because he was a victim of injustice but because he was a perpetrator of injustice. He did not go into exile because he had seen the light of reason but because he had seen and feared a real threat of physical annihilation by a force greater than himself. Yet, unlike people who go into exile for the right reasons, Jammeh cannot remain connected in any positive way to his homeland. He cannot advocate for respect for natural justice because it was his disrespect for natural justice that landed him in exile. He cannot advocate for respect for human dignity because it was his disrespect for human dignity that landed him in exile. His exile will be much more painful than ours because he has no cause to fight for on behalf of the country and the people he has bullied and terrorized for twenty-two years. He may wallow in the lap of luxury, but he will never be able to stop or get any relief from the painful pangs of homesickness that all exiles suffer day-to-day, week-to-week, month-to-month, and year-to-year. His exile will be a much hotter and drier desert for his spirit than those forced into exile for noble reasons and who therefore hope to return home someday.

Exile is a strange form of prison. It is a prison that allows you to go anywhere you want but the place you most want to go: home. It is a prison that allows you to walk on any soil you want but the soil you most want to walk on: your home soil. It is a prison that allows you to touch anything you want but the thing you most want to touch: your home. It is a prison that allows you to see anything you want but the thing you most want to see: your home. And so the exile finds himself in the paradoxical situation of being at once a free person and a prisoner of sorts. But exile may be tolerable if you are an inmate in this strange prison for the right reasons: for standing up against despotism and injustice. If, as in Jammeh's case, you are an exile for the wrong reasons, for perpetuating despotism and injustice, for trampling upon the lives and dignities of innocent human beings, this strange prison will prove much more excruciatingly painful. For while those exiled for the right reasons may entertain and be nurtured by the hope of walking on their home soil again if they live long enough, those exiled for the wrong reasons may hardly dare to hope for such an eventuality. Jammeh knows that should he dare to step on Gambian soil, he will have to answer to a long catalogue of crimes he has committed against individuals and against the country itself, from murder to corruption.

And so as the despotic regime that forced so many of us into exile is finally consigned to the historical dustbin of infamy, we can only say to our dear little homeland that we have never really left you. Our hearts and minds have always been with you, our spirits have always slept in your tender arms and our energies have always been directed at liberating and protecting you from the clutches of a malignant dictatorship that is now history. And so we send you, dear Mother Gambia, our true and unconditional love from exile. We pray that God grants us the opportunity to see you soon and to grant us the strength, wisdom, and capacity to continue loving and serving you to the best of our abilities, however human, however limited. God bless you Mother Gambia, the Smiling Coast of West Africa.

Afterword

Worlds and Words of Migration: Exile in African History

Emily S. Burrill

WHAT'S IN A name? In the political and legal world of migration, a name means everything. In the global context of the Syrian War, the global war on terror, and the spread of the Islamic State throughout the Middle East, the massive influx into Europe of individuals fleeing danger has spawned debates over the terminology for the phenomenon of people on the move. Are these people refugees, or are they migrants? A migrant is often perceived as someone in search of something or going toward an opportunity. A refugee, on the other hand, is someone fleeing something, moving away from home. A migrant, at least in principle, has the possibility of returning home and receiving the protections and benefits that come with homeland. A refugee has lost the sanctuary of home. Both operate under constrained conditions of mobility. Such labels are important because they call attention to questions of agency and impetus for movement. But more importantly, these labels accrue a certain status within legal frameworks, which then afford certain rights of access and protection under the law.[1]

It is timely, then, to be examining exile in historical context, and above all exile as an element of African history. Most of us would agree that refugees are also people in exile: they cannot return home for fear of putting themselves and their families in harm's way. But refugees and exiles occupy overlapping yet distinct categories. Both Joanne Tague and Kate Skinner show in their chapters in this volume that African exiles did not qualify as refugees according to the 1951 Geneva Convention on the Status of Refugees. However, these legal conventions do not hold absolute meaning. Most conventional definitions of the term *refugee* emphasize the fact that a refugee is in flight, in active search, and in active peril. An exile, like a refugee, is one who has been forcibly removed or coerced from one's homeland.

Here, I suggest that there is a certain urgency that goes along with refugee status, and it is this urgency that makes the plight of refugees a humanitarian concern.[2] An experience of exile is often brought on by physical banishment and removal, but the emphasis in exile is often on the metaphysical state of being away from home. Edward Said famously gives us this frame, but it is ultimately a limited way of understanding exile, or at least, it is not complete.[3] Certainly, these labels and statuses are contentious and contested. If to be in exile is to be banished and dislocated, how is this distinction different from other displacement statuses, not only for legal reasons, but for ontological ones as well? Above all, for this volume, how does exile contribute to how we think about African history?

If we start with the assumption that exile is a state of banishment and being out of place, then this book turns on the fact that exile was a widespread and multivalent practice throughout African history. Exiles were persecuted freedpersons of African descent, willing migrants in search of new opportunity in Sierra Leone, lending new insights to how we understand Atlantic migration pathways. They were French citizens of African origin, recidivists consigned to desolate penal outposts, whose petitions in the colonial archive teach us something new about French metropolitan law within the empire of law. Exiles were entire communities who engaged in self-removal as protest against a colonial regime and as an expression of their own sovereignty. Exiles are heroes and heroines of the lost futures of colonial independence, those who championed new directions within and without empire, but were banished from the table when the work of postcolonial governance began. What we learn is that no two stories, or histories, of exile are quite the same. Nor have the practices and experiences of exile been as exceptional as we have come to believe, a historical trope against which the editors of this volume rail.

The Work of Exile: Between Erasure and Opportunity

What does exile teach us about African history? The chapters in this volume suggest that exile enhances how we understand social death and the different forms it takes. Orlando Patterson wrote that social death was a defining element of the experience of slavery, and this perspective has profoundly shaped historical analysis of slavery in Africa, as well as debates about the nature of enslavement.[4] But reengaging with social death as an element of exile reveals at least two additional aspects of African history. First, "social death" as an outcome which a colonial, or even postcolonial, administration desired reveals the fragility of the state and the weakness of its claims to govern. Second, social death as an ordeal for the person in exile, or the community in exile, reveals the experience of exile and the forms that it takes.

Carpenter's chapter on the exile of Alfa Yaya illustrates this most fully. Yaya's exile was an instrumental tool of removal and operated similarly to the *indigénat*, a penal code that also drew on forced labor and subjugation of African subjects. The Lieutenant Governor of Guinea sought to send Alfa Yaya on a path to extinction, until he was forgotten. In this way, exile as an instrument of empire is also a metric of colonial anxiety about the administration's capacity to consolidate authority and control anticolonialists or perceived anticolonialists. For adversaries to be forgotten—a form of social death—rather than mourned or commemorated, would be an erasure that worked to streamline colonial narratives of conquest and civilization. In this sense, then, social death as an erasure served a linear civilizing mission teleology that justified conquest and the rise of European ideological supremacy. Later, in French West Africa, we would see examples of relegation, or the practice of using exile as a form of punishment. *Relégués*, write Marie Rodet and Romain Tiquet, were banished, but we have records of them because of their petitions. However, *relégués* experienced a different form of erasure than they may have realized: the erasure that many experienced was a form of "drowning in the administrative lapses of the carceral archipelago," as Rodet and Tiquet describe it. This type of bureaucratic drowning maintained a fiction of a state concerned about human rights, but it also sealed the deal of elimination that so many *relégués* fought against, and which the state could use through the period of decolonization. This history of relegation is an example of the edgy securitization of the colonial state, and later, the postcolonial state—nervous states, as Nancy Rose Hunt shows us.[5] If mood—nervousness, tenseness, edginess—is an important frame for considering modes of thought and governance in colonial African contexts, as Hunt argues, it follows that exile and practices of sequestration and banishment can help us understand this nervousness as an essential element of state formation.

Did Cléophas Kamitatu experience social death while in exile in France in the 1970s? In this collection, Terretta does not use these words to describe his experience, but the French government's censorship of his written words and those of other Africans in exile reveals that censorship was part of the postcolonial diplomatic entanglement of Françafrique. Censorship of Kamitatu and other African writers was certainly a form of erasure, and like the erasure of exile in early twentieth-century colonial Africa, erasure of African voices in 1970s France was an effort to streamline a narrative of state-building and diplomacy. However, censorship as a tool of the state is also a sign of anxiety, in this case, postcolonial anxiety about opposition.

Ann McDougall writes of erasure as an experience of exile, but the form of erasure that her Mauritanian subjects experience is an entirely different form of erasure than previous examples. In Cleveland, Ohio at the end of the twentieth century and into the twenty-first, McDougall tells us that some Mauritanian refugees experienced a form of erasure when their Halpulaar identities were expunged in common narratives and understandings of Mauritanian histories of slavery. Halpulaar history complicates black and white narratives of slavery, which makes it difficult to draw a comparative parallel between American histories of slavery and Mauritanian histories of slavery. Thus, erasure was both a way of simplifying a community of exiled Mauritanians who opposed the Mauritanian government, and creating affinities between Americans and Mauritanians. McDougall writes that Mauritanian refugees in Cleveland "choose what to remember and what to celebrate," and in this way participate in their own self-censorship. This, however, is a form of self-censorship and fashioning that is generative and survival-driven. Social death, erasure, exile, and censorship all populate an African history of colonial, post-colonial, and transnational mobility and meaning-making.

While exile was an experience of erasure and social death for some, it was also an opportunity. Skinner's discussion of the independence years along the Togo-Ghana border reveals exile to have been an opportunity for new forms of solidarity and pan-Africanism. Exile created an opportunity for opposition and mobilization for those on the losing side of nationalist struggles. Likewise, Pennybacker's mid-twentieth-century London was a place where "the world of the exile often merged with that of the global political activist and the visitor." Yet, anti-apartheid exiles were welcomed and surveilled at the same time, and in this sense one can see that the opportunities in exile that London proposed were mitigated opportunities within the global context of the Cold War and its proxy struggles. Pennybacker's treatment of the exile narratives in post-war London shows how Southern African exiles could tell a story about the past—their past—in order to make claims on a possible future. However, Pennybacker tells us, just as London was a global metropolis of possibility for those involved in the anti-apartheid struggle, it was still a painful world ordered by racial and gendered hierarchies.

Ly's chapter on the Bissau revolution in exile proposes a world of possibility and survival, even liberation. The Partido Africano da Independencia da Guine e Cabo Verde (PAIGC) chose exile in Guinea as a means for survival, but it also quickly became a site for social reform, education, and the consolidation of women's involvement in PAIGC. Ly deftly compares Guinea to London in this sense, as Guinea became a site for robust pan-Africanist political education and knowledge production. Histories of exile shed light on these histories of alternative outcomes in the period of decolonization and heightened nationalism.

Literary theorist Sophia McClennen draws critical attention to exile as metaphor, and also suggests that there have been two different trajectories in literature on exile. One is the rich conceptualization of exile in social and literary theory. This is the exile of Homi K. Bhabba, Gloria Anzaldúa, and Walter Benjamin, literary and cultural theorists who develop notions of exile as an existential state of displacement with critical implications for memory and identity.[6] The other is a descriptive assessment of people in exile from authoritarian regimes, a scholarship that assesses the conditions and political implications for those in exile from authoritarian regimes.[7] McClennen's goal, as a scholar of exile, is to bridge these two tracks.[8] Many of the chapters contained within this book heed the call for new and integrated scholarship on exile, largely through historically driven analysis and interdisciplinary engagement with expressive culture and political action. But it does more than this: this volume builds an archive of exile.

The Archive of Exile: Petition, Poetry, and Testimony

What is the evidentiary basis for knowledge of exile? Is it different from other historical phenomena? While petitions form a major corpus of the archive of exile, the chapters in this book reveal the possibilities of other first-hand accounts of exile, namely through political and legal testimony, as well as poetry. Qualitatively and epistemologically, these are very different sources of experience. On the surface, one is rooted in declarations of facts and an objective to uncover a course of events, while the other is an expression of a deeply subjective experience of the felt and lived world. But when we analyze testimony of exile in context, as we see in McDougall's chapter, we see that the course of events and the declarations of facts are of course also tied to complex entanglements and subjectivities. Media-crafted and packaged testimonies of Mauritanians in exile become tied to liberal projects in the host country (the United States), namely the clarion call to "fight for human rights," which glosses over inconvenient truths about Mauritania's history. Ohioan Mauritanians, in exile from the Mauritanian state for a variety of reasons tied to different political moments and experiences of hardship, become compressed into binary identities of white (haratine) and black (bidan), and their stories come to reinforce a slavery-based country narrative that holds sway in the international human rights community and within the United States. CNN and US-based advocates orchestrated testimonies that underscored the transcendent objective of a unified Mauritania. While testimonies by their very definition are supposed to make sense of past experience, McDougall shows us how testimonies can be used to obfuscate histories. Thus, testimonies are powerful, and exile testimonies show us how they are also deeply political and politicized.

Likewise, exile poetry is deeply political, but we see in the examples discussed in this book that there is an affective subjectivity that drives the message. Sana Camara's discussion of Cheikh Ahmadu Bamba's poetics of exile reminds us that poetry was one of the most effective ways for Bamba to convey his stance of passive resistance against the incoming tide of the French colonial state. As well, there is a science to poetry that we see in Bamba's exile poems, specifically his odes, which connects him to a broader Arabic-speaking community in exile and displacement as a result of European colonization. The poetry that Bamba wrote while in exile in Gabon became a chronicle of experience that Bamba's followers would invoke for years to come (and still do). Thus, while the poetry itself, when taken at face-value, represents the mystical and deep religious engagement of an ascetic, it is also a historical accounting of the greater jihad of a religious leader during a time of political trouble.

Marina Berthet makes a case for a creative repertoire of Cape Verdean exile, a corpus of work that chronicles not the internal spiritual experience brought on by exile, as we see with Bamba, but the physical and grueling reality of forced labor in exile. Poetry and songs, write Berthet, became a literature of protest against forced labor of Cape Verdeans in Sao Tomé and Principe. The protest literature within the creative repertoire is an archive of exile that reveals agency when direct engagement with the political superstructure of exile might be prohibited or otherwise impossible. Thus, we see that the poetry and song of exile is at once a form of critique and form of connection with the broader community from which one is exiled.

In the chapters of this book, we see the petition featuring most prominently as an archival component of exile studies. Elsewhere, Lawrance has described the petition as both limited and rich with possibility—limited, in the sense that some types of petitions (i.e., asylum petitions) can be formulaic, and therefore rigid; rich, in the sense that, when faced with the dominance of European perspectives in the colonial archive, otherwise silent African voices come through in petitions.[9] In this way, petitions are useful because they illuminate the desires and the wishes of those in exile, people who, by the very nature of their condition, are discursively and physically removed from their communities. But when petitions are used as instrumental tools they also tell us about a larger process of negotiation and confrontation, as the petition was often one step in a broader bureaucratic strategy. In this way, then, the petition as instrument can shed light on colonial and postcolonial institutions of authority—namely, the gatekeepers of states.[10]

Nate Carpenter and Benjamin Lawrance note in the introduction to the volume that petitions comprise a significant part of the archive because they reveal something about the experience of exile itself. For example, Ruma Chopra demonstrates how freed Black exiles petitioned the Sierra Leone Company and complained of their experiences of racial and economic injustice. Trina Hogg tells us that one imprisoned man by the name of William Caulker used the petition as a platform to explain his rationale for theft. Jo Tague illustrates how Eduardo Mondlane petitioned the Ford Foundation for resources to support Mozambicans living in Dar es Salaam in the early 1960s.

Petitions do tell us something about the interests and desires of exiles, but here I want to emphasize that the many chapters within this volume working with petitions also reveal quite a bit about the nature of power that frames exile in the first place. Petitions are pleas and requests issued to figures of authority, but they are also protests. As an instrument, then, the petition is both a critique of power and a plea for the benevolent exercise of power. In this volume, Thaïs Gendry's discussion of the strategies of the Sanwi Kingdom in the first two decades of the twentieth century is particularly illustrative of the double purpose of the petition. In their petitions, the Sannvin people rejected French compulsory military conscription and forced labor (in the form of road works and cash crop cultivation): two of the extractive measures upon which French colonialism was built in West Africa. In their petitions, the Sannvin people reminded the French authorities reading the documents of their liberal imperative as modern Republicans. In this sense, the petition sheds light on the deeply contradictory elements of colonial rule. By the same token, the Sannvin also sought British protection, beseeching the government of Gold Coast to protect them and extend asylum. Through the Sannvin petitioning process, we see how colonial power in one instance was a force for exploitation, but it was also potentially a force for recognition. Thus, the Sannvin petitions reveal that colonial power was not experienced in a monolithic way.

The conditions and terms that most of the exiled petitioners protested cut to the very heart of colonial white supremacy in different African contexts, sometimes in unexpected ways. "Hidden in the petitions are ideas of racial difference and the inscribed privilege of the colonial institution," historian Chima Korieh writes of twentieth-century petitions to the British colonial administration in Eastern Nigeria.[11] Racial difference and attendant privileges and oppressions shaped the nature of petitioning, as well as the imperatives that drove it. In the first chapter of this volume, Chopra writes of how the free Black loyalists to the British Empire petitioned the crown for the right to settle in Sierra Leone in the late eighteenth century. Free Blacks who fled the American colonies after the War for Independence went to Nova Scotia on the promise of land, skilled labor opportunities, and protections of their freedoms. Their petitions outlined the brutal failures of Nova Scotia to uphold this promise, instead perpetuating the racist social and economic structures that many of them experienced in the American colonies. Self-exile from North America's settler societies, made possible by the Sierra Leone Company's plans in West Africa, was potentially a solution to the persistence of racism in the British Atlantic World. Thus, the petitions for exile of the freed Blacks of North America highlighted the racist fissures in the British rule of law of Nova Scotia.

While most of the petitioners we read of in this volume fought racist legal and political orders, some used the petition to fight for the persistence of white supremacy. In Brett Shadle's chapter in this volume, we read of white settlers in early twentieth-century Kenya who protested the deportation of one of their own: a white farming settler who murdered a native boy on his property. At the turn of the century, white settlers supported the deportation of other whites who undermined the fiction of superiority that made white supremacy ideologically possible. Poor whites, sexually promiscuous whites, and most especially, whites who engaged in interracial sex: all were subject to deportation. However, the deportation of Galbraith Cole for his murder of Sionga in 1911 tested the fragile covenant between the government of the colony and its settlers. The settlers who petitioned the Kenyan government in the early twentieth century insisted upon the maintenance of white supremacy, and decried a deportation that threatened to undermine it.

Closing Thoughts

Histories of exile in Africa reveal a past that defies teleology, in a sense. Through exile we see a different sort of African past that complicates how we understand mobility and migration, and the conditions under which people move across borders and are restricted from such movement. When we cast our analytical gaze on the conditions of movement in this way, we begin to see how forced and voluntary migrations as conditions of the African past and present are deeply tied to carceral and liberal states in the colonial and postcolonial context. Such African worlds of migration can be understood through a new archive of exile presented here in this volume, and they invite us to look closer. So, too, do histories of exile reveal the disciplined body—the body of the subject and the citizen—to be at the center of state-making projects. This is true of both forcible and self-imposed exile. People in exile are living and breathing testaments to the problems of the nation, and because of this they are both highly vulnerable and very powerful.

The chapters in this book, when taken as a whole, highlight the way that exile was both an opportunity and an experience of erasure. These two stark categories of experience capture, in many ways, a colonial condition to be understood more broadly. In this sense, studying exile helps us to understand the colonial African past, as well as the postcolonial past and present, more fully. Further, while we are to understand that the person in exile is an exceptional figure, exile is both a long theme within African history and a broad category of experience for many who inhabit the colonial and postcolonial world.

Notes

1. The Rights in Exile Programme, accessed March 13, 2017, http://www.refugeelegalaidinformation.org.

2. Michael Barnett, *Empire of Humanity: A History of Humanitarianism* (Ithaca: Cornell University Press, 2011).

3. Edward Said, "Reflections on Exile," *Reflections on Exile and Other Essays* (Cambridge: Harvard University Press, 2000).

4. Orlando Patterson, *Slavery and Social Death: A Comparative Study* (Cambridge, MA: Harvard University Press, 1982); Suzanne Miers and Igor Kopytoff, eds., *Slavery in Africa: Historical and Anthropological Perspectives* (Madison: University of Wisconsin Press, 1977).

5. Nancy Rose Hunt, *A Nervous State: Violence, Remedies, and Reveries in Colonial Congo* (Durham, NC: Duke University Press, 2016), 5–6.

6. Homi K. Bhabba, *The Location of Culture* (London and New York: Routledge, 1994); Gloria E. Anzaldúa, *The Borderlands/La Frontera: The New Mestiza*, 4th ed. (San Fransciso: Aunt Lute Books, 2012); Walter Benjamin, *Selected Writings*, vol. 2, ed. Marcus Bullock and Michael W. Jennings (Cambridge, MA: Belknap, 2005).

7. For a recent example that draws from many African predicaments of exile, see Alexander Betts and Will Jones, *Mobilizing the Diaspora: How Refugees Challenge Authoritarianism* (Cambridge: Cambridge University Press, 2016).

8. Sophia A. McClennen, *Dialectics of Exile: Nation, Time, Language, and Space in Hispanic Literatures* (West Lafayette, IN: Purdue University Press, 2004), 1.

9. Benjamin N. Lawrance, "*Bankoe v. Dome*: Traditions and Petitions in the Ho-Asogli Amalgamation, British Mandated Togoland, 1919–1939," *Journal of African History* 46, no. 2 (2005): 243–267; Benjamin N. Lawrance, "Historicizing as a Legal Trope of Jeopardy in Asylum Narratives and Expert Testimony of Gendered Violence," in *Politics and Policies in Upper Guinea Coast Societies: Change and Continuity*, ed. Christian K. Højbjerg, Jacqueline Knörr, and William P. Murphy (New York: Palgrave, 2017).

10. Lynn Schler, "'The facts stated do not seem to be true': The Contested Process of Repatriation in British Colonial Nigeria," *The Journal of Imperial and Commonwealth History* 42, no. 1 (2014): 134–152.

11. Chima J. Korieh, "'May it Please Your Honor': Letters of Petition as Historical Evidence in an African Colonial Context," *History in Africa* 37 (2010): 83–106.

"Exiles"

by Abena P. A. Busia

Funerals are important,
away from home we cannot lay
our dead to rest,
for we alone have given them
no fitting burial.

Self-conscious of our absence,
brooding over distances in western lands
we must rehearse,
the planned performance of our rites
till we return.

And meanwhile through the years,
our unburied dead eat with us,
follow behind through bedroom doors

Contributors

Marina Berthet is Associate Professor of African History at the Universidade Federal Fluminense, Niterói. She is the author of "Ceux qui sont de passage et ceux qui restent—L'émigration capverdienne à São Tomé et Príncipe," *New Perspectives on Migration in African Settings*, ed. Mustafa Abdalla et al. (Rüdiger Köppe Verlag, 2014).

Emily S. Burrill is Associate Professor of History and Women's and Gender Studies at the University of North Carolina at Chapel Hill, and Director of the African Studies Center. She is the author of *States of Marriage: Gender, Justice, and Rights in Mali* (Ohio University Press, 2015).

Sana Camara is Professor of French at Truman State University. He is the author of *La poésie sénégalaise d'expression française (1945–1982)* (Harmattan, 2011), among others.

Nathan Riley Carpenter directs the Center for Global Education at Northampton Community College, Bethlehem, Pennsylvania.

Ruma Chopra is Professor of History at San Jose State University and the author of *Unnatural Rebellion: Loyalists in New York City During the Revolution* (University of Virginia Press, 2011).

Thaïs Gendry is a PhD candidate at the École des Hautes Études en Sciences Sociales and the Université de Genève. Her thesis explores the making of the colonial penal system in French West Africa through the study of both repressive practices and policies of clemency.

Holger Bernt Hansen is Professor Emeritus of African Studies at the University of Copenhagen. He is the author of *Mission, Church and State in a Colonial Setting. Uganda 1890–1925* (St. Martins, 1984).

Kris Inman is currently the Technical Advisor on countering violent extremism in the Middle East and North Africa at SSG Advisors. From 2013–2016, she was the director of the Africa Research Initiative at the National Intelligence University and in 2012 she was the lead counter threat finance analyst in Kandahar, Afghanistan for the Afghanistan Threat Finance Cell.

Trina Leah Hogg is an Assistant Professor of African History at Oregon State University. Her research explores early imperialism, law, and geography.

Baba Galleh Jallow is an Assistant Professor of African and World History at La Salle University in Philadelphia. His publications include *Leadership in Colonial Africa* (Palgrave Macmillan, 2014). Before going into exile in September 2000, he was a journalist and newspaper editor in The Gambia.

Benjamin N. Lawrance is Professor of History at the University of Arizona. Among his publications is *Amistad's Orphans: A Story of Children, Slavery, and Smuggling* (Yale University Press, 2014).

Aliou Ly is Associate Professor of History at Middle Tennessee State University. He is author of "Gendered Patterns of Migration and Changes to Gender Relations in Guinea-Bissau," in *Guinea Bissau: From Micro-State to Narco-State*, ed. Patrick Chabal and Toby Green (Hurst, 2016).

E. Ann McDougall is Professor of History at the University of Alberta. She is the author of "Colonial Labour, Tawdenni and 'L'enfer du sel': the Struggle from Slave to Free Labour in a Saharan Salt Mine," *Labor History*, 58, no. 2 (2017).

Susan Dabney Pennybacker is the Chalmers W. Poston Distinguished Professor of European History at the University of North Carolina at Chapel Hill. She is the author of *A Vision for London, 1889–1914* (Routledge, 1995, 2013) and *From Scottsboro to Munich: Race and Political Culture in 1930s London* (Princeton, 2009).

Marie Rodet is Senior Lecturer in the History of Africa at the School of Oriental and African Studies (SOAS), University of London. She is currently working on her second monograph on resistance against slavery in Kayes, Mali.

Brett L. Shadle is Professor of History at Virginia Tech. He is the author of *"Girl Cases": Marriage and Colonialism in Gusiiland, Kenya, 1890–1970* (Heinemann, 2006).

Kate Skinner is Senior Lecturer in the History of Africa and its Diasporas at the University of Birmingham, UK. She is the author of *The Fruits of Freedom in British Togoland: Literacy, Politics and Nationalism, 1914–2014* (Cambridge University Press, 2015).

Joanna T. Tague is an Assistant Professor of African History at Denison University in Granville, Ohio. She is a coeditor and contributing author of

African Asylum at a Crossroads: Activism, Expert Testimony, and Refugee Rights (Ohio University Press, 2015).

Meredith Terretta is the Gordon F. Henderson Chair in Human Rights and Associate Professor of History at the University of Ottawa. She is the author of *Nation of Outlaws, State of Violence: Nationalism, Grassfields Tradition, and State-Building in Cameroon* (Ohio University Press, 2014).

Romain Tiquet is a postdoctoral fellow at the History Department of the Université de Genève. His current work draws a social and regional history of Burkina Faso and Ghana on the eve of independence.

Index

Note: Page numbers in *italics* indicate maps or illustrations.

www.ingramcontent.com/pod-product-compliance
Lightning Source LLC
Chambersburg PA
CBHW051950270326
41929CB00015B/2600

* 9 7 8 0 2 5 3 0 3 8 0 8 1 *